HV
5279
W57
1979

D0872796

STATIONS

OF THE LOST

The Treatment of Skid Row Alcoholics

With a new Preface

Jacqueline P. Wiseman

Foreword by Herbert Blumer

WITHDRAWN
VALLEY
COMMUNITY COLLEGE
LIBRARY

The University of Chicago Press

Chicago and London

66212

DEC 0 4 1987

*To the men on the loop, who accepted me as
friend, and made this study possible*

The University of Chicago Press, Chicago, 60637
The University of Chicago Press, Ltd., London

© 1970, 1979 by Jacqueline P. Wiseman
All rights reserved. Published 1970
Phoenix edition 1979
Printed in the United States of America

85 84 83 82   5 4 3 2

Library of Congress Cataloging in Publication Data

Wiseman, Jacqueline P.
     Stations of the lost.

     Includes bibliographical references and index.
     1. Alcoholics—United States.   2. Alcoholics—Re-
habilitation—United States.   I. Title
HV5279.W57   1979   362.2′82′0973   79-13632
ISBN 0-226-90307-9

Contents

List of Tables

List of Figures

Foreword

This book presents a most enlightening and incisive study of Skid Row alcoholics. It identifies the major recurring situations that face such alcoholics in their collective life and depicts most ingeniously how they cope with the run of these situations. This identification and depiction is constructed chiefly out of the experiences of the alcoholics as they carve out lines of living in their particular world. It draws also on the experience of those persons who have to deal with the alcoholics and who, in doing so, largely set the social situations which the alcoholics have to meet. We are thus given a realistic, down-to-earth account that, in my judgment, is by far the best to be found in the literature of Skid Row dwellers.

There are several notable features in the study that merit comment— features that should concern, respectively, sociologically minded scholars, professionals who have to deal with low status alcoholics, and intelligent citizens who are interested in what is happening on our urban scene.

As a form of sociological inquiry Professor Wiseman's study rests on three simple yet crucially important principles or premises. The first of these is that any given sector of human group life must be seen as a diversified process in which the participants are fitting their respective lines of action to one another. The acts of others constitute the social setting for one's own act, serving to incite, to inhibit, to temper, and to guide one's own line of action as one takes note of what others are doing or are likely to do. The acts of others *tend* to fall into regularized patterns, thus enabling one to anticipate what one may encounter in this or that situation. Yet the acting individual stands over his scene, viewing it as an arena to be used by him, to be exploited by him at given points, and to be bent by him at other points as he forges his own lines of actions. Thus, group life in any given area is a moving process, tending to follow regularized forms but allowing for both differences in individual lines of action and shifts in the regularized forms. This is a different picture from the conventional sociological scheme which depicts human society as a nicely articulated structure governed by shared values and norms and backed up by sets of sanctions to hold people in line. To see group life as process is

ix

to focus attention on the situations that have to be met, to note how participants define these situations from their respective perspectives and how they meet each other's resulting actions.

Professor Wiseman has made a most fruitful and revealing application of this approach to her study of the Skid Row alcoholics. She has identified the major situations that make up their round of life, noted the way in which they view and interpret these situations, observed how they seek to meet and exploit these situations, and caught their experiences as they acted in the situations. Recognizing that the situations that are to be met consist predominantly of the actions of other people, she has sought, in turn, to depict the way in which these other people view the situations and act in them. Thus, we are given a very revealing, indeed startling, account of the profoundly different way in which Skid Row alcoholics and agents of institutions view the situations in which they encounter each other. We note the standoff character of their relations, the wide difference between how each group views itself and how it is viewed by the other, and the hollow ring that is given to the acts of each toward the other. To expect genuine corrective or therapeutic results from the encounters is to draw a fictitious veil over reality. We see, further, the typical experiences of the Skid Row dwellers: how they organize their lives in an unfavorable milieu: how they manage to meet basic needs of food, shelter, protection, conviviality and friendship: and how they cope with the conditions that press them into a treadmill type of existence. In short, Professor Wiseman gives us an incisive account of the world of the Skid Row alcoholics—an account that enables us to see that world from their point of view.

The organization of her study to yield such an account calls attention to a second principle of importance in sociological inquiry. This principle is that to study human beings in any area of their social life it is necessary to view that area of life in terms of their experience and from their point of view. To say this is seemingly to utter a bromide. Yet, oddly enough, this principle is relatively rare in sociological studies today. Predominantly, studies are made in accordance with a "scientific" protocol which requires the adoption of an objective posture in which one identifies in advance of the study the array of objective items to be sought through precise techniques. This is not the place to spell out the details of study under this protocol. I merely wish to note here that such study means almost inevitably the fashioning of inquiry by preestablished images of the matter under study. This is a real danger, made worse by being usually unnoticed and, hence, escaping correction. One should easily understand this point. An area of social life which a sociologist proposes to study is usually unknown to him personally, or at the best known only partially. Yet it is inevitable that he will cast the area in terms of images of it—images derived from the popular stereotypes of his group or from the theories with which he works. Such preestablished images control the nature of his study, outlining the problem, dictating the data to be sought and pre-figuring their relations. However, these images of the area of life may be very inaccurate, precisely because the student does not begin with an intimate familiarity with the area. This is the chief reason why sociological studies, however meticulous they may be in observing scientific protocol, turn out so frequently to have little realistic value.

The alternative is to develop an intimate picture of the life as it actually takes place in the area. And this can be done only by working through the experiences of those who are living and shaping that life.

This is precisely what Professor Wiseman has done. She thus meets a third principle or premise, namely to assume carefully the roles of the participants, to see their world from their point of view, to identify their experiences as they have them, and to trace out their lines of action as they construct those lines of action. She has done a remarkably impressive job in carrying out this form of inquiry. She has obvious gifts in gaining the confidence of the participants, in leading them to talk frankly about the crucial areas of their experience. She has taken proper precautions to check their accounts against each other so as to dig out what is genuine in their collective life. And in doing this, she reveals abundantly the imaginative insight and analytical ability without which such a type of study remains on a low descriptive level.

The findings of her study ought to prove of great interest and value to the various professional groups that have to handle Skid Row alcoholics. These groups are many, including law enforcement officers, judges, other court personnel, custodial officials, social workers, psychiatrists and psychologists engaged in therapy, and the heads of missions catering to Skid Row alcoholics. Professor Wiseman's account would enable such groups to see how they are seen by the alcoholics and thus approached by them and responded to by them. Such knowledge ought to be the occasion for much soul searching and for endeavors to reorient their official policies and actions more meaningfully to the life of the Skid Row alcoholics.

Perhaps it is the intelligent layman or sensitive citizen who can profit most from Professor Wiseman's study. The clear analytical picture which she presents of the life of Skid Row dwellers is not merely a healthy corrective for the erroneous stereotyped images of this life that are held by the general populace. It is above all a telling indictment of the institutional complex that has grown up to take care of the social problem constituted by low status alcoholics in our cities. No one can read Professor Wiseman's account and fail to see the desultory and essentially fruitless character of the official and semiofficial apparatus that has grown up to deal with the Skid Row alcoholic. Arrest, detention, legal penalty, counselling, psychiatric treatment, other kinds of therapy, and missionary endeavors, as they crystallize into institutional forms, are alike in failing to provide an answer to the problem of the Skid Row alcoholic. We cannot expect the intelligent citizen to provide the answer. But we could expect the intelligent citizen, fortified by Professor Wiseman's study, to bring pressure to bear on professionals and officials to try to devise a more fruitful and meaningful way to handle the problem. Obviously, whatever is so devised and undertaken has to respect the collective life of the Skid Row alcoholic, and be geared to it. Professor Wiseman's enlightened and incisive account of that collective life is the proper starting point for such endeavors.

University of California, Berkeley   HERBERT BLUMER

Preface
to the Phoenix Edition

It has been over ten years since I began fieldwork on the project that eventually became *Stations of the Lost*. In an ensuing decade of social change, the most striking aspect of the life of the Skid Row alcoholic has been its basic stability. There have been some interesting changes, however, in the personal characteristics of habitues.

When this book was written, most of the Skid Row population was over forty, male, and white. Although alcoholism was a dominant problem among many inhabitants, they were essentially a law-respecting group. More recent observations, however, indicate that there have been some shifts in the demographic characteristics of Skid Row residents: The population is increasingly younger and racially less homogeneous, and there is a somewhat larger proportion of females. Some of the young people who have come to Skid Row are former flower children, the human residual of a generation that believed the answer was to turn on and drop out. Today, still clinging to their anti-establishmentarianism, many have taken the final step in downward mobility—a Woodstock Nation in tatters. Some are on drugs and involved in the various illegal activities this addiction encourages. Others, fighting free of narcotics, have turned to alcohol as a legal substitute. Current Skid Row populations in large American cities may also include a substantial number of ambulatory psychotics, persons who are unable to survive in a more competitive arena but who cannot, because of the recent wave of civil rights laws, be committed to a mental hospital.

Yet for all this influx of new types, the appearance and appointments of Skid Row and its satellite treatment areas have really changed little. It is as though this cluster of buildings, agencies, and services has a life and purpose of its own apart from the characteristics of its inhabitants. As a phenomenon, Skid Row seems able to resist the most concerted efforts by urban renewal experts, public officials, downtown merchant associations, and police to eradicate it. When the physical structures are razed, its elements coalesce and spring up mushroomlike in another susceptible part of the city.

The venerable institutions of "the loop," made up of responsible men and women who round up, disperse, sentence, incarcerate, or attempt to rehabilitate the Skid Row alcoholic are still doing business as usual. No dramatic breakthrough in the treatment of alcoholism has occurred. The high racidivism rate (approximately two-thirds) remains steady. Yet this lack of success has not resulted in innovative changes or loss of "clients" on the loop.

To be sure, from time to time, police approaches to public inebriation have been modified. Instead of the revolving-door drunk tank, non-jail detoxification houses have been tried on an experimental basis. Regretfully, unless they are part of an established organization, many of these facilities seem to have too few beds and too little funding to survive more than a year or so, despite dedicated staffs.

Some psychiatric hospitals have changed to the extent that "alcoholic wards" have been abolished or drastically cut. However, by relabeling excessive drinkers as substance (drug) abusers, hospitals are still able to admit them. Other hospital facilities have been decentralized, so that alcoholism treatment is available on an out-patient basis only.

The missions also remain in Skid Row—despite persuasive evidence that they convert fewer men than they alienate. Missions do offer the penniless alcoholic a residence or haven that is not primarily correctional or medical-psychiatric, but rather focused on religious instruction and the chance to prove self-worth through labor. However, the prayer-and-soup meetings are still viewed cynically by their beneficiaries as "singing for your supper," a fact of which most of the Skid Row missionaries are quite aware.

Skid Row alcoholics still "make the loop"—going or being sent from one institution to another, moving through the system until released. Upon release, welfare workers usually return the person with a drinking problem to the very environment that spawns recidivism—Skid Row. Cheap housing is, of course, the need that overrides many others. Sometimes, concerned ex-alcoholics have attempted to find an alternative answer, usually some sort of halfway house. The long-term success of such enterprises has been questionable, however, despite their more humane approach; the survival of established institutions and the usual policies for handling the problem drinker, on the other hand, seems assured. Part of this stability, of course, is pure bureaucratic inertia. Another factor is the unofficial symbiotic relationship between the helper, the helped, and regulating agencies. Downwardly mobile misfits must find some landing place or perish. Exploitative slumlords are happy to provide it, while the fire inspectors and public health department look the other way. City and state agencies call various approaches rehabilitative when they are actually merely cosmetic—intended primarily to reduce the *visibility* of indigent alcoholics on behalf of complaining merchants. Furthermore, since this population often does not use the "stations" on the loop for their intended purposes (as reported here in detail), the actual viability of their rehabilitation programs is not a primary concern. But increasingly I am beginning to feel that these unheralded relationships do not explain everything.

If I were to study this area again, I would take more time to learn how *policy* concerning the treatment of Skid Row alcoholics is made, funded, and implemented. *Stations of the Lost* has enjoyed a growing readership among professionals and paraprofessionals in the fields of alcoholism treatment and rehabilitataion. Many of these concerned persons have corresponded with me, discussing ways that the book has suggested to them they might improve their programs. Their ideas sound innovative and workable. Yet little change has actually taken place. An analysis of the various levels of policy-involved persons might reveal how ideologies, motivations and competing interests form a mesh of interrelationships that seem to keep Skid Row and its linking institutions frozen in time, making great portions of such classic studies as Anderson's *The Hobo*, Bogue's *Skid Row in American Cities*, and Wallace's *Skid Row as a Way of Life*, along with my own study, more current than one might expect in such a dynamic, changing decade.

University of California, San Diego   JACQUELINE P. WISEMAN viewpoint has occurred, thus, I cannot presume to know what would constitute a common meeting ground. Rather, I feel it is sufficient to bring out clearly how this *lack* of commonality nourishes the hostile feelings each group has about the other's motivations.

Three major sociological levels of analysis are of concern in this study:

1. *The interpersonal level.* Efforts to cope with repeated failure by both the Row men and the agents of social control are analyzed, since there is seldom success in attempts to help the alcoholic stop excessive drinking and regain lost interpersonal social ties so he can reenter society.
2. *The institutional level.* Here the focus is on the inevitable collision resulting from cross pressures of official objectives and the latent effects of operating a rehabilitation organization. Most studies of alcoholic rehabilitation have made no effort to analyze involved institutions in the terms in which social actors most concerned view them, although some work of this type has been done with mental institutions [1] and prisons.[2]
3. *Pure forms of social interaction.*[3] The normative rules of giving and receiving, as interpreted by the alcoholics and officials in contact with each other in a benefactor-beneficiary encounter, here cause the Row man and the agent of social control to feel betrayed. Why this is so composes the third level of analysis.

The symbolic interactionist theories of George Herbert Mead, W. I. Thomas, and Herbert Blumer[4] serve as a guide for the fieldwork and the analysis.

The methodological approach is outlined in detail in the Appendix. However, a few major parameters should be stated here. Alcoholics included in the study are those male Skid Row residents who have been institutionalized for their drinking problem three or more times.[5] Agents of social control include any person acting in an official or semiofficial capacity of deviance management, i.e., policemen, judges, jailers, therapists, welfare workers, doctors, nurses, and charity workers.

Pseudonyms are used for the situs city, county, and state, for the institutions there, for all Skid Row alcoholics, and for all agents of social control interviewed or observed. This is in compliance with the National Institute of Mental Health protocol on the use of human subjects in research. If any of the names used bear any similarity to those of real persons or places, this is unintentional. Respondents' pseudonyms are also listed in the Appendix, along with assigned numbers. These identifying numbers are given in brackets [ ] after each quote within the text, so that the reader can identify both the type of respondent and the type of institutional locale of the interview.

While this study may be perceived as a chronicle of the fate of man's best laid plans, it also offers optimistic proof of the magnificent indomitability of the human spirit, for men who fail rise to try again and again.

Jacqueline P. Wiseman

Preface

The world of Skid Row alcoholics is not bound by geography. Public rehabilitation agencies are important parts of their lives and thus of this
study. Encounters between these problem drinkers and the agents of
social control who work with them are described. The effects of the relationships that develop among these persons on the goal of getting the
indigent drinker "back into society" are analyzed.

The study begins with a description of Skid Row. Institutions of control
and rehabilitation that have a sizable inmate population of Skid Row
alcoholics are discussed, along with assumptions implied in their treatment
ideologies and inmate reactions to it. They are:

1. Jail and the courts, representing strategies of control and containment;
2. Therapy clinic at the Jail and State Mental Hospital, representing
   strategies of mental (and physical) therapy;
3. Christian Missionaries, representing strategies of spiritual renewal.

Strategies of survival used by both alcoholics and officials epitomize
and summarize what is going on in this world of drinking and drying out,
exploitation and fellowship, creativity and despair.

Alcoholics move from institution to institution and this cyclical phenomenon has a profound effect both on their lives and on the agents of
social control who man "loop stations." The repetitive and, thus, comparative nature of cyclical events structures "defining encounters" of
participants—two or more individuals assessing and reassessing each other
as a result of perceiving a meaning in their interactions. It is from these
defining encounters and their past history that the ultimate relationships
between Skid Row alcoholics and agents of social control emerge.

Inasmuch as Skid Row alcoholics and agents of social control do have
somewhat polarized viewpoints of their mutual interaction, each chapter
is divided into two sections. The perspective of agents of social control as
they attempt to cope with problems of the Row alcoholic is presented in
the first section of each chapter. This is followed by the perspective of the
inmate on the same situations, problems, and/or activities. No attempt is
made to reconcile these two points of view nor to present any sort of
objective "reality." Between the protagonists no such reconciliation of

viewpoint has occurred, thus, I cannot presume to know what would constitute a common meeting ground. Rather, I feel it is sufficient to bring out clearly how this *lack* of commonality nourishes the hostile feelings each group has about the other's motivations.

Three major sociological levels of analysis are of concern in this study:

1. *The interpersonal level.* Efforts to cope with repeated failure by both the Row men and the agents of social control are analyzed, since there is seldom success in attempts to help the alcoholic stop excessive drinking and regain lost interpersonal social ties so he can reenter society.
2. *The institutional level.* Here the focus is on the inevitable collision resulting from cross pressures of official objectives and the latent effects of operating a rehabilitation organization. Most studies of alcoholic rehabilitation have made no effort to analyze involved institutions in the terms in which social actors most concerned view them, although some work of this type has been done with mental institutions [1] and prisons.[2]
3. *Pure forms of social interaction.*[3] The normative rules of giving and receiving, as interpreted by the alcoholics and officials in contact with each other in a benefactor-beneficiary encounter, here cause the Row man and the agent of social control to feel betrayed. Why this is so composes the third level of analysis.

The symbolic interactionist theories of George Herbert Mead, W. I. Thomas, and Herbert Blumer [4] serve as a guide for the fieldwork and the analysis.

The methodological approach is outlined in detail in the Appendix. However, a few major parameters should be stated here. Alcoholics included in the study are those male Skid Row residents who have been institutionalized for their drinking problem three or more times.[5] Agents of social control include any person acting in an official or semiofficial capacity of deviance management, i.e., policemen, judges, jailers, therapists, welfare workers, doctors, nurses, and charity workers.

Pseudonyms are used for the situs city, county, and state, for the institutions there, for all Skid Row alcoholics, and for all agents of social control interviewed or observed. This is in compliance with the National Institute of Mental Health protocol on the use of human subjects in research. If any of the names used bear any similarity to those of real persons or places, this is unintentional. Respondents' pseudonyms are also listed in the Appendix, along with assigned numbers. These identifying numbers are given in brackets [ ] after each quote within the text, so that the reader can identify both the type of respondent and the type of institutional locale of the interview.

While this study may be perceived as a chronicle of the fate of man's best laid plans, it also offers optimistic proof of the magnificent indomitability of the human spirit, for men who fail rise to try again and again.

Jacqueline P. Wiseman

NOTES

1. Ivan Belknap, *Human Problems in a State Mental Hospital* (New York: McGraw-Hill Book Co., Inc., 1956); Alfred Stanton and Morris S. Schwartz, *The Mental Hospital* (New York: Basic Books, Inc., 1954); Erving Goffman, *Asylums* (Garden City, New York: Doubleday Anchor, Inc., 1961).
2. Gresham M. Sykes, *The Society of Captives* (New York: Atheneum Publishers, 1965); Donald Clemmer, *The Prison Community* (New York: Holt, Rinehart and Winston, 1940; paperback edition, 1965).
3. The term "forms" is used here in the sense that Simmel used it—to refer to the various types of social behavior that arise during the interaction of individuals over time and which may vary in content according to the situation. See, for instance, Kurt Wolff (ed.), *The Sociology of Georg Simmel* (Glencoe, Ill.: The Free Press, 1950).
4. George Herbert Mead sets forth this philosophy of human action in society in *Mind, Self, and Society* (Chicago: University of Chicago Press, 1932). Mead's entire book can be viewed as a treatise on motivation and how definitions of a situation are developed. W. I. Thomas, *The Unadjusted Girl* (Boston: Little, Brown and Co., 1928), pp. 41–44, and W. I. Thomas and Florian Znaniecke, *The Polish Peasant in Europe and America* (New York: Dover Publications, Inc., 1918–1920), p. 73, both share the same theoretical framework as Mead on the importance of the actor's subjective assessment of his situation. The term "symbolic interaction" originated with Herbert Blumer and is used to designate Mead's philosophic, social-psychological theories. See Herbert Blumer, "Society as Symbolic Interaction," in Arnold Rose (ed.), *Human Behavior and the Social Processes* (Boston: Houghton, Mifflin Co., 1962), p. 179. See also Arnold Rose, "A Systematic Summary of Symbolic Interaction Theory," *ibid*, pp. 3–19.
5. Throughout this study the terms "chronic drunkenness offender" (which refers to persons arrested for public drunkenness), "problem drinker" (which refers to persons whose drinking causes them problems primarily of a social nature), and "alcoholic" (which usually refers to persons who are physically addicted to alcohol) will be used interchangeably. Despite the very real differences in each of these definitions, the terms are applied interchangeably to all excessive drinkers by both laymen and professionals. Furthermore, these terms do not have theoretical distinction in the areas of causation or cure. Theories of why people drink too much and how they can be helped to stop are the same whether a person is called a chronic drunkenness offender, a problem drinker, or an alcoholic.

Acknowledgements

Several years ago someone told me the major purpose of an academic community is the mutual aid, encouragement, and constructive criticism its members can render each other in the search for knowledge. Until the occasion actually arises, however, it is difficult to comprehend the magnitude of this assistance or the true generosity of its givers. In my case the occasion was the compiling of this report and the help was given over a three-year period of formulation, data gathering, and writing effort.

As often is the case with a social product, it is difficult to know who has *not* contributed to its fruition. Off-hand remarks, the ideas generated by the writings of others, and apparently unrelated conversations can have a profound effect on the course of a research project such as this. Thus, I make these acknowledgements in the hope, but not the certainty, of recognizing all those who helped me with this study.

The beginnings of this research project can be traced to a number of past activities that seemed scarcely related. Long before my interest in the social situation of the down-and-out alcoholic, I was stimulated by and had profited from discussions with Herbert Blumer, Erving Goffman, and Marvin B. Scott. These discussions ranged over the nature of human group life, man's existential situation in it, and the interrelationship of theory and methodology in the study of man as a creature who confronts and deals with his environment rather than as one who merely reacts to it. From this fulcrum, in a very real sense, came my initial approach to the study of the socially-expatriated alcoholic.

The members of my dissertation committee were most generous with general advice, specific assistance, critical evaluation of all chapters, and much encouragement. Chairman David Matza spent many hours on the study design and maintained a close surveillance over the study's focus and content. John A. Clausen encouraged me to attack the problems of assessing evidence and of proving the validity of the findings, which greatly strengthened the presentation of results. Scott Briar helped me gain access to institutions early in the study and offered special help in the fields of social welfare and rehabilitation.

Brief encounters often had consequences far exceeding the time and effort expended; a wise sentence or two from a knowledgeable person several times resulted in modification of the entire study. Aaron Cicourel, after hearing a recounting of early findings, recommended for further investigation the loop, as traveled by Skid Row men. Andie Knutson suggested the scope of the study be expanded to include the contrasting viewpoints of agents of social control who come in daily contact with the Skid Row alcoholics. Irving K. Zola advised obtaining details of an average day, an average week, and an average month, which led to discovery of the importance of the loop in the lives of these men. Anselm Strauss said it would be wiser to make the rounds from institution to institution repeatedly during the study, rather than "complete" one institution at a time. Thus, the information gained at one place was used as a check against information gained in another. This cross-check served to heighten my awareness of both the contrasts and the parallels in the forms of social behavior in each of the various settings on the loop. Irwin Deutscher cautioned me about the practicalities of research relationships with agents of social control who were simultaneously *subjects* and *grantors* of privileged access to their territorial settings.

Quite in a separate class in terms of my debt to him is J. Maurice Rogers, who first suggested the study of Skid Row alcoholics, made initial arrangements for access to institutions, and offered many valuable criticisms of the manuscript. In the same category is Sheldon L. Messinger, who helped organize the voluminous data collected for this study, and whose detailed criticisms of each chapter sharpened the analysis.

Many advisors and colleagues read all, or almost all, of the chapters in early form and contributed ideas and criticisms that strengthened the final presentation. They are: Herbert Blumer, Arlene K. Daniels, Sherri Cavan, Aaron Cicourel, James H. Clark, Erving Goffman, John Irwin, Max Heirich, Kathryn T. Meadow, Lloyd Meadow, and Carl Werthman.

During the first year of this study, I was fortunate to be a seminar participant in Behavioral Sciences in Public Health, University of California, Berkeley. The seminar members—William Bruvold, Noel Crisman, Joan Emerson, David Fisher, Frank Hovell, Octavio Romano, and Richard Seiden—offered many helpful suggestions on early versions of three chapters. Seminars sponsored by the Center for the Study of Law and Society, University of California, Berkeley, also provided numerous ideas and parallel data pertinent to the research I was doing.

Earl Rubington, Thomas S. Szasz, and Joel Fort generously shared with me research material that related to my subject matter and generally encouraged me.

Norman Carlin, William Sanders, Gary Smith, and Russell Thompson are four research observers that I can publicly acknowledge. Other observers must remain anonymous. My special gratitude goes to the men who may have risked "getting busted" for keeping diaries of occurrences at County Jail for this study. Although they received financial remuneration, the rate was scarcely commensurate with the possibility that they might spend extra "penalty" time behind bars.

Nor can I acknowledge by name the men of Skid Row and the agents of social control who took time to talk about the loop and who later read chapter drafts and offered suggestions and criticisms. Many agency personnel gave hours of valuable time to aid this research, and often I was allowed a great deal of freedom in my investigation of their institutions. The openness and cooperation received from the agencies of the loop was truly gratifying.

I was fortunate to obtain the services of four professional coders, directed by Gloria Vannatter: Karen Taylor, Linda Taylor, Beatrice Hampton, and Margaret Taylor. Jean Hoy typed the taped interviews with care and patience. Mary Gaines, Clair Murphy, Noel Jones, Janice Tanigawa, Patsy Myers, and Emily Knapp also helped with many details of this study.

My husband Stan assumed the dual responsibilities of providing emotional support and editorial supervision. He never failed me nor failed to know which was needed most at any given time.

This study was supported in part by Behavioral Sciences Training Grant MH-8104 from the National Institute of Mental Health, U.S. Department of Health, Education, and Welfare, and by General Research Support Grant I-SO1-FR 05441 from the National Institutes of Health, U.S. Department of Health, Education, and Welfare, to the School of Public Health, University of California, Berkeley.

Additional financial assistance for hired observers, coding and typing staff, as well as travel expenses to various institutions, was provided by the Scientific Advisory Council to the Licensed Beverages Industries, Inc. The Center for the Study of Law and Society, University of California, Berkeley, supported that portion of the research specifically concerned with arrest, sentencing, and incarceration of alcoholics.

James H. Clark, Sociology Editor of Prentice-Hall, encouraged me at a time when encouragement was most needed and was a constant and helpful advisor to whom I turned until the manuscript was completed.

J.P.W.

I

SKID ROW
AND
SUPPORTING
INSTITUTIONS

1

Skid Row

*The Professional Overview
and the Participant Close-up*

INTRODUCTION

To the average person, the term Skid Row immediately brings to mind a grey, slum-like section of town peopled with society's misfits and cast offs, poverty-stricken men who have failed to make it in the competitive world and are now eking out an existence in an alcoholic haze amid environmental squalor and human misery. The literature concerning the subject concurs. One description of Skid Row summed up the prevailing symbolism of the area with the following picturesque statement:

> Skid Row, U.S.A. belches despair. Skid Rowers consider it "the last step before the grave." They wash their hands of themselves and say they're beyond caring what happens to them any more. Nobody else cares either.[1]

All metropolitan cities tend to develop slum areas, that is, older, deteriorated clusters of buildings where the down-and-out tend to live. Skid Row, however, is a unique asylum for the homeless man. It is thought to have first developed in the United States at the close of the Civil War when countless unemployed men, newly discharged from the army, roamed the cities.[2] Today a Skid Row is found in every fairly large American city.[3]

Skid Row, and more especially its inhabitants, has been highly resistant to the pressures of assimilation. No city has been successful in eradicating either the area or the inhabitants through social engineering alone. Some cities have resorted to the bulldozer—and the homeless male moves on geographically,[4] but does not move up socially. During good times, the Skid Row population shrinks and during bad times it grows, but never

3

does it wither away from lack of inhabitants, despite the fact that its predominantly male society is replenished almost entirely by adult recruits.

Not only has Skid Row proved tenacious as a continuing urban pattern but the area and its culture are strikingly similar from city to city and from time period to time period. In fact, the descriptions of Skid Row have been remarkably stable over the past 50 years: the filth and stench of the hotels, the greasy cheapness of the restaurants, the litter in the streets, the concentration of "low-type" bars, or "dives." All of these aspects are mentioned again and again in both the research and the romantic literature from the 1920s until today.[5]

This consistency overrides the changes in Skid Row demographic composition from itinerant workers to more stable local spot jobbers and retired men living on social security.[6] The social silhouette of these men has not changed to any degree—idle, ill-kempt, living hand to mouth. Even the special jargon used by the habitués of Skid Row is amazingly consistent from city to city and through time. This would seem to suggest both a persistence of common meanings as well as a good deal of traveling from one Skid Row to another Skid Row by itinerants.

Equally persistent—and most pertinent in terms of this study—is the fact that the majority of Skid Row residents are men alone, without families, whose heavy drinking orientation outweighs efforts toward maintaining steady employment or improving living standards. In this way, Skid Row is different from other urban low-income areas where some struggle to sustain family life and regular employment is attempted. As Wallace puts it:

> To be completely acculturated in skid row subculture is to be a drunk— since skid rowers place strong emphasis on group drinking and the acculturated person is by definition a conformist. The drunk has rejected every single one of society's established values and wholly conformed to the basic values of skid row sub-culture. Food, shelter, employment, appearance, health and all other considerations are subordinated by the drunk to the group's need for alcohol. This group constitutes the drunk's total social world and it in turn bestows upon him any status, acceptance, or security he may possess.[7]

When the existence of a phenomenon is apprehended by concerned groups as inherently bad for society at large, a great deal of professional energy usually is expended on eradication and/or prevention of the presumed problem. Skid Row has attracted its share of all types of social reformers and they (and their hired agents) have, over the years, become an integral part of the scene there. Thus, as Skid Row alcoholics view their world, they must take into account these agents of social control who, in turn, see the area within a rehabilitation framework.

The purpose of this chapter is to present descriptions of Skid Row in Pacific City as seen by two types of persons who must cope with it: agents of social control, and those male residents who are also alcoholics. The problems of each group are different as are some of their goals. The several frameworks each group develops for understanding what is going on in Skid Row are sharply divergent and yet strikingly self-reinforcing. As a result, the phenomena each group encounters are selected and sorted in radically different ways. The meaning of the situations each group apprehends and the actions planned as a result have possibly only one overlapping feature—both groups see the Row as "the bottom of the barrel."

THE PROFESSIONALS' VIEW OF SKID ROW

The general attitudes of agents of social control toward Skid Row and the Skid Row alcoholic can best be apprehended by looking at two determinants of their frame of reference: (1) *their professional training,* influenced as it is by psychological and sociological literature on the subject, including the language these studies employ; and (2) *their social background* of middle-class decency, responsibility, cleanliness, and enterprise, which most of them have absorbed. (This is not to say that there are no differences in attitude among various agents of social control. Rather, this chapter dwells on the general agreement of outlook, while the next chapter highlights specific divergences based on theoretical approaches to treatment of alcoholism.)

From a review of the literature on the subject of Skid Row, it seems reasonable to say that to social workers, psychiatrists, psychologists, and many sociologists, Skid Row is seen as a prime manifestation of social pathology.[9] Like a cancer embedded in healthy tissue, Skid Row is viewed as a potential danger to an entire city. The physical deterioration of the buildings and resultant lowering of property values of adjacent areas is but one aspect of this threat.[10] The social and psychological deterioration of its residents, inevitably resulting in added cost to the city for police surveillance and humane care, is the other.

The Physical Area and Social Environment Seen as Blighted

The language selected to describe the area, an important part of the judgmental frame of reference, includes such professional terms as "below code," "deteriorated property," "dilapidated structures," "blighted zone," "detrimental land use," and then goes beyond these to such pejorative labels as "firetraps," "depressing rooms," "dismal," and "grimy."

When an official of the Pacific City Urban Renewal Agency spoke of Skid Row, he said:

There are about 50 dilapidated hotels in the area that ought to be torn down. It is a place of dismal, grimy buildings, disreputable bars, and degrading social conditions. The alleys are dirty. The buildings are crumbling. Sanitary conditions are unspeakable. Any sort of fire would end in a disaster. On top of that, there is a bad conflict of land use here that cannot go on if Pacific City is not to suffer. There are fine stores and shopping areas side by side with Skid Row. [A45]

The Residents Seen as Pathological

If the physical conditions of the Skid Row neighborhood are accepted as not only inherently unattractive and undesirable but also as conveying a pathological gestalt, certain implications inevitably arise about the moral character, the psychological make-up, and the physiological state of the man who would live in such an environment. Thus the cited studies that speak of stench, degrading social conditions, and urban blight also describe the essential character of the residents as depressed, down-and-out, apathetic, mentally and physically ill, the dregs of society, having a dependency problem, lacking in religious belief, needing counseling and psychic support, needing rehabilitation, requiring institutional care, discouraged, and frustrated.[11]

The manner in which the appearance of the area is linked with the character of the men by agents of social control can be apprehended in the following excerpts taken from professional conference papers concerning Skid Row.

Residents of Skid Row are the most poorly housed group in the urban population. The "normal" population would refuse to live in the housing occupied by these men.[12]

The Skid Row men considered that Skid Row was foul and dirty and grudgingly uncomfortable and they hated it.[13]

It [Skid Row] still stinks just as bad, and the inhabitants wander aimlessly about, just as they used to.[14]

The physical appearance of the men is also taken as at least surface evidence that the character diagnoses are correct. The following passages, excerpted from a journalist's diary on his Skid Row adventures in Pacific City, illustrate the transmutation by the press of environmental variables into social and personality characteristics.

I have just come home from Skid Row. I have scrubbed myself with laundry soap and water as hot as I could stand. But I could not wash the stench out of my mind.

Skid Row is another world—a world of crutches, of boarded-up stores, of broken clocks, peeling plaster, cracked windows, and worn-out stairs. It is a world of flophouses, greasy hash joints, and the battered inside of the patrol wagon.

But above all, Skid Row is a world of sickness. The men I lived with there were sick with the all-pervading sickness of alcoholism. They could sink no lower on the social scale. Their goal each day was to drink enough wine to get them through the next. The next day was the same and the next day and the next day.

The men I lived with had given up and in giving up they had lost the thing which once made them men.

I have scrubbed my body until it is tingling clean. My wife says the smell has gone. But it hasn't.

In my mind I still smell with the smell of the human wreckage who accepted me as a friend.[15]

The literature of the Pacific City Urban Redevelopment program also is particularly apt to illustrate the mental connection between blighted buildings and blighted individuals in the minds of professional agents of social control. The excerpt quoted below is part of an urban renewal publicity campaign to move men out of condemned hotels that are to be replaced by a sports arena. Note how disease, disaster, and arrest statistics are used as evidence the buildings should be demolished:

Some people think it's all right for you to live in the midst of all this. Compared to the rest of Pacific City, in 1964 Skid Row had:

    4 times more fires per acre *
    9 times more deaths from fires *
    8 times more tuberculosis *
    3 times more venereal disease *
    5 times more major crimes *
    30 times more drunk arrests *
        * per 1,000 population

WE SAY YOU DESERVE BETTER.   MUCH BETTER! [16]

Another approach used to extract the moral and psychological character of a given group of people is to outline their life style as perceived by observing their daily round. Again it should be kept in mind that where a person's frame of reference utilizes depressing physical conditions as an indication of social and physical pathology, it also will tend to influence the *selection* of daily round incidents and the *meanings* attributed to them.

For instance, in his demographic and attitudinal study of Skid Row, Donald Bogue asked his respondents to describe a typical day and night. He then coded the answers into gross activity categories, of which the most frequently cited are:

Working	Reading newspapers or books
Looking for work	Getting extra sleep
Walking along Skid Row	Drinking in a tavern
Talking with other Skid Row men	Going to the reading room
Sitting in the hotel lobby	Play pool, cards, other games
Watching TV	Go to mission services [17]

From this rather neutral empirical data, plus some verbatim descriptions, Bogue reconstructs life on Skid Row as brutish and mean at the very least, with some pathological overtones, both social and personal:

> The major finding of this study is that Skid Row life is very different from what may be the popular impression. Instead of being a carefree, anarchistic seventh heaven, life for the typical Skid Row resident is boring, insecure, and often lonely. Fear of robbery, worry about where the next meal is coming from, alcoholic shakes from need of a drink, physical discomfort, despondency, and self-hate are daily feelings of these men. . . . Moreover, each day is almost like every other day, punctuated only by changing seasons or a run of unusually good or bad luck.[18]

The police of Pacific City see Skid Row and its inhabitants in a framework derived from their major experiences there. They liken it to a jungle. Although a good deal of time goes into preventing the Skid Row alcoholic from being exploited and beaten up, police feel this barely scratches the surface of such activities on their beat.

> Tough guys from the Tenderloin area come down here and take advantage of these bums. . . take them to their room and beat them and rob them. [A2]

> Taxi drivers often roll a drunk from this area. They know he can't prove anything. Restaurant owners overcharge whenever they know a guy is too drunk to know better or make a fuss. [A3]

> The men rob and beat up on each other here. One day you'll see two men being buddies, the next day they are beating hell out of each other in some bar. [A2]

> There is very little permanent buddying up here. They are too afraid and suspicious of each other. [A2]

This latter remark is also a key to a major impression of Skid Row social relationships—they are attenuated when existing at all.[19] One officer of the Christian Missionaries, a major charitable organization that works with Skid Row men, stated:

> Loneliness is their major problem. Sometimes they will come in here for help with their drinking problem, but it always comes out in the end—

how lonely they are. Sometimes they cry right here in the office. These men have no families, no one who cares about them. They don't even have any real friends. [A34]

Many studies of the daily activities of Skid Row regulars reflect a similar theme: the alcoholic ambles through the day, alone a great deal of the time, sleeping in a cheap hotel, drinking in a tavern if he can afford it, or with a bottle gang if he is short on funds. He eats in a "greasy spoon" restaurant, watches television in the lobby of his hotel (if he is lucky enough to have one), and goes to bed. If he is without a bed for the night, he goes to a reading room to keep warm or drops in on a mission for soup and salvation. Then he "carries the banner" (walks around all night).[20]

In addition to being without close friends, the Skid Row alcoholic is almost completely without the social anchorages—the personal ties—that most middle-class men take for granted. If the Skid Row man ever had a wife and children, he has long ago lost them for one reason or another and he often does not even know where they are. Most in-laws avoid him. With the possible exception of his mother, he has usually lost all track of his parents, brothers, and sisters. Friends from his previous days of semirespectability have long ago given up on him. So have employers. Hence he lacks the usual social life that accompanies most jobs. By most standards he is seen to have a very constricted social life.

It is from these characteristics, of course, that the so-called under-socialization hypothesis arises concerning the Skid Row man. His apparent lack of long-term friendships, family commitments, or steady job is considered to be indicative of some flaw in his personality and upbringing, making it impossible for him to make commitments to others.[21]

Perhaps the most important indicator of the pathological character of the Skid Row alcoholic is his physical and mental state as it is affected by ingestion of copious quantities of alcohol over extended periods of time.[22] Skid Row drunks, with their lack of permanent housing, their bottle sharing, their fights, their passing out in doorways and sleeping out in all weather, the lack of ordinary cleanliness standards in restaurants and hotels, the impermanency of sex arrangements, and the dangerous jobs they often have to accept in order to make a little money, are easy prey to all types of disease and debility.[23]

Because of these conditions, Skid Row men have high rates of tuberculosis, venereal disease, pneumonia, influenza, injuries to limbs, and eye and teeth defects, as indicated by surveys sponsored by Pacific City Urban Redevelopment Association.

Table 1, that follows, shows mortality rates, by cause, found in the general Pacific City population as compared to that of the Skid Row area.

TABLE 1. Male Mortality Rates by Cause in Pacific City and the Skid Row Area

DEATH BY CAUSE PER 100,000 *

Cause	All city (MALE)	Skid Row area (MOSTLY MALE)
All causes	1461.6	3159.6
Cardiovascular	526.8	2681.3
Cancer (malignant neoplasms)	256.9	349.1
Cirrhosis	107.7	650.9
Accidents	85.0	210.3
Suicide	34.7	23.6
Tuberculosis	8.1	47.2

* Source: Pacific City Health Department. The city-wide rates are not age-adjusted because the necessary information was not available for this computation. Rates are restricted to males to match more closely the Skid Row area (which is represented here by three Census Tracts and does not quite match Bogue's boundaries). Inasmuch as cancer is primarily a disease of the aged, the cancer death differential of the two areas can be taken as a rough indicator of the relatively slight weight added to the Skid Row rates due to its older population. Age alone then would not account for the dramatically higher mortality from other causes on Skid Row as compared to the rest of the City.

Thus a constant alcoholic haze, punctuated by blackouts, vomiting spells, and agonizing withdrawal pangs, all compounded by other physical ailments and disabilities, leaves the Skid Row man so weakened physically and mentally as to be nearly unfit to cope with the ordinary daily problems. As one public health official commented:

> You think they look bad when you see them on the streets? You ought to see them in their rooms—lying in their own vomit, no bath or clean clothes for weeks, their bodies covered with open sores from drinking. Sometimes they don't even know where they are. [49]

The Etiological Puzzle

How does a man become a Skid Row resident?

The question of etiology inevitably arises as a suggested aid in making decisions as to where social engineering intervention should be focused. In the specific case of Skid Row, as suggested by the previous discussion, there is an essential chicken-egg riddle: which comes first, the assumed pathology or the economic-social exigencies of Skid Row residence; for as Wallace has pointed out, no man is born there.[24]

This is an important question to persons committed to rehabilitation of deviants, for upon the answer hinge a number of vital decisions. For instance, should social change be instituted through urban renewal, economic aid, and job placement, or should some form of personal therapy be given to overcome "deepseated" psychological handicaps such as lack of motivation or self-confidence?

Theories to explain the etiology of Skid Row residence can be divided into two general types which are summarized below:

1. Initial entrance into Skid Row is the result of a practical, conscious decision on the part of the men, affected by such pressures as an economic need for cheap housing and food, the availability of charities if work or money runs out, and the desire for quarters where a transient or laborer will not feel out of place. The emphasis here is on Skid Row as an area that offers a solution to the tangible problems posed by poverty, transient status, and lack of familial ties. For some of these theories, "skidding"[25] as downward mobility, is scarcely considered as an important etiological element, for the man was never "up." However, this "solution" is not without its price. Skid Row norms and values are the antithesis of those needed if a man is to return to sober, responsible society. Heavy drinking, spot labor, tolerance of disheveled appearance, and absence of any routine or schedule are part of a life style that eventually corrupts newcomers.[26]
2. Initial entrance into Skid Row is the result of social or psychological failure in the outside world. From this perspective, Skid Row becomes a retreat for the skidder where the occupationally or sexually insecure person need strive no longer, where those who chafe under the responsibilities of family, kin, and friends can rid themselves of this burden, and where those who long for the dependency they enjoyed with their mother can throw themselves on the mercy of the city welfare department and the missions. Heavy drinking is viewed as a way of forgetting failure in this context.

An expansion of some of these major positions follows.

ECONOMIC AND SOCIAL CAUSES OF SKID ROW RESIDENCE Bogue sees the ultimate cause of Skid Row residence as the exhaustion of economic resources, although (as will be discussed shortly) he also accepts social-psychological theories:

> The average citizen has a great deal of security against misfortune. If he gets ill (either mentally or physically), or if he shows tendencies to uncontrolled drinking, he is sustained first by members of his immediate family. They not only care for him but will try to assemble enough money for treatment. When the resources of immediate family are exhausted, more distant relatives often lend a hand. Many employers are lenient and will assist a person in solving his personal problems. If the family belongs to a church, they can get counsel and aid there. If all of these fail, public and private welfare institutions enter the field. But when the resources of these agencies are exhausted, there is only one place left—Skid Row.[27]

Bain concurs with economic explanations of why men go to Skid Row. He lists Skid Row recruits as (1) victims of swift vertical descent; (2) migratory workers who gradually move in there; and (3) the workingman who gradually separates from his family:

> It is then entirely logical that they gravitate to a Skid Row community of failures where they can easily gain a kind of sympathy and social acceptance. Here also they can make a bare living with a minimum of effort while posing and being locally accepted as being successes.[28]

Dunham, on the other hand, offers an ecological theory that might account for the existence of a collecting place in large American cities for male misfits. He suggests that cities will always develop high-rent and low-rent areas and that the low-rent areas will attract *both* the economically and socially misfit, who come together and eventually form their own subculture. Such men usually have only a grade school education, come from a broken home, have spent a good deal of time in institutions, have no relatives or friends to turn to in a crisis, have never learned a trade, and have wandered about a great deal in their late teens and early twenties.[29]

Irwin Deutscher suggests that regardless of how Skid Row started in various cities, it eventually becomes a *reservation* for the containment of undesirables.[30] There, a higher level of deviance is tolerated than in the more conventional sections of town and men who wander out of the area are either arrested or warned to return to "where they belong," (where they can be kept under police surveillance).[31]

PSYCHOLOGICAL THEORIES OF SKID ROW RESIDENCE   Wallace summarized the current psychological theories concerning men who appear to make a permanent residence of Skid Row:

> Skid Row persons are egoless and live on Skid Row for the constant ego-lifts that this society supposedly provides. (paraphrased)[32]

> . . . men live on Skid Row because of their emotional immaturity and their lack of ability to adjust to the world. The Skid Row resident, deprived of normal social familial, relations early in life, consequently is insecure, apathetic, indifferent, passive, and intellectually inefficient.[33]

> . . . early deprivation [led] to "rage with its accompanying fantasies . . . guilt; and the paranoid blaming of others for one's miserable plight in order to escape conscious knowledge of one's self-mutilating activities." [34]

> . . . the basic problem of the homeless man is not alcohol, but a deep problem of dependency . . . a study of 100 Skid Row men revealed almost all of them came from seriously disrupted homes. Most had lost a parent; many were raised in institutions. In their late teens, 97 of the 100 had come under some form of protective "institutional" setting: CCC camps, the merchant marine, logging camps, the peacetime army, etc. It

was a situation in which the men were not required to make any decisions for themselves about food, clothing, job activities. Such settings in and of themselves do not breed dependency, but they apparently contribute to overdependency on the part of men already strongly inclined in that direction.[35]

. . . undersocialization . . . social inadequacy, inability to play secondary roles. . . .[36]

. . . retreatists [who have] relinquished culturally prescribed goals and whose behavior does not accord with institutional norms. . . . Defeatism, quietism, and resignation are manifested in escape mechanisms which ultimately lead to "escape" from the requirements of the society. It is thus an expedient which arises from continued failure to near the goal by legitimate measures and from an inability to use the illegitimate route because of internalized prohibitions.[37]

COMBINATION THEORIES   Some theorists have attempted to synthesize socio-economic-ecological theories with psychological ones. By means of multivariate analysis, Bogue arrives at some general "social psychological" reasons for what he terms "the existence of Skid Row," although he might more appropriately entitle it, "the existence of the Skid Row *man.*"

1. Economic hardship (irregular employment, unemployment, and low income)
2. Poor mental health (personal maladjustment, alcoholism, marital discord, wanderlust, and emotional instability)
3. Poor social adjustment (marginality of culture or religious belief)
4. Poor physical health, physical disability, and limited intelligence.[38]

In addition, Bogue derives what he termed a "sociological" explanation of Skid Row. He points out it is an area that "provide(s) continued survival for familyless victims of society's unsolved social problems while these persons are in the terminal phase of their affliction and after society at large has abandoned all hope for them and has ceased to rehabilitate them." [39]

Anderson equates leaving home with living on the main stem (the Chicago Skid Row), that is, he attempts to answer the question, "Why do men leave home?" as an approach to why men become migratory workers and hobos, as well as why they live in Skid Row neighborhoods. Anderson suggests one or any combination of the following could be responsible:

1. Industrial inadequacy (inability to keep the pace demanded by modern large-scale industry because of lack of intelligence, drive, physical handicaps, alcoholism or old age)
2. Dependence on seasonal occupations, with resultant unemployment forcing the men to hunt for work in various parts of the country

3. Defects of personality (here Anderson included low intelligence as well as psychotic symptoms)
4. Crisis in the life of the person (the death of a family member, disgrace or embarrassment, and fear of punishment for some offense)
5. Wanderlust—the desire for adventure, new scenes, and new faces.[40]

From these discussions it is clear that residence on Skid Row is seen as resulting from the "push" of adverse conditions, whether economic, social, or psychological, rather than any great "pull" of attractiveness to the unattached man.

Certainly, this fits with the general view of the undesirability of the area. It is the perspective shared by journalists, urban renewal experts, public health specialists, social welfare workers, psychologists, and many sociologists.

Both of the general etiological theories (outlined on pages 10–11) assume the Skid Row man would like to be "back in society." Each theory, by its very nature, prescribes a route back and involves planning for the future rather than the current municipal approach of day-to-day police surveillance to keep the public drunkenness and other deviance at a given level.

For those subscribing to the first theory, the best way to help a man out of Skid Row is to help him improve his economic condition, perhaps through assistance in finding a job, which would assure a steady income, less moving around, and eventually social roots, including a family and friends. Skid Row as an area should be leveled and replaced by structures that would be more in keeping with the commercial area adjacent. It is reasoned that destruction of the area would serve two purposes:

1. It would terminate once and for all this unhealthy gathering place for society's misfits and failures.
2. It would end indoctrination of these men into "the Skid Row way of life."

For those who accept the second theory, the best way to help the Skid Row man is to probe deeply into his psychological problems and by therapy aid his awareness as to the "inner causes" of his excessive drinking. The insight eventually developed by this approach would aid the Skid Row man in "pulling himself together" and boot-strapping his way off the Row.

SKID ROW AS RESIDENTS SEE IT

How does the Skid Row man see himself and his life? At least five factors shape his frame of reference. Perhaps the most important one is the effects of alcohol itself.

There is general agreement that the early effect of alcohol ingestion is usually a euphoric one, creating a warm glow of optimism and dulling feelings of unhappiness, loneliness, social inadequacy,[41] and awareness of unattractive surroundings or persons.[42] Achievement of this effect is, of course, dependent on which stage of alcoholism the drinker has reached,[43] and whether he is at the beginning, the middle, or the end of a drinking bout. Later stages are extremely unpleasant, approaching total physical and mental collapse.

The perception of social improvements created by alcoholic intake is illustrated in the quotes below:

> Sober, I'm rather shy and backward, especially around groups. I'm an introvert. When I get to drinking, I enjoy people more. Of course, it's imaginary; you think you are the cat's meow. [41]

> When I was a lush, I thought I was the greatest lover in the world, God's gift to women. [14]

> Alcohol is marvelous at removing obstacles for a while. Everyone gets to the point where he is just fed up and scared and worried. He doesn't know where to turn. Alcohol takes care of that. The important becomes unimportant. Your problems aren't anywhere near what you thought. [55]

Although intake of some drugs is said to heighten sensitivity to beauty in the immediate environment,[44] alcohol apparently has an opposite effect. To the Skid Row man the immediate environment becomes irrelevant:

> When I'm sober, Skid Row is a transient place—there is nothing there. When I'm drunk, I don't pay any attention to the smut and dirt, I am enjoying talking to my own kind. The scenery is in the background, I just ignore it. [40]

The term "sobering up" has more meaning to the alcoholic than merely clearing his system of alcohol. It also refers to "coming down," a change in perspective from optimism to pessimism.

> When you sober up there is a futile feeling. You begin to see yourself as you really are. You know you made an ass of yourself. You wonder what others thought of you. [41]

The state of drunkenness in the Skid Row alcoholic is prolonged and steady. It is not necessarily dependent upon a large intake of alcohol so much as a constant one. Some of the men claim to drink five or six fifths of wine per day. Others say they can maintain a high on very little, once they have their body "saturated" with alcohol. Regardless of the amount, the goal is maintenance of the "high" for as long as possible. One man interviewed about his Skid Row drinking said proudly:

> Me and my buddy, after we first met, I don't believe that a day went by for almost a year and a half when we weren't continuously drunk. *Interviewer: How much did you drink a day?* Well, till we uh, just couldn't carry no more. [58]

Another part of the Skid Row drinker's framework is the very obvious "today" or "now" orientation. Agents of social control look at Skid Row and its inhabitants with a time orientation that takes in the past (for clues to etiology), the present, and the future (as a possible time for a cure). Skid Row alcoholics, on the other hand, evidence primary concern for daily survival, a view they have in common with other economically-deprived groups.[45] This, of course, stems in part from the fact that so much daily time and energy must be spent in making arrangements (for food, housing, clothing, etc.) the average middle-class citizen handles weekly, monthly, or even yearly. Even when the Skid Row man thinks of the future, he is thinking of it in different terms than does his employed, sober counterpart, as will be seen in the discussion to follow.

A third aspect of the Skid Row man's frame of reference is his feeling of powerlessness coupled with his sense of a need for cunning to outwit a hostile and unfair world. Economically and socially impotent, he feels always vulnerable and (by his standards) persistently exploited by merchants, agents of social control, by employers, even by street friends. For this reason, he suspects that his day-to-day struggle for survival will fail except for his own talents at counterexploitation.

An important fourth ingredient in the Skid Row alcoholic's life view is his adjustment to and acceptance of impermanence. Skid Row social relationships are in a constant flux. Men come and go from the area, are arrested, are in and out of institutions, die, are kicked out of their hotel rooms, and gain and lose money, jobs, and friends with a rapidity that would bewilder the more settled citizen.

Finally, the Skid Row man's view of life is a curious mixture of extreme independence from others, coupled with acceptance of a necessary dependent status from time to time.[46] The Skid Row man finds the ordinary social obligations, commitments, and cooperation necessary to hold a steady job too vexing to be endured for long. However, he will accept the total dependence of institutional living with equanimity, rarely breaking rules, doing his assigned job, and fitting himself easily to the routine of the organization.

These factors composing the Skid Row alcoholic's framework—the inebriate state, the today-orientation, the feelings of powerlessness and concomitant need for cunning, the transient aspects of social relations, and the unlikely mixture of stalwart independence and dependent status—are best illustrated by seeing how they effect, and are shaped by, the exigencies of his daily life.

When examining the patterns of everyday living on Skid Row in the same way that the culture of remote islands is studied, the search for an etiology of pathological surroundings and behavior is put aside. Instead, we must look at the recurrent behavior systems of survival. This investigation brings an entirely different range of phenomena into focus and results in a group of categories and emotional tone that departs radically from the professional conclusions just discussed.

The Skid Row Framework in Action

People, whether or not economically and socially deprived, and whether or not pathological, must meet certain minimum day-to-day needs to exist:

(1) Eating (among alcoholics this naturally includes drinking; the acquisition of liquor is often pursued as though it were a necessity more compelling than food. It is, as a matter of fact, a substitute for it, in terms of caloric intake and slaking of appetite, if not its nutritional equivalent) [47]
(2) Shelter
(3) Attending to illness

Certain additional categories of activity are important. These categories are presented together not because they are of the same order of importance but because they are areas of living which, if not absolutely essential to maintenance of life, are still a problematic part of it. The significance of the first three, especially in Western industrial societies, is clear; the last two are important in all societies:

Earning money
Keeping clean
Obtaining clothing
Release of sexual tensions
Maintenance of social contact

Assuming a man has power over the social arrangements through which his basic needs are fulfilled, the really important area of analysis becomes how he arranges these matters. When a man has little power to create systems of supply and must cope with existing social arrangements, then the *strategies* of gaining access to and utilizing the system become the commanding issues.

The Skid Row alcoholic has little or no money, no steady job, little formal training and no recent job experience, poor health, and shabby clothes. He is in an environment that any outsider would label as bleak and comfortless, offering nothing but destitution, shame, and despair. Yet his strategies for survival indicate a remarkably indomitable and creative spirit, somewhat inconsistent with the visage of pathology presented in the literature.

How does a person, without the usual resources available to an adult male, find a way to meet his minimum needs and thus survive? Inventiveness, or creativity, is the talent with which survival tactics are most often associated. The essence of creativity is *redefinition*, that is, the ability to mentally free an object from one meaning or mental framework and then convert it into raw material to serve another purpose in another context.[48]

Edmund Love's book, *Subways Are for Sleeping*, is an unusual account of indigent persons in New York City who exist successfully by stealthily redefining facilities, objects, and general public practices for their own purposes, thus creating a hospitable instead of hostile world.[49] The title of the book refers to a man who does his sleeping in subways, public libraries, and bus stations, thereby avoiding the problem of paying for a bed.

Such strategies are essentially what the Skid Row resident uses in order to survive both physically and psychologically. He begins to locate things that can become resources to supply food and shelter if they are used in a way other than generally intended. Even the institutions and organizations created specifically to provide necessities as a charity can be redefined and "worked" so as to offer more than bare comfort. None of this redefining can be done openly, however, for taxpayers and do-gooders do not like to see their largess taken under false pretenses or used as barter for more desirable objects. Therefore the Skid Row alcoholic must utilize still another human talent—the art of deception and game playing.

Skid Row residents are every bit as inventive as Love's devious characters and often camouflage their intentions as well. This is another reason why the mere recitation of the daily round activities of Skid Row residents, such as that offered by Bogue, is inadequate to the task of apprehending all the activities on Skid Row. It is the *purpose* for which the activities are intended, plus the *emotions invested in them*, that give insight into "what is going on," so far as participants are concerned.

What follows, then, is a description of how these men, lacking in all but the barest of conventional resources, use their imaginations to obtain access to and use the social system without seeming to do so.

Food

At one time Pacific City's Skid Row was an area where a man could eat more inexpensively than anywhere else. This is not generally true today. With the advent of state and city social welfare benefits to the men, most restaurants of the area increased their prices until at present they match such low-cost eating places as dime stores, cafeterias, and hamburger stands in the more conventional areas of the city.[50] The same is true of grocery stores in the Skid Row area. Because of welfare food tickets, prices are noticeably higher than the average supermarket, with quality of such items as produce and meat noticeably inferior. The Skid Row man continues to eat on the Row, however, probably because he does not feel welcome elsewhere due to his general appearance.

As mentioned, if a man is without funds, Pacific City Social Welfare gives food vouchers worth $7.50 in groceries for those men who have cooking privileges in their hotels. For those who prefer to eat out, meal tickets are supplied. However, these are redeemable only at Skid Row establishments through arrangement with the city. (These tickets are often redefined as a source of money by means of negotiation with grocery stores and cafe owners, and so will also be discussed under that category rather than strictly as a food source.)

For the independent resident with a little money of his own, obtaining a meal becomes a matter of knowing where to go to get "the makings." For instance, the ingredients for a stew can be collected piece by piece at various wholesale establishments or from restaurant discards. As an "old hand" of 16-years' residence on Skid Row put it:

> Go to the produce market and get some vegetables, go to the meat house and get some meat, and make up a stew. Go to a place where they throw out bread and get a couple of loaves of day-old bread. [52]

The charitable missions in Skid Row are exploited by men who do not care to do their own cooking, who do not qualify for welfare checks, or who have traded their tickets for cash. Furthermore, because of competition among the missions for the needy, it is possible to obtain food throughout an entire day, day after day in this way. This is because most mission workers on the Row see their role as primarily one of aiding the moral salvation of men who are wasting their lives on alcohol. Material sustenance is furnished along with the spiritual for two reasons. It is a needed bit of charity in an area where men have meager or no incomes; more importantly, those who come to eat may be possible converts. The missions are quite practical about this and usually do not dispense the food until after the religious service.[51] There are many missions in Pacific City, but they do not schedule meetings or meals at the same time of the day. This presumably is to avoid competing with one another.

Out of this situation, the enterprising Skid Row resident creates a small circle of specialized restaurants. As one put it:

> Here's what I'm telling you you can do. This is what most of us do. There's breakfast at the Our Savior's, lunch at St. Joseph's, dinner at

Beacon in the Darkness, and then you can still run over and get a late sandwich at Miss Nightengale's. Then, for variety, there's Brother Peter's and Sister Caroline's, she gives a pretty good show. Besides that there's the Waterfront, which serves three days a week, and American Mission which serves two. A guy has to be a fool to go hungry down there (Skid Row). [52]

Men also use the missions for delicatessens. As they go through the food line, they often have a concealed jar in their jacket, or sack under their arm, or both, where they dump extra helpings of beans, soup, sweet rolls, or bread for another meal. As one explained it:

We can get a pretty good midnight snack together by making the missions and putting any leftovers in a jar, or going back for seconds and taking it home. [49]

Of course, while the missions can be used to sustain life, not everyone is equally enthusiastic about the quality of their food.

In my opinion, the missions don't help you out a bit. They don't give you any substantial food, just watery soup, stale bread, made-over coffee. I went to St. Joseph's and all I got was some old beans, a side dish of cabbage, some old fruit and some stale bread, made-over coffee, and powdered milk. The only time I favor those missions is Thanksgiving day and Christmas day. Then they have turkey dinner. You can *exist* with the missions, but it's not really eating. [18]

Drink

Earlier it was said that the culture of Skid Row revolves around liquor. On Skid Row, getting a drink is seldom a problem. The down-and-out men use a sort of cooperative socialism—from each according to his ability, to each according to his need; a share-and-share-alike ethos. As some of the men put it:

Anyone who can't get a drink in Pacific City for free, well there must be something wrong with him. You can always get a drink on Skid Row, even when you can't get food. [48]

Men on Skid Row say that when they are stoney-broke someone will always let them have a drink in a Skid Row bottle party or will even sometimes stand them one at the bar. If they have "a penny up" (i.e., can prove they have *some* money, even a penny), they can buy into a bottle party (discussed under money). If they are living in a partying-hotel (and almost all hotels on Skid Row are), the men can join the party group; in fact, several men report that "if you don't join the party, someone may break your door down and actually drag you over," all in a spirit of friendly, boisterous, good fellowship. [39, 48, 49]

Party time was all the time. In that hotel (on Skid Row) there was a continual drinking spree. [39]

One other source of a free drink deserves mention, although it is close to being in the same class as the dope pusher who gives free samples to neophyte users: some bars on the Row offer a free drink at 6 A.M. to the potential all-day drinkers. (This may be viewed by the men as a kindness, however, since to a heavy drinker with the shakes, the "hair of the dog that bit him" is badly needed the morning after.)

Shelter

When a middle-class man thinks of shelter, he automatically includes in it storage space for personal possessions, and for this reason he conceptualizes a somewhat permanent abode. To sleep in a different place every night or even every week would be a great inconvenience, involving much time-consuming packing and unpacking of valuables. Such mobility is the pattern of shelter for most Skid Row residents, however. They "travel light" and think of a room in terms of sleep primarily, although they may also use it for drinking if they are trying to avoid arrest. "Traveling light" in the down-and-out vernacular means with the clothes being worn, what little money or jewelry is actually in possession, plus a safety razor and blade, and perhaps needle and thread, all kept in a tobacco pouch in the pocket. [48]

Shelter is a constant problem for the penniless or near-penniless alcoholic man, especially since he would usually prefer to spend what little cash has on liquor. However, to be without a bed for the night means to risk getting arrested as a vagrant, or even worse, getting rolled while drunk.

The most obvious source of shelter in Skid Row is the hotel, or flophouse, as it is sometimes called. The prices are low—from $5.50 to $7.50 per week. Despite the dismal, often dirty rooms,[52] men with enough money prefer Skid Row hotels to many other shelter arrangements, such as the missions, so they can retain independence.

Aside from the unsanitary conditions, the men have other problems with commercial establishments that sometimes lead them to seek accommodations elsewhere, however reluctantly. The practice by hotel owners in the area of "turning over" room occupancy as often as possible, thereby double or tripling their nightly income, is a major complaint.

The Davis Hotel owner gives relief recipients a bad time, so he has the excuse to kick 'em out at the least little thing. If you paid your dollar, they won't say "boo" to you, but if you are there on [Welfare] vouchers,[53] that's different. He wants a big turnover. He wants to get as many vouchers for the same room as possible. It don't do no good to complain to the Welfare. They know what is going on. But they figure you just might be drunk and carrying on, so rather than make trouble they send you to another hotel. [42]

In a lot of these places you can be sitting drinking with a few friends quietly minding your own business when the management comes crashing into your room. They do that anytime they take a notion. They then claim you are drunk and throw you out. What can you say? [38]

Most of these hotels won't give you any receipt if you pay in advance. Then, when you come around later to claim your room, they deny you ever paid for one. They say you were probably drunk and were at some other hotel. In this area it's hard to prove you weren't drunk. [51]

Once I checked in and I was pretty drunk and I had a new little blue zipper bag with just about everything in it—new shirts, some jewelry, handkerchiefs. I paid a week in advance. And the next day I started to my room and the manager said, "Where's your rent?" And I said, "Paid a week in advance." And he said, "You only paid for yesterday." And the upshot of it was he held my bag for the rent. Well, I went out and panhandled the money and came back and said, "Here's the money," and he pretended like he didn't know anything about my bag at all. He said he had never seen me before. [53]

The men who have "graduated" from vouchers to a monthly welfare check also claim that the various hotel managers steal from their checks. These checks are mailed directly to the hotel manager so that he may cash the check and get his rent money first. Many men claim they are shortchanged in the process, especially if they seem drunk.

Another thing, the Welfare often sends the checks direct to the hotel—to ensure the manager will be paid. He cashes the Welfare check and if the man is a bit tight, he will take out more than the rent—short change him, if you know what I mean. [20]

A Skid Row hotel clerk who served as a guide during the first stages of the study confirmed this:

I've seen those Hindus [many Skid Row hotel owners in Pacific City are Hindus] shortchange a drunk man time after time. They get his Welfare check first and they make him sign it and take out his rent and a little more. [2]

Inasmuch as there are inexpensive housing arrangements that can be made in other parts of the city, such as rooming houses in workingman's districts, and cheap hotels scattered around, why doesn't the Skid Row man select one of these? The answer usually given to this question was:

> You see, you don't feel welcome in any other part of town. Landladies don't like to rent you a room because sometimes a guy looks pretty rough. And if he has no luggage—that's all, brother. In those neighborhoods you can't go for a walk without attracting a lot of attention. You are a man without a family, a fifth wheel, suspicious. On top of that, there's no one to be with, nobody you know lives there. Everyone is married, so they don't have no time for a lot of talking. If you're not working they wonder why not. If they find out you drink, they ask you to leave. Why bother in the first place? [56]

There are, however, many creative ways of finding shelter. Such shelters may not be even as comfortable as a flophouse hotel, but they avoid the hotel's risks. They may not be as clean as a non-Skid Row room, but they lack the hostility of the working-class neighborhoods and require no expenditure of money. Further, these no-cash solutions to the housing problem are attractive to the Skid Row alcoholic because of the opportunity they afford to play a game with established (square) elements of society.

For instance, some of the missions provide bed facilities, although usually only on a nightly basis unless the man decides to accept the rehabilitation program that is offered. One man conjured up a picture of Skid Row alcoholics playing a sort of gigantic musical chairs with this resource:

> Actually, you could get a free bed every night if you went to all the churches and missions around here. You could get by taking a different one each night. [43]

At some missions, however, to get a bed requires the "taking of a dive," that is, pretending to be spiritually moved by the sermon and making a public avowal of this fact. Men who take a dive too often are shunned by the other Skid Row inhabitants as "sellouts." [54]

Although the men, without exception, profess to hate the County Jail, they are not averse to spending a night in City Jail for its warm, dry accommodations. A rather tragic-comic scene sometimes takes place when the alcoholic practically begs to be arrested, and the policeman either refuses brusquely, or complies somewhat reluctantly.

> I had just been treated at City Emergency for withdrawal and I walked over to a policeman standing in the hall and said, "I understand you've got a hold for me." He looked at his papers and said, "No, we haven't got any hold for you." I said, "You gotta have a hold." I mean I needed

some place to lay down; this is 10 o'clock at night, they kick me out of the hospital see, and I said, "You gotta have a hold." So it was the most ridiculous thing, we're standing there in the corridor, me trying to convince him he should take me back to jail. [40]

Furthermore, as is discussed in more detail in chapter 3, knowledgeable men seeking shelter will wait on the paddy wagon's scheduled route, and by their posture (i.e., leaning against a building, sitting or lying in a doorway) invite arrest in order to get a night's warm lodging.

Parking lots also can be retranslated into hotels, although this necessitates getting to know the parking-lot attendant and obtaining his sympathetic help. As one man put it:

Many cars are left on the lots all night, and if you know the right guy and he gets to know you—knows you won't vomit in the car or something— he'll point out those cars that you can stay in. You can just crawl in the back seat and sleep all night and stay warm and dry. [48]

I spent the nights in a truck, too, and sometimes they let you sneak into a bus that is not going out on a run. That's pretty nice because you have the whole back seat to yourself, or maybe there's a couple of guys there. [46]

There are other miscellaneous areas that can become shelters when necessary. In warehouse and loading locations, large boxes can be arranged into overnight accommodations. Public buildings are natural sleeping places, especially in cold weather, because they are warm, open to the public, and usually provide seating accommodations for patrons. The bus depot, the train depot, the public library, and even the YMCA in some cities have their share of men who come in to get out of the rain, to warm up, and even to sleep, if it is not too risky. Police watch for bums who congregate in public places, however, so the men must learn to sleep while appearing to read, or to sleep in snatches, or to look sufficiently well-groomed that they will be seen as tired, middle-class commuters or as businessmen catching 40 winks before their bus comes to take them to suburbia.[55]

Of course, for lodging that is a little more private and more permanent, there is always the possibility of building a "nest." Goffman first noted that people in total institutions (where inmates must spend 24 hours per day under administrative control) have a proclivity to create "nests" when they lack access to regularly-designated private areas.[56] Skid Row residents apparently do the same thing on their "reservation." Condemned buildings, half torn-down buildings, bridges under super-highways, heavily-weeded areas in parks—all these can be turned into nests, some of which are apparently protected and held as personal territory for months or even years. Note the following descriptions:

Me and my buddy had the cutest hideout you ever saw. There was a mansion that was torn down, but the steps remained. We put an old mattress under the steps and made a door with an old tarpaulin. We used to snuggle up together in overcoats and a jug and to hell with the world. [49]

Two or three of us used to go under the bridge in a place where it forks off, one side to the highway and the other across the water. There's a sort of a place in there. The fellas used to hang out in there. We had bed rolls, canvas, and we could cook there. [54]

A veteran of 16 years in Pacific City's Skid Row (although he had also lived in Skid Rows in Denver, Seattle, St. Louis, New York, and Chicago) claimed that he had spent most of his time sleeping under the freeway.

Myself, I usually sleep under the bridge. I have fortification against the cold, a half a case of that wine. Keeps you warm. Then I have a bedroll and a piece of plastic sheet to keep out the rain. [52]

However, nests under the highway can become too popular, as illustrated by the following comment:

We found a place under the freeway entrance and stayed there about six months. But see, too many people got to know 'bout it. The next thing you know, we had half the city livin' with us. There was John, Bob, and Pots coming up there, and one night Polock came up there, him and Rickey. We had a houseful. Most generally we'd all drink together then. We really had to move out. So many men living in one place attracts the cops. [43]

Because of Pacific City's comparatively mild climate, the city park becomes a hotel at night, as does any area with weeds or bushes that can be used to camouflage a bedroll. One man told me that what amounts to a colony of Skid Row alcoholics invades the park after dark; territory is actually staked out and claims are respected. The location of good weed areas are jealously guarded, as witness the following conversation:

Well, like I was doin' for, oh, three weeks of that month, I'd been sleepin' in the weeds. I had a couple of coats and a blanket. *Interviewer: Where are there any big weed patches in this city?* Well, I'm not goin' to reveal that. [41]

Every now and then the Skid Row alcoholic makes a contact that results in a permanent, or "temporarily permanent," conventional room. Usually this is some "deal" in which board and room are offered in exchange for work. Men report they are asked to move into the homes of Skid Row merchants whom they get to know to stay with mentally-ill family members, to help landladies run large boarding homes or hotels, or to work as craftsmen-helpers in cottage labor arrangements. Although such accommodations are probably far better than any he has had for some time, the down-and-outer rarely stays long. In the first place, he knows he is to some extent being exploited, since on the regular labor market a salary would have been thrown in for inducement. Additionally, the regularity of the arrangement soon bores him. He becomes tired of the confinement and the lack of cash and absence of compatible friends. Very often he gets drunk, and again disappears into the familiar environs of Skid Row.[57]

Female nurses and social workers sometimes "adopt" a favorite alcoholic and take him home to live with them for a time. This will be discussed under sex rather than shelter, although it obviously is a way of obtaining both.

As described by one man, finding shelter is a sort of game in which the object is to discover which areas can be safely used and which cannot.

> After you've bummed around for a while you develop sort of an instinct so you know where you'll be safe overnight; and when it's dark there are many places you can hide without people seeing you that you wouldn't have dared to go in the daytime. So you sleep under a bridge, under an awning, on a loading platform, or in a patch of weeds, having your bottle with you. And you don't have to take chances on them kicking you out of your room if you get drunk; you're not botherin' anybody else if you want to talk to yourself or sing a song or something like that. [21]

Illness

Every society develops mechanisms to cope with illness, either out of charitable feelings for the victim or fear of spread of contagion.

Pacific City Hospital offers a full range of medical and surgical facilities to all citizens of the city at a nominal charge and to the indigent, free of charge. Additionally, there are numerous charitable clinics operated in Skid Row that offer free eye examinations, chest X-rays, aid with minor ailments and so on. These are operated by established religious institutions and some of the missionary-type organizations.

It is, therefore, always theoretically possible for the Skid Row alcoholic to get some aid on an out-patient basis for his physical ills, at reduced cost, or at no cost at all.[58] Furthermore, the hospital can be used as a place to get much-needed food and shelter.

Money

Although food and shelter are the first-rank essentials of life, money is exceedingly useful in any advanced society because of its flexibility. Clearly, money is negotiable power.[59]

To be without money has serious implications for both the efficient allocation of time and the problems of social vulnerability. A penniless man *must* plan to devote a certain portion of each day to finding a way of obtaining food and shelter.[60] Furthermore, without money, he cannot handle such emergencies as an arrest, the need to telephone for assistance, a doctor or an ambulance, or such a mundane matter as getting caught in the rain without transportation. Petty but necessary items such as cigarettes, toilet articles, movies, or candy, all require money.

When the average middle-class person thinks of getting some money, he thinks of a steady job or an assignment for which fees may be charged, or possibly an inheritance or a gift. When the Skid Row man thinks of getting money he again must show ingenuity in creating something out of nothing. Thus, he thinks in terms of objects, relationships, or short-term tasks that can be converted into enough cash to take care of current needs—liquor, food, shelter, incidentals.

Convertible objects include welfare food tickets, which are worth $7.50 in food items at grocery stores. These also may be illegally sold to a grocery store at a $3.50 discount, which gives the Skid Row man $4.00 in cash to spend as he pleases. Store owners who engage in this practice justify the large discount (nearly 50 per cent) as the difference between the retail and wholesale value of the groceries they sell, and they claim that the profit they make on this illegal transaction is due them.

Other convertible objects include bus passes from welfare, bed tickets from various churches and charitable agencies, or extra food or clothing, all of which can be peddled on the street, in the lobby of hotels, or in some of the Skid Row business establishments.[61]

Stealing is another way of getting money or objects that may be converted to money. Usually only petty theft is attempted. Crime depends on access as well as motivation. Skid Row alcoholics do not have access to areas where they can embezzle large sums, nor do they have the equipment or organizational abilities to pull off a burglary or robbery that would net them an amount worth the time and risk. (Furthermore, most do not care to risk getting "hard" time or "big" time in state prisons for a felony since they would be forced to stop drinking, perhaps for years.)

Small objects, usually relatively inexpensive, are most often the target of the Skid Row drunk. This is not because such thefts are less in cash value than the amount necessary to qualify for grand theft in the state ($200). It is because the items taken are inconsequential enough in the lives of the victims and among the crimes handled by the authorities so as not to demand a police complaint or vigilant detective work. Quite commonly, items are stolen from a parked car, from a man who has passed out, or from the lobby of a hotel or other public building.

Alcoholics do not exempt each other from this petty thievery:

The nicest guy in the world, who wouldn't be dishonest under, uh, non-drinking conditions, will take the shoes right off your feet if he needs a bottle and you're asleep. [49]

A rather distinctive type of theft is the *caper*. Here, the spirit of the game is the most important thing; the item stolen is secondary to the manner in which the theft is handled. This allows a man, or men if more than one is involved, to hold the center of attention during a bottle party while expounding on his caper. Below are three samples of capers:

I was staying at this hotel run by a Chinese and he had a cuckoo clock in the lobby. One day when he was out I stole the clock and hocked it for $10.00. Then, when he came back and missed the clock, I offered to hunt it down for him. After I had been out a while, I went running back to him and said, all out of breath, "I almost caught the guy who took your clock. But he got away and took it into a hock shop. I waited until he came out, jumped him and got the ticket. It will cost $10.00 to get it out, plus a $5.00 reward for me." And do you know, he paid it. He was that glad to get his clock back. [49]

Other examples include:

My buddy and I spotted a bowling ball in the back seat of an unlocked car. It had the name of the owner inscribed on it along with some contest he'd won. We knew it was no ordinary bowling ball. Well, we took it and then we ran an ad in the paper saying we had found it. The man answered the ad and we told him to come get the ball. We had it up in the hotel room right up on top of the dresser, so it was the first thing he saw when he came in. He rushed across the room all smiles to get it and we said, "Wait a minute! We had to wrestle this ball away from a thief we saw take it out of your car. See how our coats got torn in the fight." (We had pulled out some seams in our sports coats before he came up.) Then we said, "It's going to cost $5.00 apiece to get these coats fixed." So he paid out $10.00 to get his ball back. [3]

Three of us were driving a truck and collecting (donated items) for the Gladhand when we hit on the idea of splitting the take between the Gladhand and us. Every other piece of furniture, we'd take and store in an empty loft where we were living at the time. We had plans to sell it a piece at a time for booze. One day Fred fell off the truck and got hurt. A police ambulance took him to City Hospital and by mistake Fred gave the address of the loft. We figured the police would be there in 24 hours and that we had just that amount of time to get all that stolen furniture out of there. So my other buddy and I took the stuff piece by piece, mirrors, sewing machines, tables, and so on, and went up and down Main Street selling stuff for a quarter or 50 cents. In less than 24 hours we got rid of everything. That's how I failed in the furniture business. [As told to A43.]

Cheap watches, cameras, and other fast-selling items can be both obtained and sold at Thieves' Market. Various wholesalers in the area also specialize in these resalable items.

Thieves' Market is an area located in Skid Row that operates much as the country market of medieval times. All large metropolitan cities seem to have them, although some are better known than others.[62] In many ways, this is Skid Row's major recreation on Sunday, a notoriously slow day for panhandling, there being few commuters and little traffic. The Skid Row men bring what they have either repaired, stolen, or purchased, and then bargain with the others over a trade or sale.

In Pacific City, Thieves' Market is held in a downtown parking lot, which normally stands empty on Sunday. Men sit on the raised wooden car abutments and barter, or they walk around peering into each other's sacks and making offers. Major bartering items are both standard and transistor radios, watches, sport coats, cameras, electric razors, and clocks. These items are sold in both good repair and unrepaired condition. Those persons buying an item that needs repairing will take it to their rooms, fix it, and return to Thieves' Market the next week to sell the refurbished merchandise at a mark-up. (Every now and then a well-dressed man in an expensive car will drive up and get out and buy large quantities of available items. I am told these are second-hand store owners.)

In such an atmosphere of petty larceny and floating domicile, the Skid Row man has a real problem of how to keep his own money safely: if he keeps it on his person in cash he is likely to get rolled when he is drunk; if he takes it to a bank, he is likely not to be able to get it out when he cannot make his current handwriting match the signature on the file due to the trembling and shaking.[63] In addition, he has a tendency to lose bank books, to forget which bank his money is in, or to feel overwhelmed by the bank officers.

Skid Row men have developed certain strategies for handling this problem. One solution is to put their money in traveler's checks. A second approach is to ask a trustworthy friend, sometimes a bartender, but usually a middle-class nonalcoholic, to keep a part of his cash. A more inventive approach is to use the pawnbroker as a bank. This involves buying an expensive piece of jewelry, usually a man's diamond ring, which can be used as collateral for obtaining small loans. One man, using such a ploy, reported that he owned a $500 diamond ring, which he often hocked for sums as low as $17.00. When he was in the money again, he would reclaim it. The interest is 10 percent of the amount loaned, however, so the men find it wise to use hock shops for very short term loans only.[64]

Parts of the body can also be converted into cash. Human blood, which can be sold to the blood bank for anywhere from $5.00 to $20.00 per pint, is a commodity that can be utilized every two to three months depending on branch policy. A branch of Pacific City blood bank is located in the heart of Skid Row, convenient to their most faithful donors.[65]

Hair on the arm may be sold for $1.00 per arm to artificial arm makers, who carefully shave the hair off the Skid Row alcoholic and place it with the aid of tweezers in the manufactured plastic arm. Hair on the head may also be sold, but few Skid Row men can bring themselves to deface their appearance to this extent. Some claim that other men (not they, of course) sell homosexual favors to young servicemen and to "perverts from the Tenderloin," a honky-tonk, homosexual, and criminal hideout area adjacent to Skid Row.

Convertible relationships vary all the way from the brief encounter a panhandler has with his victim to exploitative relationships with women met in the course of making the rounds of bars or institutions. Panhandling is considered the quickest and most flexible way to get cash, for it does not require the possession of an object nor a customer. Neither does it require time spacing as does the selling of blood or hair. Furthermore, it does not produce the guilt conflict involved in homosexual favor-selling; nor is it as risky or demanding as hustling. It is possible to get busted [arrested] for begging, but the cautious man usually is able to avoid this. As one man put it:

> An opportunist on the bum, what's he gonna do for money? . . . The easiest thing. As a rule, he's not concerned with any super-con game or any long-term return. He wants it now. He wants a drink now . . . And how can he get that drink the quickest? By panhandling, that's the idea. [51]

Stemming, or panhandling,[66] requires several talents for success. First, the man must concoct a story or an approach that will cause a stranger (the "mark") to part with money voluntarily (that is, so the mark won't call for the police.) [67] Second, he must be able to do this without feeling a tremendous shame. Some men are unable to panhandle unless in their words, they "have a heat on" (are high on liquor). Some are unable to bum at all. As one said:

> I can't do it, I just can't. It makes me feel so low. I'd rather do without, or even steal. At least, if you steal, you have your self-respect. [48] [68]

> So you got steam [are drunk]; then you don't care; your inhibitions have gone. You can talk to anybody, say anything; you don't give a damn what you say. [56]

Third, the panhandler must be able to distinguish, almost as if by an inner divining rod, those pedestrians that are "live ones." A live one is a person who has, and is most likely to part with, money. Recognizing him is considered an art rather than a craft, and only the most nebulous characteristics were enunciated by the men:

> You can tell a live one by the way he walks. [48]

> There's a certain look in his eye. [2]

> It's the way he holds himself. [44]

Those men who are able to panhandle seem to have licked the problems of technique and embarrassment by converting the activity into a game and, simultaneously, the mark into an adversary.

Techniques for stemming reveal their users to be shrewd students of common sense psychology. The following statements will illustrate:

> I always try to get a man with a woman. Men hate to look like a cheap-skate to a woman companion. A man with *two women* is even better; a real pushover. [38]

> Women alone are good bets. They get so nervous. I had one woman give me a bus transfer she got so excited. [49]

> I always ask for a nickel. They're ashamed to give me so little when I look so bad and my request is so small, so they give me more. [49]

> I tell them I need six cents or 12 cents or some uneven amount in order to make bus fare home, or coffee, or something like that. [17]

> I tell them outright it's for a drink. They are overwhelmed with such honesty . . . Some give, the others weren't going to give anyway. [41]

> I like to find them [the victims] in a place where they can't back away from me. Like sitting in a parked car or something. They can't run down the street. [48]

> I catch them coming up from the commute stations. They are in a hurry and often give me something to get away from me. (I block their path.) This makes women especially nervous. [46]

It seems inevitable, with such diverse tactics, that arguments might arise as to the best way to stem. This is indeed the case, and just as such disagreements are settled in the sporting world, so they are settled here—with a contest.[69]

> It becomes a game among a bunch of oldtimers when they get together and one tries to outdo the other. "You take one side of the street and I'll take the other," they say. [45]

> Sometimes there's three or four of us get together and have a race to see who can make the most. We each take a different street. The loser has to buy the first bottle. [48]

Here at the home [Welfare Home for Homeless Men] the conversation is either on sex or the most successful ways to panhandle. I mean that's 40 percent of the conversation. They even have panhandling contests here. [37]

Although a good deal of the stemming that goes on is done across class lines (i.e., the lower-class bum hitting up the solid citizen), more than might be imagined occurs between the men themselves—one Skid Row alcoholic hitting up another for assistance. Men who could not force themselves to stem outside their peer group will do so without shame among "their own kind."

If you are out of money you can often make out better with the guys like you. They know what it means to be on your uppers. [51]

I go after people who are in the same boat. I keep track of when they get a pension check and then I hit them up. [49]

A relationship with a woman is often quite lucrative for the Row man. This includes the relationship some men are able to manipulate (or perhaps have thrust on them) with professional women working in various positions in rehabilitation around hospitals and social welfare. This has already been mentioned as a source of shelter and it will be discussed at greater length in the section on the sex life of the Skid Row man.

Relatives are also good for some money. When contacted by an alcoholic kinsman they have not seen for some time, there is a bit of implicit blackmail in the conversation—"either pay me off or I'll be around in person to renew our relationship"—a situation seldom desired:

If I really get desperate, I call my brother-in-law collect. He is always glad to send something to get rid of me. [45]

A slightly different type of relationship is necessary for the pooling of resources, perhaps the most frequently-used approach to get money. The purpose is specific and communal—to obtain liquor for a group. Each participant in the group contributes what money he has into a pot. When it reaches the amount needed for a bottle ("the baby is born"), someone is elected to be the "runner" and go make the purchase. The man is carefully selected for honesty and relative sobriety (so he does not get arrested before returning).[70] Then the bottle is passed around until it is gone. If a man has no money, but has contributed in the past, he may be allowed to stand in on the party anyway. However, he must contribute when he comes into money at some other time or he will be called "a dino"—a man so low he must panhandle winos. [48]

For men who lost or quit their last steady job long before (often many years), *spot jobs* are seen to constitute a source of extra money but not of regular income. When a man is deep in the drinking culture, with its lack of commitment and its "now" orientation, jobs are not sought on any regular basis but are accepted when they crop up. Here the more unpleasant aspects of the steady job are mentioned by the men to buttress their decision to avoid such entanglements. The following quote from a Skid Row alcoholic was reported by a welfare worker who had arranged a job for him that involved aiding with daily delivery of merchandise:

> You mean I'll know what I'm going to do Monday and Tuesday and Wednesday and Thursday and Friday *every week?* No thank you! [A41]

Another man explained his reluctance to seek regular employment this way:

> A guy on Skid Row has no family, no payments, doesn't really have to get butted on the chin. He has no real stake in anything. This is the bottom of the barrel. No point in putting up with all that. [48] [71]

The jobs that are accepted include such short term tasks as delivering handbills (bill hiking), cleaning out basements, painting walls, cleaning up vomit in hotel halls, picking fruit, loading merchandise, and other unskilled work. Many of these jobs are obtained by standing on the street waiting for potential employers who need temporary help. Such employers reportedly drive slowly by in their car and say, "Hey, Buddy, want to earn a little cash?" This informality has its drawbacks in terms of mutual understanding as to what is being paid and how much work is involved. As one man said:

> But nowadays I always find out how much they are paying. I used to be too shy to ask and as a result I'd clean a whole back of a restaurant and work four to five hours and then they'd hand me a dollar. [26]

Alcoholics are well aware that the wages they are paid in most of these arrangements are well below any normal or legal scale and that they are being exploited because of their drinking habits:

> I went to work for this hotel for my room, and my goodness, I worked there for about four weeks and they almost killed me. They had me moving beds and furniture and plastering . . . just for my room rent. [42]

> The manager offered me a mickey [small bottle of wine] to clean up the vomit in the hall. I told him where he could go. [2]

> I have known the time when I was glad to paint several rooms and a hallway for a couple of bottles of cheap wine. Those hotel men know when they've got you. [20]

The most dependable source of money is the government—city, county, state, or national. Those persons who receive welfare checks, disability checks, social security, pension, or other forms of regular payment are considered to be in an enviable position. They are also marked men when it comes to intramural panhandling. (Methods of getting these stipends will be discussed in connection with institutions that have major control over their award.) The day before the first of the month, when the checks are due in the mail, men on Skid Row meet each other with the greeting, "Tomorrow's the day! Tomorrow's the day!" [72]

As a bartender told me:

> What you ought to do is be here tomorrow night. The place will really swing! Why, I've seen as many as seven fights going on here at once on a payday, besides the bar being full with men who are so busy drinking they don't even turn around to watch the action. [1]

Keeping Clean

The Skid Row alcoholic has ambivalent feelings about cleanliness. On the one hand, attempting to emulate the cleanliness standards of persons with jobs and families seems like an exercise in futility. On the other hand, to allow personal appearance to fall below a certain level of respectability is to risk arrest for drunkenness or vagrancy, as will be seen in chapter 3.

Most persons have a "backstage" area where they may prepare in private the image they are going to present to the public.[73] However, the Skid Row alcoholic who travels light is truly without a backstage.

One of the problems inherent in the lack of permanent quarters is that of keeping clean. Anyone who has camped out knows the problem of finding facilities for personal washing and clothing maintenance. The facilities that the average person takes for granted are missed after a short time in the deep woods. The average Skid Row man is in just the position of the camper, but without his excuse, i.e., that he is temporarily "roughing it."

Keeping the body and clothing clean and presentable then, takes a certain amount of planning. If a man has a hotel room, community bathroom facilities, however dirty and inadequate, are available. If he does not, then he must search out alternative means. Here the missions receive attention again, for they usually offer a place to shower and shave. Bus and train stations often have booths where a person may shower and clean up, although there is usually a charge for this. Most filling stations in the Skid Row area keep their washrooms locked, giving the key to customers only, thus depriving Skid Row denizens of the favorite freshening-up facilities of the middle-class citizen who is traveling.

Skid Row also has laundromats, which receive heavy patronage from the men. There are cut-rate dry cleaners in these areas as well. For the man traveling light, however, the use of public facilities is somewhat problematic unless the establishment can offer him a booth or a robe while he waits for his clothes to be processed.

Cleanliness and neatness are two different things, however, and the Skid Row man must also consider the problem of shaving and getting his hair cut. Fortunately, this is more easily solved than some of the other problems of "traveling light."

Barber schools use the indigent population on Skid Row for student practice so that a man may get a free haircut and shave of sorts at any time. In fact, according to some testimony, he may get one whether he wants it or not. Police often go to the soup lines and give out "haircut coupons" to men standing there with the admonition to "go out and get a haircut with this [coupon] and don't come back until you do." [48]

Clothing

Acquisition of clothing varies in importance in the life of a Skid Row man. If he is drinking heavily, a Row man usually does not try to amass a wardrobe because it is too difficult to move from room to room or place to place with a lot of luggage and no money for a taxi. However, since clothing often doubles as blanket or mattress, it is important to have some things, especially in cold weather. If, on the other hand, the Row man is attempting to put up a "front" and get a job, he must try to get some decent items of clothing.

Clothing is purchased with money gained in the various ways previously discussed in this chapter. Clothing can also be obtained through bartering so that the penniless man need not go without necessary items of apparel if he is able to come up with a tradable item.

One of the best ways to get clothing is to go to Thieves' Market. Here men are selling suits, sportcoats, or sweaters, either stolen, or purchased elsewhere at a lower price and marked up slightly for Skid Row.

If the down-and-out alcoholic cannot barter a piece of merchandise for clothing, he can literally barter his immortal soul—at least on a temporary basis. Men who "take a dive" at the Christian Missionaries are often given a choice of clothing in the mission salvage shop as a reward for their show of support. A less hypocritical way, as most of the men see it, is to stay after the meeting voluntarily and help put chairs away. Sometimes this gesture will earn them a chance to pick up a sportcoat or pair of slacks. When all else fails a man can always go to an institution for a time.

Almost all institutions of rehabilitation—even the jails—have second-hand clothes that they give inmates, either upon entering or upon leaving. Although it is hardly likely an alcoholic would seek to be sent to one of these institutions just for the clothing, this is a possible bonus for spending time in one.

Sex Life on Skid Row

In most studies of exotic cultures, it is to be expected that the local sex rites and marriage customs will play a prominent role, for these phenomena provide the major means of recruitment of new members to the society. However, Skid Row men are usually without wives or families. Sex and family life therefore cannot be viewed as unitary for them. This absence of familial ties may account in part for the widespread belief that the Skid Row alcoholic has no sex life or else is limited to brief homosexual contacts.

From the testimony of the men and some related testimony by agents of social control, however, it is clear that the life of the Skid Row man is not either as sexless or homosexual as it has often been portrayed. Although sex life for a down-and-outer on Skid Row may be more sporadic than it is for unmarried men with funds and more opportunities to meet women (e.g., at work and in bars during cocktail hours), it is not utterly void of female contact.

In the course of outlining their daily round of activities, many of the Skid Row men discuss women friends (usually drinking companions), whom they claim to have lived with for considerable lengths of time. If the woman has enough money, or shelter for two, they would share resources and dispel their mutual loneliness. Such women usually have clerical jobs, are well past middle age, and have "been around." Most of these liaisons last anywhere from one night to six months.

It should not be assumed that these arrangements are always sexually and economically exploitative by either party. Men reported they often cared for these women when they became ill. (One man became so worried about his female partner's heavy indulgence in tranquilizers, that he quit a job to stay home and see that she did not fall asleep with a cigarette in her mouth and set fire to herself. [39]) Some of these women, of course, enjoy the opportunity to mother a sick, helpless, albeit alcoholic man.

The Skid Row alcoholic men also indicate a continuing interest in women by discussing them at great length in bars, jail, and welfare home bull sessions, a phenomenon not unknown to men in the armed services, or other all-male gatherings. When alcoholics go to coeducational institutions, they often make female friends with whom they spend a great deal of their free time. They attend institution-sponsored dances and, in general, seem to enjoy all types of heterosexual social activity.[74] (The pin-up collection on the walls of the clothing supply room of one of the alcoholic wards at the mental hospital is extensive and graphic.)

Also, as previously mentioned, female agents of social control were reported to be another source of female companionship and perhaps sexual gratification as well. Early in the field work, the claim was made a number of times by the Row men during interviews that unmarried, middle-aged nurses, social workers, and even women doctors and psychologists often invite a Skid Row man to live with them. In my first encounter with this phenomenon, a respondent said, with obvious pride:

> So you're a sociologist, eh? Well, I have been living with a lady psychologist. What do you think of *that?* [49]

This sort of testimony I at first discounted as mere braggadocio. Subsequent interviews with various agents of social control, however, suggested that at least some of the stories of soft-hearted professional women may be true. According to a male social worker at City Alcoholic Screening:

> You have to watch some of these nurses and social workers. When we release a guy, they worry that he is going right back to drinking and they will take him into their apartments and keep him there in order to "save" him from himself. They don't seem to realize that some of these guys could be dangerous. [A36]

This was also mentioned by a male social worker at County Jail:

> Some of the women social workers get carried away by the alcoholic men. The men are really charming when they are sober and difficult for a middle-aged babe to resist. They take 'em right in their homes. *Interviewer: How does it seem to work out?* Oh, I guess all right for a while, and then the guy gets tired of it and takes off. I've never heard of any of those gals getting hurt or robbed doing this. [A50]

A researcher at a large hospital in Pacific City who was engaged in a study of patient environments also corroborated both facts—that Skid Row alcoholics often live with working women and that they are often taken in and cared for after discharge by female hospital personnel.[75]

Of course, a third source of female companionship is the women alcoholics and prostitutes in the area, who are always eager to earn drinking money. One hotel is reputed to cater primarily to aging women prostitutes whose prices are low enough for the Skid Row man. With these resources available, the men claim they shun the well-known homosexual bars in the Row. Further, it is documented that they complain when located near the "drag queens" in County Jail. (See chapter 5.) This is not to say that Skid Row men do not engage in any homosexual activities but rather that when they do, it has some of the character of a money-making enterprise or some of the make-do sexual gratification reported in prisons. As one man put it:

> Sure, I've gone with some fags—when I couldn't afford women. [18]

Social Contact

Although many of the studies already cited have referred to the Skid Row man as lonesome and undersocialized, any observer who spends any period of time on Skid Row will be struck by the general air of open conviviality there.[76]

A walk on Skid Row on a passably nice day is different from a walk in almost any other part of the city—even ignoring the obvious physical deterioration of the area. The difference is that social life, which in other areas is usually conducted in homes, restaurants, cars, shops, and other more enclosed spaces, takes place on Skid Row on the sidewalk much as it does for children playing in a suburban cul-de-sac. In other parts of the city, the sidewalk is used by adults as a pathway between a point of origin and a point of destination so that it presents areas of continual, on-going movement. On Skid Row, however, the sidewalks are used as areas for conversing, drinking, watching traffic, and panhandling. As a result, the purposeful pedestrian gets a feeling of moving through a private outdoor area (not quite as private as a national forest campground—which is often like walking through a series of bedrooms). It is more comparable to some of the characteristic use of outdoor space that might be found on a college campus.

Bain, whose study of Skid Row at times approaches an ethnography, reflects some of the small pleasures of outdoor life on Skid Row:

> Singly and in small groups the Skid Rowers swagger to their favorite meeting places, being careful to first line their stomachs with their main grease-heavy meal of the day. Their faces are flushed and their eyes excited as they converse and call to each other in jocular fashion. In brief, their whole attitude is one of eager anticipation of an imminent, highly pleasurable, esoteric event.[77]

It is suggested that many parallels between Skid Row and a college campus are obscured by the fact that in one area the dominant enterprise (getting educated) is considered worthy, while in the other area the dominant enterprise (conviviality and getting drunk) is not. Note the following parallels:

> Both students and Row men use outdoor space for conviviality to a far greater extent than do adult persons in conventional middle-class settings.

Groups of men will utilize sidewalks, stairways, railings, the grass, doorways and windowledges, dark alleys and lighted street corners for talking and drinking. (This latter use exposes participants to arrest. When I asked one why he drank in an alley with friends instead of in his room where he was immune to police surveillance, he replied, "Why do you eat out when you could eat at home?" [4])

Skid Row residents or students instantly have something in common that allows them to be friendly toward one another without seeming unduly forward or losing status. On Skid Row it is the need for alcohol, discussions of experience with the police, hotel owners, and bartenders. On the college campus it is sharing of similar classes or experiences with certain professors, or mutual interest in campus social or political events.

Both Skid Row residents and students have flexible schedules and can sit and talk for hours without anyone thinking it odd. For the student, his schedule of leisure is dependent upon his class commitments; for the Skid Row man it is dependent on whether he has some "arrangements" (for shelter, etc.) to make, a spot job, or some panhandling to do.

Both areas offer a great deal of acceptance and friendship; that is, by the very fact a man is *in* the area [of Skid Row or the campus], he is extended some friendship. Many persons remember this about their college days more than any other feature. Note the following remarks, which were made by Skid Row alcoholics about the area, but could, as well, be about the average college campus:

> There's more friendship down through there and that's why it draws the people down there more. [30]

> It's the kind of area where people talk together and take walks together and everything like that. [19]

> You don't have to worry, you can make friendships. People just walk up and make friends with you. [30]

> People on Skid Row are so open. It's a good place to drink. [44]

> It's a very comfortable environment. The men are not judgmental. [25]

> There's a lack of pretense . . . straightforwardness, no airs, no make believe . . . no hoity toity business, you know . . . direct. [41]

> They aren't constrained or acting in a certain way, wearing certain kinds of clothes. You don't feel like a fifth wheel. [53]

There are other parallels as well:

Skid Row alcoholics or students both live on very little money and rely on special part-time or idiosyncratic ways of making money.

Both groups find that they can get almost all things they need at a lower cost: food, shelter, clothing, infirmary services, barber shop.

As with a campus, there is always something doing on Skid Row that anybody can watch or join. Life is both spontaneous and communal. Just as college can be utilized as a four-year moratorium on becoming adult, so Skid Row is an area in which adult responsibilities can be held in abeyance. The "college Joe" stereotype of the student who does not allow his studies to interfere with his social life has its parallel with the Skid Row alcoholic who said:

> It seemed that the hours between eight and five interfered with what you might call the playboy life. Work interfered with the other things. I couldn't get anything done in the form of pleasure and the type of work I did was always physically hard and I'd come home in the evening and I'd be exhausted. So finally I quit to devote myself full time to partying for a while. [39]

The air of expectancy that is part of any exciting environment (things are happening, things are about to happen) is certainly present both on the campus and on Skid Row and reflects what little future orientation the Skid Row man does exhibit. Its contrast to the middle-class type of future orientation is striking. Among the middle class, future orientation usually refers to more or less explicit *plans* for the future, accompanied by delayed gratification in order to make these plans reality. On the other hand, when Skid Rowers think of the future it is in terms of *chance* not of plans—the hope for a better tomorrow without much idea of how this improvement is going to be accomplished.[78] Witness these comments by men as to why they consider Skid Row an exhilarating place to live:

> You go to Skid Row to get drunk. It's no good to drink alone. You go to see the action. See someone bat someone in the eye-ball. That's why the guys return—to see what's happening. [51]
>
> . . . . Like a guy might get a heat on and throw a brick through a plate glass window. [39]
>
> . . . . Like a guy I saw who was drunk, and he climbed up the scaffolding on the outside of a bank where they were cleaning it, and they had to get the fire department to get him down. I wouldn't have wanted to miss that. [48]
>
> You might be standing on the street, and a guy will come up and offer you a job, or pay you back the $2.00 he owes you. You never know what might happen there. [12]

Bain noticed the expectant attitude on the Chicago Skid Row also:

> The daily promenade along the street is a characteristic and highly visible aspect of Skid Row life. Beginning early in the morning, while most of the

city is still asleep, the sidewalks begin to fill with men. Although many have a specific destination in mind, such as going to work or to the employment office, a fair proportion are just drifting along *out to see what is happening on "the Row."* By 10:00 on a fair-weather morning, the sidewalk is crowded for the entire stretch of West Madison Street, from the Northwestern Station to Ogden Avenue—walking seems to have a primarily social purpose. (Emphasis mine.) [79]

The subject matter of Skid Row conversations covers a wide range and is by no means limited to, or even centered upon, descriptions of past glories, as some studies of Skid Row infer.

I heard the following topics discussed:

The possibility of flying saucers and men from other planets
The harmfulness of drug-taking as opposed to drinking (This attitude is very
    prevalent among Skid Row alcoholics.)
Ways in which the police can be outwitted
Ways in which the police show humanity
The current low level of morality in the country—especially that of youth
Skid Row characters and their activities
Ways of panhandling or making a little money
The current state of the County Jail
American foreign policy and what should be done about "subversives and
    shirkers" (Skid Row men are very patriotic.)
Who is on the Row, who is sick, who has died, who is currently in an insti-
    tution
Capers they have pulled or that have been pulled by others
Women, good and bad ones; how to meet them

The list is endless. It is a mixture of everyday conversation and subjects specific to their way of life.[80]

A Skid Row man told me that among his cohorts the conversation is:

. . . evenly divided between sex and women talk and talk about how to
get by. These guys try to live off of someone else and they got every little
racket and scheme that you ever heard of, just to get a hold of a little
money. [38]

An Average Day

Through the aid of multivariate analysis, Bogue characterized the average day of a Skid Row alcoholic as boring, insecure, often lonely, filled with fears about robbery, worry about the next meal and the next bed, and overridden by physical malaise caused by alcoholism.

Within their perspective, how do the alcoholics themselves describe a typical day? Two samples are presented:

On good days, I get a buddy and we walk all over town. We see all the tourist sights [he names them], carry a bottle with us and drink along the way. Sometimes we go sit in the town square, watch the people go by, window shop and as long as we don't openly loiter or panhandle, the police leave us alone during the day. They have to, there are too many of us—just keep your eyes open and you'll see us all over the city. [51]

In the evening, go to the movies, the girly shows and in between, "socialize," party, sit and talk in the bars, alleys, or sometimes read. We eat at odd times during the day if we got money. If not, then we eat when the missions put it out. My buddy and I once stayed drunk for six months straight living like that. [44]

Another gave his day in an orderly, chronological fashion:

6 A.M. Get up and hit the stores. I sweat it out until 6 o'clock many a morning. After I get a bottle, I pass it around. There is a great deal of comradeship then.

Don't have no breakfast or coffee. After I've finished my 6 o'clock bottle, I go scouting for someone with a bottle or with a check.

10 A.M. Probably I'm loaded again by this time.

Noon Go to a mission for a meal.

Afternoon Hustle for bottles, panhandle, or steal. Personally, I'd rather steal, I got some pride.

Evening Go to a mission for an earbeating [sermon] and a meal. Sometimes take a dive and get a bed. If no bed, then walk around till 6 A.M. again, or join a drinking party.

Most of us get about two to three hours sleep a night. Wine keeps us going. Four, five, or six bottles per day is nothing for a real wino to drink. [48]

A man who claims to have lived under the bridge (a highway viaduct) for 16 years gives his day as follows:

5 A.M. Get up and have a drink. I don't go to the stores then, there's too many standing in line. I save a bit of my last bottle for first thing in the morning. Then go back to sleep. I can tell the time by a big insurance company clock on the building across from me.

6:30 A.M. Go to stores, get a bottle and take a drink. Then I have some breakfast.

9 A.M. Have some coffee at a cafe and then hit the streets and panhandle the early morning crowd. I make from $3.00 to $10.00 a day this way.

Noon Go to a movie and stay there until 4 P.M. Eat dinner in the movie, usually a hot dog.

Rest of day until evening Drink. I join the bottle parties, but I bring my own bottle because nobody likes the kind of wine I drink.

Evening Have a bowl of soup and then go to bed. [52]

MULTIPLE REALITIES AND THE "INSIGHT PHENOMENON"

Which view of Skid Row is the "real one"? Is it a pathological area— a dirty, miserable, smelly firetrap, peopled by ill, discouraged, and even desperate men? Or is it a warm and friendly but ragged campus, abounding in opportunities for socializing, camaraderie, making deals, playing games, and getting by? Are the men exploited or are they the exploiters? Are they lonesome or surrounded by sociability?

Must there be a choice made between these two frames of reference or could they both be correct? Does the hangover that follows overindulgence mean that the party itself was no fun? Do meanings and images remain the same, or do they, like the ambiguous figures used as illustrations in psychology books, change and then change again before our very eyes as in the famous Rubin vase figure-ground or the Schroeder reversing stairway illustrations? See Figure 1.[81]

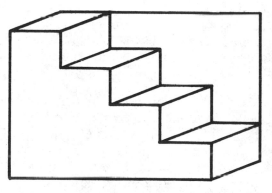

FIGURE 1

Psychologists imply by such illustrations that ambiguity (or shifting definitions) is the special province of certain objects. Actually, the change in appearance and meaning is the result of the application of different frames of mental reference to the same phenomena. In everyday life, such a change in meaning is usually viewed as "an insight," and to have an object revert back again (which it often does) is sometimes quite surprising and enlightening.

In the discussion of professional frames of reference for assessing Skid

Row, it was earlier suggested that a major reason the area is seen as pathological is because it is being compared with middle-class living arrangements. This assumption seems to be further justified by the reaction of men to Skid Row when they first go back to the area after having spent some nondrinking time in the hygienic atmosphere of some institution. *Their* perspective becomes, for a time, *middle-class*:

> My room was awful. It was cold and I was afraid to get into the bed, so I sat on the edge of the bed all night with a blanket around my shoulders. It was just filthy. The whole place was filthy. [45]

> I'll never forget one place the Welfare sent me. I went to use the bathroom and there was no water in the commode, and it was full of what a commode's used for. It turns your stomach. [43]

On the subject of friendship versus loneliness on Skid Row, they are equally ambivalent. On the one hand, they claim that Skid Row offers them the only companionship available, that they are either shunned or harassed when off the Row. On the other hand, most of them readily admit that they have no close friends on the Row, that the men are too transient, too many are out to take advantage of a drunk. However, even the shallow character of secondary relationships expressed through conviviality, although not like primary links with family and friends, may be preferred to no relationships at all. As one man put it:

> Skid Row accepts anyone, I don't care who you are, they'll drink with you. Of course, it don't pay to make close friends—they are here today and gone tomorrow. Just good drinking companions. But its better than the way I lived off the Row, I like to nearly die I was so lonesome. [30]

Interestingly, men from Skid Row indicate during interviews that they are sometimes aware of their ambivalent and changing attitudes. Temporary dislike or even intense hatred of the Skid Row area and its activities, followed by vows never to return all seem like natural reactions to the men when they are sober. Also seen as natural are the attractions of the area and their eventual capitulation to its seductive qualities.

> It's a funny thing. Sometimes you'll be at a party and it seems as though everyone is speaking brilliantly. Then, when you sober up and think it over, it isn't brilliant at all. In fact, nobody made sense, including myself. [39]

> I can only stay there (in Skid Row) so long. I have been on benders on Skid Row that might have lasted, like, two or three weeks, a month, something of that kind, uh, but uh, this acceptance of the area lasts only as long as the drunk lasts. Once I, so to speak, come to and see where I am, I can't stand it after two or three days. [40]

Often such comments are prefaced by:

"Now I see that . . ."

"Then I began to think that . . ."

"All of a sudden it looked different to me . . ."

They sometimes see their lives through the eyes of others:

It's when I think of my family that I know how far I've fallen. I wouldn't want them to know where I am now—at the bottom of the barrel. [53]

Bogue quotes a member of a metropolitan police force, who also noticed the change in perspective that Skid Row drunks undergo as a result of temporary separation from the area:

I have noticed that when these men go to jail for a good stretch, 15 or 20 days, they act like strangers to Skid Row for a while when they first get back. It's as if they got a chance to see how bad it really is. And they don't drink. Then after several days they fall in again.[82]

2
Making the Rehab Route
Dual Perspectives
on Rehabilitation Agencies

INTRODUCTION

Much of the literature on both excessive drinking and Skid Row living contains testimony about the socially-isolating results of these activities. For instance, Clapp describes the gradual narrowing of the alcoholic's social world:

> Potential alcoholics live in a progressively smaller and smaller pasture with increasingly higher and higher fences, almost as though they were following some pre-designed pattern, and their view of the world constantly diminishes until they spend most of the time looking at themselves. In due course, the fences get so high that nothing can be seen over them and the pasture becomes so small it can't contain anything but you and alcohol. When that happens—you've had it, you're an alcoholic.[1]

The geographically-restricted life of the Skid Row alcoholic has been discussed in the previous chapter. It was suggested that Skid Row functions as a reservation or collecting place where homeless deviants feel welcome, but with rather well-demarcated boundaries beyond which the men may not go without risking suspicious, hostile stares, and possible arrest if their appearance is too far below middle-class standards. Although all this is true, it is not the complete story.

It has been mentioned that public concern about a perceived social problem tends to create among other things, public institutions that will ameliorate the problem. Certainly this is true in the case of the Skid

Row alcoholic. A quick glance at the list of correctional, welfare, charitable, and public health-sponsored rehabilitative agencies for alcoholics in any metropolitan area will confirm this.[2]

As an unintended consequence of such proliferation, the life space of the Skid Row alcoholic is not nearly so geographically and socially constricted as might be supposed.

There is evidence to indicate that Skid Row is better described as an urban reservation with accessible satellites in the form of agencies and institutions concerned with the alcoholic's problems. Viewed from this wider perspective, cultural, social, and geographic variety is available to the Skid Row man since a substantial proportion of the clientele of these satellite institutions are from Skid Row.[3]

The major purpose of this chapter is to briefly describe and codify the general constellation of Pacific City public institutions devoted to the control, care, and cure of alcoholics, first as seen from the point of view of agents of social control and then by alcoholics themselves.

Basis for the codification will be the ideological position the particular institution takes on alcoholism causation and control, and their rehabilitation methods, since these factors, in turn, set the cultural atmosphere of the organization. The relationship between the Skid Row man, the agents of social control, and the various institutions will also be described.

A few remarks limiting the scope and general applicability of this discussion are in order here.

Focus will be on public institutions in and near Pacific City, inasmuch as the many private institutions for alcoholics are not normally available to the Skid Row man. Alcoholics Anonymous will not be counted as a public agency but rather as a *resource* used by the public agencies.[4] In this capacity, however, AA functions as an important contributor to alcoholic rehabilitation culture. It must also be emphasized initially that the way in which the Skid Row alcoholic perceives his reception and treatment in these institutions is not necessarily the same as that of the middle-class alcoholic—nor are the problems the agents of social control have with Skid Row alcoholics likely to be the same as those encountered with middle-class alcoholics.

CONTROL AND CONTAINMENT VERSUS THERAPY AND REHABILITATION

Two major themes dominate public action toward problem drinkers. First is the primary concern with keeping order in society. Here activities can be classified as strategies of control and containment of the public drunk. The second dominant public approach places emphasis on methods of therapy in order to rehabilitate alcoholics (i.e., turn them into sober, responsible citizens) and thus eventually do away with the necessity for control and containment.

Underlying each approach is a theory or theories, implicit or explicit, as to (1) the cause(s) of excessive drinking, (2) the essence of the alcoholic's moral character or personality, and (3) a prescription for the type of defining encounter that takes place between the alcoholic and agent of social control, at least initially. (It will be noted that these theories are specific to *alcoholism* and differ, to some extent, from theories concerning the genesis of the *Skid Row man*, outlined in the previous chapter.)

The existence of varied approaches to alcoholism, of course, reflects the intellectual turmoil in the field itself. Whether the theories regarding alcoholism and the nature of alcoholics are myths or have some empirical basis is less at issue here than how the theories tend to shape rehabilitation efforts. Ramifications of such belief systems have an appreciable effect on the existential position of the Skid Row problem drinker.

Control and Containment through Punitive-Correctional Strategies

This is a stop-gap approach in Pacific City, intended to keep public drunkenness within manageable bounds until some of the longer-term rehabilitation efforts begin to show an effect.

A drunken man is both a social annoyance and a danger to the sober citizenry. He has deliberately altered his consciousness so as to be less alert and less responsive to the communications of others and to the normal hazards of urban life. As a consequence, he is more likely to engage in nonnormative, "senseless" behavior.

Implied in the control and containment approach is that such behavior is sheer self-indulgence. It can be halted only by a decision to stop on the part of the drinker himself. Punishment of the offender by threat of jail or actual jail sentence is thought to help "straighten him out." [5] It is also considered a way of forcibly imposing abstinence from liquor, hopefully assisting him back "on the wagon." More importantly, it gets the drinker off the streets where, as the arresting ordinance suggests, he might be a "danger to himself or others." [6]

A man who is repeatedly arrested as a drunk is assumed to need increasingly severe punishment (i.e., length of jail sentence) to stop his immature and reckless behavior pattern. Sometimes an attempt is made to reform him through explaining the inevitability of this future punishment, as well as the effects of steady drinking on the body. Pacific City Alcoholism School, which is conducted once a week, consists of lectures on the unpleasant facts of continuous overindulgence in liquor. Attendance is often made a condition of probation.

Defining encounters between agents of social control charged with maintaining the public peace reflect this emphasis on order and on the efforts to contain or suppress the generally annoying characteristics of the Skid Row alcoholic. As two policemen explained it:

> If we didn't round these guys up regularly, pretty soon they'd be lying all over the sidewalks in doorways, bothering merchants and commuters or starting fights and getting hurt. [A2]

> They tend to congregate in a place and start drinking. Pretty soon there's a fight. We have to prevent this. [A3]

Thus the settings the Skid Row drunk encounters at the control and containment extensions of Skid Row are the police stations, the courts, and the jails, where he is cast in the role of a misdemeanant.[7] A list of these agencies can be found in Table 2.

TABLE 2. *Punitive Correctional Institutions*

Behavior Setting	Official Purpose	Average Stay
City Jail ("drunk tank")	Sobering up	Overnight
City Jail	Punishment for public drunkenness, drying out	Anywhere from 5 to 20 days
Alcoholism School	Education on evils of alcoholism	One night a week for four weeks
County Jail	Punishment for public drunkenness repeaters; breaking drinking cycle	10, 20, 30, 60 or 90 days (sometimes 120 days)

Rehabilitation Through Strategies of Therapy

There are two major strategies of rehabilitation, each based on a different theory of alcoholism causation. One approach centers on the psychological (and physiological) problems of the alcoholic, the other on his moral and spiritual problems with additional emphasis on development of good work habits.

MENTAL THERAPY AND ALCOHOLISM A major theory of alcoholism causation is that this behavior stems from some type of personality or psychological problem. This redefines chronic drunkenness from an action into a symptom and the drinker from "a problem person" to "a person with a problem." Because of this different outlook, amnesty is granted by society to the drinker for a period of time. The personality and situational forces that compel the individual to self-destruction through drink are then sought through the help of a professional analyst or therapist. The goal is self-understanding for the alcoholic so that he can develop more "mature" responses to his problems.[8] Accordingly, he is treated more kindly. The implication of the therapeutic approach is that the alcoholic lacks or has underdeveloped adult insight into his situation, and thus should not be judged too harshly.

Therapy for mental problems is presumed to be a joint undertaking of the hospital staff and the drinker, and it centers on gaining "insight" into the alcoholic's "real problems." As one therapist put it:

> Drinking represents an escape for these men and we'd like to help them find out what they are trying to escape from. They are sick and need help. [A17]

As an adjunct to therapy for psychological problems, medical aid is also given for physical symptoms brought on by an extended period of heavy drinking.

Ingestion of large amounts of alcohol affects a drinker adversely by causing extremely unpleasant and undesirable physical[9] and mental symptoms[10] quite different from the pleasurable euphoria and tension reduction that alcohol initially induces. For this reason, therapeutic institutions in Pacific City include a concern for the physical condition of the alcoholic. Treatment can vary from emergency aid during an alcoholic overdose to the one-to-five day detoxification routine needed to avoid delirium tremens, hallucinations, and possible seizures. If the drinking has continued over a long period of time, the alcoholic almost always has problems with his liver, stomach, or brain, and may need lengthy hospitalization.

MORAL WEAKNESS AND SPIRITUAL REJUVENATION   Although this approach is therapeutic and rehabilitative in orientation, it is based on a different view of the essential character of the alcoholic and cause of his excessive drinking. Emphasis here is on the man's lack of self-discipline and, in one sense, this focus has some rapprochement with control and containment theories because of the belief that man is responsible for his own actions and cannot blame them on some unknown, uncontrollable defense mechanism.

However, in philosophy, if not in fact, the moral weakness view is in opposition to both punishment and medical therapy as a way to rehabilitate the problem drinker. The presumption of the former is that the alcoholic lacks sufficient self-discipline and religious ideals to resist overindulgence. His best chance for survival as a social and economic man is to experience and ultimately embrace a well-ordered life following God's commandments.

Major advocates of this approach are the men and women of the missions that dot Skid Row. To quote a staff member of the Christian Missionaries:

I scc Skid Row alcoholics essentially as men who have lost their way. They are rudderless, and have nothing to guide their lives or to cling to. We try to bring Jesus Christ to their lives so that they can be born again and will not need to drink. [A34]

An encounter frequently reported by both alcoholics and some of the mission staff is for the mission officer to say to the drunk who has come in for help:

Get down on your knees by my desk here and we will pray that you will be saved by God from your sins. [18]

These implications concerning the moral character of the problem drinker have an effect on both the culture he encounters in the missions and defining encounters with the staff members. For example, religious and AA meetings take up large blocks of time at the mission. The rest of the day is spent in hard work and clean living, although not all missions put an emphasis on work. Some focus on prayer alone. However, the largest and best known mission organization combines the two.

We try to offer the men a highly-structured program, with very strict discipline so that they can get practice in disciplining their lives again. They are alone. They have no one who cares and so they care for no one. We try to change that. [A32]

Listed in Table 3 are some of the many rehabilitative institutions for alcoholics of Pacific City.

TABLE 3. *Therapeutic Institutions*

Behavior settings	Official purpose	Length of stay
State Mental Hospital	Psychological therapy; detoxification; drying out	90 days recommended
Jail Branch Clinic	Psychological therapy; detoxification; drying out	Length of jail sentence (usually 30 days or less)
Out-patient therapy center	Personal psychological therapy on an out-patient basis	No time limit—varies with interest of patient
* Welfare Home for Homeless Men	Aid with detoxification; drying out; AA meetings	90 days recommended
Christian Clinic	Detoxification (out-patient basis)	No stay
City Hospital	Detoxification	1–5 days (also operates as out-patient clinic)
City Emergency Hospital	Emergency aid for alcoholics suffering from DT's, seizures, etc.	1 day (more often handled as out-patient)

TABLE 3. (Cont'd.)

Behavior settings	Official purpose	Length of stay
Chronic Illness Center	For older "hopeless" chronic drinkers with physical complications	Several months to several years to death
Christian Missionaries * Work and Residence Center	Spiritual renewal and . . . Employment for unemployables in exchange for room and board	6 months recommended †
* Beacon in Darkness	Emergency dormatory and permanent halfway house	Overnight and up to 6 months recommended †
* Shepherd's Home	Hotel (single rooms) for alcoholics. Work in community	6 months recommended †
* Barabas' Abode	Recidivists from County Jail (may or may not be alcoholics)	6 months recommended †

* These institutions also function as halfway houses (residences for men who have undergone treatment for alcoholism and are not yet ready to function on their own). Halfway houses are not treatment centers as such, although they often sponsor AA meetings. For this reason, they are not included in this list of treatment stations, although they do function as part of the loop.
† The range of stay is so broad at the missions that an average is somewhat meaningless. Dissidents leave in a week or so; others stay for years. (See chapter 7.)

None of the three approaches outlined here is utilized in an ideologically pure form by its staff. For instance:

Jails have facilities or arrangements for emergency medical aid to problem drinkers and offer group therapy as well. Alcoholics Anonymous groups also hold meetings at the jail.

Mental Hospitals offer chemical therapy and the City Hospital offers "psychiatric examinations." Both have a punitive tinge in terms of involuntary commitment in the case of the former, and 24- or 48-hour holds in the case of the latter, plus other restrictions on freedom. Both offer a stress-free environment (at least from conventional stresses) with strict rules. The Mental Hospital offers employment possibilities and, despite ideological differences, encourages Alcoholics Anonymous to hold meetings on the grounds.

Christian Missionaries offer semisheltered living, hire psychiatrists, give personality tests, and organize therapy groups. They are served by Alcoholics Anonymous, as well.

Such eclecticism perhaps indicates an awareness on the part of officials at each of these rehabilitation stations as to the highly problematic nature of their approach to a cure; offering subsidiary services drawn from other ideologies leaves them less exposed to charges that they are ignoring a possibly better method for the rehabilitation of alcoholics.

All agents of social control who work in the field of alcoholism are faced with the constant spectre of failure. The Skid Row alcoholic shows a great resistance to any approach that seeks to curb his excessive drinking—whether containment and control or therapeutic. Thus a regular complaint of the professional is:

I keep seeing the same guys over and over again.

THE ROUTING DILEMMA

With so many institutions devoting all or part of their facilities to some rehabilitation attempts on problem drinkers in Pacific City, it can be seen that the life space to which the homeless alcoholic man has access is greatly expanded. The next logical question would seem to be: Which alcoholics go where and on what grounds?

One possible answer is that each of the three rehabilitation philosophies is admirably suited to a *certain type of problem drinker*. For instance, it might be assumed from the different way an alcoholic is treated at each behavior setting that these approaches arose from an obvious differentiation in the drinkers' characteristics and responses to rehabilitation efforts. Thus some drinkers might respond best to punishment, some need aid in drying out before they can break away from drinking, some need self-insight, while others thrive best in an environment of strict rules and spiritual guidance.

An alternative is that although each of these philosophies represent viable theoretical approaches to chronic drunkenness, none has proved particularly applicable to a special type of drinker and, in fact, no particular effort is being made to segregate these particular types and to shuttle them to the most appropriate treatment center.

If this latter is true, then being punished or being given either psychological or spiritual therapy for drinking may often be the result of chance, or of factors not directly connected with current theories of alcoholism or the character of the alcoholic. The lack of anything approaching even modest success by any of these agencies leads to the conclusion that a large scale, continuous mismatching of services and clients may exist.

Both institutional agents and Skid Row problem drinkers are aware of this surfeit of rehabilitation activities and agencies, and of the lack of any empirical guidance as to the consignment of cases. Each sees the manner of routing characteristically in keeping with his own perspectives and experiences. The official version will be presented first.

Institutional Referral System

Institutions must often be bureaucracies. Bureaucracies provide themselves with needed internal services by setting up departments or subdivisions assigned to specialized tasks. Separate agencies, all dedicated to the same goal may sponsor (or have forced on them) external departments or agencies that act in the same capacity as internal departments do within a single organization. This is exactly what has been done to aid the placement of a problem drinker. Special screening facilities have been created to sort alcoholics for differential treatment. These formal sorting and routing facilities are outlined in Table 4.

TABLE 4. *Sorting and Routing Facilities*

Municipal Court	Responsible for County Jail sentences, probation, alcoholism school directives, as well as referrals to Christian Missionaries and City Screening Facility.
Superior Court	Responsible for involuntary commitments to State Mental Hospital and to County Jail. Arranges for attention at psychiatric ward of City Hospital.
City Screening Facility	Officially the major screening agency. Designed to refer problem drinkers who come to them voluntarily or by "police assignment" to the proper agency or another screening facility.
Social Welfare	Responsible for physical maintenance of qualifying indigents and referral to other agencies.

Such screening activity has at least five official purposes and is a crucial location for defining encounters. Ostensibly, the first is to sort the alcoholic population needing aid into groups of similar drinkers who could presumably benefit from a specific approach to their problem. Second, in the case of proposed *involuntary commitment*, the decision to do so and the length of such incarceration must be decided. Third, where agencies have entrance requirements, the eligibility of the men voluntarily seeking help from the institution must be established. Fourth, the ever-pressing search for the "most hopeful cases" as distinguished from the "hopeless" has become an important part of screening.[11] Fifth, clients are sometimes screened for readiness to "make it on their own," especially if welfare aid or referral to another agency is involved.

The first activity, sorting, is possibly the least frequent in occurrence. Superior Court judges sometimes must decide whether County Jail, the State Mental Hospital, or the Out-Patient Therapy Center is best for the man with a compulsive drinking problem. But in most cases the judges will send the man where he asks to go. City Screening Facility attempts to get physically-ill alcoholics out of the jail and into hospitals, and thus supplies data for Superior and Municipal Court decisions about where to send a particular defendant.

Involuntary commitment to jail is primarily a function of Municipal Court. Currently, Superior Court makes few involuntary commitments either to the mental hospital or jail, although this is one of its functions. Eligibility requirements, the third focus of screening, revolve around residence, economic status, and sometimes general physical condition and is handled by each institution individually as well as by screening facilities.

It is the last two screening activities (both concerned with the search for "successful" clients), that are possibly crucial in their effect on the Skid Row man's destiny. These screening functions are given the least amount of official mention and are dependent on the most nebulous criteria. The presumed presence of "sincerity" of desire to stop drinking opens certain doors, allows entry to therapy groups, prevents involuntary incarceration, and prevents or enhances premature discharge. Possession of "a plan" to "make it on the outside" often ensures welfare and job-seeking aid. All screening facilities are involved in these activities.

The official flow chart in Figure 2 is a plan for the orderly process

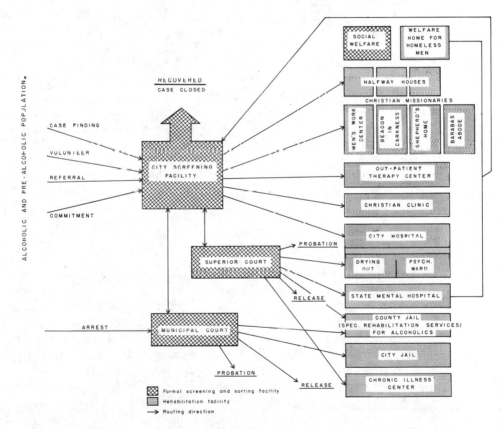

FIGURE 2 *Flow Chart Depicting Official Processing System for Alcoholics in Pacific City*

Adapted from diagram of a proposed system for coordinated community and state alcoholism facilities and services (later adopted). Private facilities and Alcoholics Anonymous groups have been omitted (although they are on the original chart), the former because they are not available to indigent alcoholics; the latter because they are not used extensively by Skid Row drinkers.

of screening and referral of each case of problem drinking that comes to the attention of a referral facility, as well as links between connecting institutions. An important aspect of this chart is the presumed resolution of referred cases as "Recovered, case closed." The following steps seem to be implied as standard procedure:

Step 1. Case finding: The alcoholic is sent by others (or goes by himself) to a sorting and routing facility.

Step 2. Case screening: The alcoholic is referred to some rehabilitation station.

Step 3. Character reform takes place: The alcoholic undergoes the treatment offered by the agency to which he was referred.

Step 4. Reevaluation by City Screening Facility: The alcoholic's case, along with his "progress in treatment," is reviewed and further referrals for his disposition are made.

Step 5. Return to Society (or retrace Steps 2, 3, and 4): Hopefully, the alcoholic stops excessive drinking and becomes a sober, useful citizen.

In regard to Step 5, since the recidivism rate is high,[12] the professionals in rehabilitation are not so unrealistic as to expect a complete cure in all cases, or even a substantial number of them. They see the same men too often. While the alcoholic is out of a given institution, however, there is always the assumption he is in a state of remission, trying to "make it" on the outside. As we shall see, this is the "more realistic" goal set by the agents of social control. Thus the phrase "case closed, recovery" on the flow chart is a general ideal rather than a specific factual result in most cases.

UNDERGROUND CONVEYOR SYSTEMS

Undoubtedly, the referral and processing plans of Pacific City institutions are intended to assist what are thought to be the bulk of *alcoholics*, that is, middle-class men, who do, in fact, constitute a majority of heavy drinkers (see page 65) but only a minority of institutionalized men. How are the "best laid plans" described above, perceived and utilized by the *client* majority—the Skid Row chronic drunkenness offenders? What sense do these men make of the master plan for rehabilitation that confronts them and that is such an important part of their life space?

The fact that informal structures develop within formal or official institutional organizations is certainly no new or startling discovery.[13] In fact, it was a part of folk wisdom long before it became standard sociological theory. Almost everyone who has ever tried to "learn the ropes" of some institution knows that there is much more to social action than its official chain of command chart or the annual report.

Informal constructs of organizations are retained in the minds of the persons who discover their importance in guiding action. They seldom are made available as part of a job description or rules book, although they often have more validity, in terms of prediction of action, than the formal structure.[14]

However, of the studies that are fairly representative of the issue (see footnote 14), all are analyses of informal social networks that spring up *within* a given institution. The development of informal inter-institutional networks has received far less notice. Nevertheless the phenomenon does occur.

For instance, institutions may be mentally rank-ordered by employees according to pay scale, promotions, prestige, and on-the-job experience offered, and then used as stepping stones in professional advancement. Both corporation men and college professors use the routes provided by this approach to success. This practice is also common among candidates for political office, as the political club chairman is elected City Councilman and then, after a period of service, seeks higher office.

Each of these arrangements is "real" and useful to the arranger, just as informal intra-institutional arrangements are. Each has some effect on the formal set-up. It seems safe to suggest also that the more and varied the institutions dedicated to the same purpose, the more complicated the inter-institutional linking through informal interaction. Thus, although the organization of sorting and routing centers is perceived as entirely orderly and logical by agents of social control, this is not true for the Skid Row problem drinker. He sees little rhyme or reason as to why he is sent to one institution rather than to another. This failure to comprehend the formal inter-institutional organization is primarily because the alcoholic experiences movement from one institution to another that is not a part of the official plan.

> You can get picked up by the police and sent to jail, from there picked up and go to the hospital, maybe from there be sent to the mental hospital, and after discharge to a mission. There doesn't seem to be any reason for you to be one place more than any other. [13]

Regardless of the lack of logic in the unofficial order within the official inter-agency links, however, the Skid Row alcoholics make their own special brand of sense out of what appears to be happening to them. Briefly, the Skid Row man perceives this constellation of available institutions as linked in so many ways that a man may pass from one to another (with visits to Skid Row in between) indefinitely. Time spent in one institution very often becomes a bridge to another. Structurally there is always some type of informal linking between institutions in the form of recruitment or referral negotiations on the part of the staff or the men themselves.[15]

Skid Row, in this context then, is a home territory for the indigent drinking man. It is a special environment that has become, for many problem drinkers, a sort of "central station"—a dispatching and receiving area in relationship to outlying public institutions. That such circles of institutions for problem drinkers exist in all major U.S. cities is well known on Skid Row, and the more adventurous man will "patronize" more than one locality.[16]

Going to one or more institutions is known among Skid Row down-and-out men as "making the loop" or "making the circle." As noted, the stations become part of the expanded Skid Row environment, and as such are utilized to make it better. Comments such as the following are typical of the feeling that game-playing the loop is part of being on Skid Row.

> I never worry when a friend of mine is missing [from Skid Row]. I know he's out making the loop and will be back. [48]

> Do you know, there's a whole underground of guys doing the circle here and then going to other cities and doing it there. They are always "seeking help." That's how they do it. They wear out one area and then move to another. They know how to play the roles expected. They know games Dr. Berne hasn't heard of. [A47] [17]

> You know, you get in a rut making the rounds from State Mental Hospital to County Jail, to Welfare Home. When you leave one of those places, you go back to the City and hit the same spots and go back to Skid Row because that's the only section of the City you know. You just go down there, that's all. [45]

> Well, let's see, I've been staying here at the Mental Hospital five weeks. The time before that I stayed at the Home [Welfare Home] eight weeks. Then I spent six weeks with the Christian Missionaries and 30 days at the Welfare Home for Homeless Men again. Of course, that's just this year. [29]

The men are aware of the importance of defining encounters as a ticket of admission to the various stations on the loop:

> You can get on the circle by going to City Hospital and then claiming you hear voices telling you to commit suicide and that you have a drinking problem. They will send you to a State Mental Hospital. When you get out of there, you can continue your treatment at the Out-patient Clinic in the city, and sometimes they arrange for you to stay at one of those halfway houses. I stayed at one of the church ones. [37]

> Where you go depends on who is looking at you and how you act. I once rubbed a judge the wrong way and he sent me to County Jail instead of State Mental Hospital like I asked. [26]

There is also an awareness of the way the loop can be used to "make out" in time of stress:

I got so sick from drinking I had to do something. So I got on a bus and committed myself to State Mental Hospital. I used to go to General Hospital for that, but lots of time they won't even let you lie down—they just give you a couple of pills and turn you out. The first time I stayed in State Hospital it was only till I got on my feet—eight days. When I got out I had no job, and after a while I started drinking again, so I ended up in County Jail. [43]

After I had been drinking heavy for a time, I got me a room at the Hawthorne Hotel on Skid Row. I felt bad about living there, but I wasn't going to spend money on rent that I could use for wine. When I got sick, someone at the hotel said to go to the Welfare and they sent me out to the Welfare Home. After I get better, I'll get my choice of hotels back on the Row. Oh, you get your choice. They have a list of all those hotels there [on the Row]. [42]

Well, I've been a patient at the Out-patient Clinic and I go to AA meetings and I've been to the State Hospital and Emergency Ward and County Hospital and out at the Welfare Home three times. My landlady holds my room in between. [37]

The Skid Row drinker is sensitive to the fact that imputations concerning his moral character differ from institution to institution. As far as he is concerned, his behavior is no different when he is sent to jail than when he is sent to the mental hospital. Quite naturally, he has a preference for the most favorable definition of himself and attempts to go where the prevailing treatment philosophy will reinforce it. Some stations offer other advantages of which he is well aware also.

I like it here [the Welfare Home] better than any other place I've been because they treat you o.k. In jail you are treated like you committed some crime and at the State Mental Hospital they want to put you in with the M.I.'s [mentally ill]. At the Christian Missionaries, home they stuff religion down you. Here, they leave you alone for the most part. [45]

Since 1955, I've been in the County Jail three times, and that's three times too many for that hell hole. I lost 30 pounds there the last time. After your sentence, they take you and dump you out at the Hall of Justice. You are right near Skid Row and with your old buddies, so you say, "Why not?" . . . and start drinking again. I got lot better treatment at the Welfare Home and at State Mental Hospital. I been there three times too. They don't do anything for your drinking, but food isn't too bad, and they have women alcoholics, which is nice for the dances. Some of my buddies told me about this place [Welfare Home] and I come here instead of State Hospital. [56]

There are several patterns of travel through the Pacific City loop. Not all stations are made by everyone, every time. Patterns may change over time as men "get wise" to the advantages or disadvantages of certain agencies on the loop. Ability to negotiate passage to a particular station on the loop is equally dependent upon the judgments of officials, the desires of the men, and the action as it develops during their encounters. Relatively naive Row men probably have different patterns than men who are "old hands."

For instance, sometimes the passage from place to place on the loop may be at the initiative of others:

After you've been picked up for being drunk on the streets too many times, you get sent to jail and could go to County Jail. That's one of the ways of getting started on the circle again. [47]

My wife arranged to get me arrested for drunk—imagine that! Then I was picked up in jail and taken to City Hospital where they gave me some stuff to help with the shakes. A social worker interviewed me to decide what should be done. Then I was taken to this court—right in the hospital. The judge there sentenced me to County Jail, for therapy, he said, which is a laugh. When my sentence was about up this guy from the Christian Missionaries came and interviewed me and offered me a job working in the salvage shop. I took it, because I wasn't going home after what that bitch did to me. They furnished food, and a bed, and paid only $4 a week to start, which is slave wages. [49]

As one man put it:

Different guys, they do different things. One will do a small circle—to jail and out and back. Another will alternate institutions—jail, hospital, missions, welfare—he just moves around. [41]

In a special subsample of 20 men, an attempt was made to trace patterns of movement through the loop over the years.[18] The following emerged:

Seven men alternated City Jail, County Jail, and Welfare Home for Homeless Men. (Some sporadic visits to City Hospital and free clinics also occurred.)

Four men alternated visits to jail and Welfare Home for Homeless Men with visits to two state mental hospitals and the psychiatric ward of City Hospital.

Two men spent their institutional time with the Welfare Home, the Christian Missionaries, and the jail.

Seven men had been to almost all stations on the loop several times and, in fact, had been to so many so often that they were unable to sort out very successfully length of visit or year of visit at each.

Once a homeless male alcoholic has made the loop, he is likely to make all or part of it again. This is due to a combination of the advantages he thinks are available to him there and the hardships he encounters in society.

Well, let's see, I've been in the State Hospital four times, every time self-committed. Never been committed by a court. I was in the halfway house twice and Welfare Home for Homeless Men several times. Don't ask me how many times I've been to jail because I've forgotten those. With the exception of jail, it isn't so bad. You get a chance to get your breath and dry out while you are in one, get some food and build yourself up. You know, regular hours and all that. You know it's pretty rough to try to make a go of it after you have been drinking for a long time. Lots of these places give a guy something to go back to when he fails on the outside. [19]

Like men who have made crime a career and have friends in every penitentiary and county jail,[19] Pacific City Skid Row alcoholics have friends in almost all institutions on the loop and every reentry is accompanied by a reunion of some kind.

Well, I got friends up at the State Mental Hospital, in fact, sometimes a bunch of us go up there together. Then, I always run into someone I know at the Welfare Home and at the missions, and in the jail—I've never been there when there wasn't some friend there too. [42]

This is the world of alcoholic rehabilitation centers as the Skid Row drinker himself experiences it. He sees a far more complicated and contradictory structure than does the most sophisticated screening and referral agent or professional staff person limited to the confines of his "station" on the loop. The down-and-out drunk has mobility (some of it enforced), and he can experience many correctional and therapeutic approaches. Officials at each station, as in the fable of the seven blind men and the elephant, usually experience only *their* portion of the total constellation. It would take a discussion with the elephant to explain to these persons how it feels to be worked on by seven blind men in succession.[20]

A schematic diagram of the informal routing system of the loop, as experienced by the Skid Row alcoholic, is shown in Figure 3. Both its chaotic nature and the ease of access from one institution to another should be contrasted with the apparent orderliness of the official flow chart (Figure 2, page 55).

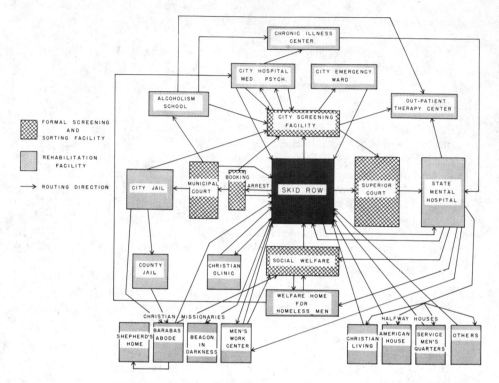

FIGURE 3 *Flow Chart Depicting Processing System for Alcoholics in Pacific City as Experienced by Skid Row Alcoholics*

Thus, although the world of the urban male alcoholic appears to close down as his continued consumption of alcohol increases and he loses such conventional ties as family, friends, employers, and co-workers, a new environment of rehabilitation agencies, serving the same clientele in rotation,[21] opens up to him. If the Row man is adroit, he is not limited to just one of these agencies for sustenance, but can travel from control agencies to therapeutic agencies, to spiritual renewal agencies, returning to Skid Row in between institutional sojourns.

It is not intended to suggest here that public agencies are an adequate substitute for such social anchorages as a wife, children, friends, and a job. They are, however, a wider horizon than the Skid Row man has been presumed to have. On the other hand, as will be seen in chapters to come, these stations on the rehabilitation loop also have a further narrowing effect on the Skid Row man's conventional contacts. Eventually, public institutions become the only territory outside Skid Row open to him.

II

STRATEGIES
OF CONTROL
AND CONTAINMENT

3

Policing Skid Row
and Keeping the Peace

The Dilemma of Handling
The Socially Unattached

INTRODUCTION

As a specialized type of collecting place—where the residents are seen as pathological and some deviant behavior is the expected norm—Skid Row naturally is subject to rather heavy surveillance by police. The job of initiating the punitive-correctional approach to alcoholism control lies with these officers who operate there with a rare mixture of almost paternal indulgence, strictness, and ad hoc decision-making not found elsewhere in the city.

Skid Row drunks are thought to comprise only 3 percent of the total population of alcoholics in a given city.[1] Yet in Pacific City (and many other cities as well) by official police statistics, Skid Row men make up 40 to 45 percent of all arrests for public drunkenness.[2] In raw, rounded figures, 4,200 of the 9,800 arrests for drunkenness made in Pacific City every year are in the Skid Row area. These arrests are further concentrated on a few men: 75 percent of the 4,200—about 3,200—are repeat arrests. There is no indication of how many *repeaters* this involves.[3]

Concentration of the punitive approach on one small segment of the alcoholic population is not too surprising, since these men are the more visibly objectionable among drunks as a class of deviants living, as they do, on the streets. They are usually shabby, often filthy. They sometimes beg money from passersby.

Additionally, defining encounters between police and Skid Row alcoholics are an important aspect of this study because these contacts are an informal avenue by which the drunk can reach formal screening agencies—the courts—and through them get on the loop. On the other side of the coin, the police are simultaneously an element in the Skid Row environment along with the merchants and missions, while being a means of entry to the loop. As a result, every time he acts, the police-man must consider pressures from Skid Row business establishments and from loop institutions, as well as the needs of the inhabitants themselves. These pressures shape arrest patterns of alcoholic men in the area. Skid Row men are aware of these cross pressures, although they may interpret their effect differently than the policeman does.

This chapter will be devoted to an examination of the factors that both the police and the Skid Row alcoholic must take into consideration in a mutual encounter.

THE POLICE VIEW THEIR ASSIGNMENT

Practically speaking, *total* control of a population of approximately 5,000 homeless, jobless, heavily-drinking men would be an impossible task even were the whole police force to concentrate its efforts there. Certain types of illegal behavior—petty theft, minor public fights, and begging—occur there more frequently than in an average middle-class neighborhood.[4] More importantly, there is great *potential* for serious crimes such as muggings, indecent exposure, fatal beatings, rape, and grand theft. This menace is ever-present, especially in the minds of businessmen who operate there, residents of nearby areas who may be disturbed by Skid Row boisterousness or panhandling, walk-through shoppers, and com-muters passing through on their way to and from work.

Two policemen, in discussing what they feel to be their job, said:

> We have girls going to work at the Telephone Company here. They have to walk through this area. We have to provide them with an area they *can* walk through. [A2]

> Primarily, the reason you pick up drunks in the daytime is the mer-chants up there. They complain. [A3]

For the police, then, the problem is not really to "clean up" Skid Row but to keep the area in a state of *relative* safety with the least expenditure of manpower.

Egon Bittner, who did extensive field work on Pacific City police in Skid Row, calls this maintenance of a given level of deviance "peace-keeping." [5] A further implication of his work is that the major thrust of police peace-keeping in Skid Row is not *control* of excessive drinking behavior per se, but avoidance of excessive public annoyance growing out of such drinking behavior. The arrest practices seem to bear this out.

Thus, police protection on Skid Row is of a different type than in most other areas of the city. Elsewhere peace-keeping is usually done on behalf of the residents of the area. On Skid Row, however, police work is done primarily for the benefit of the nonresidents. Furthermore, law enforcement in other areas is much more oriented to prevention or detection of a specific crime and apprehension of a specific criminal than it is in Skid Row.

At the same time, the peace-keeping on the Row can be said to be at least secondarily for the benefit of residents, but more in the manner of the parent who disciplines a child for his own good. Most police consider a drunk arrest to be somewhat benevolent:

> At night we pick up the drunks for protective custody. Ninety percent of drunk arrests are really this sort of arrest. Either they are lying in the street, against a building, or walking in a way that they'll be a detriment to themselves in passing traffic. [A1]

How then do the police manage, with a minimum of manpower, to keep Skid Row from exploding into a serious trouble spot?

There are two levels on which police tools of prevention can be discussed:

1. The actual manpower and machine utilization—that is, the distribution of foot patrols, car patrols, and paddy wagon forays;
2. An awareness of what might be called the psychological, social, and structural components of coercion which can be used strategically for making the most of the resources available. Bittner emphasizes this.[6]

The Tools of Peace-keeping on Skid Row

MACHINE AND MANPOWER UTILIZATION Ideally, according to one police captain, the number of men on duty in Skid Row at any one time are nine during the day and twelve at night. The night shift increase is in expectation of violent crimes, primarily because of the influx of hustlers from the Tenderloin area. The deployment of men for the Row area, approximately 30 blocks, is as follows:

TABLE 5. *Policemen on Skid Row Duty*

Daytime	Nighttime
3 radio cars (1-man)	3 radio cars (2-men)
2 men in wagon	2 men in wagon
4 beat men	4 beat men
9	12

These assignments fluctuate with the need for police in other areas of the city. When trouble hit in the park district, with an influx of hippies and drug dealers, the Skid Row law enforcement contingent was reduced, for example.

The patrol wagon makes five to six regularly-scheduled roundups (as they are referred to by police) on Skid Row; it also stands by to appear on call. The roundup schedule is as follows:

1. 7 or 7:15 to 7:30 A.M.
2. During day when needed (i.e., if called by merchants)
3. 11 A.M.–12 noon "sweep" of the area
4. 2:30 P.M. another "sweep" depending on conditions
5. 4 P.M.
6. 7 or 8 P.M.
7. Midnight

When the wagon is out, drunk arrests take on the character of a sort of human ground patrol. Potentially bothersome men are removed from open view on a regular schedule, and just as apparently are unmolested by police between paddy-wagon visits.

But not all men who could be arrested for public drunkenness (by police judgment) are arrested. Police say that they pass over ten "arrestable" men for each one picked up. In addition, only three of every ten arrestables are even contacted and warned. (Field work indicated that because of certain other conditions, which will be discussed, the number of actual arrests and contacts may be even further reduced.) As one policeman on the beat put it:

> Everytime we go out, we could take in the 40 to 50 men. As it is currently, the total take is about 15 to 25 per day. Generally a wagon comes in with five to eight men. A full load is considered to be 12. If you get over that they fight and vomit on each other. [A3]

What criteria do the police use to determine that some of the Row men are arrestable, with a small number actually worth the time to check out, and an even smaller fraction somehow "qualifying" for arrest? In the answer to this lie the social, psychological, and structural components of police peace-keeping on Skid Row.

SOCIAL PSYCHOLOGY AND THE STRATEGIES OF COERCION   First of all, for a patrol to be effective, it is essential to "know the territory." For the Skid Row patrolman, this commandment breaks down somewhat like this: he must be able to spot Row people—the chronic drunks of the area, as against a possible visitor. He must be able to recognize situations or scenes that will be trouble spots in the future; he must know that certain men getting together or certain gathering places spell trouble.

The seasoned Skid Row policeman is proud of his almost mystical knowledge in these areas, and proud of the empathy he has for the Skid Row residents and their problems:

I can tell an alcoholic from across the street. [A3] [7]

A green policeman has a tough time telling who is who. You are looking for the confirmed alcoholic. How can you tell one? Well, he doesn't look like a banker. He has a dirty shirt, disheveled hair, dirty fingernails. Unkempt is the word. This is number one. Of course, there is the flushed face and the sallow complexion from cirrhosis. He is in poor physical condition. Those are the ones to arrest. [A4]

A Skid Row policeman lives with these people. You have to get to know them and be one of them. You have to know how they feel. We know the hangovers and the dry heaves ourselves.[8] Consequently, we know them and have compassion for them. [A3]

You see a fellow who is slipping and going down, down, and we help him out—which sometimes means to get him 30 to 45 days at County Jail. [A4]

Secondly, because the wagon could not possibly handle all those who could be arrested, the patrolman has other ways of controlling his territory. The officer must know the men who drink heavily so well that he can warn them of the impending arrival of the wagon and get them off the streets before it comes—sometimes before they even get drunk. So far as the policeman is concerned, this accomplishes the same thing as the arrest, but with much less work than later in the evening when he might be confronted with lifting a prone man, breaking up a drunken brawl, or answering the complaints of merchants:

When I was on the beat I knew the guys. I knew that pretty soon they'd be lying in the street and I didn't want to have to pick them up. [A4]

If a man looks like he can make it home and he lives in the neighborhood, he is told to "take a hike down the pike." [A4] [9]

Police will actually deliver men to the mission or some other halfway house rather than arrest them. If they look clean and have been at the Christian Missionaries before, we might take them there to see if they can get in. [A3]

Another approach sometimes used by the police is to concentrate control measures on certain portions of territory through frequent arrests, thereby forcing men to scatter, spreading the deviant behavior over a larger area and making it less annoying to the public. For this reason, considerable police action is focused on three one-block lengths of street where Skid Row drinkers prefer to congregate. Similarly, if some commercial establishment becomes a gathering place for drunks, a ferment of constant trouble, the police move it up on their mental list. It is heavily controlled, either by continually "busting" (arresting) its customers or, in the case of noncooperative management, closing the establishment.

> We also have to deal with places where these men congregate, get tanked up, and then go out and make trouble. The Blue Sky cafe used to be a haven for these guys. The owner didn't care. He wouldn't cooperate. We busted guys there regular, but it didn't do much good. Finally, after trying to get the cafe owner's license revoked, we hit on putting him out of business by giving him *no* police protection. He'd blow his whistle and call for the police and we'd just stand across the street and pretend we didn't hear. The alcoholics got in fights, broke the place up. He was out of business in three weeks. [A3]

There are other important factors of which the policeman must be constantly aware as he maintains the peace in Skid Row. For instance, how much leeway does he have in applying various city ordinances to actions of men on the Row? What is the court's policy of reinforcement of the arrest decision? The current state of occupancy at the jail and the particular judge likely to try the case are also factors to be considered.

Applications of the Drunk Ordinance

The Pacific City drunk ordinance offers many administrative problems because of its vagueness. The prohibitions listed in the city code are concerned not with the *act* of drinking but rather with the physiological-psychological *state* of being drunk and its possible consequences. The charge does not require the policeman to decide whether the person in question has *done* something in violation of the law, since neither drinking per se, nor excessive drinking in public, are illegal. Instead, the officer must ascertain whether the drinker is in such a state that he is, or *potentially* is, a danger to himself or others. The words of this ordinance are similar to others throughout the United States:

> Every person who commits any of the following acts shall be guilty of disorderly conduct, a misdemeanor, who is found in any public place under the influence of intoxicating liquor, or any drug, or the combined influence of intoxicating liquor and any drug, in such a condition that he is unable to exercise care for his own safety or the safety of others or by reason of his being under the influence of intoxicating liquor and any drug, interferes with or obstructs or prevents the free use of any street, sidewalk or other public ways.

It is, therefore, unusual for police officers to catch a man in the act of *literally* violating the public drunkenness ordinance. Rather, the policeman must *infer* from collateral actions and circumstances (usually not illegal in and of themselves) that a suspected "drunk" acts as though he is under the influence of alcohol and is now, or sooner or later will be, a danger—perhaps a traffic hazard. Just what constitutes a danger or the blocking of a thoroughfare is not clarified but is left to the "common sense" of the officer.

This very vagueness, as may have been intended, provides the officer with a lever for using the drunk law as a tool for the maintenance of order in as arbitrary a manner as the situation requires.

While it might seem from the account above that more arrests would be challenged in drunkenness cases than where the police decision rested firmly on more empirical grounds (i.e. possession of stolen goods, possession of a deadly weapon, or narcotics), the fact is, however, that few suits grow out of Skid Row drunk arrests.

How is it the arbitrary decisions of police to arrest drunks are so unchallenged? Bittner suggests one reason: this freedom to use the drunk arrest as a peace weapon stems from the fact that the Skid Row derelict is almost always guilty of many minor charges at all times—to live on Skid Row literally means to live a life of drinking, panhandling, and disturbing the peace. Therefore the police can, with impunity, arrest on any of these charges in the interest of preventing future escalation of trouble with the assurance that the apprehended man is probably guilty of something.[9]

Another reason the police are able to interpret the drunk ordinance for their own purposes without fear of challenge is that the men arrested have no resources to fight the charges either at the time of arrest or in court. They have no families, no friends, no finances.

When such a man is taken in, the policeman can count on the fact that the municipal judge is unlikely to question his decision, for the man who has had a record of successive arrests and jailings is a "known drunk." This, combined with his personal appearance, makes him the type of person the judge expects to see before him on such a charge. Police must have such judicial support when peace-keeping depends on an arbitrary and random arrest system. What happens when this support is diminished will be discussed next.

Relationship of the Courts and the Jails

Policemen somewhat naturally like to see their arrest decisions receive the official seal of judicial approval by being translated into jail sentences, since it is frustrating and disconcerting to arrest men who are released shortly afterwards. This is why the current occupancy rate of the jail and the general ideology of the judges enters consciously or unconsciously into every defining decision between police and the Skid Row drunk. There is a definite relationship between the number of men the police arrest and the level of occupancy of the jail. One officer affirmed this fact as follows:

> When the jails are crowded, out of 20 arrests, maybe one or two go to jail; one or two are sent to the Alcoholism School; many get kicked out by the booking sergeant before they ever get to court. The rest get a "kickout" by the judge. [A2]

This is below the usual proportion who go to jail, which over the past five years has hovered around 20 percent.[10]

During the course of this research the Pacific City jails became crowded with hippies, civil rights demonstrators, and other youthful offenders.[11] In times like these, the police consciously cut down on the number of other Skid Row peace-keeping arrests they make. The police methods used on Skid Row during these times tend to reinforce the theory that the underlying basis of the control and containment approach is not concern over public drunkenness per se, but peace-keeping at certain levels of containment:

> We used to handle 300 to 400 drunk cases Monday morning. Now we only have about 50. The sergeant of the city jail lets 'em out. They have it [the jail] full of hippies and civil rights demonstrators right now. [A4]

> If they lay in an alley—ignore them. If they lay in a street—arrest them. That's my rule now. [A3]

> If drinking in a group, I let them go, unless there is a complaint from merchants. [A3]

> If sleeping in a doorway, arrest only if a complaint; or if kids are coming home from school; or if his pants are open and this might create a morals case—then I arrest him before it does. [A2]

> I could go down the street and send 30 to jail. But there's no room. Now I just take the bad ones—lying in the street—or the arrogant ones. [A3] [12]

An alternative to the pick-and-skip plan is to frighten the potential troublemakers off the streets:

> There is only one patrol wagon usually available for the area. Therefore, if it is busy, officers merely try to get the men to get off the streets by threatening them. [A1]

A more unorthodox approach to territorial peace-keeping is the following:

Actually, we don't want to arrest men if we can help it because there is not enough room for them now at the city prison. The city prison is so full that they turn prisoners away. Sometimes, when the patrol wagon comes in full of winos—too drunk to be left out for their own good, and they are turned down by the city prison, the wagon takes the drunks out to a vacant lot at the edge of the city. Then at least they are off the streets and out of the way of muggers and robbers. We just dump them there. They can sober up walking back. [A3]

Two types of Pacific City officials can thwart the policeman in his job of getting some drunks temporarily off the streets (and in the jail). These are police booking sergeants and the municipal judges. Of the two, the booking sergeant's actions seem most understandable to the Row policemen, one of whom commented:

They know these guys and they do what they have to do: when the jail's full up, they let a few go. [A6]

Two booking sergeants and a former booking sergeant were interviewed about the grounds they may use to free a man at the booking desk, with no charges being filed officially:

If you have a drunk and he's sobering up, it's really not necessary for him to be in court—there's no complaint, etc. Sometimes, we let them go. There are various reasons. [A7]

If they are sick and need hospital treatment, we send them there; we place no hold on them either, because we don't want to be bothered going to get them.

On a weekend or a holiday, when we get so many we can't hold them, we throw out those who came in a day before to make room for the new ones.

On the other hand, if a man has been in two or three times recently, [and] we know he got a suspended sentence, then we know the judge wants to see him, then we keep him. [A6]

A former booking sergeant who has left police work said:

When I was on the desk we let a few out because we knew them, they were friends of ours, or because their wife came down and she was sweet and pretty and pleaded with us to let her take him home. Why not? It gets a few more out of here. [A5]

The judges vary, too, in their willingness to sentence the men. The police clearly believe a lenient judge can make drunk arrests a waste of time:

It's really no use arresting them. We aren't getting time on these people. The judge keeps letting them loose. They should give them some time and have them go through the jail rehabilitation program. [A3]

Before the jails got so crowded, it used to be that drunk court was one court where a policeman could step up and speak off the record to the judge. I'd say, "This man's been drinking all week and he needs some medical attention. He should get time." So the judge would give him time. [A3]

Police also have their own assessment of the judges:

Judge Darlington blows hot and cold. He'll sometimes let them all go. Other times, everybody goes to jail. He has no set system. Once when someone stepped on his leg and broke it, *everyone* went to jail for a long time. He always asks the men to hold out their hands. You can tell what he's going to do with the whole lot after you've seen him on the first ten. [A2]

Judge Grey makes fast decisions. He's very good. He is more likely to send them to jail than Judge Darlington. [A4]

Skid Row, during the latter part of this research, was in a state of uneasy peace, with few drunk arrests because of an overcrowded jail. With observation times spread throughout the day and week, observers on the Row reported quite a few "possible drunks," but very little police action. In checking this with the police, it was confirmed that they were "going very light" on the Row and would continue to do so until other trouble areas of Pacific City were under control. (See Table 6.) [13]

TABLE 6. *Possible Drunks and Police Activity on Skid Row*

Observations made		Possible	Police	Ultimate outcome	
Day	Hours	drunks *	contacts	Arrest	Other
Monday	2–5 P.M.	47	0	–	–
Tuesday	10 A.M.–1 P.M.	(Not noted)	4	1	2—talked to 1—noted
Thursday	12–2 P.M.	(Not noted) †	2	0	1 put in ambulance 1 sent to hotel
Saturday	1–4 P.M.	59	3	0	–
Saturday	10–12 P.M.⎫	12	–	–	–
Sunday	1:30–3 P.M.⎭				
	TOTAL	118	9	1	5

* Possible drunks were men who, by the police criteria discussed on page 69, looked as though they were heavy drinkers and presently under the influence of alcohol.
† The total excludes, of course, the number of drunks on the days the observers neglected to note "possible drunks." If these followed the pattern of other days, they might add 80 to 100 to the total.

Some observer descriptions of police contacts give a little of the flavor of everyday law enforcement action on Skid Row:

Tuesday

Contact No. 1. Woman, about 50, obviously had been drinking. Policeman stopped and spoke with her. Did not overhear conversation. Policeman and woman separated, walking in opposite directions.

Contact No. 2. Man, about 50, leaning on wall of building, obviously drunk. Officer stopped and spoke with him. Then walked on.

Contact No. 3. One-legged man in doorway sleeping. Parking meter policeman passed, paused, and saw man from cycle. Did not radio. Man was still there one hour after first observation.

Contact No. 4. Man passed out. White, about 40, dark glasses. Squad car with both uniformed officer and plainclothesman stopped, examined, and then called wagon. Wagon arrived 20 minutes later. Officers walked man to wagon at man's own pace.

Thursday

Contact No. 1. Policeman spotted older man in doorway. Man dirty in appearance and looked as if he had been badly beaten. Both eyes were discolored and swollen. Officer examined and then called wagon from neighboring hotel. Wagon arrived 20 minutes later. All three examined the man and decided he needed an ambulance, which they called. Ambulance arrived about 45 minutes later.

Contact No. 2. Man staggered and fell in view of officer. Man got up and staggered into a hotel. Officer made no attempt to pursue.

Saturday

Contact No. 1. Standing drunk, about 45, poorly dressed. Officer stopped and told man to go home. Man staggered down street. Immediately afterwards, wagon passed and officer exchanged waves with those in the wagon. Man was still in view at this time. Wagon drove slowly down street observing drunks on street but did not stop.

Contact No. 2. Four drunks on corner of street. Officer stopped and exchanged greetings with three of men. Asked fourth who he was. Three chided officer while fourth man dug in pockets and presented identification. Officer then left and four waved goodbye to him.

Contact No. 3. Man lying passed out on sidewalk. In fifties, unshaven, and poorly dressed. At 3 P.M. motorcycle policeman parked cycle and walked within ten feet of man and entered a bar. Glanced at man while walking into bar. While officer was in bar, three different motorcycle officers drove by and two patrol cars. All looked at man. Officer came out of bar 35 minutes later, stopped, looked at man, and then left. One other officer passed after this. By 4 P.M. man had staggered to feet and left scene.

Neutralizing the Arrest Process

No one knows better than the Pacific City police officers assigned to Skid Row that their drunk law enforcement activities are concentrated upon a small minority of heavy drinkers of the entire city. They also know procedures used in the arrest of drunks will depend on extra-legal factors.

Jerome Skolnick has pointed out that the policeman works within a framework of value conflicts in which the rule of law emphasizes the rights of individual citizens and places constraints upon the initiative of legal officials, whereas the ideology of good police work emphasizes intelligent initiative rather than disciplined adherence to rules and regulations.[14] The policeman also is under pressure to "produce," that is, to be efficient rather than legal.[15]

To solve this value conflict, and to still be able to see himself as a worthy person performing a needed service, the Skid Row policeman must mentally be able to neutralize or negate the extra-legal aura of his actions by seeing it as a means to a desirable end.[16]

Bittner found that the police justified their action in applying preventive arrest to Skid Row alcoholics on three counts:

1. An early arrest forestalls more serious trouble in the future (where more men or respectable citizens may become involved).
2. The police action is actually for the protection of the man arrested.
3. Arrest is of slight consequence to men who have nowhere to go, no schedule to meet, and nothing really pressing to do.[17]

Police officers tend to objectify the Skid Row drunk by standardizing and simplifying his characteristics to a sort of silhouette. The Row drunk is seen as a predictable shell of a man unable to cope with the world because of his almost constant condition of inebriation.

The officer is usually not apologetic but proud of his preventative police work in Skid Row:

> If they [the Skid Row drunks] weren't arrested, they would soon be in a fight, or else they would be leaving bottles in front of some merchant's doorway and I'd get a complaint. This way, that doesn't happen. [A3]

> Actually, if I let them get falling down drunk they might be hit by a car and then some innocent motorist would have a manslaughter charge stuck on him, and for what—some wino who is a nobody with no home and is better off in jail! [A2]

The alcoholic's claim to the civil rights of any adult citizen are effectively neutralized by making his known alcoholism and its debilitating effects, plus his essential homelessness, the major characteristics of his personal identity:

> They aren't full of booze. All they have to have is a couple of swallows of wine to set them off. It's in their system. With 60 to 65 cents worth of

wine, they can get high because they have been drinking so long and so heavily. [A4]

We seldom lock them up if they are not drunk. They *are* or will be in the next ten minutes. They only need two or three swallows and they are drunk. [A3]

The way these guys live would make you sick. Sometimes they lay in a stinking bed drinking for two-three weeks at a time. The jail is an improvement. [A2]

Similar claims, of course, are made by all officers who work on any detail in which the major characteristic of persons arrested is considered to be mental incompetence; for instance, this occurs in the juvenile detail where emphasis is on the lack of adult sophistication, or in the case of the mentally ill where the lack of contact with reality is central. The following statement could, with few changes, fit the arrest of either of the above categories:

We pick them up for their own protection—they'd die on the streets if we didn't. I think it should be unlawful to incarcerate an alcoholic . . . *but without other facilities to take care of them, it's inhuman not to incarcerate them.* Some men here admit they're alive today because we picked them up and dried them out. (Emphasis mine.) [A2]

Thus the police officers believe the arrest of an alcoholic is actually doing the man a favor, possibly even saving his life by getting him off the streets. This is undoubtedly true in many cases.

This self-image of being the sometime Good Samaritan receives reinforcement from time to time in the form of the outright requests to police officers to arrest and jail an alcoholic, either from him directly or from his family.

For instance, as mentioned in chapter 3, some men on Skid Row do get so desperate for a place to stay, particularly in bad weather, that they wait in the street to get picked up, or they ask to be taken in.

As one policeman put it:

Lots of these guys actually want to be arrested. They have no place to stay and are in bad shape. I try to help them out when I can. [A3]

They sometimes sit out and wait for the wagon. Really! You take a cold night and they're better off in jail. [A2]

Distraught members of the drinker's family (where he has one) often call and ask to have a man arrested "as a favor." This usually occurs when the wino's family has the lingering hope of retrieving their relative from Skid Row "if he could only be forced to stop drinking." The actual police pickup can be handled in one of two ways:

1. A spouse or mother, worried about the drinking habits of a husband or son, has him arrested in order to stop a drinking spree. Some relatives even go one step further and call the judge requesting a jail sentence for their loved one. The judge usually acceeds to these requests.[18]
2. Officials of the City Screening Facility, which has facilities for helping *voluntary* alcoholic patients, or for patients transferred from City Jail because of their poor physical condition, will recommend that spouses *arrange the arrest* of a drinking husband or wife so that the Screening Facility Staff can see the drinker. This is the only way alcoholics can be seen at the facility involuntarily. (Emphasis mine.) [19]

Most persons have their drinking relatives arrested in good faith, assuming there will be some sort of rehabilitation program available in the jail or, if not, at least the enforced abstinence will prove beneficial to the drinker.

These requests help to shore up any possible apprehensions the police officer may have as to whether he is doing the proper thing using somewhat extra-legal methods to accomplish socially-approved goals. Further, such requests reinforce the less-than-responsible citizen image of the alcoholic.

On the practical level, the policeman has the most substantial proof of all that his approach to peace-keeping is not contrary to good law enforcement practice. As mentioned, the judge seldom, if ever, questions the arrest or the grounds on which it was made; further, the men arrested *plead guilty* to the charge almost invariably. From this background of successful defining encounters comes continuing reassurance for similar decisions in future encounters.[20]

THE ROW MAN VIEWS THE POLICE

Once the chronic drunkenness offender becomes aware of the manner in which the drunk ordinance is applied, he is inclined to become angry that almost all of the police criteria for arrest seem extraneous to whether he is, in fact, really drunk. He knows that danger of arrest is highly dependent upon geographic, social, and bureaucratic factors, and the knowledge galls him.

> Arrest for drunkenness depends on where you are, who you are, what you look like, and if they need you to fill the wagon. [41]

A discussion of these perceived criteria for arrest follows.

Where You Are . . .

Skid Row men are quite bitter about the fact that no other area receives as much attention as theirs from police drunk patrols.

> Of course, just being in the Skid Row area makes you automatically suspect. I was walking up the street there, and it was rainin'; and I crossed the alley, you know; and I been drinking a little bit, but I knew everythin' that I was doin', and I didn't pick up my foot high enough (the rain was on my glasses) and I bumped my toe, you see, and fell down. And a policeman came by and called a wagon and took me to jail. [9]

> If you are in some of the restaurants which they roust regularly, you can be arrested along with everyone else even though you are only drinking a cup of coffee. I been in the Blue Sky Restaurant where in the next booth there was a bunch passing the bottle around and the police came in and arrested everyone there, even me, and I wasn't with them. (Statements of this type are frequent.) [52]

Who You Are . . .

A Skid Row man gets the feeling of being a "marked man" after a few arrests.

> Once they pick you up drunk, they know you and will pick you up whenever they need you. They will just say, "Come on, let's go." They avoid picking up educated people; just winos. They can tell by how they [winos] talk. [44]

> After a man has been arrested several times, he gets picked up automatically if he happens to be around during a regular cleanup—he's picked up whether he's drunk or not, just as a matter of course. [10]

> I've heard guys say, "But officer, I wasn't even drinking," and the officer laughs and says, "But you soon will be . . . This saves us both time." And, of course, the officer was right, but I still don't think he should have done it. [43]

> Some guys are so well-known that if the wagon is filled when they are spotted, the officer riding on back will call out, "I'll be back for you, Louis." [38]

What You Look Like . . .

The Skid Row man is certain he would be afforded different treatment if he could dress so as to "look like he was somebody instead of nobody."

If you dress well, they won't pick you up unless you are falling-down drunk on the sidewalk. If you dress poorly and look beat, you don't even have to be drinking to get picked up. Why I've seen men getting off the van coming from County Jail where they just served time, and looking pretty bad in their donated clothing, get picked up and arrested again before they walked a couple of blocks! [15]

I've been trying to get some decent clothes before I left here [jail], so I wouldn't have the dirty, filthy clothes that I had on, you know what I mean, to go on the street, and I can't blame no officer whatsoever in the condition that I looked like. He'd say, "Well, there's a guy that's got no business on the street, he should be locked up." You know what—I had been out of jail a week when I was attacked and robbed. Following this I had a drink. The police saw me with my head all cut up and liquor on my breath and didn't bother to ask any more questions. I am now doing 30 days. [16]

Testimony from a Skid Row alcoholic who claims never to have been arrested for drunk, although in fact he was often drunk, confirms the effect of a rough appearance on the chances of arrest:

I ain't never been arrested by the police, I'm proud to say. That's because I kept myself clean-looking all the way down to the gutter. [42]

The Feelings of Personal Powerlessness

Skid Row men feel absolutely helpless in the face of a police officer's decision to arrest them. (Many voice a fear of violent reprisal if they argue or resist, but policemen emphatically deny this.) Often from the alcoholic's testimony, the police fail to explain the charge.

Interviewer: What do they say when they arrest you? They say "Get in." And they point to the wagon. "All right, get in."

Interviewer: Don't they tell you what for? They don't have to. They just tell you to get in the wagon.

Interviewer: What if you try to explain that you aren't drunk? Well, you might get a mouth full of fist or they would just pick you up and throw you in. They don't take any back talk. [49]

We were sitting in the park, drinking a carton of buttermilk, I swear that's what it was, and we were sitting alongside two other fellas who had a bottle, and the policeman came and he just pointed his finger and said, "Come on." We said, "What are you talking about? We're not drunk, we are drinking buttermilk." "Come on," he said. You don't argue with 'em. If you do you're liable to lose a few teeth.

Interviewer: You couldn't even ask them to look in the carton? You don't ask 'em nothin'. When he tells you to get in that wagon you just might as well get in it. [43]

There's no use complaining that you aren't drunk. You are outnumbered anyway. Besides, if you complain too much he will lay for you next time and really get you. [38]

Sometimes the police will catch a guy with a bottle of wine and they will take it from him and they say, "Do you want a drink?" Then they will pull at his belt and pour the wine down his pants. [48] [21]

Skid Row men are also quick to point out that some of the police are quite fair in that they will give a man a chance to "take a walk" rather than arrest him. However, there is no arguing with that dictum either, at least not in the way that a non-Skid Row citizen might argue.

Then there's this one patrolman, oh, he's a great guy. He'll put guys in hotels where they're livin' and say, "Get in there and go to sleep. Get off the street or I'll run you in. Go on, get off the street." He gets 'em off before the wagon comes around. [49]

The feeling of police irrationality and vindictiveness in handling drunks is intensified for the Skid Row alcoholic in that he cannot demand a blood-alcohol test to disprove the policeman's judgment that he is drunk (this is reserved for motorists, murderers, and others who commit more serious acts under the influence of alcohol).

Interviewer: Can you ask to take a test to prove whether or not you have been drinking heavily? They'd give you a test all right. One will hit you between the eyes with his fist or something like that. [37]

Oh, the people that demand tests are the people they bring in for some other charge and have a reason for proving they weren't drunk; but if he's a *drunk*, the judge and the police don't care whether he is drunk that time or not. [50]

This is not to say that the alcoholic denies he was drinking at the time of arrest. More than once, after registering outrage at the way they are handled in the arrest process, an alcoholic will admit:

Of course, I had really been drinking pretty heavily. I won't deny that. But I wasn't making any trouble for anyone. [17]

I was never arrested but what I hadn't been drinking. But that isn't the point really. It's how they do it. [26]

Although angered by the personal appearance criteria for arrest, Skid Row alcoholics seem unaware, on the other hand, of the effect a crowded jail has on their chances for being picked up. Rather, they attribute the mysterious fluctuations in arrest practices to the existence of some unadmitted "quota" that is changed from time to time. The following opinion was echoed by many:

When the wagon's out they must have a quota or something because sometimes they will go right into a restaurant and pick up a guy who is sitting eating, or maybe he has his head down on the table. I've even been arrested when I was in a laundromat minding my own business. [38]

Skid Row alcoholics do confirm police assertions that Row men ask to be arrested sometimes when they have no place to stay (as mentioned previously). But the alcoholics see this as expediency only, and strongly feel this practice should not be used as part of the police justification for other arrest procedures.

As one man said about his buddies:

Lots of guys actually arrange to be arrested. They go lay out against a building when they hear a paddy wagon coming. Usually they have no place to stay that night. [40]

The following description from a field observer in the jail also illustrates that some drunks have learned how to use the police arrest criteria (i.e., public nuisance) to get themselves arrested at their convenience:

There was one alcoholic I talked to who said he has been coming here [the jail] for 15 years. He stated that every time he came out here he had turned himself in and asked the judge for time. He said that when he was on the street he knew where the wagon would make its regular stops. One time he said he waited for three hours for the wagon to come. And when it did, it was on the other side of the street. He said he had to yell at the driver to wait for him.

He will stay sober for weeks on end, but when he starts drinking he can't stop. The only way that he knows of getting sober is to turn himself in for drunk and come out here. He stated he was drunk on election day once and he went to the police station and wanted to turn himself in. There were two officers out front who knew he was drunk but told him to get lost. He still wanted to be arrested though so he went to the bus depot and laid on one of the benches. Sure enough he got arrested. At first I found his stories hard to believe, but I talked to one of the bulls [deputy] he has known for many years. The bull says that his stories are all true.

For the Skid Row man, the booking and bailing procedure he experiences is certain evidence of the corruption of the authorities. First, he knows the booking sergeant often frees a Row man informally so that he need not face the judge on a drunk charge. Although this is seen as compassion, it is also seen as pointing up the unnecessary character of the arrest in the first place. As one Skid Row drunk put it:

Those booking sergeants will often tell you to take a hike—which means they are letting you go. Now I ask you, if I was really drunk, would they do that? The arrest wasn't really necessary, you see. [49]

At other times Row men complain the booking sergeant often steals their property as part of the arrest procedure. Representative is this statement:

> At the booking desk, the last piece of property I had was taken from me. They took my glasses, my nail file, my pen, and so on, and on the property slip they wrote "junk." If you complain they will throw you in the hole. I never got anything back, because my property slip said "junk." [18]

A number of the Row men interviewed also said they are refused a chance to make a phone call, although this privilege is part of the state penal code. With such a call, a man can sometimes get a friend, or family if he has one, to come and bail him out. Without it, the Skid Row alcoholic must stay in jail overnight, pending a court hearing. According to some of the Row men:

> If you ask to make a phone call after being arrested, they say: "To hell with you. We'll make it in an hour" . . . and the hour never comes. [18]

To the Skid Row drunk, the bail bond system is a plot to exploit the down-and-out homeless man. Because persons charged with violation of a state law or city ordinance are not allowed by law to post their own bail bond money, $35.00 in the case of a public drunkenness charge,[22] arrangements must be made by a family member or a friend. This places a great hardship on the homeless man who has severed all primary relationships, for he has also effectively cut himself off from outside help in the case of arrest. He usually has no family or friend to bail him out, to hire an attorney, or to protest his treatment. This means that if the Row man is to get out at all, he must obtain the professional assistance of a bail bondsman. The premium payment to obtain a $35.00 bail bond is 10 percent plus $10.00, a total of $13.50. Normally, bondsmen do not post bail bonds for drunk arrestees. This is because bailable arrestees must show some means of subsistence—bank account, pension—so as to be considered a fair risk on the guarantee to show up on court day. Few Skid Row men can meet these requirements.

This is how one "revolving door" alcoholic feels about it:

> The whole bail system for drunks reeks with corruption. You can have $500.00 in your pocket and still not be able to get out of jail. You must pay out money to a bondsman. [18]

One chronic drunkenness offender reported that he got around the no-self-bail, no-phone-call problem by paying a bonus to a caretaker at the jail to bail him out.

The most important effect of the homeless drunk's bonding difficulties is that he literally cannot risk pleading not guilty if he cannot obtain bail. Demanding a trial is a luxury for him as this is tantamount to signing up for 90 days "dead time" [23] in jail while waiting his day in court.

On the other hand, if he pleads guilty and takes his chances, he will most likely get a "kickout," a suspended sentence, or perhaps a 10- or 30-day sentence. Rarely are 90-day sentences given for public drunkenness. This is also how he accumulates a record. Said one Row man:

> Everybody pleads guilty to avoid a long wait for trial. I suppose that a stranger walking into court would think, "There's a lot of guilty people. They just admitted it." [40]

Apparently Pacific City is only one of the many cities in the United States where the penniless, homeless man arrested on a drunk charge faces more time in jail if he pleads innocent than if he pleads guilty. One man's conclusion about this practice is as follows:

> Look, this happens all over the country. On a drunk charge, if you plead innocent, you spend more time in jail than if you plead guilty. If you travel around long enough you finally find you are up against a brick wall. They want you in jail. [12]

4

The Judicial

Screening Process

Reinforcement of
the Policeman's Decision

INTRODUCTION

When a man's drinking brings him repeatedly to a state of public drunkenness, arrest, and a court appearance, the average layman feels the man
has sunk as low as he can go. Sentencing, as such, is almost a formal,
rather than legal, recognition of his social disgrace.

Skid Row alcoholics, however, are no different from other American
citizens in the mental picture they have of proper trial procedure. They
expect that the case against them will be judged on its merits, that the
charge will be compared with the presentation of the evidence, and that
they will be presumed innocent until proven guilty.

Similarly, municipal judges who sit on cases of public drunkenness
feel that their role should be one of thoughtful attention to individual
wrongs and individual needs. Said one:

A judge . . . should rule with his heart as well as his head. I don't mean
to say he should disregard the well-established principles of law; but
compassion for human beings should have great weight in making a determination in a case.

Being a judge is probably one of the greatest responsibilities that could
come to any individual. Rulings affect the welfare of people and may
determine the manner of their existence for a lifetime.[1]

The municipal court assigned to the handling of public drunkenness cases is one of the most important screening facilities for access to the loop. Five morning sessions each week are devoted to sentencing the men arrested the previous 24 hours under the city's public drunkenness ordinance.

Yet drunk court, as it is popularly known, processes 50 to 100 men within the period of an hour, actually sentencing platoons of 10 to 25 men at a time. Furthermore, assignment to this judicial department is considered such a disagreeable task that judges rotate it each week.

This chapter will be devoted to a discussion of the structural pressures—on both judges and Skid Row alcoholics—that bring about such a situation of assembly-line justice.

DRUNK COURT—THE ADULT PARALLEL TO JUVENILE COURT

The distinction that Peterson and Matza draw between two basic types of court procedures—the legalistic court and the so-called socialized court —is especially pertinent to the operation of the drunk court, as will be seen from the following brief outline:

> *Legalistic courts* operate under an adversary system, by which a state attorney and a defense counsel plead a case before a judge and/or jury. The purpose of the trial is to determine whether the defendant in fact committed the crime with which he is charged. Great stress is placed on formal proceedings and rules of evidence, very little on information regarding the defendant's character and background. If he is convicted, the defendant is subject to fine, imprisonment, or execution. The punishment fits the crime, not the particular individual.

> *Socialized courts* usually exercise jurisdiction either over juveniles, both neglected or dependent, and delinquent or criminal; or over family law or in some jurisdictions, over both juvenile and domestic problems in one omnibus court. Its methods and procedures have made greatest inroads in the juvenile court. Here, the adversary system is replaced by one or more social workers' reports, which emphasize information regarding the character and background of all parties. Judicial procedure is informal; rules of evidence do not apply. The purpose of the hearing is to determine whether a serious problem exists—whether, for example, a child requires help—and to provide the means to meet the needs of the individuals involved.[2]

Although not officially designated as a socialized court in the statutes, drunk court sessions are almost always operated along the latter lines. However, the drunk court judge faces unusual administrative and decisional problems that have a gross distorting effect on its more informal and humanized ideology.

Unlike other cases in other courts, where guilt or innocence of the defendant is the issue, the judge's decision in drunk court is almost always the sentence alone. As previously mentioned, with but rare exceptions, the men plead guilty. The judge, therefore, has no official reason to assume the men are other than guilty.

Sentencing men who plead guilty to a public drunkenness charge, however, presents a real conflict to a judge who wishes to see himself as compassionate, wise, and just. Because of the widespread discussion of alcoholism as a social problem and a physical illness, a judge must take cognizance of both the need for efficient administration of sentences for public drunks and the theoretical causes of alcoholism. As a collateral matter, he is also aware that Pacific City's ordinary male citizens sometimes "tie one on," perhaps do damage to themselves or others, and are arrested by police. Such men usually have jobs and a family. A jail sentence for public drunkenness would be a severe blow, both socially and economically.

In other words, with each man who appears before him the judge must ask himself whether he should view the defendant as merely an "overindulgent social drinker," or as a "chronic drunken bum," or as a "sick alcoholic."

In the first of these possible definitions, the judge must make a decision about whether the defendant is a wayward, but basically-solid citizen. If this is the case, the sentence can be suspended and the person let off with a warning. On the other hand, if the defendant is the type the judge tends to mentally characterize as a "childlike, hedonistic, willful, chronic drunk," he must be dried out for his own good, since he is a menace to himself and society. All the while, the third possible definition creates great decisional pressures, because the judge is aware that he must consider the prevailing public opinion that alcoholism *per se* is an illness, even if some of the acts of the person who drinks too much may legally be defined as a crime.[3] If the judge accepts this latter view, he is forced to consider the possibility he is sentencing a man who may be ill to jail. The implied inhumanity of this act must be explained and justified, even if only self-justification is involved.

This decisional picture is further confused by the fact that the judge must consider not one but *two types* of illness. The first type is the temporary, acute *physical distress* caused by repeated overindulgence in alcohol which, in cases of continuous heavy drinking, is serious enough to cause death if left unattended. The second type is based on the assumption that some mysterious psychological compulsion forces a man to drink and, like the plea, "not guilty by reason of insanity," the chronic alcoholic is not responsible for his excessive drinking. Each type of illness demands a different kind of concern and treatment, although in judicial discussions these are often blurred together.

If a judge were to think aloud, he might explain the chronic drunk sentence dilemma and his solution to it something like this:

Alcoholism may be an illness or it may be a weakness. Whatever it is, all alcoholics need help to quit drinking. One of the surest ways to help an alcoholic quit drinking is to separate him forceably from any supply of liquor. However, jail is a drastic penalty for being found drunk and therefore should be used only after other methods fail. This is because if a man is sent to jail, he may suffer undesirable social consequences, such as jeopardizing his job or causing his wife and children great embarrassment. Some men are so upset about being arrested, that is all the punishment they need. It serves as adequate warning. Others should be educated about the dangers of overindulgence through forced attendance at Alcoholism School. Others need a short sentence, but suspended, to scare them a bit; still others need a short sentence to see what jail is like so they don't want ever to go back; and some repeaters need aid in getting off the bottle which can be supplied by a longer separation from it—say 30, 60 or 90 days. The jail is set up to give these men both medical and psychological therapy through the Jail Branch Clinic of the Out-Patient Therapy Center, so they are well taken care of. Transients can be handled by telling them to leave town.

Matching sentences with men who plead guilty is thus the judge's true concern. This task must be handled within the pressures created by restricting drunk court to a morning session in one courtroom, regardless of the number of men scheduled to be seen that day.

Up until last year (when drunk arrests were temporarily reduced because of the large number of hippies and civil rights demonstrators in jail), 50 to 250 men were often sentenced within a few hours. Appearance before the judge was handled in platoons of five to 50. This meant the judge decided the fate of each defendant within a few short minutes. Thus judicial compassion attained assembly-line organization and speed.

As a court observer noted:

The Court generally disposes of between 50 and 100 cases per day, but on any Monday there are 200 to 250 and on Monday mornings after holiday weekends the Court may handle as many as 350 cases. I would estimate that, on the average, cases take between 45 seconds and one minute to dispose of.[4]

Later, with drunk arrests drastically curtailed, the court handled no more than 50 cases in an average morning, and perhaps 125 on the weekends, according to the observer.[5] Right after a civil rights demonstration that resulted in many arrests, only 33 persons were observed in drunk court. This reduction in the quantity of defendants, however, did not appear to increase the length of time spent on each person. Rather, it seemed to reduce it. The observer noted the average length of time per person was 30 seconds, although the size of platoons was reduced from 50 to 15 or 20.

Sentencing Criteria

How is the judge able to classify and sentence a large, unwieldy group of defendants so quickly? The answer is he utilizes social characteristics as indicators to signify drinking status—just as in an arrest situation the policeman looked for social characteristics to identify alcoholic trouble-making potential, combined with the arrestee's legal impotence. The effect is essentially the same: the men are objectified into social types for easy classification. In the case of the judge, the legal decision process must be more refined than for a policeman's arrest, no-arrest decision. Therefore, the judge's sentencing criteria are more complex, as they must include all possible decision combinations.

From court observations, plus interviews with court officers and judges, three primary criteria for typing defendants in drunk court emerge:

THE GENERAL PHYSICAL APPEARANCE OF THE MAN   Is he shaky and obviously in need of drying out? Here, some of the judges ask the men to extend their hands before sentencing and decide the sentence on the degree of trembling.

Physical appearance may actually be the most potent deciding factor. As one court officer put it, when asked how the judges decide on a sentence:

> Primarily by appearance. You can tell what kind of shape they're in. If they're shaking and obviously need drying out, you know some are on the verge of the DT's so these get 10 or 15 days [in jail] to dry out. [A10]

One of the seasoned judges said that his criteria were as follows:

> I rely on his record and also his "looks." Their "looks" are very important. I make them put their hands out—see if they are dirty and bloody in appearance.[6]

PAST PERFORMANCE   How many times have they been up before the court on a drunk charge before? A record of past arrests is considered to be indicative of the defendant's general attitude toward drinking. The longer and more recent the record, the greater the need for a sentence to aid the defendant to improve his outlook on excessive liquor consumption. (This is in some contradiction to the presumed greater need the man must have for drying out, since previous recent jailings mean that he could not have been drinking for long.)

The previous comment, plus the answer by a court officer to the question, "Who get's dismissed?", illustrate this criteria for sentencing:

> A person with no previous arrests [gets dismissed]. If they have had no arrests, then the judge hates for them to have a conviction on their record. *The more arrests they've had and the more recently they've had them, the more likely they are to get another sentence.* (Emphasis mine.) [A10]

THE MAN'S SOCIAL POSITION   Does he have a job he could go to? Is he married? Does he have a permanent address, or will he literally be on the streets if he receives a dismissal?

For these data, dress is an all-important clue, age a secondary one. A man who looks down-and-out is more likely to receive a sentence than the well-dressed man. According to a court officer:

> If they look pretty beat—clothes dirty and in rags, then you figure that they need some help to stop drinking before they kill themselves. [A10]

> If they're under 21 we usually give them a kick-out. If they are a business man or a lawyer we have them sign a civil release so they can't sue and let them go. [A10]

An observer reports that a judge freed a young man with the following remarks:

> I am going to give you a suspended sentence and hope that this experience will be a warning to you. I don't want you to get caught up in this cycle. [A9]

Transients form a category of their own and get a special package deal—if they will promise to leave town, they draw a suspended sentence or probation. The parallel between this practice and the police policy of telling some Skid Row drunks to "take a walk" need only be mentioned. The following interchanges are illustrative:

> *Judge:* I thought you told me the last time you were in here that you were going to leave Pacific City.
> *Defendant:* I was supposed to have left town yesterday. I just got through doing time.
> *Judge:* Go back to Woodland. Don't let me see you in here again or we are going to put you away. Thirty days suspended. [A8]

> *Defendant:* I am supposed to leave with the circus tomorrow. If I don't go, I will be out of work for the whole season.

Judge: You promised to leave three times before. Thirty days in the County Jail. [A9]

By combining the variables of physical appearance, past performance, and social position, a rough description of social types expected in drunk court, and matching sentences for each type is shown in Table 7.

TABLE 7. Paradigm of Social Types and Sentences in Drunk Court

Social Type	Probable Sentence
A young man who drank too much: a man under 40, with a job, and perhaps a wife, who has not appeared in court before.	A kick-out or a suspended sentence.
The young repeater: same as above, but has been before judge several times (may be on way to being an alcoholic.)	Suspended sentence or short sentence (five–ten days) to scare him, or possible attendance at Alcoholism School.
The repeater who still looks fairly respectable. (Image vacillating between an alcoholic and a drunk.)	30-day suspended sentence, with possible attendance at Alcoholism School.
Out-of-towner (social characteristics not important as they have nonlocal roots.) Therefore not important as to whether overindulged, a chronic drunk, or an alcoholic.	Suspended sentence on condition he leave town. Purpose is to discourage him from getting on local loop and adding to tax payer's load.
The middle aged repeater who has not been up for some time. (May be an alcoholic who has relapsed.)	Suspended sentence with required attendance at Alcoholism School or given to custody of Christian Missionaries.
The derelict-drunk who looks "rough," i.e., suffering withdrawal, a hangover, has cuts and bruises, may have malnutrition or some diseases connected with heavy drinking and little eating; a chronic drunk; seedy clothing, stubble beard, etc.	30–60–90 day sentence depending on number of prior arrests and physical condition at time of arrest. (Has probably attended Alcoholism School already.)
The man who looks gravely ill (probably a chronic alcoholic).	County hospital under suspended sentence.

These first two categories in Table 7, and sometimes the third, have not been, in Garfinkel's terms "made strange." [7] They are treated as though they are full-fledged persons who may have overindulged. The remaining types are stripped-down persons, on the "other side," so far as they are perceived by the judge.

A total of 180 men were observed in drunk court and tabulated according to the social types outlined in the table. Observations were spread over three days. Two different judges presided. The results are shown in Table 8 below:

TABLE 8. *Distribution of Drunk Ordinance Social Types in Court*

Social Types	Percent (N = 180)
Derelict who looks "rough"	38
Young repeater	15
Recent repeater who looks respectable	15
Middle-aged repeater who has not been arrested for some time	11
Young man with wife, job, first offense	11
Out-of-towner	8
Man who looks gravely ill	2
TOTAL	100

Of the total tabulated, the Skid Row alcoholics category would include the derelict (38 percent), the middle-aged repeater who has not been arrested for some time, probably having been in the loop (11 percent), the out-of-towner (8 percent), and the man who looks gravely ill (2 percent), for a total of 59 percent. This is quite near the usual 40 to 45 percent of Skid Row men represented in the total arrests for drunkenness in Pacific City.

The detailed pattern of sentencing was also tabulated and is illustrated in Table 9.

TABLE 9. *Distribution of Sentences in Drunk Court*

Sentences	Percent of Defendants (N = 180)	
Kick-out (no sentence, warned only)	2	
County hospital		
With hold	—	
No hold	2	
		74 (non-jail sentence)
Suspended sentence		
10 days or less	—	
11 to 30 days	23	
31 to 60 days	28	
61 to 90 days	19	
Over 90 days	—	
Sentenced to County Jail		
10 days or less	1	
11 to 30 days	23	
31 to 60 days	2	26 (jail sentence)
61 to 90 days	—	
Over 90 days	—	
TOTAL	100	

As can be seen in the table, only 26 percent of the men received sentences to be served in County Jail. This is quite close to the yearly average of 20 to 25 percent.[8]

Most pertinent to this study, however, is the distribution of sentences among social types of defendants. This is shown in Table 10.

TABLE 10. *Distribution of Sentences Among Social Types of Defendants in Drunk Court*

PERCENT OF DEFENDANTS BY SOCIAL TYPES

Sentences	Young man with job, wife, 1st offense	Young re-peater	Middle-aged respect-able re-peater	Out-of-towner	Middle-aged re-peater, not recent	Derelict who looks rough	Man looking gravely ill
	(N = 19)	(N = 27)	(N = 26)	(N = 15)	(N = 20)	(N = 69)	(N = 4)
Kick-out (no sentence, warned only)	21	—	—	—	—	—	—
County hospital							
With hold	—	—	—	—	—	—	—
No hold	—	—	—	—	—		75
Suspended sentence							
10 days or less	—	—	—	—	—	—	—
11 to 30 days	59	22	11	60	15	13	25
31 to 60 days	10	22	35	—	60	30	—
61 to 90 days	10	37	35	33	25	3	—
Over 90 days	—	—	—	—	—	—	—
Sentenced to County Jail							
10 days or less	—	4	4	—	—	—	—
11 to 30 days	—	15	—	7	—	54	—
31 to 60 days	—	—	15	—	—	—	—
61 to 90 days	—	—	—	—	—	—	—
Over 90 days	—	—	—	—	—	—	—
TOTALS	100	100	100	100	100	100	100

From Table 10 it can be seen that the derelicts who look rough or men who are repeaters (regardless of age or appearance), are most likely to serve time and get the longest sentences. Furthermore, the derelict who looks rough is the least likely of any social type to escape jail.

A word should be said about the suspended sentence. Judges sometimes give exceedingly long suspended sentences to drunk ordinance defendants—often 90 days or more to repeaters. This places a weapon in the hands of the court that is greatly feared. If at any time within the following 90 days (or whatever the length of the sentence), the man is picked up on a drunk charge, he may be sent directly to jail without trial for the entire length of the suspended sentence. Many men, upon receiving a long suspended sentence, and realizing their vulnerability to arrest, will "take out insurance" against being incarcerated for that length of time by seeking admission to another "more desirable" station on the loop. Favorite "hideouts" while waiting for the suspended sentence to run out are (in approximate rank order): Welfare Home for Homeless Men, State Mental Hospital, and the Christian Missionaries.[9]

Other Sentencing Assistance

Even with the aid of a simplified mental guide, the judge cannot be expected to assemble and assimilate sufficient material on each man, review it, mentally type the man, and then make a sentencing decision in less than a minute. Thus, it is not surprising that almost all drunk court judges employ the aid of one assistant and sometimes two court attachés who are familiar with the Row and its inhabitants. These men are known as court liaison officers. Because of personal familiarity with chronic drunkenness offenders, the liaison officers are able to answer questions about each accused person quickly and to recommend a case disposition. Such persons obviously operate as an informal screening board.

The most important court helper in Pacific City is a man who knows most of the Row men by sight and claims also to know their general outlook on alcohol and life. Known to the defendants as "the Rapper," this man often sits behind the judge and suggests informally who would benefit most from probation and assignment to Alcoholism School, who might need the "shaking-up" that jail provides, and who ought to be sent to alcoholic screening at City Hospital and perhaps on to State Mental Hospital. As each man is named, the Rapper whispers to the judge, who then passes sentence.[10]

In Pacific City, the man who was the Rapper for a period of time was an ex-alcoholic who could claim intimate knowledge of the chronic drunkenness offender because he had drunk with them. A relative of the Rapper was highly placed in city politics, and the Rapper made no secret of the fact that his appointment was politically engineered.[11] During the course of the study (several times in fact), the Rapper himself "fell off the wagon" and underwent treatment at Northern State Mental Hospital, one of the stations on the loop. While there, the Rapper told about his recent job with the court and how he helped the judge:

> Each man arrested has a card with the whole record on it. We would go over the cards before the case came up. We see how many times he's been

arrested. I could advise the judge to give them probation or a sentence. Many times, the family would call and request a sentence. I would often arrange for them to get probation plus clothes and a place to stay at one of the halfway houses. Oh, I'll help and help, but when they keep falling off—I get disgusted. [A51] [12]

The Christian Missionaries also send a liaison man to the drunk court sessions. He acts as Rapper at special times and thereby also serves in an informal screening capacity. Sponsorship by this organization appears to guarantee that the defendant will get a suspended sentence. For instance, this interchange was observed in court several times:

Judge, turning to Missionary representative: "Do you want him [this defendant]?" (Meaning, "Will you take him at one of your facilities?")
Missionary: (Nods "Yes.")
Judge: "Suspended sentence." [A8]

Another observer discussed this arrangement with a veteran judge:

Interviewer: Isn't there any attempt made to consider the men for rehabilitation?
The men are screened by the Christian Missionaries usually. The Christian Missionaries send someone down to the jail who tries to help them. They talk with the men and screen them. Nobody does the job that the Christian Missionaries do in the jails.
Interviewer: The Court abdicates the screening of defendants to the Christian Missionaries, then?
Not completely. We try to keep a record. Some of these men we can help, but most we can't. I know by heart all of their alibis and stories.[13]

Another important informal court post is filled by an employee who is known to some of the men as "the Knocker." The job of the Knocker is to maintain the personal records of the men who appear before drunk court and to supply the judge with this information. A court observer reported the following:

The Knocker spoke to the judge in just about every case. However, I do not know what he said. He may just be reading to the judge the official records, or he may be giving his personal judgement about the possibility of the defendant being picked up again in the near future. One thing seems clear: the judge receives his information from the Knocker just before he hands out the sentence.

Sometimes it is difficult to distinguish the Knocker (who merely gives information to the judge) from the Rapper (who "suggests" the proper sentence.) In 1963, two of these court liaison officers worked together. An interview with one partner is quoted below:

Interviewer: What do you do?

Up here we act as a *combination district attorney and public defender*. We are more familiar with these guys than the judges are. The judges alternate. We have the previous arrest records. A lot of times, guys will give phony names. It may take us a while to catch up with them. We try to remember if we have seen a guy before. (Emphasis mine.)

Interviewer: How does a judge decide whether to sentence the men and if so, for how long?

We help him out on that. If a guy has been in three times in four weeks, they should get a minimum of 30 days. They need to dry out. You know, if a man has been arrested three times in four weeks, you ask yourself the question: "How many times has he been drunk that he wasn't arrested?" Also, you look at the condition of a man—he may even need hospitalization.

Interviewer: You mean you can tell whether a man ought to be sent to jail by looking at him?

Some of them look a lot more rough looking than others. You can tell they have been on a drunk for more than one day. They are heavily bearded. They have probably been sleeping in doorways or on the street. You can tell they have been on a long drunk.[14]

Thus perhaps the most revealing aspect of the sentencing procedure is the virtual absence of interest in the *charge* and the judge's role as spokesman for the court officer's decision. This may account for the fact the judge seldom discusses the case with the defendant, except in a jocular, disparaging way. (This tendency to treat alcoholics as misbehaving children is discussed in chapter 3.) The following interchanges, which illustrate this attitude, were witnessed by observers:

Defendant: I was sleeping in a basement when a man attacked me with a can opener.
Judge: Did you also see elephants? [A8]

Judge: What is your story this time?
Defendant: (As he begins to speak, Judge interrupts.)
Judge: You gave me that line yesterday; 30 days in the County Jail. [A9]

Court Atmosphere

The above exchanges between the judge and the defendant would seem to suggest the atmosphere of drunk court is more informal than most courts of law. From the reports obtained from all observers, this is true. Drunk court is not taken as seriously as other sessions of the municipal court, or other departments, and a great deal of levity and antic behavior is tolerated (in full view of defendants), an attitude not allowed in other Pacific City courts. Excerpts from observer's notes illustrate this unserious aspect of drunk court:

> Bailiff came in today and asked other court officers in voice audible to all, "When does the parade [of defendants] begin?"

> There is open flirting between a police matron and police before court starts.

> The Knocker and bailiff put a sign, "The Flying Nun," over the judge's name before court started. Removed it when judge appeared.

> Judge comes in the front door of the court, walks very casually, often presides without robe. Unlike other courts, bailiff asks everyone to *remain seated* when judge appears. Judge is always five to ten minutes late.

> Just as the judge was about ready to start, there was a gasp and a thud. (This didn't seem to shake anyone except me.) One of the defendants had fallen over near the front of the line, and the other defendants stood there like this wasn't anything to get upset about.

> The judge asked, "What was his number?" and the Knocker told him. Then one of the court policemen said that he thought the guy was dead. "This man has had an alcoholic seizure. We're going to take him to the hospital," the judge said.

> The bailiff asked what should be done about the man's case. The judge dismissed it. It was the only kick-out that day.

From this it can be seen that the operational ideology of the judge in drunk court, although much like that of juvenile court, is lacking in the compassion often shown for juveniles. An attempt is made to sentence the man in terms of his characteristics and not the criminal act he is accused of. Extenuating circumstances of all types are used in arriving at decisions. There is no lawyer or advocacy system in operation. The defendant may be discharged to "responsible" persons in the community (this means some member of his family if he has one, or the Christian Missionaries if they exhibit an interest in him).[15]

Far from freeing the judge to make idiosyncratic personalized decisions, the result of the drunk court system is to standardize drunks on the basis of social types and then with the assistance of court aides objectify them in such a way as to fit the predetermined types. Thus the decision of the patrolman in typification of the Skid Row drinker is not only accepted in the court without question—it is reinforced and embellished.

Justifying the Sentencing Process

How does the municipal court judge, serving in drunk court sessions, allow himself to be a party to such extra-legal activities as platoon sentencing, the heavy reliance on advice from "friends of the court," and the utilization of extraneous social characteristics in setting the sentence? Why is there not a conflict with his self-image of judicial compassion for the individual and scrupulous attention to legal niceties?

For some judges, this conflict is resolved by falling back on the alcoholism-as-an-illness view of drunkenness, and by redefining many of the men who appear before him as *patients* rather than defendants. Thus, when asked to describe their duties, drunk court judges often sound like physicians dealing with troublesome patients for whom they must prescribe unpleasant but necessary medicine, rather than judges punishing men for being a public annoyance. As an example of this:

> I know that jail isn't the best place for these men, but we have to do something for them. We need to put them someplace where they can dry out. You can't just let a man go out and kill himself. [A8]

> This is a grave and almost hopeless problem. But you have to try some kind of treatment. Often they are better off in jail than out on the street. [A52]

The drunk court judges sometimes add the wish that the city provided a more palatable alternative to the County Jail, but then reiterate the view that it is better than no help at all.

Court attachés have essentially the same attitude:

> Some of these guys are so loaded that they will fall and break their skull if you don't lock them up. Half of these guys have no place to stay anyway except a dingy heap. They are better off in jail. [A10]

> The whole purpose of the law is to try to help them. It's for the protection of themselves and for others, that's the way the law reads. For example, say you're driving through here [Skid Row] and you hit a drunk. He could get killed and if you don't stop and render aid, you could become a criminal. [A10]

> Giving them 30 days in County Jail is sometimes a kindness. *You are doing them a favor, like a diabetic who won't take his insulin.* Sometimes you must hurt him to help him. (Emphasis mine.) [A35]

Like the Skid Row police, the officers, the judge and his coterie are reinforced in their definition of the situation as clinical, and of themselves as diagnosticians and social internists, by the fact that relatives often call the court and ask that a man be given time in jail for his own good. The judge usually complies. Furthermore, as has been mentioned, there is at the jail a branch of the Out-Patient Therapy Center that was originally established to work for the rehabilitation of alcoholics. (This facility will be discussed in detail in chapter 6.) Having this jail clinic allows the drunk court judge to say:

I sentence you to 30 days and I will get in touch with the social worker at the County Jail and she will help you. [A8] [16]

I sentence you to therapy with the psychologists at the County Jail. [A9] (Also reported by court observers.)

Creation of the Pacific City Alcoholism School also allows the judge to feel that he is fulfilling both judicial and therapeutic duties, giving the defendant a suspended sentence on the condition that he will attend the lecture sessions.

Where the name of the social worker or psychologist of Alcoholism School is not invoked as part of the sentence, an awareness of alcoholism as an illness is frequently used as an introductory statement to indicate the reasoning of the courts for giving a jail sentence.

We realize that you men are sick and need help. Any action I might take, therefore, should not in any sense be construed as punishment. Jail in this case is not a punitive measure, but to help you with your alcoholism problem. [A9]

However, the uneasiness of the judge with the jailing of alcoholics has other indicators. The captain of the County Jail, for instance, reports that inmates serving time for public drunkenness have only to write a letter requesting modification of sentence and it is almost always granted, something not true for modification requests of prisoners convicted of other misdemeanors.[17]

That drunk court's methods and procedures of handling the Row men go against the judicial grain also seem to be indicated by the fact court officers claim a new judge must be "broken in" to drunk court before he operates efficiently. When the judge first arrives, he will sentence differently from an experienced judge and in the direction of greater leniency. This upsets the established pattern.

The result is he is taken in hand and guided to do "the right thing" by the veteran court aids. As one court aid put it:

Most of the judges are pretty good—they rely on us. Sometimes you get a new judge who wants to do things his way. We have to break them in, train them. This court is very different. We have to break new judges in.

It takes some of them some time to get adjusted to the way we do things.[18]

The high rate of recidivism of chronic drunkenness offenders leads some experts to question the value of jail as a cure for alcoholism or chronic drunkenness.[19] Publicly, at least, the judges appear to hold to the view that the current arrest and incarceration process *can* be helpful, but that often the alcoholic simply does not respond to "treatment" permanently and needs periodic "doses" of jail-therapy. As one judge put it:

Some men have simply gone so far that you can't do anything for them. They are hopeless. All we can do is send them to jail to dry out from time to time. [A52] [20]

(The question of whether the judge actually *believes* his public pronouncements about the jail is discussed at greater length in chapter 9, footnote 50, pp. 333–34.)

SENTENCING AS AN ASSEMBLY-LINE OUTRAGE

Although the chronic drunkenness offender makes many trips through drunk court, it is not too surprising that he never becomes completely accustomed to the way he is treated there. The mass sentencing, the arbitrariness of the judge, the extraneous factors that seem to go into sentencing decisions, all these shock and embitter him.

Of the group-sentencing procedures, the Row men have this to say:

It's law on the assembly line. That's how it really is. No judge would admit it though. He's got a nice, soft, plush $15,000 or $18,000 job which hinges on this. [18]

I mean there's no concept on the part of anybody that goes into drunk court, that this is a court of law, that the judge is going to weigh the pros and cons. . . . [40]

Let me tell you, he's handling 50 guys in a period of an hour or less. Do you think he has time to, uh, to say, "Well now, why do you drink?" and like that? [12]

The situation here [in jail] could stand a lot of improvement, but the court situation is much worse. When you go down there to court each individual in the courts of the United States is entitled to individual and separate trial. You go down there and they run you into these courts, 30 or 40 at a time, and they sentence you accordingly. The front row first.

I was in there one time, I don't remember who the judge was, when we got in he ran off about seven or eight names, "You people have 30 days in the County Jail." Then he says, "The rest of you in the front row can plead guilty, not guilty, trial by court, trial by jury." [27]

Here is how they describe the seemingly unrelated factors that appear to go into the judge's decision:

If you haven't been picked up for a long time and you've been in town all that time, you'll get a kick-out; but if you've been out of town, you get a sentence, because they figure you were probably drinking all the time. [37]

. . . If you've been [picked up], say, a couple of times in a week or more, why you're subject to be sent to County Jail. [54]

On Monday before court, we all 15 of us shaved on one razor after being picked up on Friday because we knew that if we were whiskery we'd go to County Jail for sure. [27]

Of those arrested before Christmas, everyone who had an address other than Skid Row—even a Beatnik area—got a kick-out. Others like us went to County Jail. [27]

Judge Darlington is a no good son-of-a-bitch. He says to us, "Hold your hands out." They have been holding you in the drunk tank for about eight hours, no beds there, just concrete. After that you go to a holding cell. They line them up ten at a time in front and ten in back. After three days in there, worrying what's going to happen to you, you shake a bit. If you do, Judge Darlington says, "Sixty days." [18]

The fact the judge acts on advice from an ex-alcoholic, a nonprofessional who clearly is drawing his views from personal (and possibly petty) recollections of the men, further confirms the picture of totally arbitrary power with little concern for justice.

There's this guy they call "the Rapper" and he has the ear of the judge. He actually sets the sentence whenever he's there. I'd like to get my hands on him sometime. [49]

We call him "the Rapper." He has the power of life and death for the men. He sat up next to the judge and would say, "probation," "30 days," "90 days," and that's what you'd get. Is that legal? I don't think anyone should be allowed to play God like that. [43]

We were all glad when he slipped. He looked for the worst of himself in others. (Comment on the fact the Rapper had recently fallen off the wagon himself and was at State Mental Hospital.) [24] [22]

The Christian Missionary Rapper was no more popular with the men:

Jim Brown, a reformed alcoholic who has no use for another alcoholic, is the Rapper. He will hang a man if he doesn't like him. I was at Barabas

Abode and Beacon in the Darkness. We speak to each other, but he's a double-crossing, no-good son-of-a-bitch. Absolutely no good! At 6 A.M. he and the court liaison officer go through the records and *they* decide what each man shall get. They see my name and say, "Give that bastard 60 days!" [13]

The Row men are also aware that there are sometimes drastic differences between the sentences received one day in court and those received another. Empirical evidence of this can be seen in Table 11, where sentences received during a time when County Jail was normally full, and during a time when it was beyond normal capacity because of a recent demonstration are compared. (Arrests were also below average for that day, as well.) [23]

TABLE 11. *Comparison of Sentences Given in Drunk Court When County Jail was Full and When it was Beyond Capacity*

| | STATE OF COUNTY JAIL | | | |
Sentences	*Full* (N = 180) PERCENT		*Beyond Capacity* (N = 36) PERCENT	
Kick-out (no sentence, warned only)	2		8	
County Hospital				
With hold	—		—	
No hold	2		—	
		74		91
Suspended sentence				
10 days or less	—		5	
11 to 30 days	23		70	
31 to 60 days	28		8	
61 to 90 days	19		—	
Over 90 days	—		—	
Sentenced to County Jail				
10 days or less	1		3	
11 to 30 days	23		6	
31 to 60 days	2	26	—	9
61 to 90 days	—		—	
Over 90 days	—		—	
TOTAL	100		100	

As shown in Table 11, only 9 percent of the men received a County Jail sentence when the jail was beyond capacity (as compared to 26 percent when it was merely very full.)

Skid Row drunks explain such disparity not as a function of jail capacity but as evidence of graft among agents of social control. Collusion is assumed to exist between the police, City Hospital, the Christian Missionaries, the jailers, and the judges in the Municipal Court, and between the judges, the police, the jailers, and the social workers in the

Superior Courts. This reinforces the idea of a powerful system beyond the control of a penniless individual. The Row men cite the following evidence (so far as they are concerned) as proof of this.

> Sometimes, if you get smart with the policeman, he tells the judge and you get a bigger sentence. [28]

> When I was arrested for drunk, they took me first to the hospital. A social worker came around, and she had a folder, and she said, "Let's see now, uh, you won't have any way to pay for your stay here." I'd only been there [in the hospital] a day and a half, and I says, "Well, how do you know?" And she said, "Well, where you're going, you won't be able to pay anyway." So I says, "Well, how do you know where I'm goin'?" She says, "Well, you're goin' to County Jail for 60 days." I says, "Well, how do you know? I haven't even been before the judge yet!" She said, "Oh, it's right here in your folder." I hadn't been to court yet, see, and sure enough, as soon as I went before the judge—60 days at County Jail. I told the judge about it after he sentenced me and he said, "You're being irrelevant," or something like that. In other words you're going for 60 days, and you just don't argue. He said also, "Well, sometimes that's court procedure." [26] [24]

This cooperation is oftentimes suspected by embittered Row men to serve the purpose of enriching unscrupulous agents of social control or at the very least maintain them in their jobs by keeping the jail population at an assigned level:

> The key to the whole situation is the cut on the food taken by Sheriff Smith and Captain Jackson and the judges. They are all getting their cut by stealing from the food appropriations to the jail. They make $1.50 a day on each one of us. I think they have a quota at County Jail. If they are down 50 men, you can bet that 50 will go out on the next bus. [18]

> What a lot of people don't realize is that this institution and most jails need labor and the alcoholic furnishes that. When I was a trusty in Minneapolis, I'd hear the superintendent call the judge and say, "We are short 150 men here"—and in three days the courts would send us our 150 men. [12] [25]

Maneuvers to Escape County Jail

Lacking the power to fight a drunk charge legally or by means of forfeiting bail, the Skid Row alcoholic has developed other ways of avoiding the County Jail, which is hated more than any other locale on the loop. It should be emphasized that if such avoidance tactics are successful the Row man is still incarcerated, but in another (and more desirable) area.

For instance, a "regular" (i.e., chronic drunkenness offender) may get a job at the City Jail as trusty if he is known to be a good worker and is popular with the guards.

> After you're sentenced, then you go see the head man there [at City Jail], and if you've been there before, which most of 'em have, then he'll say, "Yeah, you can stay here and work for me." It's who you know that counts. [38]

A second means of avoiding County Jail is for a man to act psychotic so that he is referred to the City Screening Facility at the hospital, and perhaps even to the psychiatric ward there. Often this results in a five-day hospitalization or a sojourn in the Northern State Mental Hospital rather than a jail sentence. As one man put it:

> One good way is to act or talk suicidal. That scares them sometimes. Do a lot of yelling and pretend to hear voices. This will often break them [the jailers] down and you'll get to go to City Hospital. [37]

That the Row men can avoid a jail sentence by promising to live at the Christian Missionaries' Work and Residence Center has already been mentioned and will be discussed at greater length in chapter 7.

The Feeling of Unfairness

The judge may feel righteous because he is saving a man from drinking himself to death by sending him to jail to dry out, but the Skid Row alcoholic is neither convinced this alleged judicial "good will" exists, nor is he grateful even if it does. With the exception of those Row men who have settled on the jail as a second home, most believe there is great inequity in the way Pacific City courts are operated. They point to other state jurisdictions that deal with the drunk far less harshly:

> You take Alabama, Georgia, any place, they'll give you a ten dollar fine. Texas, you get two days in jail. You can get in jail ten times and you'll still only get two days and more chance the judge'll let you go. [10]

> Chicago doesn't treat its alcoholics like this city, neither does New York. Most of the time they keep you overnight or a couple of days. They don't send you to jail for a month or more. [14]

The alcoholics' opinion of being sent to jail for drunkenness is perhaps best summed up in this quote:

> As far as the jail goes, all jails are the same. Nobody likes to be in 'em regardless of whether they give you steak or, uh, filet mignons, or what-

ever it is, nobody likes to be in jail. They don't beat you or nothin' like that. Like any place, it's a place of detention; that's their job, that's what the judge said; we're just taken away from the public. As far as gettin' here, it's for drunk, and as far as the sentence goes I believe that's quite a price to pay. Even if it's ten days, I think it's too much myself—even ten days, takin' ten days away from your life for gettin' drunk. [12] [26]

5

County Jail as
a Station on the Loop

The Alcoholic in the Multipurpose Jail

INTRODUCTION

When a Skid Row alcoholic goes to County Jail to serve a sentence, relatives, friends, and certainly many agents of social control sigh with relief and satisfaction, for despite the shame of it all, one of the problem persons in their life is being removed to an environment of presumed safety, abstinence, and possible rehabilitation.

Alcoholics constitute a special class of prisoners at Pacific City County Jail. According to the captain and the guards, alcoholics are quite docile while in custody. They do little fighting, do not take part in antijail demonstrations, work hard on their jobs, shun homosexual contacts, and generally, if sometimes sullenly, obey the rules. In comparison to other offenders in the County Jail, they are almost viewed as nonprisoners.

The off-hand attitude toward the custody of the alcoholic as a convicted criminal is well illustrated in this statement by the jail captain.

> We have some few every year that simply walk away. We don't do anything about it. They are very docile and 95 percent of them create no problem to others. We may punish them mildly for walking away if we pick them up again (maybe a one- to two-day lockup). If he is an antagonistic person, we'd give him a longer punishment. If a nice guy, and most alcoholics are, then one to two days . . . perhaps no outdoor assignments. [11]

On the debit side, the chronic drunkenness offender often has a bad hangover, or worse, may be undergoing physical withdrawal as a result

106

of being suddenly cut off from his liquor supply. Within one to seven days after arrival at the jail, the alcoholic may suffer delirium tremens, or experience an alcoholic seizure [1] in which he becomes dangerously violent; certainly a problem to the deputies. One man described his seizure, which occurred at County Jail, in this way:

> All of a sudden I thought I was at the top of a church steeple looking down over the city of New Orleans. And these men were trying to knock me off so I would fall clear down to the street, so I was fighting them off to save my life. Actually, they were the guards at County Jail trying to hold me down. They told me later that they opened my cell door and I flattened one guard on the way out—just walked right over him. [27]

In addition to the immediate problem of alcoholism withdrawal, these men are frequently weak, sick, and old. As mentioned in chapter 1, the chronic drunk usually has long-term health problems related to his drinking, such as open body sores, malnutrition, liver damage, stomach ulcers, chronic insomnia, and epilepsy. Many Row men arrive at the jail with serious cuts and bruises, the result of recent street fights or muggings. One prisoner in ten has lice and other vermin infesting his clothing. They often have skin rashes of undetermined origin. Except when in residence at some institution on the loop, many of them have not worked or kept regular hours for months or even years.

According to an official bulletin [2] of Pacific City, the jail provides chronic drunks with a setting that will be helpful and even rehabilitative for their specific problems. However, the treatment that the alcoholic receives in the jail, like the conditions of his arrest, is subject to other organizational pressures that have nothing to do with his lack of criminal tendencies or his presumed need for health care and therapy.

The agents of social control who operate the County Jail naturally tend to see the alcoholic inmates as only a portion of their total assignment and its accompanying problems. Alcoholics, quite understandably, are less interested in the problems of operating a county jail than in their own specific treatment. These two perspectives—and the effect they have on defining encounters between the two groups—will be discussed in turn.

The focus of this chapter is not upon the County Jail as an institution of detention. The problems of operating a prison, or any total institution, and the agonies of being an inmate in one, have already been ably recounted in Sykes' classic study of a maximum security prison, *The Society of Captives*,[3] in Goffman's *Asylums*,[4] and in *The Prison Community* by Clemmer,[5] to name but a few. Although the County Jail ordinarily is not considered to be like a maximum security prison or a mental hospital, many parallels apply.

The main consideration of this chapter is to view the County Jail as one important result of the arrest process—a way-station on the rehab route for the Skid Row alcoholic, and a link to other stations on the loop, especially the Christian Missionaries, the Out-Patient Therapy Center, and the social welfare organizations.

THE JAILER'S DILEMMA

When a jailer is asked his short-term goal on the job, it usually does not coincide with the public view of what should be done for the alcoholic there. Like the policeman who sees his mandate on Skid Row as peace-keeping, the jailer sees his duties as designed to "get through the day without incident." [6] These specialists in custodial care are expected to handle any problem connected with the imprisonment of large groups of men in a way that creates a minimum of public concern. Jailers, therefore, walk a narrow path between leaving themselves open to accusations of either treating the prisoners too well (after all, jail is not supposed to be a country club), or too harshly (it is not supposed to be a concentration camp either). [7]

While attempting to maintain a trouble-free institution somewhere between the extremes of comfort and cruelty, the County Jail manager must deal with two major contingencies: budget limitations and the problems of maintaining custody over a mixed population. Both of these factors, in turn, have an effect on the way alcoholics are treated. These factors also tend to modify the official goal of special rehabilitation efforts, which in turn affect the status that alcoholics, as a group, are accorded within the jail society.

Budgetary Limitations

The budget of County Jail is controlled from the central headquarters in Pacific City. If quality of medical care, food, or the physical plant is any indication, administration is tight-fisted indeed. First, the jail is not equipped to function as a withdrawal unit in the same way as the six-bed ward in City Hospital. The budget simply would not allow it. The doctor is scheduled to come in only three times a week; and then he can devote little time to alcoholics undergoing withdrawal because he has the medical problems of a 600-man jail with which to cope. By the testimony of many inmates, the doctor often does not make a call even twice a week. There is no registered nurse on duty. Cases felt to be serious in the judgment of the deputies are taken to City Hospital. [8] Drugs are administered primarily by the guards upon the general prescription of the doctors. Even the drugs used are representative of the general level of care that the jail is able to give. According to the chief County Jail psychiatrist:

We have to use a cheap DT mix here. We really ought to use Thorazine, it's much better for DT's. [A16]

The lack of special infirmary facilities for alcoholics was also mentioned by the guards, one of whom said:

It's a big joke to have the alcoholics here. Some are in DT's; some are so far out they don't know what they are doing. We put them in with everyone else. [A12]

Food is purchased in bulk by the headquarters central supply department and allotted to the county facility. Complaints as to its quality and quantity are universal and have been the focus of both jail demonstrations verging on riots and several grand jury investigations.[9] Complaints have been made by jail officials as well, since they naturally are aware that well-fed prisoners are more easily managed. Said two officers about the quantity of food supplies:

We are out of coffee, beans, and a lot of other essentials. The storehouse is almost empty, the cook is just about frantic. Sometimes we have to truck in emergency supplies from the other jail. It's ridiculous. [A12]

The problem is to feed more than 600 men on 60 cents per man per day, plus what comes in from our farm. [A11]

It is impossible for us to serve certain things that have eye appeal, like fried eggs, because we have no mess hall. [A11]

As a plant built during the depression to contain a maximum of 600 men, the County Jail is totally inadequate for today's occupancy level. Officials complain about the lack of shower facilities (only 27 shower heads to serve all inmates), a central dining hall, and a gymnasium.

The jail looks somewhat rundown on the inside. It is maintained, the captain said, within the limits of his budget:

We have paint crews out every day painting some part of the walls. They go as far as our paint budget will allow. The reason the walls look dirty is because of the bad light in here. We need more lighting fixtures. [A11]

Thus the physical environment into which alcoholics arrive offers little in the way of psychologically-encouraging quarters. In fact, it is just the opposite. This is in contrast to other cities in the state, several of which have developed special barracks-type, minimum-security plants in which to house their alcoholic inmates. Men who have made the loop often allude to these facilities, causing the captain to remark:

One of the things that makes this jail so hard for the men to take is that they have been to the jails in Southern City and West Coast City where there are barracks and more outdoor space available. We just don't have that. [A11]

Controlling a Mixed Population

Men sentenced for public drunkenness comprise at any one time 40 to 45 percent of the County Jail population (and 60 percent of the admissions). The remaining 55 percent include such assorted felons as drug users and drug dealers, bank robbers, embezzlers, persons convicted of assault and battery, civil rights demonstrators, sex perverts, rapists, homosexual prostitutes, and persons convicted of homicide but who have had their sentences reduced to manslaughter and are serving a year or less.[10] According to the captain:

> While the maximum sentence here is one year, you can find a cross-section of the state penitentiary in every county jail. We have everything from murderers on down. [A11]

As a result, a wide range of inmate activities that structure jail time as a social experience for the alcoholic are shaped to cope with men in for more serious criminal charges, rather than by the needs of alcoholics. This includes general rules of conduct, the strict security measures that are imposed, the in-jail jobs available, the degree of contact with persons on the outside, the type of jail clothing alcoholics are issued, the quantity and quality of food, and the help obtainable from the social workers. A more detailed discussion follows.

The pressures to run an establishment with a minimum of public friction and headline-causing trouble, coupled with the need to control such a polyglot criminal population, have inevitably resulted in a series of strict written and unwritten rules to cover every conceivable area of conduct in jail. These rules are designed, not to make life miserable for the inmates but to ease problems or eliminate potential trouble for the administrators. In keeping with the pressures for simplicity, the rules apply to everyone, even persons who are health, education, and welfare commitments.[11] (These HEW commitments will be discussed in greater detail in the next chapter.) It should be mentioned here, however, that Skid Row men get fewer lockups and other "busts" than do other prisoners in the jail.

In addition to the physical bleakness of the jail, the social restrictions that are applied are a good deal like that of the penitentiary. There are approximately five security counts per day (maximum security prisons have seven). The men are searched for contraband when they come in from working outside, and cells are shaken down periodically. Other security measures resembling those used in the state prisons must also be enforced to avoid running the obvious risks: for example, a man convicted of a serious charge might escape or run amok because of use of marijuana, LSD, heroin, or other drugs smuggled inside the premises.

In addition to rules regarding personal cleanliness and cell neatness, the following posted rules of social conduct are enforced through an arbitrary system of lockups and privilege denials:

1. Each inmate must stay on his tier or at his job, unless he is paged and told to report to some particular place. When he has finished his work, he shall return to his tier. Do not visit other tiers or other places.
2. Fighting or horseplay will not be tolerated; no wrestling, singing, or loud talking at any time. Radios must be played in the cell only, not in corridors.
3. Only two books per inmate will be allowed.
4. Magazines, books, candy, food, and tobacco may not be brought or mailed in by friends or relatives. Magazines must be subscribed for and mailed directly from the publisher. All other articles can be bought at the commissary.[12]
5. Letters are to be written on two pages and on one side only. Put return address and name on upper left corner of envelope. Money should be sent to you by money order.[13]

Until recently, playing cards and gambling were not permitted, but this rule was rescinded as one of the concessions made after an inmate riot.

These written rules are only the beginning. At the guard's discretion almost anything (including hoarded sugar, unfinished boxes of cornflakes, etc.) can be called contraband and possession will result in the prisoner being "busted," that is, given a penalty in the form of a lockup or loss of "good time."[14] Breaks in proper decorum that might embarrass prison officials, such as shouting out the windows at women visitors below, or speaking when not spoken to, are also taboo.

Communications between the inmate and the "outside world" are drastically curtailed.

All mail is censored by the deputies. Any letters that contain scurrilous references to the jail, or attempts to make appointments with ex-felons, or love letters to women the deputies doubt are close to the inmate, are returned to the writer with the statement that they will not be mailed until the objectional matter is removed. The writer must put his name and address on the envelope so he cannot hide his current status from others.

Phone calls are not allowed. Emergency phone calls will be made by the social workers, but they resist demands of this type unless connected with family troubles, and urge the inmate to write letters concerning the details of problems having to do with unfinished business at the time of arrest, or new developments in his life while in jail.[15] The Skid Row inmate without family seldom has anyone to contact anyway.

Visitors are limited to Saturday and Sunday afternoons. The visiting room is crowded and little privacy is afforded. Again, this is an academic problem so far as Skid Row alcoholics are concerned. Most do not have visitors; the County Jail is difficult to reach by public transportation and few Skid Row men have automobiles.[16] Thus these alcoholics serve their time without even the breaks in monotony that other prisoners enjoy through weekend visits with friends and relatives.

Social Status in the County Jail

It might be supposed the alcoholic, because of his easy-going nature and his willingness to conform, would be given the high-status jobs in the jail and therefore would be among the social elite there. In jail, however, as on the outside, this is denied him. Again he is low man.

Because of the nature of the nonalcoholic jail population, and perhaps compounded by the low budget that does not allow for unnecessary jobs, work appointments are not given on merit or to afford inmates needed training and experience. Job assignments primarily must conform to the limitations set for the remainder of the jail population. As a result, the alcoholic must take the employment *leavings* in jail.

For instance, alcoholics rarely become trusties at Pacific City County Jail, nor are they given the better inside jobs (clerical, technical, or more advanced culinary work.) [17] These must be saved for the inmate who cannot be allowed outside, whether because of the seriousness of his crime, or because there is a hold on him from police of another jurisdiction, or because he is a drug user and might make contact with a pusher in this way.

Out of a total of 40 kitchen jobs available, alcoholics held, on the average, eight of these jobs, according to the captain, although they compose almost half of the jail population. Furthermore, since the average Skid Row man's sentence is 30 days, it is difficult to be promoted to a better job when another inmate serves his time and leaves. In addition, performing most kitchen jobs requires some training, and there is a jail rule that no one gets such a job if he has a sentence of less than 30 days. Again, this hits the alcoholic hardest, as he is most apt to have a short sentence. (As noted in the previous chapter, his average sentence is approximately 26 days.) [18]

The distribution of jobs in County Jail means that alcoholics rarely have an opportunity to wear ego-gratifying pressed clothing, or to eat employee's fare in the kitchen instead of inmate food in their cells.

If the alcoholic is able to work, he is usually given a lower-status, outside job or, in a few cases, a kitchen job.[19] Outside jobs may be either "landscaping" the jail lawn and grounds, or working on the farm.[20]

Alcoholics also do the dirty inside jobs that no one else will take, and they do them well. According to the captain:

> The alcoholics do excellent work in culinary work. They do well in janitorial work. They will do the dirty work others won't handle. [A11] [21]

However, manual labor that alcoholics provide in the County Jail serving Pacific City is by no means gratuitous "make-work." If the public drunkenness law were modified so alcoholics would be kept overnight and then released,[22] or taken to a hospital ward for a five-day drying out and then released,[23] the entire work structure of the County Jail would have to be revamped. According to the captain:

> Do you know what would happen if the alcoholics no longer came here? They are 90 percent of the farm labor. If we lost them, we'd have to close this place down. Once in a while, I think what would we do without them? I don't know. It would take a complete reorganization. [A11] [24]

Relations between social workers and alcoholics will be discussed at greater length in the next chapter. Suffice for now to say that the domination of these rehabilitation services by the nonalcoholic inmates maintains the pattern described above.

Thus the alcoholic, by virtue of other administrative problems, is reduced or degraded to the lowest of the jail inmates, although he has committed possibly the least serious crime of all those incarcerated.

Justifying the Alcoholic's Jail Term

Like most other agents of social control working with the alcoholic, the jailer is plagued at times by ambivalence as to what sort of person the man serving a sentence on a public drunkenness charge really is, and what sort of treatment he should receive. Again, as with the police and judges, the image of a helpful, rehabilitating process occurring in the jail is evoked along with the definition of the chronic drunk as a patient rather than a prisoner.

Most jail administrators believe they are doing the chronic drunkenness offender a favor by keeping him sheltered and separated from his liquor supply. These services alone are thought to override other contingencies of his jail experience. The captain of the County Jail puts it this way:

> We think we do as much as the state [mental] hospital for the alcoholic. Men come down here and dry out. They are built up physically.[25] If it

weren't for this institution, the lives of these men would be considerably shortened. The laws of the jungle would catch up with them. It's our experience that most of the men eat very little and live nowhere in particular. This [jail] is actually, in effect, their home more than Pacific City. [All] [26]

AN INMATE'S PERSPECTIVE ON SERVING A SENTENCE

For the Skid Row alcoholics, the entire incarceration experience presents a nightmarish challenge to survive the official juggernaut that seems so harsh and predictable in some ways and yet so idiosyncratic in others.

Jail to him bears little relationship to his condition *as an alcoholic*. Rather it is a world in which he feels deprived of the most basic goods and services, a condition attendant to all jails.[27] That it may be cleaner than his Skid Row surroundings seems beside the point to the alcoholic arrestee, for in many ways jail is a magnification of the hated parts of his Skid Row life without many of the compensations.

For instance, although Skid Row is a world upon which outsiders look with disgust and disdain, the Skid Row man has some status *within* it: he has drinking companions, he is included in parties, he is accepted. And he need not associate with those "square Johns" who look down on him. In the jail, the alcoholic's status is low for a number of reasons, but he is unable to escape the effects of this labeling. He must constantly associate with those who look down on him.

A more detailed discussion of the County Jail from the Skid Row alcoholic's perspective will be presented below.

THE CONSTANT DISAPPOINTMENT IN MEALS   Meals at Pacific City's County Jail are considered to be poorly prepared and inadequate by both alcoholics and others, and complaints about the food are the first item mentioned whenever an interviewer asks about the jail.[28] The wide difference between the food given the prisoners and that which the deputies eat is well known, and the basis of considerable jealousy and bitterness. The fact there is no central dining room and inmates must eat in their cells is also galling to the alcoholic men.

It's the only jail I've ever been in where when they have breakfast, as soon as breakfast is over, they're talking about what they're gonna have for lunch. And then when lunch is over they want to know what they're gonna have for supper. You're always perpetually hungry out there—continually hungry. [59]

You get very little to eat at County Jail. I come out 134 pounds, went in at 150.[29] In the morning you get a plate of mush, two slices of bread, and coffee. You get that every morning but Sunday. Sunday morning they give you two packages of either cornflakes or sugar smacks. Lunch is a bowl of soup and a couple of slices of bread, and coffee. And at night, it's supposed to be the best meal of all—it could be hash or something. [56]

The food is bad enough as it is shown on the menu. But the way it is served—it's just a mess dumped on a plate. I once had hot buttered noodles and then they put my jello right on top that. [18] [30]

I'm an ex-restaurant man. I know the cost of food wholesale. They claim to spend 60 cents a day on us. That's a laugh. If they spend 20 cents, that's all. [18]

The portions are very tiny. If you want more, you'll have to trade the trusties something for it. Like a cigarette or something like that. Negro trusties run the place. [50] [31]

You can buy extra snacks at the commissary if you have money, but not many of us come in with money, and very few of us [those on social security] have any coming in. The other guys get money sent by their families. [16]

One of the things you usually have to buy is sugar. An alcoholic craves sugar, and you don't get any here, not even on your cereal or in your coffee unless you buy your own. You get mush or oatmeal every morning with no sugar on it.[32] You have to buy it. You eat in your cell. There's no dining room, you just eat alone. [9]

I was once in the hole for five days for throwing food. But I had my privilege. I told them what I thought of it. It was worth it. [27]

LIVING QUARTERS   The six-by-nine-foot cells are furnished with a bunk, a sink, a toilet, and a stool to sit on. In Pacific City County Jail as mentioned previously, the cell walls need cleaning, the paint is chipped, and there are various graffiti written on the walls.[33] In some ways it may be likened to living in a bathroom, since the toilet and sink are constant companions.

During crowded periods, not every inmate can have a cell. Mattresses are put in the aisles on the floor at night. These makeshift accommodations are often given to the alcoholic because he is the least likely to be a security problem. (Mattresses are not cleaned between inmate usages and are extremely dirty-looking.) [34] The sleeping situation is a major complaint among the alcoholics:

Sometimes it's so crowded there are men sleeping on the floor on mattresses. The mattresses are filthy. They are just filthy. [56]

Things are very crowded on my tier. There are 60 cells, only 57 in use and 81 inmates on the tier. [10]

Today, finally, the men that were sleeping on the floor got a cell. The number of inmates leaving is starting to surpass the ones that are coming in. Now there are no more men on the floors . . . About April and May it will again get crowded. (Notes of jail observer.)

Medical Care

The medical situation is viewed with panic by the Skid Row alcoholic. Adequate medical care is very important to an alcoholic, who often feels that his problem is primarily a medical one demanding the attention of a skilled physician. The lack of a resident doctor, or even a nurse, at County Jail is cited by the Row men as one more sign of the heartlessness of the society that will send an alcoholic to jail instead of to a hospital:

A doctor comes in once or twice a week. Even when he does examine you, he scarcely looks at you. Most of the time there's no doctor here; no nurse at the infirmary either; just inmates. They call the officers if there's a man sick; but it's gonna take 'em a good time to get you down. Well, let's put it this way, you gotta be very bad and look like you're gonna die to be lucky enough to go to the hospital. [14]

When there is an emergency, they usually take you to City Hospital in a matter of hours; but again this is not the case always because there are men that will fake illness and consequently others will suffer for this. They have no medical officer or anyone capable of the responsibility for the infirmary. The doctor was here March 15 and didn't come again until today (March 21). (Notes of jail observer.)

They take our prescribed medicine away from us, that helps us keep from having seizures, and then they make us wait maybe a week for the doctor to come in and say it is okay to take it. In the meantime, we have a seizure that could have been prevented. [16]

The doctor just left and I didn't get to find out why the guards will not give me back my prescription. And he won't be here again 'til Friday. (The day was Monday.) [9]

The fact that the jail is in violation of the state penal code on medical care is taken by the Row men as further evidence that as inmates of the County Jail they are beyond society's concern:

We have a doctor comes in once, maybe twice a week. There's no regis-tered nurse on duty out here. All these people are sick, you can't get no medication—epileptics and all this kind of thing, and *I know the law re-quires that a registered nurse be on duty in a place of this kind 24 hours a day, seven days a week.*[35]

Men have seizures and fits here and everything, up there in the "squirrel cage" [36] in Three North, beatin' their heads against the bed, climbing up against the bars and the walls. Things like that and they can't get nothin'.[37] [12]

I looked up the county jail penal code in the prison library and it says that there is to be a physician available at all times if there is a daily average population of more than 100 persons. We have over 600 here and we are lucky to see the physician once a week. I am going to get a writ against this place and expose it. [10] [38]

Constant Status Deprivation

If it is true that the social structure of an institution generates the social roles available to those within it,[39] and if a positive self-image is a pre-requisite for rehabilitation, then it is doubtful that County Jail can ever aid alcoholics to feel a part of society.

To the alcoholic, both formal and informal jail procedures reduce him in status. Starting with admittance procedures, the alcoholic feels he is constantly degraded. First of all, he is disturbed because he is treated like a criminal (which he stoutly believes he is not); second, he is denied the "good jobs"; third, he finds that he is a low-status criminal as well, the unkindest cut of all.

INAUGURATION INTO INMATE STATUS   Woven together from many inter-views and presented below is a representative picture of what seems im-portant about the jail experience to the Skid Row alcoholic. To them, each situation bears a message about what jail authorities think of the Row man; the message is not encouraging.

Routine admittance procedures, intended primarily to prevent the en-trance of narcotics or vermin into the jail, convey the first message of the jail experience: "You are now a criminal or jailbird and will be treated like all the other inmates here." [40] Below is a description of this experience at Pacific City County Jail:

First of all you arrive in a van, and you strip down and they search under your arms for narcotics and so on; and they put your clothes in a basket and issue you blues. (Most confirmed older alcoholics do not use narcotics and do not approve of their use. Therefore, to be searched for them is considered insulting.) [60]

You take a shower, they spray you, delouse you, and then you dress. The clothing they give you then is nothing but a pair of coveralls that look somewhat like mechanic's clothes and one pair of socks that are either too large or too small. The shoes are all torn up and for laces you are lucky to have a piece of thread or string to keep them from falling off. By the way, you receive no undergarments. [60] [41]

They take you to Three North,[42] the "fish tank." Three North is also the place where the homosexual queens are and we have to stay with *them* for several days. Why they put drunks and homosexuals together, I don't know, but you can imagine that it is not very pleasant to be around them.[43] It's the worse place I know to be just when you are about to go into the DT's. [56]

All the way through admission you are treated just like a criminal—and we're really not criminal. [49]

CRIMINAL HIERARCHY IN JOB ASSIGNMENTS   Just as in the "outside world," where occupation generates status, privilege, and personal self-satisfaction, so also in jail does the work assignment fill this deep human need. Alcoholics are bitter because—as the least dangerous of prisoners—they feel they ought to get the best work assignments. As previously noted, the Row men in fact get the worst job assignments in the jail and thus miss out on the accompanying privileges.

On top of that, if you get some of the inside jobs, you have all sorts of privileges, like making your own coffee, cooking, and eating. You can't do that on other jobs like farm crew. If we made our own coffee we'd get the hole for five days! Why should it be like that? [9]

They give you old, patched-up cotton pants and shirt. They aren't even pressed. You have to get an office job or a kitchen job to get to wear pressed stuff. [15] [44]

The Row men suspect they are passed over because of their status as virtual paupers. As a consequence of being ineligible for high-status jobs, the alcoholic must take orders from those men whom he looks upon as "the real criminals."

I know a guy who got a front office job. His family fixed it up with a guard for $40.00. (Corroborated by a jail observer.) Of course, we've got no money to do anything like that. [17]

If you want to work, you mostly get the outdoor tasks. Mostly the trusties are the guys who are going to be there three months or longer. If you get under 30 days, you often don't get a work assignment and can't get out of your cell. So, get this, the guys who have reduced felonies are *in charge of us*—and we aren't even criminals. Those guys are in for narcotics use, petty theft, larceny, strong-arm robbery, and so on. [10]

This latter complaint is reinforced by some other grounds on which status is awarded in jail—the "worthiness" of the crime.

Because alcoholics are in jail for a reason that other inmates define as not worth going to jail for, they are considered stupid. Men who consider themselves to be in jail on "worthwhile" raps such as burglary, embezzlement, and strong-arm robbery look upon their jail sentences as a hazard of their profession. They make no secret of their contempt for a "wino" who has to serve time because of too much boozing. The alcoholics are aware of this:

> Those guys think they are somebody and they treat us like dirt; call us "dirty winos" and other names I won't mention. In jail, the top guys are the guys with the stiffest sentences. [50]

> Here's the idea, you see, they're in there for something, what you might say, worse than we've done. All we've done is get busted for drinking, which they consider foolish. Now they've got to have something to look down upon to build their own ego up; so a wino, we're nobody, so they can push us around and this makes them feel big, as a general rule. [17]

> If something's messed up on the tier they point to one of us [winos] and tell us to clean it up because we messed it up. And we clean it up, not because it is our fault, but because we know what would happen to us if we didn't. [16]

> Yet, these are the same people [inmates in on more serious crimes] the jailers seem to trust the most. They get the best jobs. They have access to little things like sandwiches. They have the "makings" for just about everything. We get nothing. We are low men around here. [16]

The Jail Atmosphere

To the Skid Row alcoholic, County Jail time is time served in an atmosphere of gloom, boredom, arbitrary exercise of power, exploitation, and violence. Because of his lack of relatives and friends in the outside world and his low social status in the jail, the Row man feels he faces these things totally alone. These elements are discussed, primarily in the alcoholics' own words:

> County Jail is a gloomy, desolate, dirty place and there's no incentive for a man there; he, uh, he's continually gloomy. There are no recreational activities [45] and they list it as a rehabilitation center; but they're in error because it's really no place for a drunk to go or to get well. [46]

PRISONER OF THE POWER PATTERN For the alcoholic, Jail rules are not mere administrative formalities, nor are they limited to those posted in the cell. Rules are seen as extensions of the persons who enforce them and are just about as idiosyncratic as individual personalities. Therefore, the network of formal and informal sanctions can be discussed in conjunction with those who create and enforce them.

Pacific City County Jail can be grossly stratified into four official levels: at the top are the deputies (who serve as guards), next come the trusties (inmates who help in some form of jail routine), followed by inmates who have some sort of job, and inmates who have no job. Alcoholics fall into the latter two categories. Thus they have at least two levels of authority above them at all times.

Perhaps the greatest complaint of the Row men is that the enforcement of the rules is not predictable. If there is a pattern, it is difficult to detect and it varies by level of official as well as by person. It makes the world within the jail, for the alcoholics at least, unpredictable and insecure.[46]

The deputies don't beat you around. They're nonchalant; they're impartial. It's just a job to them. But they treat us just like the other criminals —which we're not. They bust us for the least little thing. It would be easier to tell you what is *not* a bust than what *is*. And a lot of it you have to learn the hard way. There is no indoctrination period to warn you; for instance, I was given a five-day lockup because I tried to smuggle in two green onions under my arm from the farm. I was going to put them in the food to jazz it up. They called it "contraband." I know a guy who got busted for feeding bread to the seagulls. [27]

Most people are not aware of the great power which is invested in the guards. They are not guards as such—they run the place. They can lock you up on a whim, like if you say "Good morning" at the wrong time. [38]

You find that even though there are specified rules you are to follow, the enforcement of them fluctuates with the member of the staff that happens to be on duty. Some bulls will let you get away with one thing while the others may bust you for it. After a period of time here you get to learn with which bulls you can do certain things. An example of this is you are not supposed to write letters in ink. Most of the bulls will not say anything if you do, but then there are those that will. After you get to know the shifts that the bulls have, you know just when you can write in ink, and when you can't. (Notes of jail observer.)

Getting busted means take away some privileges: like commissary, ban you from the yard, keep you from visits and mail, or take away your good time. If they want to, they can lock you up in a cell. The hole is solitary. [12]

They can also take away the five days "good time" and days work time you earn each month after the first 30 days. They can take all or part of that. [12]

The particularistic aspect of the system of rules and sanctions at the jail also leads the inmate to doubt the essential humanity of his keepers and their supposed impartiality in administering the rules.

There are one or two that are sadistic and enjoy watching a man suffer under their power. Their superiors are aware of this but don't seem to care as long as there is no real trouble. (Notes of jail observer.)

Then there are the ones who just do their job and stick to the rules. But even then what can you think of such a man that would take a job like this, to see every day tormented, miserable, unfortunate, human beings. There has to be something wrong with their thinking. Most are too lazy to get a real job or they are afraid to steal, so this is a perfect spot for them. (Notes of jail observer.)

They treat you just like a criminal—you are a criminal. You're behind bars; you're counted five or six times a day; you get no privileges, no rights, no nothing. [16]

The trusties who dish out and distribute the food, lock and unlock cell doors, and hand out the towels hold power over distribution of petty but important items of everyday creature comfort. As mentioned, at County Jail, a majority of the trusties assigned to the tiers with alcoholic inmates are Negroes. There appears to be no love lost between these two low-status groups. Each tries to put the other down. According to the alcoholics:

The Negro trusties try to degrade us through words and actions. They will say such things as, "Get out of my way, tramp." They also give you very small portions of food—just a tiny piece of meat and a little potato about this big and they say, "If you want more, you'll have to pay a cigarette or candy for it." If you don't have money to buy cigarettes or candy to trade for the food, then you starve. And you can't complain to a deputy. Then they [the trusties] *really will get you.* [17]

The above comment is substantiated by deputies who said:

The Negro hypes [47] run the jail. They are the schemers. They are really in charge, wheeling and dealing in pressed shirts and commissary. The alcoholics never get in on this. [A12]

The trusties cheat the winos on food, and you can't fink on a trusty. They tell these old men that if they squeal, either they [the trusties] will get them or their buddy will. [A13]

Negro trusties confirm the feeling they have for the alcoholic, but deny that they cheat them. Said one trusty of the Skid Row bum:

They are sick. They ought to be put in a sack and dropped in the bay. They have bad health habits. I wouldn't accept something from a wino. Once he touches it, I don't want it. He don't have nothing. If you give a wino a cup of coffee and mush, he's satisfied. They are about the lowest people in the jail. They don't bathe—and have a foul odor. [A53]

As to the food, we don't hold anything out. If we have three weiners left over, how are you going to divide that among 60 men? So the trusties divide it. They [the alcoholics] eat better here than they eat on the streets. [A53]

VIOLENCE AND INTIMIDATION   Perhaps the most frightening and men-
tally-debilitating aspect of the jail experience for the alcoholic is being
trapped in a world of violence from which there appears to be no escape
and which seems to reproduce the terrors of the slum street increased to
the nth power. Here are some of the comments the men make about
this:

We are stuck here with burglars and others of the same type that rob and
kick us around on the street. [10]

At noon today a man was attacked sexually by another inmate. When the
guards found out about it, they put the inmate who attacked the other in
the hole. (Reported by jail observer.)

Things can get pretty rough. If you go down to the commissary and buy
something, you'll get robbed [by other inmates] before you get back up to
your cell. I've seen 'em rob a guy of stuff and cut a guy all up. You don't
dare report it to a guard, or they'll get you even worse. [11]

(Because of the problem of robbery on the way from commissary, the
captain advises the men to buy only one day's needs at a time.)

I just went down to the showers. Again there was another fight. One of
the men taking a shower asked one of the laundry men for some clean
clothes. The men in the laundry said "no." The one taking a shower
again demanded some clean clothes. When the laundry man said "no"
again, the other one shoved him and reached for the clothes himself. That
was how that one began. It was broken up before the bulls got there.
(Notes of jail observer.)

If you don't do what they say, they threaten to "get you off the tier."
Getting a guy off the tier is just the short process of everyone on the tier
beating the hell out of him. Then he will go down to the captain and tell
the captain that he wants to move to another tier because he doesn't get
along with the people on this tier. But he will not go down and tell the
captain that a bunch of inmates jumped on him, because he knows if he
does, he will get the same thing all over again, except he will come out in
a little worse shape. (Reported by jail observer.)

You run into all kinds of people out here. All you can do is hold your
breath. [16]

Few alcoholics, older men in shaky physical condition, are any match for
their fellow prisoners.

Once I saw two of them, a Negro and a Mexican, and they went into the
cell of an old guy over there that was more or less psycho, but on a good
pension and everything, a retired engineer, and, uh, I seen 'em go into his
cell and work him over and walk out with all kinds of cigarettes and
candy, just because he wouldn't give it to them. These were the trusties

that did that. Even if you told the captain about it, all he would do would be to bust 'em for a few days, or give 'em a lockup, and they would get even with you later. (Notes of jail observer.)

Again, this is substantiated by some deputies who say:

These alcoholics are the victims here. If they have money, the younger element takes advantage of them, takes their commissary from them, threaten if they tell the deputies then they will get them. Some of these guys are here on assault with a deadly weapon. The colored punks take these winos real bad. I know they bled one for about $50.00. I've seen them cut with razors in my presence. [A13]

They [the young Negro drug users] take the commissary stuff from the winos right after they buy it. Then threaten to cut him up—cut his throat. It's mostly these 20-year-old guys picking on the old men. If a man is here for only 15 to 20 days, he decides to go along with the program. [A12]

FEELINGS OF ISOLATION AND HELPLESSNESS   The fear of physical violence is magnified by the knowledge of complete isolation from the outside world. The Skid Row alcoholic, without family, friends, or money, knows he has no one to turn to should he suffer an injustice or be in serious danger. If he needs medicine and does not get it, there is no one to whom he can complain. If he is beaten up, he is afraid (on pain of more beating) to complain. If he does not get enough food, there is no one to tell. He cannot even write about these things in a letter, for they are censored out. Besides, he has no money for stamps. He is totally without social reinforcements that even most criminals take for granted.

We have no real contact with the outside world while we are here. No phone calls are allowed. No one comes to see us. No one sends us money or writes us. We can't even afford writing paper or stamps. *You know, if something awful happened to us, no one would even miss us.* [18] [48]

EXPLOITATION   Even the alcoholic's experiences of being exploited on Skid Row because of his economic powerlessness are repeated in jail. As he sees it, other criminals and the guards use him to their advantage.

For instance, in an attempt to "get in" with those men who really seem to run the jail, the Skid Row alcoholic will often jeopardize his freedom by serving as a "drop" for narcotics.

Sometimes the drug users will offer me tobacco if I will bring in a package left in the bushes outside. There is not only dope in this jail, but needles and knives. The drops are made outside and we bring them in. [14]

Deputies are aware that the alcoholic prisoners are used in this way.

The winos are used for drug pickups. They are bribed with tobacco. They don't have any money to buy tobacco, so they will do just about anything for it. [A12]

Cheap jail labor is used by both citizens and guards.

I mean, take Valley City; now it's a known fact that when they start pickin' that fruit out there at harvest, well they go around makin' pickups because they work out of jail. Prisoners go out of jail to work on the harvest, pickin' peaches or cucumbers; though they get paid; they get a dollar and a half an hour for eight hours work—they call it the "work furlough." The sheriff gets $5.00 a day, on a counting out of your wages, you probably know that—he gets $5.00 a day for every day you work and you get $6.32. [54]

Moreover, the entire jail operation is seen by the Skid Row alcoholic as dependent upon his presence:

Here at County Jail—we have a year-round operation. We got a farm to run, lawn to keep up, we got to furnish year-round jobs for the guards. If the population falls below a certain point—it has to be brought up—to get the work done and keep the guards. [17]

Listen, any policeman, any guard at the jail, any judge can tell you what's going on with the drunks. It doesn't help to send them [the drunks] to jail. They [police, guards, and judges] all know that. But they are in it for the money and the graft. They aren't going to upset a good deal. As a man who has spent 20 years in and out of jails for drinking, I know what I'm talking about. They use us. [18]

The End of the Sentence

When a man has served his sentence, he is given back his clothes, or some donated clothing from a charitable organization, plus 15 cents carfare.[49] This is so he can take the bus home, if he has a home, after he is transported back to Pacific City. For most of the Skid Row alcoholics there is no home to go to. He may have made arrangements while in jail to go to the Christian Missionaries Work and Residence Center, or he may have hopes to get into the Welfare Home for Homeless Men. Usually the 15 cents is all he has to show for his jail time and he needs some sort of shelter.

The men report (and a series of observations confirm) that the Row men often pool this transportation money with a friend and buy a bottle. The whole process begins again.

Most of us leave jail feeling very bitter. We feel like we need a drink after that. [14]

Perhaps the best summation of the arrest, sentence, and jail experience came during a series of research observations of interviews with inmates conducted by Brigadier Gomez of the Christian Missionaries. These interviews were for the purpose of aiding the inmates in getting modification of their sentence or gaining admission to the Work and Residence Center. After listening to a man explain his situation, the Brigadier turned to the author to explain:

This man is scared because he feels he is caught up in some kind of a system where he is helpless. [A14]

III

STRATEGIES
OF
REHABILITATION

6

Mental and
Physical Therapy

Realities and Adjustments
at Two Loop Stations

The practice of sentencing drunks to jail, whether as punishment or for drying out, has been labeled inhumane and has been a target of social reformers for many years. It is their contention that alcoholism is a disease [1] of a psychological nature and therefore can be properly controlled only by some type of mental therapy.

Today, in addition to medical aid for the acute symptoms of alcoholism and the general physical debilitation that accompanies it,[2] undergoing some form of psychological treatment for the assumed mental problems that caused the continued heavy drinking is standard, despite the lack of empirical evidence to substantiate alcoholism as an illness, or any therapy as a viable cure for it.[3] Additionally, the illness theory is embraced by many alcoholics, who testify to the personal helplessness they experience if they try to stop drinking without professional assistance.

Current psychological efforts concentrate on group therapy, but hypnosis, LSD and CO_2-assisted therapy, aversion therapy, and other psychological-pharmacological approaches have been attempted in the state hospitals, primarily on an experimental basis with small groups of volunteers.[4]

The sum of all this effort, if the rate of recidivism is any acceptable indication, is an unenviable record of failure to attain the avowed twin goals of mental and social rehabilitation.[5] Recidivism among Skid Row

129

alcoholics is extremely high; with discouraging regularity they return to the mental institution or therapy center that so recently discharged them, or move to another institution on the loop.

In an attempt to understand how psychological therapy is experienced by alcoholics and their therapists, two institutions on the loop will be examined in this chapter. Both facilities were organized to offer psychological aid in addition to medical therapy to alcoholics. Substantial proportions of the patient population in each are Skid Row alcoholics. (See chapter 2, footnote 3, page 298.)

First focus will be on the County Jail Branch of the Out-Patient Therapy Center (hereafter referred to as the Jail Branch Clinic). Discussed second will be the Northern State Mental Hospital (hereafter referred to as State Mental Hospital).

These institutions can be reached by a number of routes. The Jail Branch Clinic is considered to be part of the County Jail and therefore accessible to inmates serving time there. Additionally, an alcoholic could be *committed* (on a Health, Education, and Welfare order) to the Jail and Clinic by a Superior Court judge as an alternative to State Mental Hospital, although this latter practice has been dropped recently.

State Mental Hospital can be reached through Superior Court commitment (sometimes with the aid of a referral from the Alcoholic Screening agency) or from Skid Row directly as a voluntary commitment. Sometimes staff members at other stations on the loop make referrals to the hospital when they have a man they feel they cannot manage.

Before discussing the perceptions of agents of social control and Skid Row alcoholics about therapy at these two stations, two subject areas must be outlined in detail inasmuch as they are major aspects of mental treatment on the loop. They are: (a) group therapy, practices, and claims, and (b) the ever-present spectre of failure of group therapy as a treatment for alcoholics. Together, these phenomena structure many of the interactions on the loop. Group therapy is the most widely-accepted psychological approach among professionals and forms a major part of the rehabilitation services at the jail and the mental hospital. The high rate of recidivism that both therapists and alcoholics continue to experience forces some adjustments to failure, which in turn affects the climate of these stations on the loop.

Group Therapy as an Approach to Alcoholism

The term "group therapy" refers primarily to the application of or adaptation of individual therapy techniques, often psychoanalytically-oriented, to a small group of people. The ultimate goal is the same for both individual and group—to aid the person with emotional problems to attain a better understanding of himself—his motivations, anxieties, and conflicts

—so that he will gain greater mastery over himself, making better use of his psychological strengths, and will be less overcome by his psychological deficiencies. Group therapy as an approach to alcoholism assumes that drinking is merely a *symptom* of underlying emotional forces and social conflicts, the nature and the influence of which may or may not be known to the man. Basic to the group therapy approach is the belief held by its advocates that once an alcoholic understands both the presence of his problems, and the fact that drinking has become his method of coping with them, he will be in a position to stop over-imbibing and attempt a more acceptable mode of adjustment. Therapists often make remarks about the goals of group therapy such as the following:

> It [group therapy] should strip the person down to his ego, the true person. He will then see himself as he really is, without his facade. Then he can recognize what his hangups and *real* problems are and do something about them. [A24]

This confrontation of the person with himself is assumed to be accomplished through what is often referred to as the "dynamics of the group," exemplified by Bion's description below:

> The therapy of individuals assembled in groups is usually in the nature of an explanation of neurotic trouble. . . . Sometimes it *turns mainly on the catharsis of public confession.* One hopes to accomplish some of the same things that you would in individual therapy, that is, to help the person become more aware of his feelings, but because he is in a group, to convey his feelings more openly and by interacting with others perceive their feelings more accurately and become more sensitive to . . . their reactions to him. (Emphasis mine.) [6]

Another assumption of group therapy is that when the average person has his true self revealed to him, it will be under conditions of great stress—outward displays of emotions such as shouting, gesturing, and crying are welcomed as signs of a fruitful session. Among group therapy leaders, statements like the one below are typical:

> I consider a session successful only when people get deeply involved emotionally—pound the table, and so on. This is good for them. Otherwise, they are merely intellectualizing, holding back, keeping it deep down within themselves. [A17]

Of a session considered highly successful, another psychologist said:

> Sometimes even the therapist gains from these sessions. Dr. Golden cries when he reveals the truth to himself. [A28]

As Bion suggested by his use of the phrase "public confession," it is assumed that the truth about any person will be neither pretty nor flattering, and this leads to a systematic search (with accompanying accusations) for shameful deeds and terrible desires, especially in the area of sex and self-aggrandizement.[7]

To elevate members of a group to this emotional, empathetic, and confessional pitch, leaders claim therapy groups should be limited in size (approximately 4 to 12 members) and have frequent, regular contact with each other (a minimum of 8 to 12 weekly meetings lasting an hour or more.) [8]

Like all psychotherapeutic efforts, and unlike most medical treatment, the effectiveness of group therapy is not apparent during or shortly after treatment (if future cessation of heavy drinking is the goal).

Adjustment to the Failure of the Therapeutic Ideal

A number of studies have dealt with the adjustment of individuals when their belief systems—and the somewhat idealistic plans based upon them —collide with the hard exigencies of execution. The impact has been aptly called "reality shock." [9]

For those who survive and continue operations in some form, rigid adherence to principles is usually not the primary reaction. Rather, there is a juggling of ideas and values, methods of approach, blame of self, and blame of others, until a new definition of the situation and a belief system emerges that seems to "work." The process by which this is done can be arbitrarily divided into steps as follows:

1. Original ideals and purposes (original definition of the situation); failure to achieve goals within framework of ideals

2. Identification of barriers to success

3. Strategies to circumvent these barriers

4. Resolution (redefinition of the situation).

As is obvious, these steps open the way to any number of alternative decisions so that the ultimate resolution is by no means predictable at an early stage. In fact, as will be seen, staffs and patients of the two institutions to be discussed resolve the problem of failure in divergent ways because their different intermediate decisions reflect attitudinal reactions to pressures and access to solutions unique to each.

Perhaps the most crucial part of this chain of reflection and readjustment is step 2—Identification of barriers to success. Some of the possibilities both professional therapists and their patients must consider are (a) the patient failed to or was incapable of cooperating in therapy; (b) exigencies beyond the therapist's control (for instance, budgetary problems, housing problems, medical problems) made the therapy unworkable; (c) the therapist lacked the requisite skills for helping this particular patient; or (d) the therapy itself is useless.

In making such a decision, attitudes toward the self and the sponsoring institution are obviously jeopardized. To admit either that a given therapy is a failure or that the therapist is not sufficiently skilled is a serious blow to the professional; on the other hand, for the alcoholic to admit that he is not amenable to therapy is to face the possibility of being incurable, or at the very least, uncooperative and not motivated. To see the institution as militating against that which it professes to encourage is to develop cynicism, rebellion, or apathy whether one is staff or the patient.[10]

Both the staffs of the Jail Branch Clinic and the State Mental Hospital experienced failure and "reality shock" when faced with the high rates of recidivism of their alcoholic patients. Naturally, the patients experienced this as failure as well.

How barriers to success are perceived by both staff and patients at these two institutions and the strategies employed by each to overcome such perceived barriers (and to overcome each others' counter-strategies), make great differences in the ultimate resolution by both groups at the two institutions.

These resolutions serve, of course, as a general description of the state to which the therapeutic ideal has evolved, at least on the loop in Pacific City.

REALITY ADJUSTMENT OF THE
JAIL BRANCH CLINIC STAFF

Failure to Achieve Original Ideals and Purposes

When Pittman and Gordon published *The Revolving Door* in 1958,[11] they concluded with a series of recommendations for a "new approach" to the problem of the police-case inebriate. The basic concept was one of treatment and rehabilitative effort rather than punishment and custodial care, and encompassed medical, physical, psychological, and social therapy.

In 1959 a branch of the Pacific City Out-Patient Therapy Clinic was established in the County Jail as a demonstration project.[12] Staffing was financed by a grant from the State Department of Public Health Division of Alcoholic Rehabilitation. State funds allocated for work with the mentally ill were later redirected to support this effort after the original grant period expired.[13]

This development was described rather optimistically in a state-sponsored house organ devoted to mental health efforts:

Alcoholics arrested in Pacific City this month begin being "committed to treatment" at County Jail rather than sentenced, in a revolutionary plan to stop the "revolving door" sentencing of drunks long criticized by sociologists. . . .

Until now (quoting a judge who was instrumental in getting the program started) a state hospital was the only place we could send alcoholics. This does not necessarily work out. An alcoholic can be taken care of better and is more apt to be rehabilitated if he has available to him a county program in the area in which he lives.[14]

Treatment approach at the Jail Branch Clinic emphasized group therapy, led by psychologists and social workers. A psychiatrist was included among the professionals to aid in prescribing drugs for men undergoing withdrawal and to coordinate staff efforts.

Another important part of the clinic's official service included a psychological evaluation of each alcoholic so that the best approach to his individual problems could be instituted:

Two hundred and fifty "drunk-related" admissions are made to the [County] Jail each month. Each person is interviewed and most are given psychological tests. This evaluation leads to some estimate as to recommended treatment, rehabilitation, or other courses of action.[15]

As is apparent, the program boasts of many positive features: It seeks to catch the chronic alcoholic at a most vulnerable state—during and immediately after withdrawal. It was believed there would be no problem of losing patients; the clinic would literally have a captive audience for both evaluation and therapy. Furthermore, it might be assumed the alcoholic men would appreciate a program offering aid for their drinking problem, while simultaneously differentiating them from the remainder of the inmate population.

Despite this optimistic beginning, the clinic staff experienced repeated failure. The men who were given extensive counseling and group therapy continued to return again and again to County Jail on drunkenness charges.

Identification of Barriers to Success

In analyzing the cause for recidivism among their patients, the staff of the Jail Branch Clinic blamed both the chronic drunks' lack of amenability to group therapy, and the jail system in which a therapist must operate.

When chronicling their tribulations with the chronic drunkenness offender, the professional staff said they had to contend with apathy, hostility, cynicism, insincerity, manipulation, and an unrealistic or downright disinterested attitude toward the causes of drinking behavior. Such characteristics are, staff members agreed, scarcely those that make for good group therapy participants.[16]

> They [the alcoholics] are seldom sincere about wanting to stop drinking. Most of the time, they join therapy groups just to get out of their cells. [A18]

> Some of them won't admit they have a drinking problem. They say they are here on a bum rap. Now I know that is probably true, that they might not have been drunk when they were picked up, but they *do* have a drinking problem, nevertheless. They get very angry if you remind them of that. [A19]

> They are both apathetic and hostile. Of course, part of that is due to the fact that they are orally dependent characters and they just want attention, but not attention which would help them understand themselves. They are too immature for that. [A15]

> When they know *why* they want tranquilizers or other pills, I seldom prescribe them because I know they [the alcoholics] are just manipulating me. [A15]

The intense preoccupation of the alcoholic with immediate mundane problems of living—the "now" orientation—is also taken by the rehabilitation staff as a sign of disinterest in treatment. Thus, requests for help with lost suitcases of clothing, repossession of a car jeopardized by their arrest, general living conditions in the jail, or problems of withdrawal, instead of concern about the long-term problems caused by drinking, spell insincerity to the staff. Social workers as well as psychologists have adopted this stance.[17]

> Seven out of ten alcoholics are only interested in some favor. They want you to call a hotel to keep their clothes, or call up Welfare to tell their worker why they won't be in. They are not interested in treatment. At any one time I am helping only about two or three who really want help in stopping their drinking. [A18]

> They want us to do something about this jail. I tell them, "That isn't your main problem. Your main problem is why you are here." Then they say that is the fault of the police and the judge. What can you do with attitudes like that? [A17]

> They are great at asking for pills, but that is not going to help them with their real problems. On top of that, the easier they come out of a bad one [withdrawal and attendant problems], the more likely they are to go right back to drinking without any worry about the next one or any attempt to discover why they drink. [A15] [18]

As if the perceived patient attitude toward their drinking problem were not discouraging enough, Branch Clinic staff feel they also are forced to cope with an arrest and sentencing system that supplies too many patients at one time for the size of the staff and releases them again too rapidly. Both of these factors militate against individual attention to patient-inmates and the development of successful therapy groups.

For instance, as described in the Public Health bulletin, one of the major tasks of the original rehabilitation demonstration project at the jail was the diagnosis or evaluation of each alcoholic. However, the small part-time staff,[19] faced with an average of 50 or 60 men coming and going daily, was forced, with but few exceptions, to abandon this service.

Currently, those diagnoses that are made are not based on clinical tests. In the case of drunkenness offenders the diagnoses are made under the press of time and are based on the police charge. This system reinforces the built-in bias against the Skid Row man first created at the time of arrest. Under it, the diagnostic mandate is surrendered to the police in somewhat the same manner and for the same reason that it is surrendered earlier by the judge. According to one psychiatric social worker:

> The psychiatric diagnoses of inmates here that appear on the state form are taken from police records. If men are picked up for public drunkenness then they are diagnosed as "alcoholism addictions." If they show mental deterioration, cloudiness of thinking, judgements, and memory impairment, then they are diagnosed "chronic brain syndrome associated with alcoholism." [A19]

Additionally, given the size of the average therapy groups, the small branch staff who are dividing their efforts between three jail buildings could not possibly handle more than a fraction of the total alcoholic population at any one time. In actuality, eight therapy groups, with an average of six to ten men in each, were meeting once a week. This means that out of a population of 250 or more alcoholics, the optimum number possible in rehabilitative therapy groups would be 48 to 80 men, or only one-fifth to one-third of all the alcoholics in jail at any one time.

Whether or not this represents the full capacity of the staff is another question. Of all the stations observed on the loop, the Jail Branch Clinic evidenced the least amount of activity or actual contacts between the therapist social worker and the alcoholic inmate. During observations at City Screening Facility, a steady stream of men, most of them older and obviously impoverished alcoholics, came in for help. Interviews with administrative personnel at the Welfare Home for Homeless Men and the State Mental Hospital were constantly interrupted by patients. On the other hand, entire mornings or portions of days went by at the Jail Branch Clinic without anything apparently happening with the exception of clerical activity.

An even more serious obstacle than the alleged shortage of personnel to lead therapy groups with alcoholics at the jail, is that a majority of the men arrested as drunk receive a sentence of 30 days or less. With therapy meetings scheduled weekly, this allows the leader barely enough time to work a man into a group before he is gone.

As staff members put the situation:

> Most therapy groups do not have alcoholics in them. First of all, alcoholics don't get long enough sentences to qualify. If you meet once a week, you will only see a man who has a 30 day sentence three or four times at the most. You can't do anything in that length of time. I do all my recruiting from people who are here six months or more. [16]

> Group therapy depends on prolonged contact of the same people. And then it should go on out of jail. We are thinking of starting a group for alcoholics. [A56]

Staff Strategies to Circumvent Failure

How are the jailed alcoholics kept out of a program that was ostensibly started especially for their benefit? Like the studies of reality shock previously cited, the attempts to circumvent failure usually contain an effort to do well that which *can* be done well [20] and to drop what appears to be impossible.[21] Screening is the tool used, and it is described by the staff as deciding who would probably "benefit" from group therapy and who would not.

Major screening criteria developed by Jail Branch Clinic staff as to amenability of inmates to rehabilitative therapy literally block most Skid Row alcoholics from a place in a group on one or more counts:

1. Four to nine months sentence so that there will be time for the group to develop feelings of intimacy and relatedness

2. Being youthful enough to be able to change (under 35 years of age)

3. The presence of a "sincere desire to be rehabilitated." [22]

Staff explain some of these screening criteria as follows:

> Very few older men are in my group because they are selected out. Basically, I try to get people between 25 and 35. Sometimes I go up to 40. At 25 they are in a position to discern a pattern of failure, but are still young enough to change the pattern. [A19]

> Therapy groups are filled in the following ways. A patient's form is sent to all men who are going to be here nine months or longer. (This is usually about 60 men.) From this we get on the average of 24 replies. Then we screen out and keep those who are the most motivated. In this way, you get a group of eight or ten. [A15]

The elusive quality of "sincerity" or "motivation" is perceived by what is termed a "psychiatric examination." This is an informal discussion with the prisoner-patient concerning his motives for desiring therapy. It averages 15 to 30 minutes in length, according to clinic staff, and naturally is not available to many inmates.

> It [the screening procedure] is a psychiatric evaluation, an assessment of a person's total functioning as a person. It is done on the basis of my personal knowledge of people, what they tell me, their affect, and so on. No personality tests are used. As to length of time spent in evaluating any one person—if I have half an hour, I can get some idea. We limit these groups to those we feel are most *motivated*. Motivation is very important. [A17]

As previously mentioned, attitudes of the individual thought to indicate his sincerity are primarily focused on an expressed concern with his drinking habits and what they are doing to his life, and what other problems may be causing his excesses. Furthermore, a man must be willing to discuss these things freely. As some of the therapists [23] put it: "I look for . . .

Openness . . .
I look for emotional investment in wanting to stop drinking. In flat affect, I assume insincerity. I might feel they aren't quite ready to get in and tackle this. Therapy means talking directly about themselves—sharing themselves in an honest and open way with me. Do they know why they need alcohol? Do they consider it a real problem?

An awareness of his problem . . .
Sometimes a man will come to me and say: "Mr. Kennedy, I've had it. Can you help me?" Then I know he's sincere.

I think a man is probably insincere when he is seeking to tell me about his life, but is not disturbed about its pattern.

An attitude of self-blame . . .
If they talk about present circumstances ("And this is the reason I drink," they say), I try to find out how much they project their predicament on others and how much they blame themselves. If a man blames others, then he isn't ready for therapy. He must blame himself.

Also excluded from therapy on other grounds are male alcoholics who receive 60-, 90-, or 120-day sentences for drinking (thus being eligible for groups so far as long-term availability is concerned); however, they constitute the heavy-loser group—older chronic drunks who have appeared before the judge many times.

The outcome is as might be expected. The screening criteria have drastically curtailed the number of Skid Row alcoholics eligible for, or participating in, the rehabilitation program. When the records were checked during the six-month period of the jail portion of this study, out of a possible 200 to 250 alcoholic patient-prisoners available for therapy at any one time, there were only two or three to be found in a group.[24]

During one month (January 1967), for instance, a total of 31 men in jail on public drunkenness charges were seen by the Jail Branch Clinic for any reason. Table 12 indicates the treatment these men received while in jail that month. Forms that must be filled out for the state agency that controls funding provided the data.

TABLE 12. *Chronic Drunkenness Offenders Seen by Jail Branch Clinic Staff* *

NUMBER OF FACE-TO-FACE INTERVIEWS
(N = 31)

One	17
Two	10
Three	2
Four	2

TYPE OF SERVICE PROVIDED
TO OR IN BEHALF OF PUBLIC DRUNKENNESS INMATE

	Number of Encounters				
	One	Two	Three	Four	None
Admission services (orientation meetings) (N = 31)	18	4	—	—	9
Evaluation, diagnosis, or testing (N = 31)	—	—	1	—	30
Individual interview therapy (N = 31)	5	1	1	—	24
Drug therapy (N = 31)	—	—	—	—	31

PSYCHIATRIC CONDITION † AT DISCHARGE
(N = 31)

Not treated	20
Treated and unimproved †	4
Treated and improved †	4
No answer	3

REFERRAL SUGGESTIONS
(These are actually "paths out")
(N = 31)

No referral, patient withdrew from program, etc.	14
Referral to other facilities (on loop)	17

* Source: State Mental Health Fund Forms, January 1967. (These were the most recent forms available to me. Previous ones had been filed with the state. More recent ones were not filed or in evidence anywhere.) The categories used are provided by the form.
† No criteria for improvement provided.

Another indication of the de-emphasis of service to the alcoholic patient relative to other types of patients at the Jail Branch Clinic is obtained by calculating the proportion of contacts with alcoholics in comparison to other patients at the Jail and then to compare this proportion with that found in other mental health institutions offering aid to alcoholics in the city.

TABLE 13.* Patient Contacts † at Three Mental Health Institutions Serving Alcoholics in 1966

(SHOWING PERCENT ALCOHOLICS OF TOTAL CONTACTS)

| | Voluntary | | | | | Involuntary | | |
| | Outpatient Therapy Clinic | | | City Screening Facility | | County Jail, Clinic Branch | | |
MONTH	ALL PATIENTS	ALCO- HOLICS	PER- CENT ALC.	ALL PATIENTS	ALCO- HOLICS	PER- CENT ALC.	ALL PATIENTS	ALCO- HOLICS	PER- CENT ALC.
July	537	339	63	149	105	70	97	43	44
August	215	136	63	190	133	70	179	79	44
September	155	102	67	182	127	70	35	16	46
October	184	116	63	198	134	68	36	16	44
November	553	327	59	170	119	70	148	65	44
December	175	104	59	163	114	70	79	35	44

* Source: Official statistics of Out-patient Therapy Clinic (of which the City Screening Facility and County Jail Clinic are branches).
† "Patient contacts" is a gross category referring to any type of contact with patients and is not indicative of the number of patients in treatment. Each patient-contact counted as one unit. No effort was made by these facilities to keep track of multiple contacts with the same patient, so the total patients involved cannot be reported.

As is evident from Table 13, 60 to 70 percent of the patient contact load in the two voluntary out-patient facilities were alcoholics. Although at all times there was a captive population of around 250 to 300 alcoholic inmates available for treatment at the Jail, only 44 to 46 percent of the total caseload at the clinic were alcoholics. This figure, furthermore, includes the group orientation sessions during which 15 to 25 men are addressed at one time. Many of these are alcoholics. (Some reported that they go to the orientation sessions whenever they are jailed, primarily because it affords opportunity to get out of their cells.) Other mental health institutions do not offer group orientation sessions as part of their program so that their patient-contact count reflects persons seen individually or in group therapy.

Help for the alcoholics in County Jail has not been entirely overlooked, however—at least officially. Rather, success has been redefined. The new Chief Psychiatrist has suggested that the "unrehabilitatable" Skid Row alcoholic needs help in getting referrals for other stations of the rehab route more than he needs group therapy:

I would like to see something done about these men's [the Skid Row alcoholics] existence. Get them on welfare, and so on. To try to make the alcoholic inmates independent is crazy. Why not make them *appropriately dependent*. It's much cheaper to keep them on welfare than in here [in jail]. (Emphasis mine.)

You can't attempt character change in 30 days. But you can help them here and get them on welfare when they get out. They aren't ever going to be creative individuals, in the therapeutic sense of the word, and I think we should stop pretending that's what we can do here for them. [A16]

However, even this effort seems to touch very few of the Skid Row drunks. Although the Branch Clinic functions both as a referral and arranging agency for the Christian Missionaries and other such facilities on the loop, the number of actual arrangements are miniscule. Table 14 shows the number of referrals in a month.

TABLE 14. *Loop Referrals of Inebriates in January, 1967* *

Referral to	Number (N = 31)
Out-patient psychiatric clinic	1
Out-patient Therapy Center †	7
City Screening Facility †	1
Social Service Agency (usually for two weeks' welfare checks and a hotel room in Skid Row) †	5
Chronic Illness Center †	2
Psychiatric ward of City Hospital †	0
Employment service	1
No referral, patient withdrew on own or against medical advice	9
Further care not indicated	4
Other	1

* Source: State Agency forms
† Other stations on the loop

In March 1967 the Branch Clinic at the County Jail was granted power by the Pacific City Department of Social Welfare to arrange economic aid for those men who were willing to continue group therapy with the main Out-Patient Therapy Clinic after release from jail. The following memorandum (posted on the bulletin board of the Jail Branch Clinic) announced this new link between two rehab route stations:

MEMORANDUM

The Social Welfare Commission, as reported in the previous memorandum approved the giving of general assistance (goods, rent orders, incidental expenses) to persons just released from County Jail who otherwise would not qualify. (Ordinarily to qualify for general assistance a man must be a resident of this state for three years and of [Pacific City] for one year, have no resources, and be unemployable.) An ex-inmate may now receive such assistance for two weeks after release from jail, *provided he is accepting out-patient services at either our Center (for therapy) or the Prisoners' Association.* (Emphasis mine.)

What the Department of Social Welfare intake worker needs is a statement noting (1) date of release, and (2) the fact that the ex-inmate is seeking help at one of the two aforementioned agencies. . . . In order to fulfill our agreement with the Department of Social Welfare, the latter approach should only be used with <u>highly reliable patients</u>. (Underscoring in red.)

Again, however, the Skid Row alcoholic does not often qualify as a "highly reliable" patient. According to the social worker, a "reliable patient" is:

Someone in long-term treatment. They shouldn't seem to have a record of a lot of failures and a lot of arrests. Some of the alcoholics who come in every 30 days over and over wouldn't qualify. They seldom have the motivation to follow through and go to the Out-Patient Therapy Center in the city, or whatever plan you set up for them. I possibly give 25 such referrals to alcoholics each month, and they must go to the Out-Patient Therapy Center to show good faith, and only about one or two ever show up. [A18] (*Note:* the records do not indicate that anywhere near 25 referrals are made per month.)

Redefinition of the Situation

Under the circumstances, it would seem the Jail Branch Clinic staff might have screened themselves right out of existence. Such is not the case. They merely switched to what they term to be "more satisfying patients." This re-direction was facilitated two years previously when a new General Psychiatrist-Director [25] of the Out-Patient Therapy Centers expanded the clinics' purposes, both in the city and the jail branch. The expansion changed the focus of the clinics from dealing exclusively with alcoholics to dealing with drug users, marijuana users, cigarette smokers, sexual deviants, prostitutes, criminals, delinquents, gamblers, and potential suicides. This broadened scope allowed the professional staff members greater latitude in selecting patients who meet the criteria for possible success in group therapy. At the present time it is apparently the more glamorous and interesting inmates who fill those therapy sessions that are offered.[26]

REALITY ADJUSTMENT OF THE ALCOHOLICS TO THE JAIL BRANCH CLINIC

Inmate-patient Ideals and Failure

Reactions of inmates to the Jail Branch Clinic vary with attitudes toward the fairness of the arrest and jail sentence itself, and whether or not treatment for drinking was actually expected. This latter, in turn, is affected by judges' promises at sentencing and previous jail experience.

Although they do admit to a drinking problem, many Skid Row alcoholics consider a great proportion of their arrests to be unjustified, that a few beers or even being drunk does not constitute recidivism. The men, therefore, differ from the Jail Branch Clinic Staff in their perception of failure. As far as the Skid Row men are concerned, most of the failure lies with the system that incarcerates them on reputational grounds under the pretense that there will be therapy for them at the Jail.

The first-timer is likely to accept at face value the "sentence to treatment" he receives from the judge; therefore if he receives none, he feels robbed.

> After I was arrested for drinking, the judge told me that I was going to get treatment for my drinking problem in jail, and that they had those psychiatrists there to help me. Why I was pleased and so was my wife. I really thought they could help me stop this thing. But it didn't do a bit of good. Their treatment was just sitting talking about my problems with other drunks. No help at all really. [26]

The sense of outrage is enhanced considerably if the alcoholic is sent to jail via the City Hospital-Superior Court route (see chapter 5), for quite often his appearance before the judge is voluntary and his request (and expectation) is for commitment to State Mental Hospital.

> My wife convinced me I should be committed to State Mental Hospital and I went before Judge Lilly of my own accord, mind you, and do you know that bastard committed me to jail instead! I didn't speak to my wife for a month after that—I thought she had planned it that way. In the jail you are treated just like all the other prisoners. It's not like State Mental Hospital at all. [39] [27]

Incidentally, both Skid Row alcoholics and City Hospital personnel involved in screening alcoholics for Superior Court sessions suspect that the judicial choice between commitment to State Mental Hospital and a sentence to County Jail often rests solely on the attitude and past record of the supplicant. Said one such official:

If the man seems to be using State Mental Hospital as sort of a resort and going there over and over, the judge may commit him to jail for therapy. Also if he seems *insistent* that he wants to go to State Mental Hospital and says it is his right and smarts off to the judge that way, he'll end up in the County Jail for his therapy. [A36] [A38]

An alternative explanation was proposed by a city mental health official:

State Mental Hospital was getting so many alcoholic commitments that it looked bad on the annual report because it was higher than any state in the country. It made the state look as though it had a very bad alcoholism problem. By siphoning off some of these men to County Jail, alcoholic admissions to the hospital could be brought back in line with other like institutions. [A49]

Regardless of whether he arrived at the jail via the arrest route or Superior Court commitment, the Skid Row alcoholic is quick to condemn the jailing system.

You see a jail is a jail. You can't get around that. There ain't no amount of treatment going to take away the bitterness of being cooped up in a cell. Sometimes when I get out of here I go take a drink because that is all that will make the bitterness go away. [15]

Inmate Identification of Barriers to Success

Held primarily responsible for the failure of the jail to aid alcoholics is the welfare worker-therapist. The first timer, expecting treatment, blames the therapists for their lack of attention to him.

I filled out one of those slips asking for an interview for therapy and I never got one. I tried a couple of times. They have their favorites here, I think. [12]

The seasoned, revolving-door type inmate, inclined to be cynical about his arrest and jailing by now, seldom complains about the lack of therapy; rather, he accuses the Jail Branch Clinic staff of callously ignoring his most pressing here-and-now needs. When he discusses the shortcomings of the Jail Branch Clinic, the chronic drunkenness offender talks about the staff's apparent heartlessness concerning withdrawal problems, mundane details of living, or problems connected with the jail and his sentence, all of which he feels are tied to his subsequent drinking behavior.

They don't care about your physical problems . . .
When I came in I had some pills with me for withdrawal that City Hospital gave me, and the guards took them away and I didn't get anything

until the doctor came around. He took a couple of days to get to me, too, and I went through hell waiting, I'll tell you. They can't care much about rehabilitating you if they treat you like that. [9]

They took my Dilantin away from me. I needed that for my epilepsy. Then I had a seizure and there was no doctor to even care for me. One of the trusties put a wallet in my mouth so I wouldn't bite my tongue off. I tried to tell those social worker about needing my medicine, but they wouldn't listen. [17]

They don't care about your personal problems . . .

They won't even make a phone call for you. I asked them to call my social worker [on the outside] and tell her where I was and they suggested that I should write a letter. [15]

I came in without money and I can't get even stationery and an envelope and stamps to write my wife. Recently I heard my father died and I wanted my wife to write and inquire about it. I asked Mr. Benton [a social worker] for stationery and stamps but he said I had to buy my own. He said stamped envelopes are available on the tier. But they're not. They have been out a long time. [11]

They are very slow to do anything for you . . .

I put in one of those chits [requesting aid] just to have someone to talk to. That was three weeks ago and I haven't heard from them. [13] (A repeated comment.)

I went to them for help with modification [of sentence] and they fooled around and didn't do anything until it was about time for me to leave anyway; then they called me in and suggested I just finish out my term. [12]

Perhaps the most annoying to alcoholics, and the most serious accusation of all against the therapist welfare worker is the worker's refusal to admit awareness of general living conditions in the jail or in other stations on the loop. As one respondent put it during an interview (shouting and pounding on the table):

Why don't they [the social workers] see what's *really* going on here. How could they be so blind? Why do they say they are trying to help you and then ignore what is happening to you? How can they be so mean? [10] [29]

In the orientation session they try to tell us that the Christian Missionaries have a *treatment program*. Are they blind? Don't they know? Did you hear that girl say that she has heard some complaints that the Christian Missionaries work you to death and pay you a *pittance*? Then she went on to say that you should look at it as a treatment program which pays you while being treated. Either she doesn't know, or she thinks we don't know. [18]

Patient inmates describe therapy and the therapists as follows:

In general, group therapy is . . .
Fried ice cream and wolf tickets. (Wolf tickets are a Southern Negro term referring to selling tickets to a wolf hunt that is never held.) Both terms refer to something that is useless. [14]

Just something that is a substitute for television. [10]

Specifically, group therapy lacks meaning . . .
Group therapy may help you with your personal problems, but it does not help you stay away from alcohol. [43]

Therapy groups are all right, and I enjoy talking about my problems, but when you hit the street . . . all of a sudden it's stark real. You have to do what you know how to do if you don't get help. [10]

The therapists are both square and sadistic . . .
How can a person sit down and say to me, "Why don't you try this and that?" He's never experienced any of this! The only way for him to understand what heavy drinking is like is to try it. We should all sit around here and get stoned and *then* talk about it. [15]

They [the therapists] try to *reduce* you, to make you give up all your codes and your principles about what you should talk about and what you shouldn't—things that you've done and you know others have done. They try to tell you it will make a better person of you, but it doesn't. Not on your life. [10] [28]

Thus with every move he makes, the therapist at the jail appears to the chronic drunkenness offender to be inept, cruel, or at the very least not helpful. A willing puppet of the jail establishment in the Row men's eyes, the therapist lends his professional presence to an activity called "group therapy" so as to convince the humane-minded among the public that rehabilitative efforts are being made in the jail, when actually they are not.[29]

So I said to the psychiatrist, "What do you mean coming out here and trying to make men *adjust* to something like this? How can you live with yourself?" He didn't know what to say to that! [18] [30]

Therapy is something people like to think is offered in jails so that they can look at themselves in the mirror in the morning when they shave and not cut their throats. [12]

Inmate-patient Strategies

To the chronic Skid Row jail repeater, acceptance of therapy would be tacit admittance that he is being properly treated and that jail confinement is helpful for his drinking problem.

Failure, in this context, would be to join a group and cooperate with the Jail Branch Clinic. The Skid Row alcoholic, powerless as he is, refuses to play this game, to be a "sell-out" in his own eyes and the eyes of other seasoned Skid Row drunks. Instead, he uses a tactic often employed by persons who see themselves as unjustly treated by someone whose power is far greater than theirs—he turns "sour" [31] and uncooperative.

> Those therapists can take their groups and shove them for all I care. I don't talk to them anymore than I have to, and when I do, I don't tell them anything. [12]

His attitudes no doubt are apprehended as the cynicism, hostility, or apathy that the staff experience in connection with the chronic drunkenness offenders.

Inmate-patient Definition of the Situation

The Skid Row alcoholic is convinced of staff hypocrisy or an establishment conspiracy against him. He does his time and leaves the jail filled with a sense of the injustice of sending a man there for mere over-imbibing in public and, so far as he is concerned, the dishonesty in promising him "therapy" when none worthwhile is available.

> You see, they shouldn't have alcoholics there [in County Jail]. Alcoholics need medical help and sometimes the doctor doesn't show up for a couple of weeks at a time. As for therapy—that's a laugh. There isn't any. They call sitting and talking therapy. It takes more than that to overcome this drinking habit. No one I know is in any of those groups.
>
> Judges know there isn't any therapy here—but they know it sounds better if they say they are sending us to get some. [18]

REALITY ADJUSTMENT OF THE STAFF AT THE STATE MENTAL HOSPITAL

Failure to Achieve Original Staff Ideals and Purposes

The State Mental Hospital also accepts alcoholics as patients and its record of recidivism (on the basis of visible repeaters) is no better than that of the Jail Branch Clinic. However, the approach of hospital staff to this failure and the decisions made in coping with it have been quite different from those of the Jail Clinic staff, with concomitant differences in interaction between alcoholics and agents of social control at this station and in reception of group therapy by Skid Row men.

Historically, three state mental hospitals, (Northern, Central, and Bay) served those alcoholics of Pacific City who could not afford intermittent sojourns in private sanitariums. Judging from the treatment most Skid Row alcoholics reported having received from these institutions in years prior to this study, their staffs had long ago undergone a reality shock concerning the amenability of the chronic drunk to the psychiatric services of the hospital.

Primary complaint of the professional hospital staff concerning the alcoholic men centers about the resistance these patients exhibit to being defined as mentally-ill persons. The remarks recorded below were overheard by the observer, not gathered in interviews. They come from Northern State Mental Hospital staff members who worked with alcoholics in the past, and they epitomize mental hospital staff attitudes in general.

> It's simple. I hate alcoholics. I'd rather work with the *real* mental patients. [A nurse]

> They are not mentally-ill, just weak-willed. Once they are dried out, they are in complete touch with reality. They don't belong in a mental hospital. [An orderly]

> Alcoholics think they are better than anybody. They think they are better than the mentally-ill; they think they are better than the drug addicts; some of them even think they are better than some of the staff! Teach them a little practical nursing (one form of "industrial therapy"), and pretty soon they are telling you how to run things. [An orderly]

An apparent lack of gratitude on the part of the chronic drunks for the therapeutic efforts expended on them, compounded by a willingness to manipulate or take advantage of their benefactors, is also a sore point with mental hospital staff members.[32]

> They can't be trusted. They go out on pass and get drunk; they smuggle liquor in. [A24]

> They're not grateful for all that is done for them. A staff member can work and work with an alcoholic and he will repay him by picking up one day and taking off without a word. [A25]

> Alcoholics are manipulative. They pretend to go along with you and with the program when they really don't. They are the world's best actors. They are out for what they can get, and so are insincere. [A22]

> These guys pretend to go along with psychotherapy, and for another end —to get out of work, to borrow money, to get a suit of clothes, to not be held responsible for anything. (*Interviewer: How can you tell if they are sincere?*) If their story brings tears to *your* eyes, it's probably a sociopathic one. If he cries, maybe there is something there to work with. [A26] [33]

With such a list of complaints, it would not be surprising if the mental hospitals also attempted to screen out all but the most "hopeful" men among those alcoholics who apply for admittance. Indeed, this is often the case. Hayman, in his study, *Alcoholism: Mechanism and Management*,[34] reports that in a nationwide survey of state hospitals 25 percent of such institutions were reluctant to admit alcoholics. Hayman goes on to say:

> The program for alcoholics has not been too successful in the state hospital. Patients do not want to go there, state hospitals do not want to receive them, and psychopathic courts do not want to send them there. Thirty-eight percent of the alcoholic patients of psychiatrists are refused admission to state hospitals. They are a burden to the psychiatrists and other personnel, they are often demanding and their return time after time is extremely frustrating to the personnel.

Such rejection of alcoholics, however, is not the case in Northern State Mental Hospital. In 1965 the hospital had an opportunity to enter into an agreement with Central State Mental Hospital as to allocation of patients for a wide area, including Pacific City. The result was that Northern State Mental Hospital became the sole resource for alcoholic patients for Pacific City, while Central State Mental Hospital agreed to take all other mental patients from that city.

Financially, the decision was a tremendous windfall for Northern State Hospital. As one of the psychologists explained it:

> We realized that alcoholics are like money in the bank. You see, we get our funds from the state on a per admission basis. The alcoholics come in more often, stay a shorter time, and give us more admissions to report. On the other hand, mental patients have far less turnover. Central State Hospital got the worst of the deal. We can use the extra money for research, for speakers, for special therapists, and so on. [A22]

Other staff members concurred that the high admission rate of the alcoholics was of benefit to Northern State Mental Hospital's budget which is based on a combination of patient admissions and average in-hospital patients. However, they complained that the money did not benefit the alcoholics directly because it went to the General Fund of the state and could be dispersed only for staffing. The director of the experimental program said:

> . . . the alcoholism program did not reap the benefits of extra budget or staffing drawn by alcoholism admissions; it was used to start an adolescent program, enrich a geriatric service, or provide staff for continuous treatment wards. [A23]

An added windfall results from the fact that the state now considers alcoholism as a disability and pays the hospital a monthly sum for the care of men thus disabled.

This decision to accept all alcoholics made screening the alcoholic out of Northern State Mental Hospital impossible. It further meant that, like it or not, the staff would be confronted daily with their most frustrating patients. The situation seemed to be one where a new approach to treatment would have to be found that would change the attitudinal picture. If this were not done, the administration would have to risk the emergence of cynicism (a) in staff members who would have to treat patients for whom they felt contempt, and (b) in the alcoholic patients who are cognizant of staff feelings toward them.

Staff Identification of Barriers to Success

Having accepted the alcoholics as bona fide mental hospital patients, the next decision of the State Mental Hospital staff was how to treat the 2500 who would be received (mostly on a voluntary commitment basis [35]) each year at a monthly rate of 150 to 200. The decision of the staff at State Mental Hospital was the opposite of that at the Jail Branch Clinic. They decided it was the treatment, and not the patient, the staff, or the institution, that was to blame for the high rate of recidivism of patients with drinking problems. In other words, the absence of a certain cure for alcoholism was openly acknowledged and made an integral part of the program.

Because the hospital is research-oriented, the decision was to institute an *experimental program* that would offer many types of treatment for alcoholism in the hope that some effectiveness modalities might be discovered in this way. The director of the experimental program for alcoholics described the decision:

Multiple symptomotology, obscure etiology, and the obvious limited efficiency of specific treatment procedures argues strongly for a multidimensional approach which employs a wide variety of personnel whose efforts are integrated in a team arrangement. [A23]

Staff Strategies to Circumvent Failure

Briefly, the multidimensional approach is as follows: beginning with the generally-accepted notion that there are many types of alcoholics,[36] as well as many stages of alcoholism,[37] administrators of the program are attempting to develop a typology of alcoholics through the use of psychological tests such as the Minnesota Multiphasic Personality Test (MMPI). At the same time, many different approaches to rehabilitative therapy are made available to the chronic drunkenness patient. After the typologies of alcoholics are developed (through the aid of IBM electronic data processing machines and factor analysis), it is planned that an attempt will be made to correlate *types of alcoholics* with the types of therapy to which they respond best in terms of extended periods of sobriety after release.

The new program for alcoholics is designed with frank awareness of the various criticisms leveled at mental hospitals in general, especially in their treatment of alcoholic patients:

1. That alcoholics are treated as step-children in most hospitals where they are accepted at all [38]

2. That many mental hospitals are too highly stratified, resulting in a lack of communication between the staff members, who have the most contacts with patients, and the doctors, who control therapeutic efforts [39]

3. That the day-to-day living situation in the hospital can affect rehabilitation progress [40] and

4. That the institutionalized patient is often separated so drastically from the community that he finds adjustment to it upon release difficult if not impossible. [41]

The hospital staff has much more control over system exigencies than did Jail Branch Clinic therapists, so that the following innovations could be inaugurated at State Mental Hospital specifically for the alcoholics' program:

1. Alcoholics were to be treated as full-fledged patients, and a major force in their own treatment. This resulted in making the alcoholic eligible for group therapy where formerly he was ignored. Furthermore, an effort was made to weed out unsympathetic staff and to recruit personnel who had positive feelings toward an experimental program with the chronic drunk.

2. A general relaxation of class (and even caste, i.e., staff-patient) lines among staff was instituted; technicians were taught group therapy techniques; first names were instituted in wards, etc. Natural leaders among the patients were to be developed who could be on a peer status with regular staff members. As one highly-placed professional staff member put it:

   We want a closeness between staff and staff, and staff and patients. We want *everyone*, technicians, ward doctors, people in research, to take one patient individually. We hope to level out status distinctions

—of the doctor who "knows" and the technician who "does." *Everybody* does the same thing.

The implication is that therapy can be done by everyone. The proposal is to give technicians short training as counselors or in handling a therapy situation. [A27]

3. An attempt was made to have each unit democratically self-sufficient, with the patients making some of their own rules, issuing passes, and setting punishments for rule infractions.

4. Integration of the patient with the community was attempted through various training programs, which ranged from training men to work as community rehabilitators of non-committed alcoholics, to doing work for nearby farmers at less than union scale, to donating labor to the indigent of the community. Additionally, frequent passes were issued so that the patient could visit his family (in the fairly rare cases where he had one). An information program on half-way houses available in various communities was maintained.

5. Patients were urged to stay 90 days to get the most benefits from the program and a great majority of them do this. (The hospital benefits financially as well from this longer treatment period. It receives state disability payments in the sum of $12.00 per day for 20 days, for men staying over 30 days. This money comes from employer-employee contributions to the State Disability Fund. It is $3.00 per day more than the hospital spends on patients in the alcoholism program—the $9.00 a day spent is slightly over half the state average. However, inasmuch as most alcoholics stay more than 20 days, the hospital is hardly making a profit on the transaction.)

Although the connection between eclecticism in therapy, democracy in the wards, and the compulsion to drink has never been fully established,[42] the experimental program described above is an important part of the staff belief system, seemingly so logical that its logic is never questioned. When asked to describe how the program for alcoholics will help these men, staff members involved in it speak in generalities, relying on the flexibility and general looseness of the program to prove why it should be constructed that way: [43]

At present, the program is to find out what the program is. Everyone goes their own way. They are given free rein. But it all comes out in the end. [A27]

Patients are a main force in their own treatment. In a practical situation, treatment programs are not assigned rigidly, just suggested. If no interest is shown in a group—it is dropped. Patients are made to feel that they determine their own program—that they have a choice. [A23]

They [the patients] are the teachers—we are the students. It means we value their experiences. We use what will work. They are most willing to join a cause. This gives them a chance for a meaningful role too. [A24]

The main point here is, let's not get carried away with our own idea as to what to do. *Let's ask the patient.* What we have here is unique—a patient organization that constantly reflects what is going on. Involvement is the key. We call it the Northern Mental Hospital atmosphere. [A22] [44]

With this heavy accent on an experimental approach, formal therapy at State Mental Hospital could take many forms; however, the two dominant ones at the time of the study were the old standbys, industrial (work) therapy and group therapy.[45]

Medication is available to help a patient get through the DT's, seizures, and other withdrawal symptoms. This, plus adequate diet and sleep, are considered to be an important but intermediate means to the greater goal of helping the patient adjust to a regular work schedule again and to perceive and understand his "true" problems.

After undergoing detoxification, alcoholics at State Mental Hospital are assigned to what is known as an I.T. (industrial therapy) task. The jobs in this category are the standard ones assigned to mental patients: janitorial, such as mopping and waxing floors; grounds maintenance; laundry room; and kitchen duty. In some cases, I.T. assignment includes practical nursing of mentally-ill or senile patients. Once in a while a man may have an opportunity to revive an old trade, such as painting, electric work, or playing musical instrument at the Thursday night dances. The men receive no pay for this work.

Industrial therapy takes little or no professional staff supervision. Whether or not it is therapeutic is seldom questioned or even discussed by staff. The Patient's Handbook for the Hospital has this statement about work assignments, which is an exemplar of all statements uttered on the subject by staff:

You will be assigned to a job soon after arrival that will occupy several hours of your time each day. Not only does your work help the hospital, but you can benefit from learning on the job and find interest and satisfaction in being a working member of a therapeutic community of 2,400 people.

Industrial therapy is sometimes combined with occupational therapy by giving the alcoholic an opportunity to work for townspeople (as mentioned, at reduced wages) or by projects that attempt to develop fairly verbal alcoholics into salaried "community resources" to help with the alcoholism problem in surrounding communities.

The ultimate importance of the psychological, while not ignoring the physical, is also emphasized in the Patient's Handbook.

KALAMAZOO VALLEY
COMMUNITY COLLEGE
LIBRARY

A Sound Mind in a Sound Body

Restoration of your physical health is of primary importance. A physician will see you soon after arrival for a complete medical checkup, and the Unit Coordinator will explain the program to you and get better acquainted with you. Later you will have a more intensive interview with the Psychiatric Consultant or Unit Coordinator with a view to *reaching a deeper understanding of your problem.* (Emphasis mine.)

Greatest hope for making inroads into the problems of alcoholics is pinned on group therapy, which can and does run the gamut from ordinary one- or two-hour sessions to 24-hour so-called gut-level therapy meetings.[46]

Redefinition of the Situation

In any research program, success is defined in terms of information gained. From this point of view, the failure of a hypothesis is almost as useful in providing information as if it had succeeded. The experimental ethic applied to the State Mental Hospital program means that success is measured in terms of research effort, not low rates of recidivism.

In the meantime, until a cure for alcoholism is found, work with the alcoholic is redefined as ameliorative. Currently, the chronic drunk's general prognosis is described by sympathetic hospital staff in somewhat the same way advanced cancer is described: hopeless until a cure is found. Staff members feel that they are doing something for the alcoholic, even if such efforts do not have any long-term effects.

Patients who drink after therapeutic efforts of staff are not seen as failures, either to themselves or their therapists. Rather, such backsliding is to be expected, and there is no agonizing reappraisal of the situation. Discussion of recidivism takes on a resigned tone:

> The alcoholic, like a cancer patient, may look well, but is only experiencing a remission. Thus, the chance of a recurrence is always present and is not the fault of the therapist, who should actually be congratulated (as one might congratulate the cobalt-ray therapist) for giving the patient as long a symptom-free period as he had. [A22]

> The fact that they drink again isn't necessarily failure. If they turn toward help sooner than the last time—then they are improved. They have learned they can terminate their illness at one point. Actually there is no time limit on when an alcoholic can be pronounced cured. Alcoholism and the reaction to alcohol is a progressive disease which goes on whether they drink or not. Even after 20 years of sobriety, they could tumble. [A26] [47]

> You can expect to see these guys over and over. The best way to look at it is to be glad that you can do something for them to lengthen their lives. [A38]

REALITY ADJUSTMENT OF THE PATIENTS
AT THE STATE MENTAL HOSPITAL

Failure to Achieve Original Goals

To the Skid Row alcoholic, the first trip to a mental hospital is a drastic step indeed, but those who do overcome their fear of going there (or are committed) develop great expectations as to the hospital's ability to "cure" them, especially if it is their first visit. Furthermore, they are hopeful that the hospital interval will convince significant others of their sincere desire to stop drinking.

The fear with which the uninitiated views a mental institution is well expressed by these Skid Row alcoholics who had not yet been in one:

> Well, I believe that most state mental hospitals, they take you there as a nut. If you're an alcoholic, you have to be nuts, they put the drunks in with the nuts. They are all in the same ward. So I ain't got no use to go there [to a mental hospital]. I ain't nuts yet. [12]

> Well, I figure they [the hospital staff] might put you in a cell or a straitjacket or something like that. I didn't want that. [58]

For the average alcoholic, the term "mental illness" is reserved for those persons who are completely out of contact with reality—something that happens to him only during withdrawal or when he is extremely "high." When he is through these crises, the alcoholic believes the mental hospital staff should acknowledge that he is more rational than the average patient there.

> Once I'm over the shakes, I know what's going on just as well as any doctor. I'm not an MI, you know. [25]

> I'm here on an MI commitment, but I'm not one. I'm an alcoholic and my family arranged the MI commitment to keep me here longer. The hospital lets me stay here in an alcoholic unit so I don't have to live with those guys [the "bona fide" mentally ill]. [24]

Coupled with this fear of the "nut house" is a sort of awe as to the type of treatment it might offer to qualify for its title as State Mental Hospital. Certainly, it is expected to have experts offering very special therapy—perhaps even a "sure cure."

> I supposed they [the hospital staff] had some special methods by which they could dry you out and show you how to keep dry. I was expecting to

come back out and never care about having a drink again. I thought I was going to be cured, just like if I had the measles or the mumps or something. That's what a hospital is for, isn't it? [59]

Well, it wasn't what I expected, although I don't know quite what I expected. They just dry you out and give you a rake or a broom and that's therapy. I thought that they would cure me of this thing [chronic drinking]. [57]

What the alcoholic finds is that while the State Mental Hospital is not so fearsome as he supposed, neither is it so efficient. Staff members readily admit to him that there is no cure for alcoholism and that their program is experimental.

The final disappointment is that the time spent in the mental institution does not impress others of the alcoholic's motivation to stop drinking and thus ease his road back to social acceptance. Quite the contrary, his stay leaves him with a permanent stigma that further reduces his already questionable job-getting ability. Occupations requiring bonding, security clearance, liability insurance, a license to operate a public vehicle are barred to him as a man who has been in a mental institution. That he had gone in more often than not voluntarily, and for a drinking problem rather than a "mental problem," makes no difference.

As the men explain it:

By golly, that State Hospital has come up a couple times in government jobs, at the shipyard, and up where they have that special electronics lab. Some people realize you're no more than an alcoholic, at that, but you're still put in one category, because you've been in a State Hospital. When you come out of there you've got that label on you, you know. [45]

Once you get a state mental hospital on your record, you can't be bonded. [58]

You have to lie. If you go for a job any place, and they ask you if you've ever been in a mental institution, you put down "No." [48]

I was all set up for the military ship transport at Fort Madison but, boom, that State Hospital pops up and I lost the job. [59]

I had been on a job as an accountant and doing well when one day they called me in and said that my work was satisfactory, but perhaps I would have more chance for advancement elsewhere. I was furious. "It's my mental hospital record, isn't it?" I said. They didn't answer and so I said, "You haven't the guts to admit it." [41]

On city, county, and state jobs, you're dead if you have a mental hospital record. In fact, I'd go so far to say in a way you're worse than an ex-con in one sense of the word. They have a government program for bonding ex-cons, but nothing for alcoholics. [59]

Patients' Perceptions of Barriers to Success

Despite their disappointment in the power of the mental hospital to cure them of alcoholism, Skid Row men are ambivalent about placing the blame on the hospital or its staff.

First of all, the Skid Row drunk enjoys the concerned, courteous treatment accorded him at the hospital. For those who had suffered rudeness or even cruelty in other institutions, the overtly friendly atmosphere that is part of the experimental milieu seems more in keeping with the drunks' idea of themselves and the way in which they ought to be treated when "sick" or sober. Rather than the bitterness they exhibit toward the Jail Branch Clinic, the men appear ready to cooperate with the staff of the State Mental Hospital even if they are not completely sold as to the usefulness of the program. The following statements are typical:

> Here at State Mental Hospital the treatment is real good. One of the psychoanalysts said, "Well, one thing we believe in doing here is treating you like a human being," which they do here. That's very true. [26]

> This is the only program where there is any kind of off-hand acceptance for the alcoholic. [30]

Attitudes are mixed toward a hospital program where its promoters do not claim it will cure at least some of the patients.

On the one hand, the fact that the staff admits there is no sure cure for alcoholism can be taken as an explanation as to why a man might start to drink almost immediately upon release from the institution and this is rather consoling:

> All this is an experiment here. The hospital staff admit themselves that they know very little about the problem of chronic drinking and they are trying different methods and doing the best they can. But they can't be certain that anything will help us. [29]

On the other hand, the bland admission that the program is experimental is also disappointing:

> Well now, if they don't know how to cure alcoholism, what do they send us up here for or encourage us to come up here and commit ourselves? What's in it for us? [19]

Coupled with ambivalent feelings toward the experimental nature of the hospital program is a combination of doubt and praise for group and industrial therapy. On the one hand, Skid Row men want to feel group therapy offers them some hope for aid with their drinking problem; on the other hand, they do not see how mere "talk" can do this and, further, they have empirical evidence (in the form of their own stubborn return to drink) that group therapy does not, in fact, work. There is, however, little of the hostility toward professionals at the hospital such as was exhibited towards therapists at the jail, even though most of the men have experienced both institutions. It is as if the men wish to cooperate at State Mental Hospital in exchange for courteous treatment. Men who would not accept group therapy from the Jail Branch Clinic, even if they were offered a chance to participate, are found sitting in the same type of groups at Northern State Mental Hospital with apparent equanimity. Thus, such diverse comments as the following are heard:

> Well, there must be something to all this group therapy or they [the staff] wouldn't waste so much time with it. [25]

> As far as this group therapy goes, I've seen too many guys stay in therapy for four-five months and then go get a drink. [43]

The more inexperienced the patient, the more likely he is to embrace group therapy as possible aid for his problem. Indeed, it is these new patients who provide the hospital therapist with the reinforcement he needs as a professional in the form of interest in and praise for therapy sessions. Such patients are also more likely to blame themselves for failure:

> I think I failed because I hadn't changed anything really. And this may be the reason that I'd fall on my face again and again, because I didn't change anything. [19]

Some men, whether newcomers or old hands, decide that insight is a matter of waiting things out.

> If it takes me six days, 60 days, or six months, I'm going to find out something before I leave here; because I've been around it enough and I know enough about it. I don't know . . . for some reason or other I've always been able to help somebody else, but I never can help myself. I want to know the reason for this drinking pattern that I've been on for the last 15 years. [29]

> The average guy has to come back to the hospital two or three times before he makes it. [21]

Some men feel that if they can only continue the group therapy program outside of the hospital, maybe it will keep them from going back to drinking.

Well, since you can't really talk to people on the outside like you do in therapy, I thought it would be good to continue in a group. There was a man here from the Out-Patient Therapy Center and he told us that we could keep going there. [28]

I'm going to stay in a group after I get out *because I'm afraid not to.* But I'm not sure that this isn't perpetuating something too, and I'm going to do it as a practical necessity, and I'm going to try to let it be a help to me; but it will be, in a sense, perpetuating this thing; it will still be reaffirming the fact that I'm an alcoholic, which I have to do really. I don't have too much alternative. I can't pretend that I can go out and pick up where I was 15 years ago. [26] (Emphasis mine.)

We've even talked about having our own therapy sessions. One of the counsellors at State Mental Hospital suggested that when we're out, three or four of us get together and talk things over. (*Interviewer: did you ever try it?*) Oh yeah, we do it all the time here [Welfare Home for Homeless Men] and down on Skid Row. We get together and shoot the breeze. [59]

Like the therapists, some alcoholics who are sympathetic to therapy in the hospital setting tend to assess the effectiveness of group therapy in terms of secondary or intermediate goals rather than the primary one of helping a man to stop drinking. For instance, the men will say that group therapy . . .

Gives insight on how you should have handled family situations:
When they talk about the family, and then when you look back on it, you realize that you were goofing it up in certain ways . . . which you could have made a little different, see; but you weren't trying to handle anything. [26]

Gives a warning as to what might happen to you if you persist in your present ways:
But here's the thing, you're sitting in these groups and you see a young person, or even an experienced drinker; he may be your age, but maybe his problems have only gotten acute in the past three years and yours have been going on for ten years. And you think, "Why, he's doing and saying and thinking the same way and doing the same things as I did." And you think, "Gee, if I can only tell this poor bastard what he's doing." [21]

Unfortunately, sometimes the insights come too late for ameliorative action:

Sometimes it's too late for you to correct the things you did. Of course, you could always correct them in the future if you got a second chance.

If you still have a family, you can stop doing some of these things but sometimes things have gone so far you can't do much about things that have already happened, important things, family and money. So, well, I don't mean that it's entirely hopeless, these groups are helpful to anybody. But sometimes it's too late. [20]

It was wonderful to get a chance to talk about your problems. Everybody had a different viewpoint on it. I think it was a good thing. But here's the idea: when you leave here, uh, what got me—you're going out in the world again, you don't have a job, you don't have this, you don't have a place to stay, and soon you're back on the booze again, see. [28]

The lack of applicability of group therapy to "real life" situations often strikes the participant:

. . . When you're not getting along with your wife and family and neighbors, you can't sit down and say, "Let's all have group therapy." Right? And actually, you can't do that with anyone on the outside. So that all of this that happens in here, while it's very helpful, it doesn't exactly work on the outside. If you were as frank with people as you are in group therapy they'd fight you. Right? [26]

Although group therapy apparently does give the men something to think about, many admit that the desire to drink eventually (or quickly) overcomes any resolve not to drink:

Group therapy gives you a guilty conscience in a way, you know. If you take a little drink, you say, "I know I'm doing wrong, but . . ." Then once you start drinking, like the man said, well then you don't give a damn anyway, you know. Well, you think about it, but you say, "To hell with it anyway," you know. That's the attitude, see. You say, "Well, I'm disgusted, I'm discouraged," you know. Any alcoholic knows that he's doing wrong by taking that drink; I mean he's got a little conscience about it; he knows he's doing wrong but he blots that out of his mind anyway and takes that drink. And bang, he's on his way; goodbye job and goodbye this and goodbye that. You wind up drunk, and maybe you wind up here or back in State Mental Hospital. [60]

I had group therapy at State Mental Hospital and do you know what I thought about during therapy—getting a drink. I had one five minutes after I was discharged, and after a couple of drinks, you know, you don't think about therapy at all. [59]

When I left, I didn't think about anything. I thought about getting a drink. I put my suitcases in the bus, got tags on 'em, got my ticket, and went across the street and had a couple a' double shots and bought a bottle for on the bus and another in Porterville, and here I am—I lasted a month, I think. (*Interviewer: Did you think about anything you talked about in group therapy?*) No, not after I got that first drink; everything went by the board. [29]

Thus the men are neither sure about the effectiveness of group therapy in stopping their drinking nor that insight into their problems will result in automatic behavior change:

Well, it's one thing to say I got drunk because my mother-in-law is a bitch, or because this went wrong, or something like that. It's another thing to be able to do something about it. [23]

On the subject of industrial therapy (the other frequently used treatment), the men admit on the one hand a job keeps them busy, that the work assignment was their first opportunity for many years to apply a learned trade; for this they were grateful. On the other hand, they were annoyed that work is called therapy since they do not see it as connected with their drinking problem. That the hospital does not acknowledge how important the labor of the alcoholics is in maintaining operations is also a sore point:

I was an electrician while I was there and believe me, it was a joy to be working at my trade again. [50]

Most of the alcoholics there [State Mental Hospital] are working. They call it industrial therapy. It's really advantageous for the hospital to have the alcoholics there because they do most of the work. Mostly it's janitorial work. For instance, I worked in the dishwashing room on the machine, and lots of them work as cooks and cooks' helpers. [58]

Alcoholics are needed to run this hospital. They tell of the time they took the alcoholics on a picnic and they nearly had to shut the place down while they were gone. [24]

They gave me a shovel, a rake, and a lawnmower. I guess that was the therapy. [44]

Some are downright bitter about their job assignment:

They threw me in the terminal ward and all I did was look after patients that were getting ready to die, cleaning up feces and urine and changing the beds and washing feces off the patients. It's just a detail and it's, put bluntly, it's a feces detail. [45]

Patient Strategies to Circumvent Failure

Almost all Skid Row alcoholics who participated in this study had experienced mental hospital confinement at least once; many had been in several mental hospitals throughout the state or had returned to the same one as many as three and four times. After the first visit, they were aware of the hospital's approach to treatment but still continued to come, the majority voluntarily.

With ambivalence toward hospital-sponsored therapies, feelings of failure are considerably softened, and strategies to handle disappointment reflect this. As with the hospital staff, the patient strategies are primarily in the nature of redefining goals. Thus for almost all Skid Row men, the most important part of the State Mental Hospital is the help it offers them with the *physical* and *economic* aspects of their drinking problem and Skid Row living.

Prolonged and numerous intoxications result in such physical manifestations as passing out, blackouts, delirium tremens, nausea, the shakes, hallucinations, and excruciatingly painful hangovers, all of which reduce the pleasure derived from drinking. Additionally, the alcoholic becomes aware of two new developments in his drinking patterns: first, he finds he must drink to sober up. There is a sort of reversal of reactions—abstinence causes nervousness, jitters, and tremors, while a few drinks make him steady and bring the world in focus. Second, the alcoholic finds his tolerance for alcohol is noticeably reduced. Often he will throw up the first two or three drinks before his body will allow one to stay down.

Lillian Roth describes the torment of this stage in her autobiography:

As the years went on something terrifying happened. You couldn't hold as much. You began to throw it up. You drank and you threw up. You were sick all the time. Sometimes you vomited all morning before your stomach retained an ounce of it—the drink your body needed so desperately.

The next stage was worse. You lay in bed and drank around the clock: drank, passed out, waked, drank, vomited, drank, vomited, drank, passed out. . . .

Then, still worse, the shakes. And after the shakes, the horrors, the delirium tremens, when you heard sounds that were not there and saw things that did not exist, your being was one gigantic, inflamed, tortured mass of mental and physical anguish. . . .[48]

When this stage is reached (often referred in the professional literature as the chronic stage), the alcoholic knows he is in serious trouble. He wants to stop drinking at least temporarily, but he fears the terrible withdrawal symptoms—seizures, hallucinations—that accompany this decision.

Primary in the belief system of the Row men at this stage in their drinking is the idea that an alcoholic must be forceably "dried out" since he cannot possibly manage this feat on his own. Such aid is usually sought at an institution. Almost all men who go to State Mental Hospital, whether voluntarily or through court commitment, admit they were in desperate need of medical help because of physical addiction to alcohol. City Hospital, with a five-bed alcoholic ward, will keep a man only five days (not long enough to dry out) if, indeed, he can get in at all.[49] This often leaves the mental hospital as the only hope for the suffering drinker aside from the jail. As the men explain it:

I was afraid. Yes, I was. I'd never had the DT's but I knew I was near. I was afraid of that sort of thing. I didn't have any question about needing to get into a hospital. [46]

I told the judge, "Look I can't get off—I'm on a bender, I can't get off of it." You see, they have an alcoholic ward at the mental hospital. . . . [45]

I was at City Hospital and they had kept me there a couple of days and I said, "I've got to get off this thing. You don't want to keep seeing me here and I don't want to keep coming back here. I'll go anyplace. Look, I'll go to a state hospital or any place, it doesn't make any difference to me. I mean if that's what I have to do to be cured, I'll go. [55]

I went because I was tired of it all. I definitely wanted to get well. [39]

I came here this last time—walked in here sober. I could tell I was going down and decided to come in right away. [21]

Thus while the major emphasis of the hospital staff is on the creation of an experimental therapeutic setting in which the patient can "find himself" and gain insight into his problems, the major emphasis of the patient is on the accommodations for gaining respite from his alcoholic "addiction."

The emphasis on physical needs and the here-and-now rather than therapy [50] is evident in answers to the general question, "What do you think of State Mental Hospital?"

Concern with the medication . . .

They are very good at helping you dry out and give you medication. That is all the treatment there is. [58]

Medication and rest. That's the important treatment there. Of course, I worked my share, too. [45]

The most important thing to a man who has come here for alcoholism is a bed, good food, some medication for the DT's or a seizure, and a place where he can stay off booze for a while. I can always tell when I'll be needing that. You get to a point where you aren't eating and you are drinking all the time—up at 6 A.M. to get a bottle—and you say to yourself, "I'm going to have to quit for a while and dry out." [40]

Concern with the food . . .

Only trouble is the food. I don't like the food too well. No salt in it because of people on diets. [49]

Well, with this problem of mine [drinking], I've eaten in 40 or 50 hospitals and mind you, except for the most expensive ones, this is as good
as any of them. There's nothing wrong with it. You do get tired of it,
though. [50]

Complaints about having to associate with the mentally ill during meal-
times indicate how the Skid Row alcoholic sets himself apart from those
with mental problems:

They made us eat with the MI's and that's not very pleasant you know.
[38]

Lots of the MI's can't handle themselves when they eat. I don't enjoy
watching it. [53] 51

Concern with facilities . . .

It was a great disappointment to me. Oh, the medication, is okay; when I
checked in I was coming out of the DT's and I needed it; but the food
is bad and there were crowded conditions. However, it beats the jail. [60]

It was very crowded when I was there. Men were just about sleeping in
each other's bunks. They had 'em sleeping in the hallways. [60]

Concern with rest and recreation . . .

It's a good program. They take us to Hadley High School swimming pool.
They'd take a group over there and that was enjoyable. They had tennis
courts up there too. [60]

I just got out of there September 20th and I had a wonderful time. You
can go somewhere or not, you can go to a dance or go down and visit the
TV ward, play cards, you know, it's a picnic. It really done me some good.
They have dances every Thursday. [61]

Back in 1950 State Mental Hospital was ideal. The food was splendid and
the first night I went to a dance they broke out a fifth of wine. Sexually,
one could find satiation until the law came into effect that would send an
alcoholic to San Quentin for five years if he was found with a female MI;
but conditions at that time were really wonderful. No therapy, no medication, just a rest! [39]

The surroundings up there are beautiful. You're in a valley, in the rainy
season it rains plenty and in the summer it's real hot. But you can have a
lovely time up there, dances every Thursday, a movie every Tuesday,
plenty of recreation, go around to the various cottages. Go to the women's

cottage at night and have popcorn and play dominoes and have a get-together. Plenty of reading if you're interested. I just sort of relaxed, that's right, just relaxed. [39]

They weren't strict at all. Lots of the fellows got liquor in all the time. You just climb over the fence and get it. I didn't drink any, but I lent them my coat. I had a hunting coat, and I was always lending it, somebody was always borrowing my coat to go over the fence. [49]

Furthermore, if handled properly, going to a mental hospital can financially benefit the alcoholic patient who is usually on his "uppers." Most men are proud of the fact that they can "earn" disability payments while in a mental hospital. (So well accepted is this practice that information on how to file for disability and the amount that a man can expect to receive is posted on the bulletin boards of the hospital.) The hospital gets $12.00 per day for 90 days from any claim received, and the patient may take away with him any amount up to $500.00, a nice-sized stake.

The attitude of the men is not one of gratitude for largess received, but of matter-of-fact expectation of getting payment because they "qualify for it." [52] Additionally, they feel that they earn their way at State Mental Hospital through industrial therapy—the labor they furnish without salary —and endure this for other hospital benefits:

I was at State Mental Hospital twice and they just filed for me and the checks started coming in; when I left there I had a nice little piece of change. (*Interviewer: Did you work after you left there?*) Yeah, one day. That's enough to qualify me again, I think. [46]

You have to be careful and not go to welfare and accept help from them or you will disqualify yourself from the disability at State Mental Hospital because you withdrew yourself from the labor market. [21]

If you earn over $300 you can draw disability when you come here. I was entitled to $26.00 a week for five weeks. They're working on my claim now. I only worked 15 days last year but I earned $537.00. [29]

Patient Redefinition of the Situation

Thus the mental hospital gradually becomes defined as a desirable place on the rehab route—often by default in comparison with other stations such as the jail,[53] and the Christian Missionaries:

Lots of people wonder why the state lets us keep coming back here. What do they want us to do? Die of starvation and drinking? I tell you this place is a godsend. In fact, to some of the guys it's like a country club compared to the life they've been leading. [20]

I went to the judge and I said I needed help. "Make it a mental institution," I said, "because if you don't just as sure as shootin' I will end up in a road camp [jail with outdoor work]. I don't want to go to the road camp because it would be a record against me, and I don't have a record." [45]

I used to go to some private place for a week at a time when my drinking got out of hand, but now I can't afford that and so have to go to the public mental hospitals. [49]

I was on Skid Row sweating out an examination I took for civil service work in the United States Post Office and while I was waiting I got the district attorney to arrange a three-month stint for me at State Mental Hospital. [45]

You become institutionalized. You come back and come back. The first time I came here, I didn't believe they had open wards, etc. But they do. Before I had to dry out on my own; now I can use the hospital to dry out. [26]

I think it's terrific here. Most people use it as a crutch . . . just to dry out . . . then went on their way. It's good to know it's here. [59]

The best part about this deal is that if you're eligible for disability, why you can receive disability payments while you are in the hospital. Then you have it when you get out. This is because the state now reckons alcoholism is a disease, and it might be at that particular time. They have a man up at State Mental Hospital who does nothing but find out if you are eligible. Of course, the hospital gets some cut from this money. [58]

The psychiatrist was wonderful about it. He said, "Well, stay here until you've got a little money." [37]

Most guys will tell you they are here to get their disability. It pays more than unemployment and they save it for you here and then you have something when you hit the streets. I'm staying for 90 days so I'll have something when I leave. [21]

7

Spiritual Salvation

The Last Resort

INTRODUCTION

If jail does not rehabilitate and group therapy does not result in character-changing insight—where can the indigent alcoholic turn for help? "Come to God for help," is the message of the Skid Row missions, one of the few institutions on the loop devoted primarily to the Skid Row alcoholic.

The Christian Missionaries is a worldwide charitable organization, structured internally along semimilitary lines, and Protestant in religious denomination. Its goal is to bring material aid and the word of God and his Son Jesus Christ to homeless, handicapped persons of the earth.[1]

Row men arrive at the Missionary Center in Pacific City from many different points of departure on the loop. Some come directly from a long-term drinking spree on Skid Row that has left them weak, sick, penniless, and frightened. Others are referred by the courts as an alternative to County Jail. Rather than return to the Row with little money and less hope after completion of a jail sentence, Skid Row men may come in to the Center, where there will be food and shelter, in an attempt to "catch their breath." A few are sent over from the State Mental Hospital upon discharge, inasmuch as the Center is recommended as a halfway house to these penniless men. Men who have been to the Center before, or at other Centers around the country, often return when they fail to "make it" on the outside. Thus the Christian Missionaries get their share of alcoholic recidivists.

In order to support their work with alcoholics, the Christian Missionaries collect castoff articles, which they recondition and retail through second-hand stores in the major cities. The Missionaries' Work and Residence Center for Handicapped Men is a major way-station on the rehab route for the Skid Row alcoholics of Pacific City.

167

At the Center the Row men receive a type of treatment quite unlike that of any other station on the circle.[2]

It has been observed by other investigators, and noted in previous chapters of this report, that the official activities of service organizations or agencies substantially reflect a belief system about the type of persons that is to be aided, that is, what clients will look and act like, what their "real" needs are, what the probable causes of their problems are, and what services will be of value to them.[3] Because of the agency's Christian orientation, the Missionaries have a somewhat different view of man—and consequently of the alcoholic—than do other professionals attempting rehabilitation in this field.

Briefly stated, the Christian Missionary approach is as follows: to err (repeatedly) is an inherent part of the human condition; [4] to forgive such failure (even repeatedly) is to emulate the divine.[5] This viewpoint does not demand that the individual alcoholic rehabilitator make an agonizing reappraisal of his methods in the face of failure, that is, the high rates of recidivism. Rather, his work is based on acceptance of almost inevitable backsliding on the part of his charges. No matter how discouraging recidivism may be, the Christian Missonary worker must be continually willing to labor in the vineyard, doing the Lord's work without asking for signs of success of the type that secular institutions seek. Endless compassion for the fallen when they need help, no matter how many times they fail—this is the *real* goal.

This acceptance of the inherent weakness of man also suggests that little credence be given to individual instances of apparent reform. A man must resist sin (drinking) for a lengthy period before the presumption he is "in between slips from grace" can be set aside. Failure is the expected phenomenon; success is short-term abstinence rather than any permanent cure of alcoholism. Within such a framework, the best and safest place for a morally weak man is under the protection and tutelage of one of God's helpers and messengers.

The first portion of this chapter will describe the Christian Missionaries' program for rehabilitation of alcoholics as it is shaped by their apparent beliefs about the basic nature of man in general and the alcoholic man in particular. The effect of a collateral function of the Center—a thriving salvage business—on the central goal of helping homeless male problem drinkers will also be discussed.

Second, this chapter examines the beliefs of the Skid Row alcoholic as they relate to the Missionary Center. This arises because of the contrast the men have perceived between what they depict as the ideal religious-charitable organization and the actual operation of the Christian Missionary Center. The questionable legitimacy (to them) of the Missionaries' money-making enterprises is also important in explaining alcoholics' attitudes.

The Missionaries operate several facilities in the Skid Row area itself, offering both one-night and long-term help to alcoholics, plus a residence for men released from jail or prison. However, this discussion will focus primarily on the Work and Residence Center for Handicapped Men, the official long-range rehabilitation program for problem drinkers.

THE CHRISTIAN MISSIONARIES' HUMAN SALVAGE OPERATION

The general nature and needs of the men the Christian Missionaries help, and the goals the Missionaries set for them are described in the official philosophy of the Work and Residence Center. These goals are: to provide rehabilitation and spiritual regeneration of handicapped, unattached, and homeless men. The handicaps may be either mental, moral, physical, social, or spiritual. Dual emphasis is placed on revival of religious enthusiasm and orderly work habits so as to enable the men to return to society.

Specifically, the alcoholic's problem is seen as an excess of human weakness and lack of purpose, compounded by tortuous guilt for his numerous slips (a guilt that drives him to drink more and more in order to forget his lapses).[6]

To aid the spiritual and moral redemption of the men, the Center makes its many worship services mandatory. A Bible class is also available. Psychological problems are taken up in group therapy.

To implement the goal of helping their charges improve work and personal habits, Christian Missionaries offer a combination residence-work program to these unemployed (and largely unemployable) men. The work involves all aspects of the salvage business and the profits make the Center entirely self-supporting. This activity is so well organized and has enjoyed such financial success that it helps support other Missionary charities and thus offers the Center a collateral *raison d'être* beyond helping the handicapped, for it frees United Crusade funds for other Missionary charities.

The men's physical needs of room, board, clothing, and medical assistance for minor ailments are taken care of by the Center. The social needs of the men are considered to be fulfilled through the opportunities presented them to be with each other informally in the recreation room and at work, and through formal discussion sessions led by professionals.

The Pacific City Center has a capacity of 130 men but usually operates at around 115. The bedrooms are small but clean; the diningroom is pleasant. There are eight six-man rooms, two five-man rooms, six four-man rooms, ten three-man rooms, and 18 single rooms. There are two recreation rooms and a snack bar.

Thus the Christian Missionary approach to rehabilitation of alcoholics at the Work-Residence Center for Handicapped Men is somewhat unique among stations on the rehab route. Officially and legally, the Center is not a clinic, a correctional institution, a sheltered workshop, or a halfway house. Yet it functions to offer all these services, plus spiritual guidance and group therapy for psychological problems. According to the Chaplain-Clinical Director:

> This program helps alcoholics by providing an assortment of work, meditation, chapel devotions, and friendships. We try to get at the *whole man*. Just taking care of his physical problems and giving him medication doesn't offer him any help for the future. [A32] [7]

In order to handle a large number of men efficiently, the Christian Missionaries' organization has developed a routine for processing applicants and maintaining them as residents, including assignment to a room, to work, and to suitable therapy. This routine will be described in detail, along with an expanded discussion of the program and the rules for living at the Center that have evolved over the years and which reflect the general belief system about the characteristics and needs of the clients.

Intake Procedures

Men who apply for help at the Center must pass an intake interview with the Chaplain-Clinical Director. To be admitted to the program, men must have what the Missionaries' staff members term a "treatable handicap." Types and proportions of handicapped men admitted to the Center in Pacific City can be broken down as shown in Table 15.

TABLE 15. *Proportion of Men with Various "Treatable Handicaps" Admitted to Christian Missionary Program*

Alcoholics	80%
Ex-convicts	10
Other (itemized below)	10

    Emotional instability
    Convalescence from illness
    Drug addict
    Antisocial
    Wanderer
    Homosexual

Source: Missionary report. The terminology designating "treatable handicaps" is theirs also.

Permanent handicaps that will not *in themselves* qualify a man to be accepted for the Missionary program (but will not automatically disqualify him either) include old age,[8] amputee, crippled, epileptic, deafness, poor vision, organic disease, and mental illness. These are problems the Missionaries' staff feel are beyond the intended scope of their organization's program. If, however, these handicaps do not result in inability to work in the salvage program, the man may be accepted. The men are given a complete physical examination. (A doctor and nurse are on duty two nights a week to take care of minor physical ailments. Major problems are referred to City Hospital, and a seriously-ill man will probably be discharged from the Center until he is in condition to work.) The Center is not equipped to handle men in acute withdrawal, although men in bad shape from drinking are accepted:

> We take any man in really acute withdrawal to City Hospital. We've had men here in pretty bad shape. If they are not acute, we give them an easy assignment until they feel better. The men in the best shape are sent out to do soliciting for cast-offs, and things like that where they meet the public. [A32]

The ever-desirable presence of "sincerity for self-improvement" is another important criterion for admittance.[9] This trait, however, takes second place to the ability of a man to work in some aspect of the salvage operation since, as noted, this activity supports the Center and contributes to other Missionary work as well.

Some attempt is made to weed out "rounders" although the feelings of the staff toward them is ambivalent.[10]

The Therapy Program for Alcoholism

There are actually two staffs at the Center—the Missionaries and hired employees. The latter includes professional, clerical, and service workers. The individual Missionaries concern themselves primarily with the spiritual salvation of the handicapped men and the management of the salvage operation. On the professional staff at the Pacific City Center is a former Protestant minister with a degree in counseling, a vocational-rehabilitation counselor, a psychologist (part-time), and a psychiatrist (part-time). The latter two staff positions were first created when the Missionaries received a federal grant of $55,000 annually for five years for a demonstration project [11] of their alcoholic rehabilitation program. (This grant period expired in May 1966.) The clerical and service workers aid with the operation of the Center and the salvage operation, usually as supervisors.

The activities and rules of each of the therapies offered at the Center are described below.

SPIRITUAL THERAPY To the Missionaries, the most important type of therapy for the chronic drinker is spiritual-religious; this is intended to help a man "regain purpose in his life," to rebuild his inner strength so that he can resist the bottle. Four types of spiritual-religious therapy are available to problem drinkers at the Center:

a. Religious services twice a week—Thursday and Sunday (compulsory)
b. A short "meditation period" every morning (compulsory)
c. Bible study groups (voluntary)
d. Self-denial campaigns (semivoluntary).

Religious services are conducted by either the Christian Missionaries of the Center or Missionary officers of other charities elsewhere in the city. Additionally, ministers of various Christian denominations are often invited as guest speakers.

To help the men overcome feelings of guilt they may have about their past drinking behavior, considerable emphasis is placed on assuring them of God's forgiveness. It is hoped the men will let God and Christ become an important part of their lives. The Missionary Major puts it this way:

These men have a lack of belief in themselves and feeling for themselves. They can't believe that God forgives. Once you convince them that God forgives them, then they can forgive themselves. Then they can build on this faith. Their biggest problem is lack of belief in themselves. [A29] [12]

As the Missionaries view the problem and its solution:

When you make God or Christ a part of your life, you are going to endeavor to live a clean life—you see Christ as a personal friend. You don't want to do anything that would disgrace Him. Then you don't want to disgrace yourself and your family. [A29]

Audience participation is an important part of the Christian Missionary service. Although the Missionaries make a point of saying they do not ask for testimonials, as is done at Beacon in the Darkness Mission,[13] they do have what is referred to as "a time of sharing experiences." Such verbalizations have a standard meaning: that the original condition of the alcoholic on arrival to the Center was one of atheistic helplessness and that he found inner strength at the Center. According to the Clinical Director:

We just ask them how they are doing. There is no pressure to testify.[14] Often a man will start out with a formula sentence, "I want to thank God and the Christian Missionaries . . ." but it isn't necessary to do this. [A32]

Sometimes they say something like, "Now that I have accepted the Lord Jesus Christ as my Savior, I am no longer alone. I was wandering, and didn't know what to do with my life before." (Notes from participant observer.)

Giving testimony has other therapeutic value, according to the Missionaries:

These men are antisocial to begin with, and the reason they must drink is to relax enough to socialize. That is why we have a time of sharing and testimony . . . that is why we have Bible classes—so that a man can get practice in verbalizing. [A29]

Morning meditations are for the express purpose of reinforcing in the beneficiary's mind the fact that he is lost, but can have the hope of finding himself through spiritual renewal.[15]

These men get on a merry-go-round of drinking and never take time out to think of what they are losing in the process. We tell them the morning chapel gives them a period in which to take stock. [A33]

Bible study groups are available for those men who are considered not sufficiently "sophisticated" for group therapy of the psychoanalytic variety but who still might benefit from talking over their problems in some context with others.

The Bible groups are sort of sub-sub therapy groups. Some [men] . . . graduate on to other groups from there. [A32]

Another regular part of the religious participation in the Center is a ritual referred to as "self-denial." This device involves the internal fund-raising campaign to finance Missionary work abroad. Both Missionaries and beneficiaries are expected to donate—each according to his ability. The Skid Row man may be asked for 25 cents or 50 cents or a dollar, which must come out of the small gratuity he is paid for his work at the Center (see page 175). At the devotion services during self-denial campaigns, each man receives an envelope with his name on it for his contribution. A rocket-missile chart posted in the chapel indicates total progress towards a previously set goal for the Center as a whole.[16]

The rationale for inclusion of the men on the program in the self-denial campaign again implies a basic Christian Missionary belief about their characters: these men, who have been living a self-centered and hedonistic life for a long time, need an opportunity to sacrifice and do something for others.[17]

It makes them feel like they are contributing something to others—and this is good for them. They have been selfish for a long time. [A32]

All of these religious efforts are intended to give the handicapped man an opportunity for self-insight. The desired end-result, of course, is the moral and social rejuvenation of the Row man.[18]

Spiritual renewal is signified by a change in attitude from selfish to unselfish. A man begins to be concerned about another man in the program. He will also begin to participate in things that are not required, like Bible study, AA meetings, bowling, the recreation facilities. [A29]

WORK THERAPY   As previously mentioned, the salvage operation has a dual purpose. First, it supports the Center and aids other Missionary charities: second, it provides employment for the man who is caught in a circular trap of inability to find work because of his drinking reputation, followed by drinking because he fears he is unemployable. Steady work is considered by the Missionaries to be an absolute necessity for a man if he is to gain back his self-respect.[19] Furthermore, it gives the average problem drinker, who is accustomed to devoting his entire day to either obtaining liquor or consuming it, something to do with his time—now that he is not drinking. According to the Director:

> Work therapy provides the man with a sense of well-being and helps him to avoid morbid thinking. We make it clear to the fellows that this isn't make-work, but important. It contributes to operations. [A32]

The vocational counselor had this to say about the work therapy programs:

> It keeps the men busy. They say, "What do I do instead of drinking?" Usually, they'd be intoxicated. They don't know what to do with their time if they are not drinking. Besides, you are dealing with vanity. It helps a man if he knows that he is not getting outright charity. [A33]

Work is also seen as being a definite aid with the physiological problems of withdrawal:

> We put a man to work the minute he is accepted in the program, no matter how bad he feels. We think that the work takes his mind off his physical problems and that the sweat he works up actually gets the impurities out of his body faster. Why, when you go by some of these winos that are sweating and working, the odor from their sweat alone would be enough to intoxicate you! [A29]

The work itself includes solicitation of people's throw-aways, driving trucks, loading and unloading merchandise on the docks, sorting of donated items, and repair and cleaning of various articles and reselling them. An attempt is made, within the limitations of the operations, to place a man in the type of work he prefers. Men are expected to work a five-and-a-half-day week, from 8:00 a.m. to 4:15 p.m. Monday through Friday, and from 8:00 a.m. to noon on Saturday.

Despite the intentions of the Missionaries to give the men employment that will enhance their self-respect, the Center stops short of calling the alcoholics "employees." Rather, men who are accepted for the program are referred to as "beneficiaries." Incoming men must sign an agreement acknowledging that they are beneficiaries and not employees. In keeping with this nomenclature, they receive a "gratuity," not a salary, for their work. The amount awarded starts at $4.00 per week and may be slowly increased to $15.00 per week, with the increases being semiautomatic until $10.00 is reached. Until a man passes the $8.00-a-week point, $1.00 of his pay is given to him in the form of a ticket that he may spend at the Christian Missionary snack bar operated outside the recreation room in the residence hall.[20] The purpose of this method of payment was explained as follows:

> The gratuity is not intended as a wage but as a therapeutic tool. After they get up to $10.00, it may be raised according to progress on the program. This is judged in terms of a beneficiary's cooperation, his attitude, does he participate in activities, stay a loner, and so on. Also, a man can be lowered in gratuity if he goes "on report." This means that he was caught pilfering or drinking. (Going "on report" is the alternative to being "checked out"—asked to leave for rule infraction.) [A29] [21]

> We also have a gratuity meeting in which the supervisors, the residence manager, the chaplain, and others come and discuss how a man is working out, the pros and cons on him, et cetera. Is he cooperative? Hard to get along with? This is how it is decided who gets the increase. It normally takes about six months to get up to $15.00 per week. [A29] [22]

The Missionaries also believe that a man has more self-respect when he has some money via the gratuity to buy little necessities. The $1.00 snack bar ticket is to aid him in putting aside a small sum for "extras" like cigarettes, gum, and candy.

The staff acknowledged, however, that the men often complain about the amount of their gratuity. When they do so, there are a number of rejoinders developed by the Missionaries:

> When they complain about the amount of the gratuity, they forget about the board, the room, the suit, dress coat and slacks, white shirt, sports shirt, and pay for medical care and psychiatric treatment which we supply.[23] If you figure it up, they get just about minimum pay. If they are up to $10.00 to $15.00 gratuity, then all they have to buy out of that is cigarettes and shaving lotion. They get one-third off clothes at our stores. They can have a savings account and we bank it for them. Many men, who have been here a year or more, leave with $100.00 or $200.00 in savings. [A29]

> After a man's been here about two weeks, he stops being grateful and begins to feel he's being taken advantage of. He forgets he was unemployable. He demands to be paid what he is worth. I had a man come in and tell me he was turning out $1,000 worth of upholstery work a day

for $4.00 a week. I told him to remember that he couldn't get work on the outside. They want to be treated like full-fledged employees when they really aren't. [A33]

COMPANIONSHIP THERAPY   In keeping with the well-accepted theory that the problem drinker lives an increasingly isolated life, the Christian Missionaries attempt to reverse this trend by enforced group living.

Beneficiaries are placed in five- and six-man rooms when first accepted in the program. Discussions and friendships during the dinner hour are encouraged by small four-man tables rather than long tables found in most institutions. There are recreation rooms with television, pool tables, and magazines. Bingo games are held on Saturday night (primarily to keep the men in and away from the bars). All of this is intended, according to the professional staff, to increase camaraderie among the men:

> What do we mean by camaraderie? Men can achieve a degree of acceptance with other people and other alcoholics. They don't have to be buddy-buddy, but they can accept each other.
>
> A lot of the drinking by these men has its many roots in an attempt to change their own actions. We try to teach them here to like each other, and thus themselves. Then maybe they won't feel like they have to drink to change their behavior in order to be liked. [A33] [24]

This camaraderie does not include friendship with Missionary or professional staff, however. Missionaries rarely mingle with beneficiaries either at dinner or in the recreation room or even after church services. Professional staff see the men only in their official capacity. Strict social distance is observed otherwise.[25]

GROUP THERAPY   In addition to the heavy emphasis on spiritual renewal and resocialization, the Christian Missionaries have continued to sponsor a number of psychoanalytically-oriented therapy groups, even after termination of the federal grant.

It should be mentioned, however, that group therapy and spiritual regeneration are not necessarily antithetical. Talking personal problems out is seen here as the tool that forces the patient to see himself for what he "really" is; religion then can become the tool by which he overcomes these revealed faults and assuages the guilt associated with them.

Only a small proportion of the men in residence at any one time are invited into these therapy groups (approximately 25 or less). Criteria for admittance to a group are the same as that of the Jail Branch Clinic: staff appraisal of ability to develop insight into motivations and willingness to share this insight with others, a sincere desire to quit drinking, and general sophistication to appreciate the concept of group therapy and its goals.

Group therapy is not popular with men at the Center and those invited to join a group often leave after one or two sessions. Center therapists explain this failure within the framework of their discipline and are most specifically oriented toward the view of the men as immature and unsocialized.

> Some of these men are so withdrawn from society that it is an effort for them to be in a group with others. [A32]

> They are frightened, insecure men, and therefore don't want to tell their business in group therapy. [A33]

VOCATIONAL COUNSELING THERAPY The evolution of vocational *counseling* to vocational *therapy* is an example of how activities at the Center have been shaped in response to the diagnosis of the beneficiaries as weak and spiritually lost. When originally made available, the counseling effort was not so much therapeutic as pragmatic; it was designed to help men find an outside job after they had been in the Center's program for some time. However, the man who eventually took over the job of vocational counselor forced a change in the focus of the program. "Working with the whole man" became the purpose of vocational counseling.[26] This means discussing with the alcoholic why he lost his last job, why he didn't enjoy his work, and what connection these dissatisfactions may have had with other problems, such as his sex life, his personal insecurities, and ultimately, his drinking problem. According to the Major:

> Our vocational rehabilitation plan works this way. First of all, they relearn regular work habits by working in our salvage Center. Ninety-five percent of the men don't want assistance in finding work. They know where to go for jobs and how to get them. This is why our vocational counselor works with the man on the *meaning* of his previous vocation. Maybe that was what caused him to be an alcoholic. During our research program, which went on for five years, we found that a goodly proportion of these men were in the wrong occupation. [A29]

> This is not an employment agency. We don't get them a job. We really need a job developer on the staff here. [A33] [27]

The implication of the new approach is, of course, that few of the men are ready to hold a regular job in the outside world unless and until they change inwardly.

> When it comes to planning employment, it is important to work on the treatment and adjustment aspect *first*. That comes *before* getting a job. They must try to understand and relate their behavior to past job experiences. On very rare occasions we help them find a job. [A33]

In any case, no vocational counseling *of any type* is done until a beneficiary has remained in the Center for a minimum of 90 days:

I tell them they must invest time and sobriety to get our services. [A33]

Table 16 indicates that 51 percent of the men who claim they left the Center for a job elsewhere stayed two months or less on the program, and therefore did not qualify for aid from the counseling service. The remainder did qualify for job counseling. In raw numbers, this is 51 men, or seven percent of the total admissions. No information was available at the time this study was completed as to whether they were, in fact, counseled before finding their jobs.

TABLE 16. Men Admitted to Program Who Terminated to Take a Job (1967)*

(SHOWN BY LENGTH OF STAY AT CENTER)

Length of stay on program	Percent (N = 106)	
1 week	5	
2 weeks	8	
3 weeks	6	
1 month	13	51
2 months	19	
3 months	13	
4 months	8	
5 months	9	
6 months	8	
7 months	2	
8 months	—	
9 months	—	
10 months	2	
11 months	1	
1 year	2	
2 years	4	

Source: The data were drawn from Christian Missionary records of terminations for one year. The stated time period can be taken as referring to the lower limit of the implied interval, with the upper limit being just under the next category.

* This is based on the men's claims, not on verified fact. However, inasmuch as a large proportion of the men leave without giving any reason (See Table 19, page 209), it might be inferred that this represents something near the true number of men who leave for jobs.

STRUCTURED MILIEU THERAPY   The Center's rules reflect another important characteristic of their clientele: that Skid Row men are potentially, if not actually, irresponsible and undependable. The most important regulations are listed, followed by the stated rationale for their existence.

Curfew is at 11 o'clock every night and a man who leaves the Center (to go to a movie, visit a friend, etc.) and returns after that time will find himself locked out.

Men must have passes to visit relatives, to stay away from the Center overnight, to go job hunting, or see the doctor during the day. All time away from work must be made up.[28] No weekend passes are issued until a man has been in the Center for 30 days.

All private property, such as typewriters, radios, and electric shavers, must be checked in upon arrival and stored until the beneficiary leaves or rooms alone.

Once a man has left his room in the morning, he may not return until 5:00 p.m. (This rule holds even when the weather turns cold or there is unexpected rain and he is without a jacket.) [29]

There must be no drinking on or off the premises.

Lockers are inspected periodically for stolen goods. "Girlie" magazines or liquor are forbidden.[30]

Men must wear slacks and sport shirts to the recreation rooms and a suit coat to Sunday and Thursday services. When leaving one's room, all clothes must be hung up, and the man's folding chair must be closed down and placed on the bed.

The first two rules are intended to enforce regular hours on men who have not kept them for a long time and, further, to make responsible employees of them. Curfews and passes are also intended to keep beneficiaries on the premises, away from bars, and out of trouble.

A structured environment is good for the alcoholic. He has been living in a totally unstructured one for too long. [A33]

We feel that they [the beneficiaries] need firm control over their living here. The (rule against) . . . leaving without a pass, the regulation about not drinking . . . (are needed) because obviously they aren't able to control themselves. These rules are intended to support their *supposed* desire not to drink. The 11 o'clock curfew, the rules on bathing, picking up clothes, and so on are to keep this place from becoming a flophouse. The men have been pretty thoroughly undisciplined for quite a time before they come here. [A32]

As to the 11 o'clock curfew: we work with 120 men. They would be coming and going at all hours if we didn't control this. We'd have to have someone on the desk all night. We can't afford that. Besides, a man who has only six hours sleep doesn't work well the next day. The doors are locked at *exactly* 11 p.m., not before and not after. [A29]

The rules concerning property, lockers, and restrictions on returning to rooms once vacated are primarily to prevent petty theft, which the Missionaries see as an ever-present danger from beneficiaries. Men who work with donated materials can easily slip a transistor radio, an electric razor, or other small but valuable article in their pockets. Then later they can hide the item in their lockers and smuggle it out to sell or pawn for liquor. Again, this is interpreted to be a result of their moral immaturity. As the clinical psychologist put it:

> They don't even think of it as stealing. After all, it was discarded material, things people didn't want anymore. They know that the Missionaries will sell these items for way under what they could get in a good trade down on Skid Row, so they just hold on to them. [A31]

The rules of dress and room maintenance are for the purpose of re-instilling pride of appearance and desire for clean living conditions in the men. Putting all chairs on the beds means that the mopping and waxing detail can work quickly through their daily floor-cleaning chores. The Major explains the dress code as follows:

> As for our rules, some centers aren't this rigid. You walk into their recreation room and guys are there in their work clothes, they are sweaty and there is smoke in the air. It's like a stag party. You aren't going to lift a man up very high on those standards, are you? Men must come to church in dress clothes out of respect. You would be surprised how many men are too lazy to iron their shirts unless we require it. [A29]

The rules are clearly stated at an orientation meeting scheduled soon after the admittance of a beneficiary. Punishment for minor infractions ranges from being moved out of a desirable single or double room, back to a six-man dorm, a reduction in the weekly gratuity, or having the gratuity withheld entirely for a week. A serious violation—stealing or drinking—exposes a man to being asked to leave immediately. Police are never called in such cases.

> The Missionaries don't feel that it looks right to have one of their beneficiaries arrested for stealing from them. It hurts the public image, you know. So the only weapon the Missionaries have is to throw the thief out. [A31]

Termination records indicate that the Missionaries drop proportionately very few men for violation of rules. In the past year, only 14 percent were dropped for such infractions (See Table 19, p. 209). Apparently loss of gratuity and private rooms are used as interim punishments far more often than the more extreme penalty of "checking a man out." Furthermore, pilfering accounted for only 1 percent of the terminations, while infrac-

tions connected with drinking accounted for 12 percent. Of the terminations, 2 percent were the result of miscellaneous infractions such as
fighting, use of drugs, problems with the police, and apparent gross mental
disturbance.

ASSIGNMENT DECISIONS   Assignments to therapy also reinforce the general assumptions made about the character of the Row men.

A man is given a room, a work assignment, and possibly allocated a
position in a therapy or Bible discussion group following a case conference
about his potential reaction to various types of rehabilitation efforts. The
psychological tests (MMPI, Wechsler, Interpersonal Check List [31]), plus
information on religious leanings, and past drinking patterns, which the
Row man fills out when accepted for admittance, help provide the necessary background for the assignment decisions. These decisions are made
jointly, approximately two weeks after admission, by the psychologist, the
vocational counselor, and the clinical director.

For the majority of Row men, the decision is to limit their therapy to
work, companionship, and milieu. For a few, who are considered not to
be too old or truculent, there is the possibility of getting into group therapy
after a month at the Center.

There are four therapy groups, led by the psychologist, the psychiatrist,
or the vocational counselor. Six to eight men are in each group, the optimum number possible being 32 men, although, as mentioned, the average
is usually 20 to 25. The fourth group is an orientation group for borderline
beneficiaries, i.e., men who might do well in group therapy later. As mentioned, there are also Bible discussion groups. Alcoholics Anonymous
(AA) discussion groups are set up where there is interest. [32]

Actually, it is assumed that no man is left without therapy because . . .

> The whole set-up is therapy. Companionship with the other men on a
> working-living basis is the most important therapy of all. [A32]

Length of Stay, Termination Procedure, and the Difficulties of Returning to Society

Six months is the length of stay recommended for a man to get the most
benefit from the Center's program. This is longer than other stations on
the loop. The rationale is that this is the minimum length of time needed
to give a man an opportunity to establish new habit patterns. Actual stay
recommendations vary in proportion to the individual's drinking career.
It is assumed that the longer a man has been drinking, the longer it will
take him to be resocialized. According to the vocational counselor:

> If they ask me how long they have to stay here, I ask them how long they
> have been drinking. If they say six years, then I say, "Give me a month
> for every year." If they say 26 years, I say, "Give me a week for every
> year." [A33]

However, these rehabilitation estimates do not mean that a probable discharge date is automatically put on the calendar. As a matter of fact, although entrance to the Center is programmed in some detail, termination procedure is virtually ignored along with other considerations (such as location of job and housing on the "outside") that go with termination.

Center staff members freely admit there is no formal machinery established for the termination of a "rehabilitated" Row man. That is, unlike State Mental Hospital and other stations on the loop, there is no case conference or predetermined date at which progress or possible discharge is either discussed or put in operation. Men who are in residence at the Center are considered to be in a temporarily "saved" status, but assessment of their ability to live independently, supporting themselves, is not a regularly programmed consideration.

Thus men are almost never called in and told that they seem "improved enough" to move out and get a job, and that they will be aided in finding employment or suitable housing. (There is a formal termination procedure that a beneficiary may initiate if he wishes to leave, but this decision is left up to him and does not include aid in making the transition to a new working-living situation outside the Center.) [33]

Other factors in operation also militate against the development of machinery to aid men in reestablishing themselves in the outside community:

First of all, as may have been surmised from other material presented, neither the work schedule nor the professional aid is geared to helping the men find employment on the outside.

A beneficiary must work during prime job-hunting days, Monday through Saturday noon. A man is allowed one day a week off for job-hunting only after he has been with the Center for 90 days, and then he must make up the time by working overtime. (Previous overtime does not accumulate for such purposes.) If a man can prove he has an unusually excellent prospect, he may be given two days off, although not necessarily consecutive ones.[34]

This paucity of employment-seeking time is justified by the Missionaries on the grounds that were they to grant extended periods of release-time for any reason, they would inevitably find themselves operating a residence where men could come and go as they pleased, work if and when they pleased, and drink whenever they were off the premises. With such laxness in house rules, a man could stay out long enough to return sober and successfully pass the clerk on the desk (one of his duties being to detect men who have been drinking and deny them access to their rooms).

Second, existing voluntary leave patterns almost negate the need for termination machinery. Of the men leaving voluntarily, 55 percent go before a possible official termination period without formal notice to Missionaries or staff. (See Table 19, p. 209, of this chapter.)

Fewer than ten percent of the men stay six months. [A31]

We have a 43 percent drop-out in 30 days. [A33]
(Actually, it is higher—approximately two-thirds in 30 days. See Table 17.)

We can't hang on the men. We try to figure out which ones will stay so we can concentrate our energies on them, but we can't predict too well at this time. [A32]

Finally, those few men who do stay the recommended six months have a tendency to want to remain indefinitely.

Some men, a few, are told informally that they are ready to leave. Those few are the ones who don't want to—who won't go. [A31]

Some men get institutionalized and we keep them out of charity, because that's the kind of a place this is. If a man is 61, has no social security, and so on, where can he go? [A33]

If we see a man developing a dependency on the facility, we try to get them out before they become institutionalized. But it isn't easy. Take Mr. Muller. He's institutionalized. He can't function outside of here. Slumps every time. [A33]

The link between the beneficiary and the Center is often reinforced by the Center Missionary staff's hiring the man as a permanent, regular employee,[35] or by the man marrying one of the women employees of the Center—usually a salvage sorter.

Of the 400 new men coming in 1967, the number who at any one time become Christian Missionary employees are about ten, mostly truck drivers. [A31]

Five percent of the men stay on as employees. Almost all regular [male] employees in the salvage business are recruited this way. [A32]

John is marrying a woman in the sorting room . . . a common phenomenon. [A31]

Table 17 indicates the distribution of the length of stay at the Center for the past three years. Note that 50 percent or more of the men stay no longer than three weeks, and that no more than 5 percent or 6 percent stay five to seven months—close to the desirable length of time so far as the Missionary program is concerned.

TABLE 17. *Length of Stay at Christian Missionary Work and Residence Center*

PERCENT

Length of stay on program ‡	1965 (N = 563) †		1966 (N = 674) †		1967 (N = 718) †	
1 day	8 ⎫		6 ⎫		8 ⎫	
1 week	15 ⎪		19 ⎪		20 ⎪	
2 weeks	15 ⎬ 50		18 ⎬ 53		15 ⎬ 53	
3 weeks	12 ⎭		10 ⎭		10 ⎭	
1 month	17		18		19	
2 months	12		10		11	
3 months	7		7		4	
4 months	3		2		3	
5 months	2 ⎫		2 ⎫		3 ⎫	
6 months	2 ⎬ 5		2 ⎬ 5		2 ⎬ 6	
7 months	1 ⎭		1 ⎭		1 ⎭	
8 months	1		1		1	
9 months	1		*		1	
10 months	1		*		*	
11 months	*		*		*	
1 year	2		3		1	
More than a year (2, 3, 4 years)	1		*		1	

Source: Records kept by Christian Missionaries.

* Less than ½ of 1 percent.
† The base here refers to number of men who were accepted on the program and then terminated. One man may be represented more than once if he was on the program several times in one year.
‡ Time was not divided into intervals, but rounded by the Missionaries to the nearest full day, week, month or year.

Explanations as Beliefs

Assessments of the Christian Missionary program also reflect the belief system concerning the inherent characteristics of the Skid Row drinker. Two aspects of official thinking illustrate this: explanations of the high rate of turnover, and definitions of Center (and staff) effectiveness.

OFFICIAL EXPLANATIONS OF THE HIGH TURNOVER   The innate weakness of the chronic drunk is usually considered to be the major explanation of the high attrition rate of the men after a relatively short stay. Discussion of this problem may be couched in psychoanalytic or spiritual terms, depending on the disciplinary persuasion of the person making the statement. Said the vocational counselor:

> They cannot handle the anxiety of knowing themselves as they really are. So they come in and say they are quitting, that they don't like their boss. Sometimes I can get them to discuss it openly in therapy, but more often they just take off, their anxiety is too much for them. [A33]

We are such a paternalistic organization that they come to think we should make everything right—when we don't they get angry and quit. They come to me and say, "The foreman doesn't know his job," and I'll say, "Well that happens on the outside too, doesn't it?" And they look at me like that has nothing to do with it. We are their Papa, and they expect Papa to be perfect. That's it. [A33]

According to the Major:

There are several reasons why the men leave after being here only a short time.

First, they are afraid the other beneficiaries will get to know them too well. They don't want their past known. They don't want to relate to anyone and have the responsibilities of a real friendship. Second, there are those who stay a short while and think they have their drinking problem licked—that one beer can't hurt them. They are on cloud seven, they think so much of themselves, and they go out and have a beer to prove it, and that's all. Then, we have a small proportion of men—mostly young first-timers—who only need 30 to 45 days here to realize what has happened to them, and they straighten up and go home. [A29]

The staff psychologist sees motivation for leaving as perhaps having two equally valid levels:

It is hard to tell what is the *real* reason for the men leaving here as much as they do. When they do give us a reason, it's because of co-workers or supervisors, or they think they are being exploited. We wonder if it isn't just that their anxiety gets the best of them. [A31]

The professional staff sometimes blames the profit orientation of the Center for the high turnover among the beneficiaries:

In any treatment center, the salvage operation must show a profit. All the men's centers are self-sufficient and, in fact, help support the rest of the Missionary activities. This is okay, but it can interfere with a man's therapy. A man must be working even when he feels lousy, or if he should have special therapy because he's discouraged, or if he needs time to look for work. Making X number of dollars comes before the welfare of an individual man. [A33]

The inherent problem is that a certain amount of money has to be earned here or else we go out of business. Some of the money goes to territorial headquarters for the building fund. This means that where the work assignment or the amount of time worked isn't therapeutic for a man, the Missionaries aren't structured to do anything about it. [A31]

STAFF'S ACCEPTANCE OF LIMITATIONS ON SUCCESS   It has been already decided, as a practical matter, that where the spirit is willing but the flesh is weak, there is no real sense of absolute failure when a Row man does not succeed. Rather, the staff has learned, like the mental hospital staff, to accept intermediate goals as signs of success:

> You learn to scale down your goals. If a man was in institutions 52 weeks per year and he now has it down to 40, then there is success. [A31]

> You learn to look at it this way—they achieve more abstinence here than anywhere else in the past years. [A33]

> In general, I believe the Christion Missionary Centers are a boon to mankind all the way around. They are helpful to the men and they don't use tax money. They are better than the jail and perhaps more rehabilitative than the State Mental Hospital. They are a path to self-insight if the men will only use them that way. Any problem of exploitation of the men is usually an individual manager problem—not a Missionary problem per se. [A31]

According to the clinical director:

> I have to prove to myself that the human being is worthwhile and there is the possibility of a degree of recovery. My feeling is that even if a man is here for a month, he has at least gained a degree of human respectability. It has most to do with my view of the human being. It does not arise out of theological tenets of the church (i.e., that the good are good and the bad are bad). [A32]

According to the vocational counselor:

> I go on because it feeds into my pathology. I'm a manipulator. I'm an aggressive guy. I've had enough success doing this, that it works okay. I don't see it [his cure] as the end product of being successful—but the activity itself is pretty well received. I enjoy working very hard with the alcoholic and seeing the response. Then, it's up to him. But the relationship we have at that moment when I'm working with him is very satisfying. [A33]

The Missionaries themselves see their Center as filling a need that is justification in itself:

> We try to meet a need. We aren't trying for "success" in the usual sense of the word.

> I keep myself going in this work by the fact that I'm able to help men. The religious aspect keeps me going. I feel that this is the place that God wants me to be. Man will not grow without failure. If you do not stub your toe, you won't learn anything. These men give up too soon. The

religious aspect of our program is so important because it is the man's spirit which will keep him from drinking. We are the only program which treats the whole man—physical and spiritual. [A29]

We don't define success by how many permanent cures for alcoholism we are able to effect. The Christian Missionaries go where there is a need. We fill that need. These men need us. They come here flat broke and sick and we provide a sanctuary. We offer them help with their alcoholic problem when they need it most. *That* is our success. If another agency came along and started *really* helping these men, we'd move on to other things. [A30]

BEING SALVAGED: LIFE WITH THE CHRISTIAN MISSIONARIES AS SEEN BY THE SKID ROW ALCOHOLIC

To the average citizen, the Christian Missionaries' Work and Residence Center for Handicapped Men appears to offer more real aid and comfort to the Skid Row alcoholic than some of the other stations on the loop. Food, companions, and general surroundings are certainly better than in the County Jail. There is more privacy and freedom of movement at the Center than in the State Mental Hospital, or the Welfare Home for Homeless Men, or the jail. Although the pay may seem miniscule, it is more money than most of the men have been earning, whether in treatment institutions or on the street. In addition to this, spiritual counsel and group therapy are available, and both presumably could be of assistance to a man who has an alcoholism problem.

Certainly, for a man who wants help and is "down on his luck," perhaps even faced with the problem of maintaining sheer existence, the Christian Missionaries could be viewed as a Godsend.

However, as was mentioned in the previous section, the turnover of residents in the Center is exceedingly high. Talks with ex-beneficiaries reveal most are very bitter. Vehement remarks of the type that follows are common:

I'll tell you why most of us go there. Because we're desperate. We need a roof over our heads. But I'll tell you something else. Next time I'm that bad off, I'll jump off the bridge instead of going there again. [20]

Did you ever know a junk dealer personally? They aren't the nicest characters. Well, the Christian Missionaries are junk dealers. They take in second-hand stuff and resell it. And they have a typical junk-dealer's personality. [31]

When pressed to explain these harsh sentiments, Skid Rowers sum up the Christian Missionaries individually and collectively as:

A bunch of goddamn hypocrites.

Hypocrisy can be best described, from a sociological point of view, as a betrayal of what was assumed [by the betrayed] to be *a mutual understanding* between two parties, concerning (a) the nature of their identities and, (b) their relationship to each other. More importantly, the deviating party denies any digression.[36] This act of failing to honor announced commitments, while at the same time continuing to claim them, puts significant others in the position of responding to what appears to be two sets of signals: what the proponent claims is still the basis of the relationship, and what the evidence seems to show.

Thus hypocrisy is more than the mere difference between the normative ideal and actual conditions or activities at any given time.[37] There is always another ingredient: the tenacious claim by one party or group that the ideal is indeed being lived up to despite a great deal of apparent evidence to the contrary.

The *amount* of evidence to the contrary necessary to generate charges of hypocrisy varies with the clarity and specificity of the ideal, as well as with general distribution of knowledge about it. Obviously, the more completely detailed a claimed ideal, the more likely the chance of an action being seen as a betrayal; whereas, the more indistinct the ideal and the less common knowledge about it, the more likely a given action can be seen as "fitting" or falling within the ideal.

In the case of the Christian Missionaries, the ideal "Christian" is firmly stereotyped—in detail—in the minds of most Americans, including Skid Row alcoholics, just as the Christian Missionaries "know" the universal characteristics of man in general, and alcoholics in particular.

A professional Christian should be warm, friendly, understanding, forgiving, fair, and above all, generous. Charity should be of a nonjudgmental variety, offered to all in need on the basis of genuine love for humanity. Mere belief in Jesus Christ as a personal savior does not really qualify an individual to regard himself as a real "Christian," according to the Skid Row alcoholic. Using the above criteria, the homeless problem drinker finds the Christian Missionaries as falling quite a bit below standard.

How and why does this seem so to the alcoholic, considering the services offered to him by the Missionaries in comparison with other stations on the loop? Is there a connection between this feeling of betrayal and the high turnover of beneficiaries?

H. L. A. Hart has made the point that the ascription of meaning to an action is not an exercise in recognizing the *inherent* quality of that action, but rather in subjectively deciding, from among many possibilities, the *likely* meaning. Hart also suggests such a decision is the result of the *cumulation* of evidence, with every added clue making the decision increasingly easier and every detracting incident modifying it a bit.[38]

The general verdict of the Row men that the Christian Missionaries are hypocrites is the result of such a building up of evidence, beginning with the entrance of a naive alcoholic into a Missionary residence and continuing until he leaves the Center. Each succeeding definition becomes evidence confirming the hypocrisy and makes the next judgment easier to reach as well, inasmuch as it affects perception. Additionally, the "wised up" beneficiary is eager to create and reinforce in neophytes uncomplimentary perceptions of the Missionaries. A discussion of the assessments and verdicts arrived at by the men in the process of their residency, and undoubtedly in part through contact with former residents, follows.

In reviewing these verdicts, it is important to keep in mind that they are representative of the attitudes of the dissident majority who leave the Center long before the recommended six-months time. In order to ascertain whether there is attitudinal change in a positive direction with increased length of stay, interviews were arranged with some long-time residents. Four such men [39] were located and interviewed, and where their feelings about the Center contrast with the majority, these minority views are presented.

Passing Intake

Assaults on the men's credibility in initially accepting the claimed Christian ideal of the Missionaries begins with entrance to the Work and Residence Center.

As mentioned previously, passing intake officially involves submitting to an interview designed to determine (a) the presence of a treatable handicap, (b) sincerity of the candidate's motivation to quit drinking, and (c) ability to participate in the work therapy program.

To the Skid Row men, however, there are undercurrents involved in passing intake that differ somewhat from the official policy of compassion for the downtrodden alcoholic who wants to "straighten out." This difference between stated intake policy and actual practice becomes a cornerstone in the case for hypocrisy that the men build. Getting into the Center seems dependent less on the needs of the men or their perceived determination to stop drinking permanently, than on the needs of the Missionaries to staff their salvage operations.[40]

According to the men, if an alcoholic—sick, hungry, and penniless— applies for admission on Friday or Saturday, the Missionaries will *not* take him in until Monday, regardless of his sincerity and very obvious need. Why should this be? The answer given in several interviews was:

> If you come to them at the end of the week, you can't get in—even if you are sick and cold and beg for a place. This is because they know they can't get any work out of you for a day and a half, and no work—no feed. They tell you to come back Monday. [59]

In fact, former residents of the Center are aware that a man had better not be *too* sick or *too* disabled or he won't get in on *any* day of the week. They see this as a lack of true charity, however, rather than adherence to a given program of rehabilitation that is not adapted to medical treatment.

> Let me tell you, if you can't do a job, if you can't work or something like that, you're on your way out [of the Center]. [42]

Offering a skill the Christian Missionaries need is more important than being an alcoholic in distress and with a sincere desire to be rehabilitated, according to the men.

> Now what you do is nose around and find out if they are short some skilled person—like an upholsterer, or a man to fix appliances, or what not. Then they will snatch you up, because if they don't find a guy who can do that work they might have to hire someone who can, or pay to take stuff to the dump they can't handle . . . And either way they are stuck, because putting out cash is a bad, bad word among the Christian Missionaries. [31]

The men claim, in fact, that if an alcoholic gets known for his skill, this is *all* that it takes to pass intake. They claim that a skilled person can get into the Center despite any trouble he caused during a previous stay and regardless of whether he appears sincere or not about the program.

> Well, if you work well and they know you, you can get in any time. One of the officers who was transferred to Laurel City came to me before he left and said, "Any time you come to Laurel City, I want you." Later, he called me long distance, so I left the desk in Pacific City and went down south for a while. [20]

> If you've been there before, and if they liked you, they will usually take you in again and again, even if they have had to throw you out for drinking. [45]

The obverse is . . .

> If you can't make any money for 'em, to show a profit for 'em, well you'd better figure you're on your way out. [38]

Logically, voluntary entrance seems to be essential to a program that is dependent upon the personal motivation of the alcoholic male to seek regeneration. However, this aspect of admittance does not appear to be a serious requirement, since some men who go to the Missionaries as a

Hobson's choice are accepted into the program and the sincerity of their desire for reform is not questioned:

> The judge said, "Well, if I send you over to the Christian Missionaries, will you go over there and work and stay there till you get straightened out?" And the guys up for sentencing on drunk charges say, "Oh, yeah, yeah." Of course, they'll say "yes" to anything, you know, just to get the hell out of the door. [18]

> Of course there are a lot of fellows at the Christian Missionaries under duress because they are out of a state penal institution, and they have to stay there till their parole is up. The parole board likes 'em there because it's easy to keep an eye on them that way. [18]

> Well, you can see one of their [the Christian Missionaries] court aides at drunk court and if they are willing to take you, you can escape jail—but it's a toss-up which is worse. [20]

Being "On the Program"

The Christian Missionaries rehabilitation program receives the most demerits from the men, although certain aspects of it are considered to be greater proof of hypocrisy than others. A catalog of these viewpoints follows.

HAVING RELIGION SHOVED AT YOU   Spiritual counseling and guidance is disliked by many alcoholic residents of the Center as high-pressure and demeaning—neither characteristics deemed as fitting the Skid Row man's idea of religion:

> There are morning devotions. There are Thursday night meetings. There are Sunday services. They just shove the religion down your throats . . . All they do is harp on religion. [41]

Resistance to the religious teachings of the Missionaries is tied, in part, to the definition of the beneficiary's character that the men feel is implied in the sermons. This is somewhat different than the message the Missionaries claim they are trying to convey. As may be recalled, the Missionary message is:

> Regardless of what you have done or been in the past, God forgives you. So stop feeling guilty and start building a better present and more hopeful future.

To the alcoholic, this message is perceived with a different meaning: the alcoholic is the sinner, the Missionaries are the saved, who, in turn, are now going to salvage the sinner. He is unworthy; they are worthy.

As the men explain it:

In a thousand subtle ways, they tell you how worthless you are. God is forgiving you for all the rotten things you've done. You get your ego just about demolished in those sermons. [38]

Most of us feel bad enough about our life without having someone tell us again and again that they love us *anyway*. They keep reminding us how lucky we are to be getting help even though we are worthless. [19]

Of course they try real hard. They say such things as, "It's not too late for you now," and "Jesus was more concerned with the one sheep that strayed than with the 99 in the fold." [45]

To the men the most annoying and degrading part of services is being called upon to "testify."

They want you to get up and declare that you are saved. There's quite a bit of pressure on you to do this. I wasn't brought up to act that way. Catholics don't do that, you know. [20]

When you testify you have to say something like: "I thank Jesus Christ and the Christian Missionaries for giving me hope," or "I was wandering around and didn't have any direction, and didn't know where I was going; but now I've found Jesus and I've got something to try and plan for." You know, that sort of thing. [59]

They put lots of pressure on for testimonials for Christ; and that's in the Sunday service. Once when nobody did, the Major got angry and said, "What is this, a sit-down strike?" And obviously we weren't going to get out of there until somebody testified. (Reported by observer.)

In addition to assuring termination of devotional services, there are certain privileges extended—apparently rewards for testifying, all of which are perceived as bribery by the men:

If you testify, they make it easier for you because you are considered "safe on the program." You might get a private room in which you are allowed to smoke and actually have a transistor radio. [31]

Long-time beneficiaries generally concur with the positive practical advantages of testifying, although they debunk the implication that it is a requirement of continuance on the program:

There exists in the minds of the men a feeling that a point system is kept here . . . That is, if a man cooperates and goes on with the program, he could possibly be moved to employee status. Also, the point system is like money in the bank. A plea for clemency [if you break a rule] is received better if you have shown cooperation with the program. [34]

I have not testified since I've been here. I've given a welcoming speech and read scripture, though. I never felt I had to testify, *but* the fellows who do are favored by the corps officers—they get a pass to go out, get a better room, get a transfer to a job they want. [32]

Most beneficiaries cannot believe that the Missionaries take this testimony seriously. Rather, they suspect the Missionaries must be merely pretending to believe testimonials because to do so serves other more pragmatic purposes:

Of course, the Major, he knows that the men are lying. Well, he sees the same ones over and over. But he doesn't care—just so he can put in his record that so many men were saved that night. [31]

Of course the Missionaries don't believe you; but they smile happily when you testify because it sounds good for the new fellas, and there are around 60 new ones each month on the average. [20]

Now I don't want to sound cynical and skeptical, but if I were in that position [the Missionary officers] with a good salary [42] and a beautiful home filled with donated furniture, I'd keep on trying to convert people regardless of whether I made any headway, too. [31]

Furthermore, the men are bitter because they feel the hypocrisy of false testimony is forced on them. They also must endure some teasing by their fellow beneficiaries as "sellouts":

Men who testify say, "Well, that pays for it another week," and that sort of thing, and obviously they consider it part of the payment for their board and room. [29]

Men in the audience will listen to some testimonials and say under their breaths things like, "Why you lying son-of-a-bitch. See you tomorrow and you'll be drunk as a skunk." [31]

BEING WORKED   Perhaps foremost among the perceived reasons for believing the Christian Missionaries are hypocrites, so far as Christian charity goes, is the feeling that the work-therapy program amounts to "a sweatshop, with wages to match." This is particularly galling to the Skid Row man because he believes that huge profits are being made from both his labor and his well-publicized presence as a beneficiary of charity. He ties all this together when making his judgment of the organization.

To begin with, the men see their assignments in the salvage business as hard labor:

It's very hard work. You have to lug all this stuff up from the basements and pack it in these trucks, and unload the trucks, and then it has to be processed and handled again in the Center where the trucks came in to unload. [60] [43]

The men claim the Missionaries make working conditions even rougher by a long work week with few rest breaks in a day. It is also felt there is a lack of concern shown for the physical incapacities of a man undergoing alcoholic withdrawal, inasmuch as a man must go to work the same day he is admitted, regardless of his current physical state.

> . . . it's worse than a concentration camp. I worked six days a week because they were short-handed when I was there. They almost worked me to death. I left after two months. [38]

> It's a slave labor camp. They crack the whip, believe-you-me. You're not even allowed to sit down, and, uh, you're only allowed to smoke once before lunch and once after lunch. [42]

> It's a five-and-a-half day week and you really *work*. And it doesn't make any difference how you feel. You can be so sick from drinking that you feel like you are going to die, but you still are sent out into the docks to work. [31]

> If you say something about not wanting to work more than eight hours a day they say, "Well here's the door, you can go out the same way you came in." The officers talk just like that to you. [20]

Rather than considering the gratuity as charity, the Skid Row men consider it a sign of exploitation:

> I think it's a crime that they work the men so hard and pay them so little money. [42]

> When you first go in you get $4.00 a week, $1.00 of it is a snack bar ticket to be used at their coffee bar for candy or cigarettes or whatever, and then after they say four weeks but it usually takes about six weeks or five and a half, you get $5.00, one dollar of that is a snack bar ticket. Then after two weeks you go to $6.00; two more weeks you go to $7.00, two weeks after that you go to $8.00, a dollar of which is a snack bar ticket. About a month after that you stay at $8.00, but this time they give you $8.00 cash, they trust you with a dollar not to be spent at their canteen; and if you stay around there you can eventually go to $15.00 a week, but it usually takes pretty nearly a year. [31]

There are, of course, none of the taken-for-granted fringe benefits of most jobs today. Since the men sign an advance agreement to accept beneficiary status, no overtime pay or sick leave is granted.

> There is no such thing as overtime pay, even if you work 10 to 11 hours a day. You have to make up time if you lose an hour, and any overtime you work doesn't count against that. [29]

Say you get a refrigerator dropped on your foot or something: that is *your fault*. If you are required to go to City Hospital, then you have to make up that time working Saturday afternoons. *There are no excuses.* [38] [44]

If you get the flu, they throw you out. They aren't going to keep a non-worker around. If you've been with them a while, they might arrange for the welfare to sign you to go to the City Hospital, but if you are new, its O-U-T and tough on you. [31]

That the size of the gratuity is being taken by the Skid Row men as a reflection of their true worth is obvious from the embarrassment they exhibit when outsiders discover what a small sum of money is given for their efforts:

Sometimes a friend will say to me, "What do they pay you, $75.00 a week and room and board?" and I says, "$5.00 a week." Then he says, "You mean you work for $5.00 a week? You're crazy!" [20]

I was a solicitor for a while and got to wear a suit and tie. I had a respected position and people in town treated me well. As far as they knew, I was a Christian Missionary staff man, making $150.00 a week. Sometimes they would even have coffee with me—something they wouldn't do if they knew I was getting $5.00 a week for my job. [31]

In addition to the gratuity being small, its therapeutically-oriented administration is seen by the beneficiaries as capricious and arbitrary, like the parent who uses his child's allowance as a lever for good behavior:

If you break a rule, or get caught with liquor on your breath, they can bust you back down to $4.00. Or, after working a whole week and you break some rule, they can decide they aren't going to pay you nothin'. And they can do that because it's not a wage, it's a "gratuity," if you please. [31]

Unfortunately, even good behavior will not protect your gratuity entirely . . .

You are expected to *give back* a part of that gratuity in a ceremony called "self-denial." They give out little envelopes with your name on one and and you are supposed to put back a part of the money you earned for that week. The donations are for their missions in Africa or something like that. [59]

If you don't give, one of the officers will say to you, "I don't believe that you are getting our program, Mr. Johnson" . . . so you just about have to give. They have a quota for each man based on his current rate of pay. [31]

Here's how the "self-denial" campaign works. If you want to stay there you'd better kick back a dollar or maybe 50 cents and put your name down—because whoever kicks back gets to stay. They say that if you are ever to get over being an alcoholic that you must learn self-denial and that this is good practice for you! [20]

BEING USED   The men feel that their very presence allows the Christian Missionaries to exploit several avenues of monetary return at once. As beneficiaries of charity, alcoholics aid the Missionaries to claim to be a nonprofit organization while reaping a tidy profit, and qualifying for United Crusade funds. By going to the Missionaries with their alcoholism problem, the men aid the organization in its claim to be a specialized rehabilitation outfit, thereby obtaining federal and state aid. By being designated beneficiaries of a salvage operation, the men encourage public donations that benefit the organization as a whole. Finally, the men provide free labor for the operation of an unusually well-organized business.

Do you know that being a nonprofit organization those guys [the Christian Missionaries] don't have to pay no taxes, no social security, no unemployment compensation, no nothing! No wonder they can make so much money. [18]

They are very good at throwing dinners for organizations, like the Women's League in Pacific City, to show them what a great thing the Missionaries are doing. These are the people who, when they make out their wills—and some of these old biddies have a lot of dough—will remember the Christian Missionaries. [42]

They don't even have to buy the food they give us. Merchants donate second-day bakery goods, sometimes butchers will give a whole pig or a beef carcass. [31]

Now they keep records of how many meals they serve, and how many beds they give out.[45] This is so that they can hit the United Crusade for a larger share, and when the old ladies from other organizations come to visit they will say, "Isn't it nice what they are doing for these poor fellas!" [20]

City fathers of Pacific City are so hoodwinked by the Christian Missionaries as a charitable organization that they give them buildings. They sold them the old Hall of Records a couple of years back for $1.00. What they hadn't looked forward to was that the Missionaries would fix it up a bit, and now that a branch of the freeway is going through there, they are going to make the state pay well for condemning it. [18]

The Skid Row men are not certain of the amount given by the federal and state governments for their rehabilitation, but they know a substantial sum is involved.

Did you know that the Christian Missionaries got a huge grant—$400,000 I understand—from the federal government to work out some kind of program for rehabilitating alcoholics? [45]

As I understand it, they get so much per man in residence from the state —something like $25.00 a week. Now the food is mostly donated, the clothing is donated, the salvage we work on for selling is donated, and we get paid next to nothing—so they pocket most of the $25.00, wouldn't you say? [60]

As the men see it, the Missionaries even come out ahead when they give things away:

Now the Christian Missionaries is very, very jealous of its image to the public. It does a lot of good, and shall we say is smarter in a way than the Red Cross, because the Missionaries will go to a flood area and give things, but immediately go on the radio and tell the public about this, and the public immediately responds to about six or seven times the amount required, and consequently warehouses are bulging. [31]

The business acumen of the Missionaries is considered to be antithetical to true Christian charity and, indeed, evidence of its absence. The Missionaries, their beneficiaries claim, are not so much interested in Almighty God as the almighty dollar. Charity for the Row men is seen as a facade to cover an inordinate interest in the business aspect of the organization.

The Christian Missionaries, especially in Pacific City, do not exactly operate on Christian principles. They run the place more like an auto dealership, and keep statistics, and constantly talk about quotas—either under or going over one. It's quite an efficient organization. [31]

The public have got this rather weird idea that the Missionaries are running around in bonnets and tambourines and, uh, pulling men from the gutters. That's just a minor part of their activities. They are BIG BUSINESS! [42]

To that efficient Major,[46] an accounting sheet which shows a profit is a more welcome sign than the sign of the cross. [31] [47]

Well, I'd say they are about 70 percent businessmen and 30 percent religious—if that. [18]

When it comes to a choice between "Love your fellow brother," or "shall we show a profit?" you can bet that in Pacific City, the Christian Missionaries will opt for the profit. [45]

The methodical way in which solicitation and collection routes are laid out and planned, a reflection of the fierce competition among the various charitable-rehabilitation-salvage agencies that have branches in every large city, is also seen by the alcoholics as *prima facie* evidence of the "true" nature of the Missionaries.

> When I worked for them they had about 30 trucks plus vehicles for other purposes, garbage, and so forth. And you go out in crews, and you have territories, and you cover these territories on the average of once every three months. You carry bags from the Christian Missionaries and give them out and then you go back and pick them up on the next day or so and see what people were able to dig up to put in them. You do an average of 40 to 60 contacts per day. Where people are not home you leave a bag to remind them that the Christian Missionaries have been around. [31]

> There is plenty of competition, it being of course, the St. Francis Organization, the Gladhanders, the Heart of Gold, the Veterans association; and sometimes one of these will beat you right into a choice territory. And then the going is pretty rough and the pickin's pretty slim, in which case we'll jump territory for a day or two and perhaps beat them at their own game. [31]

To the Skid Row men, the degree of organization that the Christian Missionaries show could only spring from a heart devoted to commerce. For further proof, men describe the intricacies of the profit-oriented operations and imply at the same time the gross underpayment of the beneficiaries whose labor, as the men see it, makes the whole operation possible.

> For instance, they have a guy they hired who knows rare old books and he goes through all the books donated and pulls out the good ones and these don't go to the stores—they are sold separately because they have a real price tag on 'em. Why I'll bet they make more than $50,000 a year easy just on books. [31]

> They have their outlets carefully conned. For instance, stuff that needs mending is baled and sent to Mexico and Arabia where people are not so particular about what they wear. Clothes that are worse than that may be sold to paper mills that make paper with a high rag content. Ties are baled and sold by the bale to Mexico—beautiful, expensive ones, it makes no difference—they don't sell well in the stores, so they are not allowed to take up space. [31]

> They have special stores that sell expensive antiques only. [42]

> If it weren't for drunks and poor guys like us, why, uh, the Christian Missionaries would probably starve to death, and they'd have to close up the place, see. [59]

> We subsidize them, the bastards. They pretend they are helping us when actually they are using us to do their dirty salvaging work. [48]

Long-time beneficiaries, however, do not have this same feeling of exploitation.

I don't feel exploited particularly. They [the Missionaries] claim to spend $6,000 per year per man. These guys [the alcoholics] have no conception of what it costs to run this place. Nobody goes out and recruits them. When they walk in they are praying they'll be allowed to stay. They come hungry, cold, and hung over and anything is fine. By the end of two weeks they are starting to complain. [32]

The only time I was sober was when I stayed with them. [60]

They have a pretty good program, especially when you compare it to going to jail. [33]

SEEING "THEIR MONEY" SPENT   Where does all the money go? Skid Row men would like to know because . . . "it is really the money we should be paid, plus what they get from the government and charity funds for being so good to us." Many of the accounts of how the Christian Missionaries spend their money are passed from beneficiary to beneficiary, like folk tales. They are recounted here because they form part of the grounds on which judgments of the Missionaries are made, and not because they are necessarily true.

There is a hierarchy of worthiness, at least in the minds of the men, as to what is done with "their money":

The following expenditures are considered to be "all right" . . .

Well, now they have various homes for needy people. They don't make any person pay who isn't financially able. It's a very worthwhile thing. [20]

They support missionary schools in Africa. [28]

They have a religious retreat in one of their country centers and send some of us men along with some of their officers. You spend your time in meditation and meeting and talking about the Bible or perhaps there's a subject selected, some aspect about the Bible, and it's enjoyable. [31]

A less acceptable expenditure is the maintenance of Missionary staff officers, which the Skid Row man suspects comes directly from salvage operations.

The officers get a house, car, staples, and furniture free from the stuff donated, so that even if they are poorly paid they have, in fact, $200.00 walking-around money—*our money*, really. [17]

Well, they [the Missionaries] use the money to pay the officers their small salaries—they really don't make much, $38.00 to $58.00 a week. But then they make up for it by furnishing them a home and then buy homes out in the Pacific City suburbs for them. Then, they pay all their medical expenses, their children's college education, plus letting them have the first pick of what comes in. We furnish the money for all that. [31]

Even less justified expenditures, so far as the Skid Row man is concerned, include:

Well, what do you suppose supports their officer training schools? We do, you damn well know it, don't you? They have to recruit these people, and give them uniforms, and train them, and all that takes money. [42]

Furthermore, the men suspect that some of the donated material is snatched up by alert Missionary officers not only for their own use, but also for resale to augment their rather small salaries:

This one Major had a sister in Valley City who opened a thrift shop. And he'd go out on truck calls himself, and then keep the best stuff for his sister to sell.

He'd pick out the choice things. He was finally stopped. The others got a bit jealous because he was takin' and makin' three times more than the average. (As told to observer.)

Major Davenport who lives out in the suburbs of Pacific City has his big double garage just *loaded* with stuff people have donated to charity, they think. He goes down on the docks early in the morning and picks stuff to be sent to his home . . . color TV sets and stuff like that. (As told to observer.)

The above are seen as using only a small portion of the huge profits the Missionaries make. The rest is thought to be invested for an even larger return:

Now they [the Christian Missionaries] are supposedly nonprofit, but let me tell you something. They make so much money that they finally had to set up another corporation to handle and invest it. This was partially because ever since President Kennedy stopped the shipping out of money, they couldn't send near as much abroad. So they set up a branch—the National Reclamation Company—which spends its time investing the profit of that nonprofit organization. [31]

They are so rich that they have an AA rating in Dunn and Bradstreet. [42]

They have their own seat on the Stock Exchange. They own a controlling interest in a big food store chain. [18]

Some men assume that no amount of sleuthing could account for all the money the Christian Missionaries have and all the ways in which it is diverted:

I mean that's like asking what does the Pope do with the money the
Catholic Church gets. You might as well ask that. [29]

It is on this general tone that the Skid Row alcoholic usually leaves the
subject of exploitation of beneficiaries as a sign of hypocrisy.

The long-term resident is a bit more philosophical about the use to
which the Missionaries put their profits, although he does concur that the
amount is considerable:

A lot of these guys think the Christian Missionaries make a lot of money—
and, as a matter of fact, I'm pretty sure that they do make a good profit.
But they use it wisely. They probably put out more charity per dollar
than any other charitable agency. [33]

SOCIAL STAGNATION   The men are not eager to develop "camaraderie"
with other men at the Center, although the Missionaries deem this an
important part of their therapy. Rather, they would prefer to have some
social life elsewhere, away from the Center where they both live and work.

However, house rules, coupled with the small gratuity, puts a crimp in
any outside friendships the men may try to maintain or resurrect. The
result is that free-time recreation revolves around the Center, creating a
sort of intensely institutionalized isolation that the men feel is worse than
the so-called social isolation of the chronic drunk on Skid Row.

Having any kind of real social life is out. You'd have to have a steady job
and better pay. You couldn't go with a girl friend, you couldn't do
anythin', any special activities or anythin', cause you would be workin'
all the time and you have to be in so early at night. [60]

You can't have any friends at all. You can go out after dinner and be
back by 11:00 P.M., but they purposely have dinner late so that you can't
be out long. [59]

How can you take a woman out on four dollars a week? [20]

Recreation really comes down to going to the recreation room and watching TV or shooting pool. Some centers allow card playing—some think
it is a sin. [26]

They have bingo games which last until 9:30–10:00 o'clock, and of course
by then it's too late to go out. We go to the games because it's a chance
to win $1.00 sometimes or a snack bar ticket that can be sold. When you
make only $5.00 a week, $1.00 is a lot of money. [31]

Additionally, the Skid Row men claim Christian Missionary officers
show little friendliness toward them, and this becomes another basis for
a charge of hypocrisy. Specifically, the Missionaries lack warmth, friendliness, and compassion toward their charges:

They [the officers] never mingle with us guys. They run this place and give sermons like they was better than us, and they don't come to the lounge and talk with us or anything like that. The only time I saw the Major downstairs chatting friendly with the men and making comments on their pool games and stuff like that was when there were guests for the Sunday morning service. As soon as the guests were gone the Major left, just like that, 30 seconds later. (As told to participant-observer.)

The residents of long-standing agree with this, but are not particularly upset about it . . .

Almost to a man, the officers are not consistent in their reaction to you. First, there is some warmth and then, zoom! A curtain goes down, and they are real cool. [34]

The officers remain distant, but then I don't think they should get too friendly with beneficiaries—this can lead to fraternization. [32]

PSYCHOLOGICAL AID FOR THE DRINKING PROBLEM Inasmuch as group therapy is offered only to the more hopeful cases, many Skid Row alcoholics are not invited to participate. Thus their attitude toward psychological aid may reflect the usual feelings of those who are left out.

Well, up until just a few months ago they were operating under a $300,000 or $500,000 federal grant which was awarded five years ago. They had to show some kind of staff for that so they got a couple of psychologists and two social workers—quite heavy stuff. [31]

They give you some kind of psychological test, but they never talk the results over with you, so what's the use? [45] 48

Of course, many of the men, having made the loop repeatedly, are somewhat jaded about psychologists and psychiatrists, anyway.

I didn't even try to see the psychiatrist there. I've been to so many psychiatrists in my time that I've, uh, retired, you know, I've retired from that. I figure if they haven't helped by now, they aren't going to. [40]

Long-time beneficiaries have kinder words for group therapy:

I think you will find that persons who have had group therapy are more successful than those who have not. [35] 49

JOB HUNTING AID From the Skid Row alcoholic's point of view, getting a job and thus beginning to reintegrate with outside world activities is the single most important step in his rehabilitation after he has dried out. As one man put it:

It's not the drinking that worries me. I just wish to goodness I had a job
and was making my own way. Then I'd have something to look forward
to. (As told to observer.)

When a man goes to the Christian Missionaries for help, one of the
services promised him if he sticks with the program is that of vocational
counseling. From the sound of the title, most first-timers assume this refers
to aid in finding employment on the "outside" after they have dried out
and regained their physical and spiritual strength. Some men claim they
were told that the Missionaries maintain employment files listing current
jobs available in the area.

Well, the story they gave me was, "If you stay here for six months and
have a clean record, there's a possibility we can find you employment." [45]

The men complain the vocational counselor wants to do group therapy
with them instead of finding them a job.

Furthermore, the men say that the Missionaries make it as difficult as
possible to look for a job on your own.

Well, everyone knows it takes time to find a job and go out on interviews
and they [the Missionaries] just won't let you go. [42]

Well, for one thing, what are you going to do about giving a phone
number, or an address? The minute you do that, you have two problems.
(1) The employer knows where you are staying, and (2) the Missionaries
know you are looking around. And you know what they say, "Aren't you
satisfied with the program?" [60]

I defy anyone to find a job when he has only Saturday afternoon and
Sunday free. [38]

The men are bitter because they feel forced into dishonest strategies
in order to job hunt.

Well, you can tell 'em your mother is dying and you have to have the
day off to see her, or you got to go to the dentist, or something like that.
And of course, you make the time up. [50]

Many of the men are convinced the Missionaries do not want them to
find other work for the obviously selfish desire to guarantee a labor force
for the salvage operations:

They don't seem very happy when you get a job. They say, "What's the
matter with the program? You ought to stay here on the program
longer." [45]

The Missionaries are reluctant to find you work even though they have promised to do that. They say, "We don't consider that anyone really on this program of rehabilitation can lick their drinking in less than a minimum of six months or, uh, preferably a year." You see, well, this is right away guaranteeing them six months of steady labor. That's why they drag their feet in this area. [26]

Although they promised to help me find work, they never once sent me out on an interview. Why should they? They were getting a hard day's work out of me for practically nothing! [47]

Long-time beneficiaries do not complain about the lack of job-hunting help:

There are men here who have these dreams of getting a job and starting over. I've never succumbed to these fantasies. [35]

The Rules Men Live by—
Getting "Pinched" and Getting "Busted"

LIVING IN   Unlike their attitudes toward the program, the beneficiaries have high praise for the housing, the food, and the clothing they receive, although they do not consider this, combined with their gratuity, to be adequate pay for their work in the salvage operation. Men describe the facilities in the following manner:

The residence is nice . . .
The place is real clean. The beds are the best and rooms are well heated and well ventilated. You start out six to a room. If you keep your nose clean and don't drink, you gradually get moved into a more and more private room—four in a room, two in a room, and then your own room. This takes six months to a year.

Clothing is given the men also . . .
Now when a fella comes in here, he's given a clothing order; he'll be allowed, depending on the type of job he has, a good pair of shoes, perhaps a pair of socks, an undershirt, shorts, shirt, work shirt, and for church purposes a white shirt and a necktie, if he doesn't have one.

Food is adequate, but not exciting or of gourmet quality . . .
Generally the food is okay: however there are few steaks or chops or things like that. There will usually be macaroni—the diet has a high quantity of starch. Sometimes you get ham or something like that, if a pig has been donated. For lunch you get baloney or baloney and cheese sandwiches and coffee.

Recreation facilities are available . . .
The canteen is perfect: two television rooms, one color TV and one black
and white, a big billiard table, a pool table, and reading material. There
are bingo games, checkers, and once in a while a movie is shown.

However, much of the good feeling engendered by the physical plant is
lost because the men living at the Center feel that they are treated like
children who cannot be trusted.

They actually have "sniffers" on the desk and when you go to get your
key, they smell your breath and you go on report. That means that you
have to see the clinical psychologist. If they don't like you, it's out right
now. [31]

Furthermore, punishment is not always based on the crime, but on
Center needs:

I always advise newcomers not to even make a telephone call from a bar,
for if they see you coming out, then you have had it, unless you are in a
job which is both essential and difficult to fill. [31] [50]

To be caught [pinched] with a bottle in their possession, or with liquor
on their breath too frequently, can result in being thrown out, or reduced
in room and gratuity level [busted]. This being the case, the men take
reasonable precautions not to get caught:

First of all, just be sure that you don't have a bottle in your hands. Then
you are automatically out. However, if you hide it in or around the building, who is to know whether it's yours or mine? Keep it out of your room;
they shake down your room just like in jail. [28]

The sniffers at the desk are good at catching you. Some men fool them by
using those little bottles of stuff that kill your breath instantly. I carry
a tube of toothpaste with me inside my coat and just about a half a block
away from the Center front door I put a coupla squirts of that in my
mouth, mush it around, and walk right up to the desk and get my key—
they can't tell a thing. [31]

Perhaps the most annoying thing as far as the Skid Row alcoholics are
concerned is the administration of the rules by ex-alcoholics who stay at
the Christian Missionaries. These are the men who are assigned to the
front desk or the switchboard. They are loyal to the Missionaries rather
than old drinking cronies and, like the proverbial convert, have become
stronger advocates of sobriety than their employers. This annoys the Skid
Row alcoholic much more than the perceived holier-than-thou attitude
of the Missionaries themselves. The men complain that:

The ex-alcoholics act like they are better than the alcoholics . . . These guys get a regular job with the Christian Missionaries (they are former drunks themselves) and now they are drunk with power—it's the old story of the corporal trying on the general's pants and getting a certain amount of authority. They get so they live in a very little world and it revolves around the activities of the Christian Missionaries. [20]

There's nothing colder to an alcoholic than an ex-alcoholic who has converted to the Christian Missionaries. They will actually ignore old friends of theirs who come into the place . . . pretend they don't see them. [59] [51]

I've heard the ex-alcoholics say to the men, "Why, we could clear all you bums out and fill the place up in a day." [29]

The alcoholics resent the frequent locker inspections and other precautions to prevent petty theft—even while admitting theft does take place.

You know, a guy is always suspect of stealing when he works for the Christian Missionaries. If you go in with something like a little radio or a shaver, you've got to check it until you leave. They go through your lockers, too, and if they find something and you can't explain how you come by it honestly, they assume you stole it. Why, once you leave the dorm in the morning, you can't even go back for a jacket or something if it should start to rain. They are afraid you will try to stash something in your locker or try to get something out. How's that for Christian trust? [45]

Retribution for petty theft can be devastating. A man may be immediately expelled, minus any gratuity he would have received.

I've heard men say in the dead of winter, "But I haven't got a cent." And the Missionaries say, "That's too bad, buddy. We found an electric shaver in your locker, and you have no sales slip for it. Out." [18]

Long-time residents see the rules as necessarily forced by the actions of the beneficiaries:

All the rules are here because they have been proven necessary. For instance, you can't go back to your room after you leave it because people sack out, hide out, go into the lockers of others, hide stuff they are pilfering, and hide bottles of liquor. That's why they have to shake down the lockers, too. [32]

Alternatives to "Getting the Program"

Six months seems to most Skid Row men like a dangerously long time to stay at the Missionaries. The major fear among the men is that they may become a "regular" at the Christian Missionaries—a Skid Row man who stays so long that he cannot make it on the outside, and so becomes an employee—a sort of live-in domestic for the group. This is, as many of the men see it, the true aim of "the program" rather than "straightening out."

> Some of 'em just stay there. They can't get away to hunt for a job; they can't get enough money together to go away on their own. They just give up and become a "regular." (As told to observer.)

It is true that length of stay is associated with becoming a regular employee. Of those men who terminated to take staff positions in the Missionary salvage business, 65 percent had been with the rehabilitation program six months or longer. Table 18 gives the distribution. It may be compared with the average length of stay of men who terminate to take jobs on the "outside" (see Table 19, p. 209).

TABLE 18. *Length of Residence of Beneficiaries who Become Regular Employees of Christian Missionaries, (1967)*

Length of stay on program *	Percent of Beneficiaries (N = 20) †
2 months	10
3 months	10
4 months	5
5 months	10
6 months	5
7 months	15
8 months	—
9 months	5
10 months	—
11 months	5
one year	10
two years	15
three years	5
four years	5

Source: Missionary records on terminations.

* The stated time period can be taken as referring to the lower limit of the implied interval, with the upper limit being just under the next category.
† Not all remain as employees. Some "slip" and go back to drinking.

It is generally accepted among the beneficiaries that there has to be something wrong with a man who would become a regular rather than take his chances on the street.

> I know one fella down there and he's a little mentally deficient. So the Missionaries let him wear a suit and hand out programs at night. You ask

him what time it is and he'll look at his watch and tell you, and you ask him again one minute later and he'll say, "Well, I don't know." He has to look at his watch again. Those kind of people the Missionaries probably help. [20]

I've known guys that's been with them [the Missionaries] three and four years. Of course, they are the broken ones. Oh, it's a very scary thing. [29]

Thus, to the men, being "on the program" means being exploited, being socially isolated, being degraded, and eventually being "broken"—a certain treadmill to oblivion.

On the other hand, "getting institutionalized," while not desirable, is viewed with considerable less approbation than "getting the program," although it is not judged to be an ideal arrangement by any means. "Getting institutionalized," so far as the men are concerned, refers to "working" the Missionaries and other similar shelters from city to city, rather than staying in one and seriously trying the "program" or trying to land a job on the outside. This approach is preferable to taking the program seriously because it leaves a man with a feeling he is still running his own life, even if he is doing it by playing at being "dependent." (The Missionaries, of course, are aware of this phenomenon and have their own argot for describing such a man—he is referred to as a "rounder." (See Footnote 10, this chapter.)

After a while, it seems like you get institution-wise, and fall back, and depend on them for a livelihood. [45]

Some guys make a career out of the Christian Missionaries. They go from one to another all over the country. Now this time of the year they'll come out here on account of the weather. Come summer, they'll start heading north. [41]

Those institutions get to be a crutch. In other words, it's so much easier to come here than fight it out and try to get a job. [47]

A braver alternative, of course, is to "take off"—leave the Center and try one's luck on the streets.

I'd been there a couple of months and I said to myself, "This is just plain stupid staying here. I mean working all week and getting $5.00, $6.00, and $7.00, nothin' to look forward to, and no chance of bettering myself while I'm here. If I don't leave, I'll be stuck here." [28]

Of all the stations on the loop, leaving the Christian Missionaries is done with the least amount of formal observation of the proprieties. As previously mentioned, for the most part, men merely walk off, often with-

out packing their gear. Seldom do they inform the officers of their intentions.[52]

I just took off. I took what I had on my back and that's all. [14]

Over the weekend a lot of fellas get drunk and say, "To hell with it," and
they beat it; sometimes as many as 12 are missing on Monday morning.
[29]

I just got sick of it and one night I went out a window. Someday I'll go
back and get my stuff from them. [42]

The men are always saying, "I'll be glad to get rid of this damn place."
And they might take off one night, go out on a pass and never come back.
They meet a friend on the street who says, "Let's have a few drinks," and
they're off on the bum again. They can always decide to go to another
city and another Christian Missionary Center. (As told to observer.)

Table 19 indicates the various ways in which leaving the Missionaries is
handled by the men, according to Missionary records.

TABLE 19. *Leave-Taking Conditions of Beneficiaries of the Christian Missionaries in 1967*

Leave-taking Condition	Percent
VOLUNTARY	($N = 718$)
No formal termination	48
AWOL (i.e., missing)	37
† Walk off job	5
† Walk out of residence	2
† Walk out, misc.	4
Formal termination ‡	38
Left, no plans disclosed	21
Left for employment	15
Admitted to hospital (veterans, city, or mental)	4
Became Christian Missionary employee	3
Went to school	*
Returned home	*
INVOLUNTARY	
Rule infraction	14

Source: Christian Missionary termination records.

* Less than ½ of 1 percent.
† Unlike AWOL, leave-taking was witnessed, although not formal. (Men often walk
off a job in anger.)
‡ More than one reason was possible in the formal termination procedure.

The Center as a Station on the Circle

For the "wised up" man, that is, one who has made the circle before,
there are three major incentives to becoming a "beneficiary" of the Chris-

tian Missionaries: (1) to get a temporary roof over his head and a full stomach (this means that all other approaches to these needs have failed and other stations on the rehab route are temporarily unavailable or more undesirable); (2) to make a stake so as to have some chance at a new start on an independent life, or (3) at least to get "squared away."

A ROOF AND A FULL STOMACH

First of all, it's a place to stay. You can forget the therapy and rehabilitation nonsense and the long-term, uh, aid, and all that. I mean the important thing is that you're busted and in bad physical shape. [60]

I was down to where it was either the Christian Missionaries or nothin'! [13]

The Christian Missionaries meant nothing to me actually except a roof over my head at the time. [19]

The Christian Missionaries are considered a good temporary haven also for those who plan to use their pension, when they get it, to live on.

I know fellows who have been with the Christian Missionaries seven-eight years. They get their social security and bingo, that's what they were waiting for, and they are out of there. [20]

"MAKING A STAKE"   A stake is more than moving-around funds. It is the amount of money a man thinks would give him "another chance to make it." The stake is seen as paying for a room in a decent neighborhood, and money for several weeks' food. It represents a suit presentable enough for job hunting, along with shoes, shirt, and a tie. There are back union dues to pay, and maybe a reinstatement fee. Equipment or tools are often needed for some jobs, and in the case of Skid Row alcoholics, were long ago hocked for liquor. Most men estimate that around $300.00 to $500.00 minimum is needed for a decent stake, although few men have ever really tried to budget minimum requirements in detail.

Some men actually attempt to save their gratuity—by denying themselves cigarettes, candy, gum, and movies until they have several hundred dollars. But this is an exceedingly slow process and they cannot ignore their needs for shaving cream, razors, and other toilet necessities, as well as their 50 percent of medical needs, which must come out of the gratuity.[53]

Some of the attempts of the Row men to augment this regular payment take an unusual form. Bingo is one of the profitable amusements offered by Missionaries, as well as other Christian charities of the area, that is utilized by the men to get their hands on a little cash.

Down between Third and Fourth, in an alley at the Grant Hotel, they run a bingo game and it costs 10 cents a card. And whatever is in the pot goes to the winner. You can sometimes get a couple of dollars that way. [18]

The Catholic churches have bingo games during the week and they sell tickets for a dollar or three for $2.00 and there you can really make some money if you are lucky. If a fellow makes something, he kisses the Christian Missionaries "goodbye" right now. He probably won't even bother to go back and pack. [31]

On Saturday and Sunday nights the Christian Missionaries have bingo games and these bingo games are in the form of 12 prizes. It's a long session because they use letters that are put up on a board, interlocking letters, like SA or WS and each time you win you get a dollar snack bar ticket. Well, on the sixth running of the bingo game you get a $2.40 snack bar ticket, see. You can sell these tickets to the men who have just come in and plan to stay a while. Usually the $1.00 tickets go for 70 cents. Either you save it for your stake or you can buy a whole fifth of wine for 60 cents. [31]

The men also sell services to each other. One enterprising man ran a washing-ironing service at the Center.

I done all the ironing and washin' for the guys and got paid for that. Charged five cents a shirt and ten cents for pants. Guys paid for that themselves, and besides I was drawing my $5.00 a week from the Missionaries, too. [9]

At Christmas time the men can earn $10.00 a day soliciting public donations ringing a bell over the Missionary kettles, but this offers a certain threat to self-esteem—public exposure:

It's a pretty good deal, getting a chance to ring the Christmas kettle bell. They have the city divided up into territories which they stake out. The only problem is that you keep hoping that none of your boyhood friends, your classmates, come by and see you ringin' the bell and collectin'—at least that's how I feel. [20]

Magazines collected while working on the truck are also a source of revenue.

The guys take these magazines during their lunch break and go through them furiously and pull out the coupons. You know, Lady Prell, 7 cents off with this coupon, 10 cents off this particular item and so on. They'll gather $6.00, $7.00, $8.00 worth of those coupons together and then go down to the Chinese stores downtown where he pays 50 cents on the dollar. He checks his stock and he has 30 cans of so-and-so shoe shine and they're gonna get a nickel off. If you have 40 of these coupons, that's too bad, he don't buy no more than shown on his invoice. A fella can make $2.50 easy that way, and the Chinaman gets the same profit when he turns the coupons in. [31] (Also reported by observer.)

Making headway in a savings program is, as might be expected, very slow, given the above resources.

Well, you know that *anytime you leave,* you're gonna leave there about the same as you went in, except you're gonna be a whole lot healthier and have more clothes; *but you ain't gonna have that stake.* [61]

It's sort of pitiful. You'll hear the guys talking about that they have $11.00 saved and with their next pay they'll have $15.00 or $16.00 depending on whether they have to buy razors or something like that. (Notes of observer.)

I'm about to get a savings program going to have my teeth taken care of. The Missionaries pay half. I hope to get to the point where I can spend $5.00 a week and save $10.00. [35]

Those activities that pay more range from the legitimate to the illegitimate, from the fantastic to the impossible.

A man fortunate enough to have a driver's license is eligible to drive a truck for the Christian Missionaries at $1.25 an hour, plus overtime on Saturdays, with a bonus for all the rags and clothes brought in over a certain amount. However, the recipient then must pay $18.00 a week room and board to the Missionaries.

The reason these truck drivers work for the Christian Missionaries for $1.25 an hour is that it is the only job they can get. They are ex-alcoholics and it's the only thing available. [60]

Men who have a pension (and an outside address where it can be sent) can go to the Christian Missionaries for bare necessities of life and thus save their pension for the "stake."

If you get a pension for disability or something, say $50.00 or $60.00 a month, then you can go to the Missionaries and live for nothing and bank your pension, and git stiff every weekend off the gratuity they pay you. [61]

Within this environment of miniscule opportunities, a Skid Row alcoholic working for the Christian Missionaries sees many valuable objects being donated, and often he feels there is little chance he will ever receive what he considers to be his fair share of these gifts. From time to time this temptation proves too great, and a man will risk being expelled from the residence by taking a transistor radio, a typewriter, or a portable television, hiding it in his locker, and then trying to get it out past the desk to sell it in Thieves' Market or to the fences operating in the bars near the Center.

Such activity is defined as proper by the men because, in some ways, they feel this is merely stealing what is coming to them for their work, or repaying in kind for the treatment they have to endure in order to barely survive.

Talk about stealing, if working a guy, say ten hours a day and not paying him for it isn't stealing, I don't know what is! [61]

It is through the realm of the fantastic and impossible that the men reveal the true hopelessness of their position. Most common of the hopes that circulate among the men trying to make a stake is that of the "big find" made while cleaning out a house or carrying furniture. This is the billfold or the currency found in a donated chair or under a donated rug. Such conversations run like this:

Suppose we found $600,000 in the place we cleaned out today. Why, that would be $200,000 for each of the three of us. Now, if I had that amount I'd take off for Oklahoma and buy me a little farm . . .

Suppose it was only $20,000. That still wouldn't be bad. That would get me out of here and maybe I'd get me a partner and we'd open up an eating place, nothing fancy . . . (Conversation reported by observer.)

According to men who have been on the scene, such daydreaming goes on for hours and rivals talk of glories of the past.

GETTING "SQUARED AWAY" AND "TAKING OFF"   If making a stake is next to impossible at the Christian Missionaries, a man can always check in to "get his breath," or "get squared away." This refers to an enforced period of sobriety he feels necessary in order to think out his next step. (Since this is one of the avowed purposes of the Missionaries, they have a claim for success here—even if the content of the meditation does not fulfill their hopes.)

It's a place to stay until you get squared away, until your stomach is full, and *your head is clear*, and you got some decent clothes. [59] (Emphasis mine.)

It's the place to go when you want to *think things over*—where you want to go from here. Sometimes you just go to be able to do that without worrying where the next meal is coming from. [31] (Emphasis mine.)

Most of these men, they've lost their friends and relatives and this [the Christian Missionaries] is a port in a storm. It's a *time to reassess their lives* according to their sense of values and then get out of here. Everybody wants to get out of here, that's the talk all the time along that line. (Resident in conversation with observer; emphasis mine.)

A man feels he is squared away when he has temporarily stopped drinking, cleaned himself up, obtained some clean clothes, and is generally feeling better. He becomes anxious to be back on the streets drinking with friends or trying to "make it" (neither of which he considers possible while living with the Christian Missionaries).

When a man reaches this juncture, having convinced himself of the impossibility of making that "stake" in his present surroundings, he usually "takes off."

For those who stay there is more pity than censure:

You can't blame the guys who stay there. Those Christian Missionaries got them by the balls. (Resident in conversation with participant observer.) [54]

IV

STRATEGIES
OF
SURVIVAL

8

The Return to Society

The Prodigal Son Syndrome
in Rehabilitation

And the son said unto him, Father, I have sinned against heaven, and in thy sight, and am no more worthy to be called thy son.

But the father said to his servants, bring forth the best robe, and put it on him; and put a ring on his hand, and shoes on his feet.

And bring hither the fatted calf, and kill it; and let us eat, and be merry:

For this my son was dead and is alive again; he was lost and is found. And they began to be merry.

St. Luke 15:21–24

INTRODUCTION

An oft-stated goal of all institutions on the loop is to get their charges "back into society." Indeed, this is the primary purpose of the rehabilitation of *all* social deviants—to return them to the community, much in the way the Biblical prodigal son returns to his father, somewhat the worse for wear, but contrite and reformed.[1]

For alcoholics and drug users this idea of returning to society is often broadened so that maintenance of sobriety or "normal consciousness" is equated or at least coupled with return to society; and the two are then referred to by such terms as "return to reality" or "getting these people back to the real world."[2]

The assumption, quite logically, is that sobriety cannot long be maintained without the reinforcing assistance of respectable community and peer group pressures. Likewise, reentry into society is thought not to be

217

possible unless the person is sober and "in contact" with others. Each is seen as dependent on the other.[3] This belief is actually part of the philosophy of "working with the whole man" that appears in various forms in rehabilitation literature as well as among educators [4] and medical social workers, to name but a few other professions espousing this approach.[5]

In studies and conferences devoted to the Skid Row problem drinker, as well as in the course of informal conversation with professional therapists and welfare workers, these sentiments are voiced repeatedly, albeit in different forms:

These men need help in order to get back into society. [A25]

After a man has got back into society, he is asked to report periodically on his progress.[6]

Back in society, a functioning and responsible citizen [Final caption on a chart explaining therapy for the alcoholic at State Mental Hospital]

The Welfare Home offers no guarantees of success, but it gives a man a chance to get back to reality.[7]

We must help him [the Skid Row derelict] realize that he can "come back" and resolve to try.[8]

Its [the halfway house] aim, starting with sobriety, is gradually to introduce the men to jobs, independence, and respectability in the community. . . .

It [employment] also builds up their self-esteem and self-respect, hopefully, and gradually giving them a feeling of community acceptance.[9]

Each station on the loop has a different program to accomplish this reentry into the world of accepted persons. The urban renewal expert plans to bulldoze Skid Row buildings; the municipal judge gives a "kickout" to a man with a job, and a sentence to the man without a home; the Jail Branch Clinic psychiatric social worker attempts to get the offender to "face his real problems and learn how to handle them"; and the State Mental Hospital staff arranges for some of its patients to work out in the community. At the Welfare Home for Homeless Men, employers who are willing to take a chance on the alcoholic are patiently searched out. The Christian Missionaries give dual priority to returning to God and to rebuilding socially-approved habits of working and living that should equip a man to take his "rightful place in society."

With such aid, the Skid Row man leaves almost any station on the loop cleaned up, sobered up, dried out, physically built up, psychologically investigated and "purged," perhaps spiritually renewed, and sometimes even occupationally placed.

However, despite the hopeful pronouncements of the stations and the rather elaborate programs to implement them, most Skid Row alcoholics eventually return to Skid Row, to heavy drinking, and then back onto the loop, regardless of which was the last station visited.

Professional assessments of causes for such a high rate of recidivism were discussed in previous chapters. Focus on the Skid Row men, their characteristics, and their reaction to therapy is the common denominator of all such theories.

Recapitulated briefly, these theories are:

1. The Skid Row alcoholic was not sincere about his therapy or rehabilitative efforts in his behalf. He merely wanted to dry out so that he could drink comfortably [and heavily] again. He never intended to try to get back into society or to stop drinking permanently.[10]

2. The Skid Row alcoholic stopped his therapy or treatment prematurely. If he had stuck it out longer, it would have done him some good and he might have gotten back into society.[11]

3. The Skid Row alcoholic is immature. He does not wish to face up to his true problem, which is that he is using excessive drinking as a way of coping with life. He needs to locate some source of inner strength so that he can do without alcohol as a crutch.

No alternative explanation of the mystery of recidivism among Skid Row alcoholics has been offered by the alcoholic himself. The rationale he gives for failure to stop drinking and "make it back" seems inadequate when one considers that resumption of heavy drinking and the institutionalization it brings represent a serious setback to his ultimate rehabilitation. Yet, often, when he returns to an institution and is asked why he began to drink again, the Skid Row man's explanation is extremely vague.[12]

The most frequently given answer is:

And then I decided to hell with it, and I started drinking.

Other men concur that when they took their first drink on the outside, it was no agonizing decision, but more a spur of the moment action:

It wasn't any real *decision*. I ran into an old drinking friend, and it was good to see him, and we went to a bar together, and that did it.

I had a mishap while I was out [of the Mental Hospital]. The guy who had a job for me was in an accident and couldn't use me right away after all, so I went on a toot. I waited around for a while, but I really had nothing else to do. [27]

Of all the respondents asked in the course of this study to explain how they happened to return to heavy drinking, very few offered what might be called extenuating circumstances:

I hadn't been drinking for months, and my two brothers were on their way from the East Coast to visit me, when I received word that they were both killed in an auto accident about ten miles outside of Pacific City. It was such a blow that I was lost. I just started drinking again. [49]

Such a general absence of reasonably-acceptable explanations for resumption of drinking offers no viable grounds for disagreement with professionals and lends credence to their theories of character weaknesses among alcoholics and premature cessation of therapy. However, emphasis on explaining the failure to benefit from therapy has obscured another possible avenue of investigation of the causes of recidivism—the nature of the task of getting back into society or to reality, and the assortment of problems that are encountered by a Skid Row alcoholic on "the road back."

MAKING A COMEBACK: ENVISIONED GOALS AND PROFESSIONAL PLANS

What is the society to which the professional rehabilitator would like the Skid Row alcoholic to return? How does a person who has "checked out" for several years, as many alcoholics have, gain readmittance and eventually long-term acceptance in this society?

The Society of the Agent of Social Control

In 1943 C. Wright Mills accused sociologists of having a middle-class bias in their discussions of "social problems." By analyzing their textbooks and articles, Mills was able to isolate the following consistencies in their descriptions of society:

There is a strong tendency for the term "society" to be practically assimilated to, or conceived largely in terms of primary groups, and small homogeneous communities.

What content there is [of actual life] is a propaganda for conformity to small-town, middle-class milieu.

[Sociologists] do not consider the difficulties which some [persons] face in trying to be middle-class.

[Sociologists see] the ideal person [as] "socialized," the other "selfish." [13]

If the documents of field service investigators, probation officers, psychiatric social workers, adoption agencies, and mental health hospital staffs considering discharge of patients are any indication, agents of social control have been strongly influenced by the sociologists' view of what society and its inhabitants should be like. These agents are, for the most part, middle-class in upbringing and in current perspective. The yardstick and goal for the activities of others is this all-pervasive background:

> The ideal family is the nuclear, intact family. Courts of conciliation, adoption bureaus, juvenile probation departments, to name a few, look more kindly on this form of family than any other, press for its maintenance, and favor it with decisions.[14]

> The place of the man is out working on a steady job in the community. The place of the woman, if she is married, is in the home.[15]

> The home is a single-family dwelling, or a sizeable apartment; there are ample bedrooms for the children and the parents. It is kept clean.[16]

> The middle-class ideal is the adjustment toward which most individual and group therapy is oriented. There is great emphasis on getting along with people, seeing your own faults, and being responsive and responsible.[17]

Thus the society the Skid Row alcoholic is urged to enter is a middle-class, small-town society. It is epitomized by descriptions of social relations to be found in such studies as *Middletown*,[18] *Small Town in Mass Society*,[19] *Plainville, USA*,[20] *Elmtown's Youth*,[21] and *Yankee City*.[22] It is a place where people are in fairly intimate communication with each other and have a sense of belonging together. There also, people engage in a division of labor that is not so complicated as to be outside the realm of understanding of the average person. Norms of hard work, cleanliness, sobriety, and responsibility toward others prevail and are rewarded. It is what might be called "mainstream" society, since all social deviants are either generally ignored, or sanctioned and well controlled.[23] Furthermore, it is a society small enough to notice a newcomer and formally admit or reject him.

This is not to say that the agent of social control tells the Skid Row alcoholic to "try to get into middle-class society," or that he even urges his client to get a white collar job and live in a respectable neighborhood. Quite the contrary, the Skid Row man is urged to get a very low status job.[24] If he has welfare support, he is even sent to a Skid Row hotel. However, the *implications* of subjects discussed in group therapy and in private conferences are that by following middle-class norms, even in a lower class setting, gradual movement and acceptance into mainstream society will eventually follow.

As is evidenced by the excerpts quoted, the assumption is that the Skid Row alcoholic is *returning*, perhaps to a social niche kept with faith and hope for him all these years, much in the way that the penitent and remorseful prodigal son returned to his father's home.

As one agent of social control put it:

> . . . the staff [of the New Horizon Center] make sure he [the Skid Row alcoholic] understands their interest in him *because society wants him back.* (Emphasis mine.) [25]

The Reentry Plan

How is a man to gain entrance into this society which the agents depict? Each station on the loop has a *plan*, whether stated or implied, complicated or simple, to guide the alcoholic towards ultimate reentry.

A plan is a vision of how things are going to be. A plan implies foresight and usually envisions activity and progress toward a goal. When a plan is presented and discussed, the general assumption is that if the outlined tasks are performed successfully, the goal will be reached.

Plans for the Skid Row alcoholic vary in detail. Discharge from many stations on the loop may be preceded by a conference during which agents of social control attempt to help the man formulate the steps he should take for his return to society. Sometimes a job may be arranged, as well as welfare assistance.[26] Some plans, on the other hand, are very simple. The County Jail offers very little beyond drying a man out, seeing to it that he keeps regular hours, stays away from liquor, and eats three meals a day. However, the Jail Branch Clinic does arrange for Welfare assistance for a few men. (See chapter 6, pages 141–42.)

Regardless of the institution from which the man is being discharged, the implied or stated design for return to society of the Skid Row alcoholic usually contains the following components:

1. Get a job and keep it. (Employment counseling and placement help is sometimes given here.)

2. Get a room and some decent clothes. (Welfare or the Christian Missionaries may help out here.)

3. Abstain from liquor and work actively on drinking problem. (Get help from AA if necessary. Join an outpatient therapy group. Avoid old drinking friends.)

4. *Patiently* work toward goal of reintegration.

An assumption here is that if the subparts are pursued successfully, integration into society will surely follow, although progress may be slow. Conceptually, these steps can be viewed as a means of recapturing *social margin*, which is an absolute necessity for a stay of any permanence in any level of society except the very dregs, and deserves further discussion.

The Protectorate Function of Social Margin

Social margin refers to the amount of *leeway* a given individual has in making errors on the job, buying on credit, or stepping on the toes of significant others without suffering such serious penalties as being fired, denied credit, or losing friends or family. Where a person is well known, and considered to have many likeable traits, there exists social margin to have some unpleasant characteristics as well.[27] If there is a past history of good work on the job, a failure will be overlooked, although this may vary according to the stiffness of the competition.

Thus it is not only the act of "messing-up" (violating social norms) itself that gets a person in trouble. It is the number of times the breech occurs, the way it is accomplished, and the previous reputation (margin) that a person has at the time of any given act. In the same vein, it is not actually lack of cash that keeps a person from purchasing, nor merely public drunkenness that lands him in jail. It is the width (size) of his margin or social credit. Social margin also encompasses the human resources a person can call upon in case of disaster, such as an incapacitating accident, losing a job, or being arrested. A person with margin can get help from his family, employer, or friends at such times.

Social margin, then, is an attribute that must be ascribed by others, although its ascription can be manipulated by the social actor to some extent, and is, of course, influenced by his actions. Social margin is compounded of the good will of people within the actor's ambit of influence and the time, credit, or money they are willing to devote to assist him should the need arise.

Social margin is graduated somewhat like the possession of riches. The more one has, the more he can get. As a result, possession of margin is class-bound: the higher the social class one has, the greater margin one can draw on. This is not to say that the lower-class man has no margin, but he has less than the middle-class man [28] and what he has is often dependent on his display of middle-class traits of dependability, responsibility, and future orientation. The increase and decrease of margin occurs in geometric ratio rather than arithmetic proportion. The term "my luck ran out" probably refers to the dramatic disappearance of social margin.

Consistent overdrawing of margin can result in its reduction to the point where a man is almost paralyzed, inasmuch as loss of this social leeway makes every mistake increasingly serious until a small misstep can be "the last straw" and result in disaster. This is, indeed, the case of the Skid Row drunk.[29]

Concomitant with the loss of social margin is the most serious loss of all—social grace and assurance in everyday situations. As a man is faced with increasingly serious definitions being assigned to his missteps, he is beset with "nerves" and paralyzed lest he reveal this. It is this loss of self-assurance that is most difficult to replace. Such a self-confidence gap can make the difference between being hired and not hired, kept and not kept on the job, treated as an insider or as an outcast.

Width of margin is historically determined by a person's known biography. This, in turn, affects the number of people willing to render aid in a tight spot. When an alcoholic acts in such a way that his wife divorces him, his in-laws and children avoid him, and his friends, associates, or employer sever relations with him, he has lost something besides their companionship or good will. He has lost the social margin their good will provides. By the time a man hits Skid Row, he has very little, if any, margin remaining.

At first, the drinker may not feel the loss, and may actually be relieved to be free of a nagging wife and disapproving in-laws, children, friends, or a dominating employer. He may even feel a sense of relief at no longer having to go to a hated job. As his money dwindles to a few pennies, and the hostile world intrudes, the protectorate role of these normal social connections becomes more apparent. At this point he must measure his margin in terms of today's companions, today's housing, today's economic power, which of course goes a long way to explain his "now" orientation.

In economic and power terms, there is no one from whom to borrow any substantial sum of money, regardless of the emergency. There is no credit from stores where credit has been abused, and no credit from stores that know of the abuse. There is no one to write a letter of recommendation so that a new job can be obtained. There is no one to handle bail in case of a drunkenness arrest, or to protest the loss of medicine or other mistreatment in the jail. There is no one to resist commitment to a mental institution or to offer an alternative to the Christian Missionaries.

Margin has other functions besides protecting the individual from the ultimate dire consequences of his actions or providing the basis for social assurance; social margin gives him reason for restraining himself from committing future deviant acts. That is, the possession of margin operates to commit a person to protection of that margin—a future-orientation, to be sure. Concomitantly, the loss of all or almost all margin means that the person has no stake that he need protect by conformity. In other words, margin is both protector and worth protecting. When the homeless male drunkenness offender starts drinking again, he usually has little margin to protect and can expect little protection in return.[30]

Scott Briar and Irving Piliavin touch on this social phenomenon in their article on juvenile delinquency, "Delinquency, Situational Inducements, and Commitment to Conformity."[31] They suggest juveniles should be looked at in terms of being either high-stake boys or low-stake boys.

The high-stake boys have various strong commitments to conformity that are tied in with their self-image and valued relationships and activities. In other words, they feel that they have a stake in conventional society and something valuable to lose should they be apprehended while deviating from social norms. The low-stake boys have no such deterrent. They have nothing to lose in terms of status and relationships that has not already been lost.

An allied concept to loss of margin might be that of "loose ends," a condition whereby the person has no legitimate business anywhere and therefore nothing to occupy him. Under such conditions, deviant activities, which are more accessible, can pass the time, and there seems to be little to lose, inasmuch as there is no responsibility to anyone specifically. Row alcoholics epitomize the man with a low stake, and at loose ends. Their social margin is near zero.[32]

Before reaching the loop, the Skid Row chronic drinker usually has lost his money, his job, his family, and his friends. Furthermore, he usually has depleted his wardrobe. After making the loop, however, he is in even worse shape. He has also lost his ability to appear on the street at all when the paddy wagon is on the Row; he is unable to get security clearance; he cannot be bonded; he may have lost his driver's license, union card, and seaman's card; and he is considered uninsurable. When the once-heavy drinker looks for a job, there are gaps in his work record that represent time spent in jail and mental institutions. These gaps and institutionalizations are often used to establish his current character. He is a man without any margin at all. He is a man with little to lose by further heavy drinking.

To get into mainstream society, even at the lowest respectable level, such a man must increase his margin to the point where every little misstep does not result in drastic action like the loss of a job, the severing of a relationship, or reinstitutionalization. To recapture margin he must remake his biography, a long and laborious process. This is the thrust of the reentry plan discussed earlier.

First, a menial job like dishwashing or bussing dishes must be obtained and the reformed deviant must be able to stick to it for at least six months. In the meantime, his personal credit must be reestablished by such actions as keeping up on his room rent promptly and repaying small personal loans, if he is fortunate enough to receive any. This is why many men feel they must have a reserve fund ("a beginning stake") in order to tide them over until their first payday. (See chapter 6.) Gradually, he must try to save money, start a small bank account, get an address in a reputable neighborhood, and become known as "steady and dependable."

In working his way back to a position of some margin in society, the necessity for a man to accept any job he can get cannot be over-emphasized. It is the exception that a man can be placed in a skilled position right after making the loop, as this quote from the assistant director of the Welfare Home for Homeless Men indicates:

> We had a triumph recently. We got a man who had a long arrest list through a civil service exam for draftsman. *We got the government to overlook his history.* It isn't often we can arrange that. Most of the time, it's their history that does them in. [A42]

More usually, the social workers who are trying to place alcoholics in jobs have this to say:

> What these men don't realize is that they must work very hard for a very long time before they will be treated like adult citizens again. They have to gradually work their way back to respectability. It cannot happen overnight. [A43]

Sometimes agents of social control speak with hopelessness of ever getting a man to the point where he can recapture social margin, as the captain at the County Jail who said:

> What the general public doesn't realize is that most of these men can't earn a living. They look awful. No employer in his right mind could or would hire them at union wages. They have lost practice in their skills. They have been out of a job so long that they don't know how to act. . . . [A11]

The older a man is, the more difficult this road back becomes, for social margin is closely tied to work and marriage careers, and these in turn, have specific timetables for intermediate accomplishments upon which later accomplishments are built.[33] The development of certain craft skills or executive ability, being promoted, having children, and so on, all affect opportunity for further enlargement of margin. Some of the deadlines for accomplishing these intermediate goals are imposed by social norms, some by insurance and pension contracts, some by the nature of man's physiology.

The plan to reenter society, then, must of necessity be a plan to recreate a new biography for a marginless person who has fallen drastically behind in his personal timetable. The agent of social control, while acknowledging the many difficulties, and stressing the time and patience it takes, believes new margin can be created.

How do men experience and react to the obstacles that inevitably are encountered as they attempt this task of getting margin for a "return to society?"

THE SKID ROW MAN PUTS "THE PLAN" INTO OPERATION

Return Versus Breaking-In

In the atmosphere of the institution, with the clear, friendly, logical counsel of the average middle-class professional worker, exhortations to reenter society seem to make a great deal of sense. True, much hard work is demanded; but the plans suggested also appear to offer progress and the goal seems worthwhile. Middle-class nondrinkers seem like the world's happiest people from this vantage point.

When asked what he is going to do upon release from an institution, the Skid Row alcoholic typically says:

> I'm hoping to "make it" in the outside world this time. I'm really going to try and not drink and to get back on the track. [30]

> I'm going to try to get back into society. I know that I've been leading an aimless, useless life. It's really no kind of life for anyone, there on Skid Row. [48]

> I'm going to work on my problem. I'm going to try to get back on my feet and live with the respectable world again. [23]

The Skid Row drunk is encouraged in this stance while in the institution by the professional posture of friendship offered by his therapist and other patients. Psychologists and social workers attempt to "gain rapport" with the patient. The alcoholic is also a part of the pseudo-mutual interaction that is a sought characteristic of group therapy sessions. These institutionally-created social success experiences often make the Skid Row man feel quite capable of inserting himself into any desirable primary group in the "outside world."

It is easy to forget that the environment of friendship at the institution is *contrived* [34] for the express purpose of offering the alcoholic a warm, supportive (therapeutic) community, and that the professionals who do this are actually trained to ultilize empathetic techniques as part of their jobs.[35] Mainstream society does not concern itself with being therapeutic, however, and the reaction of the man-on-the-street or the boss-on-the-job to the ex-alcoholic is often a cold wind that clears away the haze of such pretensions to easy acceptance. Thus there is minimum transfer of personal adjustment training from the institution to the outside world.[36] Often this is a reality shock of no mean proportions, one sufficient to send the recipient back to the warm unreality of alcohol.

Furthermore, the fact is that the Skid Row alcoholic is really not *return-*

ing to any niche being held for him in society in the same sense that it often is for the middle class alcoholic.[37] Rather, the Skid Row man is trying to break into mainstream society *for the first time* and he usually must do this without the support of friends or relatives as "starters." [38]

Using current occupation as an indicator, Table 20 is quite suggestive of just how much social distance there is between middle-class society, in general, and the average Skid Row alcoholic's position upon release. (Note the absence of professional, semi-professional, managerial, and technical occupations, as well as skilled workers—the backbone of the middle class. Additionally, almost half of the Row men [43 percent] had *no* employment in the preceding month.)

TABLE 20. *Social Characteristics of Skid Row Men*

(AS INDICATED BY CURRENT OCCUPATION)

Occupation (in month preceding interview)	Percent of Skid Row Men in Pacific City (N = 2,582)
General laborers and construction workers	12
Culinary workers	6
Sales and clerical	5
Hotel managers and clerks	2
Teamsters	4
Longshoremen and warehousemen	3
Seamen and stewards	3
Domestics	1
Other	15
Not reported	6
No employment in preceding month	43

Source: *Pacific City Urban Redevelopment Association Report* (1963).

Furthermore, as was mentioned (in chapter 1), the Skid Row man is much more often a man of inadequate skills and education than a man who has "skidded," in the social mobility sense of the term, from a relatively high position down to the bottom of the barrel. A number of studies previously cited indicate many Skid Row alcoholics were never in any stratum of society but were "wanderers" or working or living in institution-like settings from early youth.[39] Others relinquished their social niche so long ago and so completely that they have no one waiting for them to "return." (The possible exception is among those men who still have parents living. But here the choice is not too attractive—living with [and possibly caring for] an aged parent.) [40]

Details of Executing "The Plan"

The plan the Skid Row alcoholic is presented for his "return" to middle-class society is not only demanding, in the face of his social class and occupational limitations, but somewhat skimpy as to details. The plan emphasizes only a few of the needs that he must meet and problems he must overcome to lead any sort of satisfactory existence.

Getting a job, a room, and maintaining sobriety (partially through avoidance of drinking friends) is the gist of the plan, but these maxims do not offer a guide to fulfilling other needs and solving other problems without resorting to Skid Row tactics. What is he to do for social contact, contact with the opposite sex? How is he to get the job, the room, and avoid old friends? How can he change from a today-oriented, no-social-stake person to a future-oriented, middle-class person with margin? How is he to feel a *part* of this middle-class society?

Once the Skid Row alcoholic is "on the streets," the plan is not at all so logical or easy to follow as it seemed to be when presented to him in the institution. His framework for constructing meaning must shift from the professional formulas of the return to a society, which is substantially middle-class in concept, to that of the homeless man coping with day-to-day needs in a world that is alien and unfriendly.

This disjunction in viewpoint inside and outside the institution could easily account for the paucity of reasons offered by the Skid Row alcoholic for drinking excessively again, as well as his apparent insincerity about trying to stay dry. The Row men stop drinking while imbued with the rehabilitator's framework; they start drinking when they *see things differently* on the outside; they are at a loss to explain their lapse when they *return to the rehabilitation framework again*, for the decision to drink was not made within this framework.[41]

If these men were to give a detailed account of the framework that makes taking a drink seem like the most feasible thing to do at the time it is done, they would have to recount their life as experienced while trying to follow the reentry plan. In such a description, the following items are pertinent:

Social Structure and Employment Opportunities

Even in times of high employment, it is difficult for a Skid Row alcoholic who has made the loop to get a job. In part, this is because (as has been mentioned) his union membership has lapsed during drinking bouts, or he cannot get a job in his trade as an electrician, metal worker, or one of the other crafts because so much of this work is tied in with contracts demanding security clearance for all workers.

To be unbondable means that the Skid Row man cannot work on many jobs connected with the handling of money or expensive equipment. His status as an alcoholic (or ex-alcoholic) means he cannot work around heavy machinery because of high-risk insurance provisions. Add to this his age, his loss of current experience in his field, and the suspiciously long gaps in his job record (which are hard to explain in any case), and the picture of a virtually unemployable man emerges.

Here is what these men say about the agony of job hunting:

I know what is going to happen. Everything will be going along all right until they find I didn't work for nine months. When they ask why, and I tell them I was in a mental institution for a drinking problem—that's all brother. They say, "Don't call us, we'll call you." [48]

I wish that someone would go in ahead of me and say, "Look, this guy is an ex-alcoholic, but he's okay now. He hasn't had a drink for some time and he's really trying to make it." That would clear the air, and then I could go in and talk about my abilities. [37]

If I get the job by lying about the past, sure as shootin' they find out.[42] I've been told nine months later that my security clearance didn't work out and I would have to leave even though my work was okay. Now, I'm afraid to accept something for fear I'll just lose it. [45]

My references are so old that there is no use using them. I don't have any recent ones because all the work I've been doing is in institutions. I was an orderly in the mental hospital and I'd like to work as an orderly now, but I don't dare tell where I got my experience. [55]

A final blow to his job-getting ability is his address and lack of telephone:

Skid Row is a bad address to have to put down on job applications. Right away they suspect you. And you don't have a telephone either so they can get in touch with you. I sometimes offer to check back from time to time, but you can see they aren't impressed. [38]

What kind of employment can these men get?

The range is limited to menial jobs with low pay. Such jobs often do not involve the man's former skill, or if they do, they are combined with other, low-status tasks. Gardening and "landscaping" the grounds of the numerous colleges and universities that dot the Pacific City area is a major resource for placement of ex-alcoholics by rehabilitation agents. Custodial work or cafeteria jobs are also available at such institutions. Other non-profit institutions such as hospitals and rest homes hire these men as attendants or orderlies.

In Pacific City itself, the Row men must be willing to work as dish-washers, busboys and on other general clean-up jobs. If they are lucky, they may find employment as an elevator operator or night clerk in a cheap hotel. The Row men who were merchant seamen can try to get their papers reinstated and go back to sea.

If he gets a job, the Skid Row alcoholic finds himself torn between fear of failure and anger at what he conceives to be exploitation.

First of all, as his work experience recedes into dim memory, the Row man loses confidence in his abilities to hold a job. Mistakes and problems that cause a secure jobholder some uneasiness cause the ex-alcoholic trying to "make it" to endure true agony. As one man put it:

> You aren't "current" on your job anymore. You forget how to do it. You are certain that people are watching you and saying, "He can't handle it." [40]

Another Row man related the following as what he conceived to be *his failure*, and as the reason he ultimately resumed drinking:

> I had a good job in the filing department, it was arranged for me by the Welfare Home, and I was doing well when they put me in charge of six young high school drop-outs on a government project to train them for jobs. I couldn't get them to do anything! I worked and worked with them, but they weren't interested in learning. I felt like I was a failure as a supervisor. It made me so nervous I started taking tranquilizers, but they didn't really help, so one day I just walked out and went back to drinking. I couldn't handle that job. It was too much for me. [37]

Furthermore, the Skid Row man trying to stay dry usually feels he is treated differently than the rest of the employees. He is constantly reminded that he is lucky to have a job. He is often paid less than usually offered for the work.[43] He is asked to do things he does not think should be part of the job (such as mopping floors, when he was hired to do gardening). And he is expected to perform these extra tasks in good spirit. His experience is that if society wants him back at all (as suggested on p. 218) it is to exploit him. Often he does as he is told for a while, but the moment comes when anger at what he feels to be an injustice gets the better of him. Years of unemployment have not taught him the discipline of patience on the job, nor does he yet have enough social margin to make the cultivation of such forbearance seem worthwhile, being still "now" oriented. He quits, usually telling the boss off in the bargain (which means no recommendation for future job hunting), and the unemployment part of the cycle starts again.

Problems of Living Quarters

The problems of living quarters, once the Row man is "outside" again, come up almost immediately. Based on the type of job he can get, the Row man can usually afford only a single room, perhaps with cooking privileges, and probably near or in Skid Row. As previously mentioned, a single man who is not well dressed has difficulty renting a room, even in parts of the city that cater to laboring-class families or to single professional men. This is why the reformed alcoholic usually is resigned to living in

Skid Row or the Tenderloin, where he blends in better. However, he is living in a drinking culture again.

Skid Row men who are given welfare vouchers through arrangements with jail welfare workers, the Christian Missionaries, the Welfare Home, or on direct appeal to the Welfare office, are sent to Skid Row hotels, inasmuch as the budget for such aid is limited and cannot support numerous men in any but the cheapest of rooms.[44] Skid Row cafes are the only eating establishments that take Welfare food tickets. Thus with the aid of Welfare, the Skid Row man finds himself sent to Skid Row, a drinking culture, and told not to start drinking again.

An alternative housing arrangement is the halfway house. There are quite a few such establishments in Pacific City, but they are not popular with the Skid Row man. Halfway houses are, from his point of view, too much like an institution in their scheduling of meals, lights out, and required attendance at AA meetings. Furthermore, these facilities are used by the state parole board to place prison parolees because this solves some surveillance problems. These ex-convicts are avoided by the Skid Row alcoholic unless he has also done some "hard time." Finally, those Skid Row men who have jobs complain they are constantly "hit up" for money by those without jobs.[45] This combination of association with ex-cons and penniless peers makes the halfway house an atmosphere charged with suspicion, uneasiness, and coolness. As one Skid Row man explained it:

> There isn't much friendliness in a halfway house. You have to be careful who you speak to. Either they are broke and want to put the touch on you, or they are ex-cons and will take advantage of you. As a result, every man sort of keeps to himself. It's a cold and suspicious place. [55] [46]

Sobriety and Sociability

The resolution not to drink and to avoid old drinking companions means spending most free time alone. As many of these men said:

> I ate all my meals alone. Most of the time, I had to cook them in my room on my hot plate. About once a month, I could afford dinner out, but it's really no fun to eat out alone. [47]

> Sometimes, I'd go to an early movie, then home, read in bed a while, and go to sleep. Those four walls really close in on you after a while. [51]

> I was trying to live on Valoda Street in Gadsen District of Pacific City [working class]. It was very lonesome. I finally went to Skid Row where you know everyone. I hadn't even had anything to drink, but was picked up for drunk. [54]

As previously mentioned, most Skid Row alcoholics do not seek support for their abstinence from liquor by attending local Alcoholics Anonymous meetings or by socializing at AA clubs. AA has never had much appeal for the lower-class alcoholic. It is primarily a middle-class organization, focused on helping ex-alcoholics regain their lost status. Skid Row alcoholics dislike what they refer to as "drunkalogs," in which members tell with relish just how low they had sunk while drinking. They dislike what they call the "snottiness" and "holier-than-thou" attitude of the reformed alcoholic (or "AA virgins" as they call them). The only reason Skid Row men go to AA is to convince another person (someone who would be impressed by such attendance) that they are really trying to lick the alcohol problem. As one put it:

> I plan to join AA. Then people will believe I'm not drinking. As it is now, if I get drunk for three days, they don't count it if I'm sober for three weeks. [48]

Other Skid Row men tell of going to AA meetings out of desperation for *any* companionship and for the refreshments served. After the meeting, they feel a very strong urge to drink so that life becomes a round of early evening AA sessions followed by late evening drinking, and morning hangovers:

> It got so that I just went to AA meetings and from there would get a bottle and go to my room and drink—usually Vodka, and then sober up in time for the next AA meeting. [37]

One might ask why the Skid Row alcoholic does not make friends with co-workers on his new job—if he has found one. The answer given by many of the men is that they have nothing in common with the average worker. Experiences on the loop seem to socialize the Row man so that he is unable to enjoy the company of those who do not share such experiences as living in institutions on the circle, fooling the authorities, panhandling, and general Skid Row adventures.[47] This is especially true if the Skid Row alcoholic has been placed in a gardening or groundskeeper job. His co-workers are seldom urban men, and the Skid Row man keenly misses the presence of the "city" and the men who have knowledge of its many-faceted underlife.[48]

Of new on-the-job acquaintances, the Skid Row drinker says:

> They don't speak my language. They are square-Johns. [50]

> I got so lonesome for someone who talked my language. You can't talk to some jerks. [40]

> I want to talk with someone who knows what I'm talking about. Some guys have never done nothing. [41] [49]

The Problem with Women

A Skid Row man trying to "make it" back into society has a particularly complicated problem so far as women are concerned.

As previously mentioned, the average Skid Row man is usually quite charming and has no trouble attracting female companions on the Row or partners at the State Mental Hospital. However, neither of these types of women is seen by the alcoholic as a good influence for a man who is attempting to stop drinking. What he wants, in his own words, is "a decent woman."

The problem is, though, that he is shy and awkward about pursuing a woman of this type. As one Skid Row man put it:

> It's been so long since I been around a decent woman, I don't know how to act. [48]

Furthermore, if the Skid Row man has recently been in jail, at the Christian Missionaries, in a non-coeducational halfway house, or spending his time in all-male company on the Row, he has lost practice in communicating with women. Wallace quotes one such man's insecurity about women:

> Now, how shall I ask one of these girls for a dance? No need of introductions, that much I knew. Which would be best, "C'mon kid, let's prance this out?" Or, "May I have this dance?" How I wished these girls were men. I could talk to men.[50]

Another worry is the lack of acceptable credentials.[51]

> What can I offer a decent woman? I have no job and no prospects. If I go with a drinking woman, sure as shootin' I'll wind up drinking again. [55]

As noted, the Skid Row alcoholic does have some access to professional women who would like to mother him, but here he must relinquish any hope of being head of the house, and must settle instead for being sort of a house pet.

The Daily Routine

What is the daily round like for this man who is trying to gain some social margin so as to get in and stay in the society depicted by the middle-class professional? The mundane experiences of this project form the framework within which the Skid Row man gives up and takes a drink.

A composite description might go something like this: rise early in a lonely room; breakfast fixed on a hot plate, eaten alone in the room, or eaten alone in a cheap restaurant; ride the bus to work (often quite a distance), because an alcoholic usually has lost his driver's license or cannot afford a car and cannot afford to live near work; work all day at a boring, menial, poorly paid job with dull, unsympathetic (to the alcoholic) co-workers and an unsympathetic (to the alcoholic) boss; return at night to eat dinner alone and watch television in the hotel lobby, or read, attempt to freshen his limited wardrobe, or go to bed, knowing a similar day awaits him tomorrow.

Although he may be seeing a welfare worker or a therapist on a regular basis, the dried-out chronic drunk trying to "make it" discovers his relationship with these professionals is not the same as it was in institutions, and he has no claim on their outside social time for informal friendship.

The solitary status of the Skid Row man also affects his opportunities for *experiencing* success. Success, like margin, is an attribute ascribed by others. The Skid Row man has no friends or relatives to reinforce his determination to "make it" or congratulate him on progress. No one (except for an occasional professional therapist) seems even aware of his efforts to prove worthiness. Respectable society is not an entity, and it neither hands out keys to the city nor certificates of social integration. It seems almost impossible for a Skid Row man to know when he has, indeed, "made it." Certainly, merely going through the motions of being respectable will not necessarily elicit immediate recognizable rewards.[52]

The agents of social control counsel "patience" and that "better things will eventually come." But patience means future orientation, a psychological state of mind that is foreign to a man who has been operating for many years on here-and-now satisfactions.

The story that follows is typical. The man was first interviewed at the Welfare Home for Homeless Men and then seen about a month later, quite by chance, at County Jail. He explained his lapse this way:

> I got a job at the Green Pine Hotel in the suburbs as janitor. I was terribly lonesome. I had no friends. I was on the job there two weeks and then came down to the city. There's quite a few fellows I know around. I want to be with somebody I know once in a while. I liked the job, but I got lonesome. There's nothing to do and no one to talk to. If I had had companionship, it wouldn't have happened. You get lonesome in one room. [10]

Also revealing is the answer to the question, "How were things out there?", asked of a Skid Row alcoholic who had just returned to jail after two weeks of freedom. He replied:

> Pretty rough! Everything moves so fast. No one knows or cares if you are alive. You just don't fit in anywhere. [16]

Going Full Circle: "And Then I Decided to Hell with It"

In contrast to a return to the society and reality suggested as a goal by professional rehabilitators, there exists also the Skid Row society with its instant warmth, friendliness, and general conviviality. Here, many of the friends of the job-holding Skid Row alcoholic are living on welfare and spending their time drinking, partying, and making out. The dole in Pacific City provides a standard of living probably only slightly lower than the pay of the first menial job available to the alcoholic just discharged from an institution. The room of the "unreformed drunk" may compare favorably with the room in which the struggling "ex-alcoholic" is living. The amount and quality of food each is able to obtain varies but little, even though the unreformed man may be getting part of his daily bread from missions and other charitable organizations.

Furthermore, having once made the loop and learned its machinations, the Skid Row alcoholic trying to "make it" knows that these institutions are always available to him. Compared to the way he is living while trying to make a comeback, some of the stations that he despised and feared at first seem pleasant in retrospect.[53] Old friends are certain to be in any institutions he should choose (or be sent to). Although "admission to society" is so nebulous as to defy definition or provide any feeling of belonging, admission to an institution is just the opposite. While progress toward the goal of reintegration into society is difficult to apprehend, progress in an institution is well marked. On the inside the alcoholic is often told if he has done well on a task, and may be given a higher status job; in therapy, he is praised for "being honest and not holding back"; at the Christian Missionaries he may be promoted to a better room or a larger gratuity; he may even have "institutional margin" on the basis of past performance.[54] Outside the loop station, in Skid Row society, there are the small triumphs of making out and sharing one's cleverness with friends over a bottle.

Thus where the road into respectable society is cold and lonely, Skid Row and the stations of the loop offer conviviality, feeling of accomplishment, as well as an opportunity to forget the struggle.[55] The Row man can stop seeking an idealized society at the end of the rainbow, stop leading a treadmill existence, and return to being seen by his most significant others as a real person again.[56]

An important character in the "Return of the Prodigal Son" story is the respectable brother who stayed at home and out of trouble. In a very true sense, he epitomizes the general attitude of the average citizen toward anyone who strays from the fold too long or too completely and then expects to be granted amnesty merely by some suffering and an apology.

When asked to come to the party given in honor of the returning prodigal son, the self-righteous brother was angry and said to his father:

> Lo, these many years do I serve thee, neither transgress I at any time thy commandment; and yet thou never gavest me a kid, that I might make merry with my friends; but as soon as this thy son was come, which hath devoured thy living with harlots, thou hast killed for him the fatted calf.
>
> Luke 15:29–30

To which the Skid Row alcoholic might reply, as he gives up the fight for acceptance in the rehabilitator's society and returns to Skid Row living and inevitably a loop institution:

> And then I decided to hell with it, and I started drinking again.

CYCLING OUT

Is there any way off the loop? Besides the few who stick it out long enough to get back sufficient social margin to reclaim a lost existence, what other ways are there for Skid Row men to escape?

There appear to be three major ways off Skid Row:

1. Become a live-in servant for an institution (or, once in a while, for a professional woman).

2. Go into alcoholic rehabilitation as a profession.

3. Die.

The first has been amply discussed. Ex-alcoholics may be found at many nonprofit institutions, especially hospitals and rest homes, for some small wages plus board and room. This becomes, then, their new way of life.

The second escape route has possibly been traveled successfully by more alcoholics than is generally known. During the course of this study, the number of ex-alcoholics in positions of agents of social control on the loop was astounding. Ex-alcoholics can be found in administrative positions in the Courts, County Jail, the City Hospital, the State Mental Hospital, Welfare Home for Homeless Men, and the Christian Missionaries.

Other ex-alcoholics are to be found making a career of operating Alcoholics Anonymous clubs, halfway houses, and therapy groups. The newest halfway house for men to be started under the sponsorship of the Pacific City Department of Public Health will be manned by ex-alcoholics.

The factors underlying the success of this maneuver to get off the loop may well center about the fact that "going into rehab work" converts what is a vice in the outside world (i.e., excessive drinking, institutionalization, familiarity with other alcoholics, and absence of recent job experience) into an employable virtue. Indeed, this idea has been formally accepted by many agencies concerned with reform and rehabilitation of deviants.[57] "It takes one to know and understand one" philosophy prevails. Paradoxically, however, the assumption an ex-alcoholic will be more understanding in working with alcoholics has not generally held true if we are to accept the testimony of the men they work with. Alcoholics complain that, "There's nothing colder than an ex-alcoholic," which suggests that once a man makes it to "the right side" he no longer empathizes with former buddies but rather identifies with the associates of his newly-established status— other agents of social control.[58]

Death is the third way off the loop. Six Row men died in Pacific City during the course of this study of such causes as acute alcoholism, cirrhosis of the liver, brutal beatings in an alley, a seizure, and an internal hemorrhage. Men who get off the loop permanently in this way, have long ago given up the fight for reentrance into society. After a few such attempts they unhesitatingly take a drink the moment they leave an institution. Such men can be roughly divided into two types—both of whom accept the consequences of the bridges they have burned and the lonely life that will be their future.

They are:

1. *The so-called institutionalized man*, the perennial and resigned loop maker. This includes the chronic drunkenness offender who uses the jail as an emergency hotel in bad weather, the self-admitted State Hospital man who uses that institution for drying out and building up both physically and financially, and the mission rounder who, cursing the hand who feeds him, still goes back when forced by hunger and illness.

2. *The Welfare Skid Row man* who "graduates" to vouchers and settles down to living on what his check provides, plus what he can earn on pick-up jobs. He drinks heavily except on the days he has an appointment with his social worker. Intermittent institutionalizations keep him alive.

Both these types of Row men are trapped on the loop. Death is their only avenue of escape.

9

Benefactors, Beneficiaries, Compassion, Gratitude, and Trust

Forms of Social Relationship Between the Helper and the Helped

INTRODUCTION

It has been shown that the loop expands the world of the indigent alcoholic beyond the boundaries of Skid Row. In this enlarged territory, one of the indigent drunk's most important relationships is with agents of social control who occupy a status superior to his by virtue of their official appointment to encourage his rehabilitation. This chapter is concerned with the developing content of these relationships.

The circle, or the loop, of the Skid Row drunk can be viewed as a series of services provided to the alcoholics by a benevolent tax-paying public. It is a manifestation of the concern that man feels for his less fortunate fellowman. The proliferation of stations on the loop reflects, in part, continuous efforts sponsored by the public to discover the "right combination" of therapy and services that will rehabilitate or "cure" the chronic drinker. This same concern for humanity is no doubt felt by the agents who are hired to man the loop stations. Most professionals who go into rehabilitation are dedicated to helping humanity and have a strong emotional investment in their jobs. Although there are some agents on the loop in Pacific City who openly proclaim their hatred of the alcoholic,[1] the majority—including the police and jailers—sincerely want to help him.

As for the Skid Row alcoholics, it can be stated almost as unequivocally that they desperately would like to be cured of "alcoholism." They would like to be able to drink socially without drinking compulsively; they would like to be able to enjoy drinking without attaining the state where they suffer hallucinations and must undergo withdrawal. They would like to be, in other words, normal (perhaps "heavy normal") instead of pathological drinkers. As long as these men continue to ingest copious quantities of various forms of alcoholic beverages, however, they will desperately need medical help—drying-out facilities and the chance to rebuild their health from time to time. Thus they need and want most of the medical assistance offered by the stations on the loop.

Rather than being bound together by their mutual goals, however, Skid Row alcoholics and agents of social control are hostile toward each other, existing in what might be described as a constant state of outrage, distrust, and disappointment. In order to understand this conflict, it is necessary to engage in what Simmel has called the central task of sociology—the analysis of social associations, of the processes governing them, and of the forms they assume, and to generalize these forms to other similar social arrangements.[2] Here, the social association to be analyzed is that of the benefactor and the beneficiary.

The counterroles of benefactor and beneficiary (or helper and helped) present one of the most basic, yet complex forms of social association.[3] The variety of relationships that develop among givers and receivers can be understood, in part, by an analysis of the emotional expectations of both parties to a giver-receiver transaction. They are: (1) compassion of the benefactor—often assumed to have caused, at least in part, the action of giving; (2) gratitude from the beneficiary—assumed to be the natural response to kindness; and (3) a degree of mutual trust between the two as to the nature of the favor and its resultant good effects.

The Good Samaritan parable [4] offers a model of the emotional expectations accompanying the giver-receiver relationship in its ideal state. The story also illustrates the effect of the customary emotions on the organization or structure of the giver-receiver relationship. The charity or compassion of the Samaritan, the enduring gratitude of the traveler, the mutual trust between the two men during and after the act of kindness, all set the stage for the idealized outcome of an association of this type. So, too, history records the gratitude of the Pilgrims for the help received by the Indians. The ideal model is also found in childrens' fairy tales where the concerned hero receives the grateful thanks of the heroine he has saved from some undesirable fate. Their mutual trust is evident throughout this interlude, and in the end they often marry and live happily ever after.

As illustrated by interactions on the loop, however, real-life relationships between the giver and the receiver may not develop along such simplistic lines. Each of the emotional axes mentioned—compassion, gratitude, and trust—provide possibilities for misunderstandings and disappointments, so it is not surprising that numerous mutant forms of the giver-receiver relationship can and do develop.

In the case of the agents of social control and the Pacific City Skid Row alcoholic, the class and status difference between them set the tone or style of emotional interaction expected by each during this interaction. In general, agents of social control are middle-class and have absorbed middle-class professional ideas as to the proprieties to be observed in the giver-receiver relationship. These ideas, somewhat naturally, are not always in agreement with those of the Skid Row alcoholic man, who is predominately of lower-class origins.

With this in mind, giver-receiver forms *in general* will be analyzed, using loop relationships as illustrative of what might emerge under similar conditions *anywhere* in social life. Then, *self-perpetuating* features of these specific giver-receiver relationships will be discussed.

First, let us look at how expectations and disappointments in the area of social-emotional processes shape the helping act—perceived compassion from the benefactor, perceived gratitude from the beneficiary, and perceived trust between the two. Such an examination will show that there are no situations that are ipso facto worthy of compassion until defined so by someone; neither are there acts that universally call forth gratitude; nor can a giver-receiver role-relationship insure against betrayal. Furthermore, even if a person believes he is portraying these emotions as expected, they may not be perceived as such by others. With so many problematic areas, is it any wonder the identity of the "real" beneficiary in the transaction between alcoholics and officials of institutions is open to doubt?

EMOTIONS AND THE GIVER-RECEIVER RELATIONSHIP

Charity and Compassion

Skid Row alcoholics often claim that the agents of social control who work with them are "heartless, cold, and even cruel." On the other hand, agents of social control claim their compassion, when shown, goes unnoticed.

Certainly, the manner in which a favor is done is as important to the reaction of the recipient as the favor itself. This has been recognized by man since time immemorial. The best discussion of this perhaps is still found in St. Paul's First Epistle to the Corinthians:

Though I speak with the tongues of men and of angels, and have not charity [love], I am become as sounding brass, or as tinkling cymbal. And though I have the gift of prophecy, and understand all mysteries, and all knowledge; and though I have all faith, so I could remove mountains, and have not charity, I am nothing. And though I bestow all my goods to feed the poor, and though I give my body to be burned, and have not charity, it profiteth me nothing. Charity suffereth long, and it is kind; charity envieth not; charity vaunteth not itself, is not puffed up, doth not behave itself unseemly, seeketh not her own, is not easily provoked, thinketh no evil; rejoiceth not in iniquity, but rejoiceth in the truth; beareth all things, believeth all things, hopeth all things, endureth all things.

Yet compassion, or charity, presents complications specific to the human condition not encompassed in the Epistle. First, most persons professionally engaged in aiding others find it almost impossible to maintain a high level of compassion for all with whom they must deal. Second, some acts of compassion are not so construed by the receiver. The first is a shortage problem of the giver, the second a definitional one of the receiver.

THE RATIONING OF COMPASSION TO THE "WORTHY"   Charity and compassion are not available in unlimited supply, the Bible notwithstanding. Like so many other strong emotions, compassion cannot be called forth on every possible occasion without exhausting the giver.

This fact places members of the assistance professions in a difficult position because they are daily in situations that elicit feelings of compassion. For sheer emotional survival, they soon learn to insulate themselves against such excessive demands on their psyches. Doctors and nurses, those most exemplary benefactors, are taught from the beginning of their careers to suppress compassion for the endless stream of suffering humanity with which they must deal, lest they become emotionally exhausted and their efficiency destroyed.[5] As a result, these medical professionals pick and choose from among the individual cases those persons to whom they will offer compassion as well as routine care.

The same problem of scarce emotional resources is present for the professionals who work with alcoholics. To understand the grounds on which agents of social control deny feelings of compassion for many of their clients, their criteria for *worthiness* to elicit compassion must be understood.[6] Sympathy is inextricably bound up with the phenomenon of *identification*. This is because persons are unable to identify (empathize) with activities they cannot understand.[7] In the case of most professionals working with alcoholics, these criteria are, in part at least, a reflection of their middle-class values. And this can be seen by the basis on which compassion is generated or denied to the Skid Row alcoholic.

First, it appears that the route through which a person arrives at the point of needing aid is important to the amount of compassion he will rouse in his would-be benefactors. In order for his helpers to identify with him, his condition should be the result of "understandable factors," i.e., no fault of his.[8] *Second*, the response of the alcoholic to aid and to his benefactors should follow an "acceptable" pattern. *Third*, the actual "good" the aid seems to do him should reflect the goals of his benefactors so they can identify with the results and experience "success" in their terms.

On the first criteria, in the specific case of alcoholism, the biography of an alcoholic can work for or against his getting a portion of the sympathy available from agents of social control. For instance, if his wife or a child died of cancer or were killed in an auto wreck, if his business collapsed through no fault of his own, if his health failed for a reason other than drinking, or if he suffered some other disabling disaster, the reaction of the professional often is:

> You really can't blame him for drinking. Look what's happened to him. He's lost everything. Who wouldn't drink under those circumstances?[9]

On the other hand, sympathy is seldom extended to the alcoholic who is merely lonesome, who has lost or divorced a wife because of his excess drinking problem, and who usually has also lost his business or job for the same reason. His current existential position may be identical to the more "deserving" alcoholic previously described (he has "lost everything"), but agents of social control—and laymen as well—invariably respond somewhat differently:

> Well, if he's so lonesome, why did he walk out on his wife and family 15 years ago? Why didn't he try to straighten up and hold his job? He's getting what he deserves, in a way.[10]

The burden of proof as to worthiness for sympathy is on the alcoholic. Heider has suggested people have a tendency to equate misfortune with punishment and fortune with reward.[11] Thus there is always the suspicion ill befalls the individual who deserves it, unless he can prove otherwise.

Second, the attitude of deference with which a beneficiary responds to his benefactors, the spirit with which instructions are followed, and the repentance exhibited for past misdeeds, all help create a case for being included among the worthy clients.

For instance, the term "disreputable poor" discussed in the previous chapter, describes those persons whose reaction does not meet acceptable standards of earnestness and repentance. The disreputable poor do not try to get out of their dilemma, nor do they maintain a pose of gratitude toward those who help them. Their attitude leaves much to be desired, as far as benefactors who are also agents of social control are concerned.

What is the appropriate attitude for the worthy alcoholic? The alcoholic should appear to be trying to stop drinking (he certainly should not walk out of the institution and take a drink moments after). He is cooperative and cheerful about both work and therapy assignments. He does not try to leave before officially discharged. Above all, he does not question the motives of the institutions or their agents. In these ways, the alcoholic garners "worthiness points." [12]

For those men who do not respond satisfactorily, there are such comments as the following:

> You can work your heart out on these men and they turn right around and go out and drink. There is no point of getting all worked up helping them. [A41]

> They are sullen, they are doubting; you don't feel like knocking yourself out over them. [A38]

Third, nothing so engenders continuing identification and good will as a feeling of having done someone "good." Nothing sparks frustration and pessimism as a feeling that attempted good deeds have failed to accomplish their purpose. For instance the doctor in the novel *Intern* describes how cancer surgeons develop a great dislike and lack of compassion for patients who have a recurrence of cancer: ". . . as though they are blaming the patient for having the recurrence." [13]

In the treatment of alcoholism, the blame is felt to be even more directly attributable to the patient's lack of self-control rather than to the failure of the therapy. Thus it should not be surprising that recidivism, which robs the agent of social control of his success, should cause a substantial drop, rather than rise, in compassion toward the patient. This is true even of the erstwhile "worthy clients" with "good reasons" for pathological drinking, if they fail to respond to professional aid within what is considered to be a reasonable time.

Such comments as the following by agents of social control are not unusual:

At the emergency room of the City Hospital:

> I used to be sorry for these guys; but when you keep seeing the same ones over and over no matter what you do for them, you stop feeling so upset when they crawl in here looking so bad. [A54]

From a social worker:

> When I started in this line of work, I used to really suffer with every guy, and I used to about kill myself trying to straighten his life out and

help him stop drinking. Now, I don't succeed with very many. I try to enjoy doing what I can, but I don't go around with my heart on my sleeve anymore. I've had too many disappointments. [A24]

From a psychologist:

Working with alcoholics can take a lot out of you—if you let it. You can feel so sorry for them and be so disappointed when they slip again. I've learned to hold myself in. [A31]

It is not surprising, then, that alcoholics perceive their reception by case-hardened agents of social control as somewhat less than compassionate. However, the reasons ascribed *by the alcoholic* to this cold response illustrates the difference in perspectives between the two groups. Seldom does the Skid Row man's causal analysis include any awareness of the effects that previous disappointing clients have on professionals. Rather, the cold manner is assumed to be a manifestation of the defective character of persons hired to help men with their drinking problems.

Boy, you meet the coldest people in these institutions. Look at those orderlies and some of those nurses. Boy, they could freeze ice cubes. They are just here for the salary. They couldn't hold any other job. [29]

You go around for a while on this circle and you find it's a pretty rough world. The judges don't give a damn about you; the Christian Missionaries do, but it's just to work you to death; the jailers see you as one more body. You could die anywhere on the loop and no one would shed a tear. [9]

If the agent of social control is a former alcoholic himself, this is taken as sufficient explanation for his lack of compassion:

There's nothing colder to an alcoholic than an ex-alcoholic. [23]

ONE MAN'S COMPASSION IS ANOTHER MAN'S CRUELTY The natural compassion of the staff worker for the down-and-out male alcoholic is almost always further stifled by the restraint imposed by professionalism. One of the central problems of human relations is the nice balance of involvement and detachment required in connection with an act that is claimed to be helpful in the long run but that hurts and seems cruel at the same time.[14]
In the case of help given the alcoholic, the staff member often must prescribe disagreeable or even painful treatment. He may be required to administer the treatment himself. To be able to do this and still maintain a self-image of concern for humanity, the professional must have a strongly-rooted belief that he is meeting the "real needs" of the people who come to him for aid. This belief is usually implanted as part of his professional training. His outward compassion (in connection with the suffering of the client) must be suppressed as part of the treatment

necessary to attain the long-term goal of curing or rehabilitating the patient. To the alcoholic, however, some of the methods of therapy used to help him seem completely lacking in human compassion or, in some instances, to be actually cruel. For example, where the so-called helping act is a 30-day jail sentence, the judge may see himself as aiding the alcoholic by removing him from his source of supply, but the alcoholic does not necessarily look upon this as an act of compassion. Similarly, the Christian Missionaries perceive the down-and-out alcoholic's real needs as spiritual renewal, a feeling of God's forgiveness for leading a dissolute life, and the relearning of responsible work habits. This clashes with the alcoholic's expectation of proper help from the Missionaries. The alcoholic focuses on the here-and-now perspective of room, board, medical attention, rest, and a chance to make a stake. The agent of social control has a future-perspective that might be described as "suffer now for rewards later."

Heider suggests these dichotomous grounds for judging the positive or negative nature of a given act could be labeled "local" versus "total relevance":

> To undergo a painful treatment is certainly to suffer a negative event; but [the receiver] can desire it because of the positive consequences. By the same token, an event that may be positive in its local relevance may, because of its total relevance, be rejected.
>
> . . . in the case of benefiting and harming, the total relevance of the event and not its local relevance gives the kind of stability and order which make adaptation and expectation possible.[15]

From this study of the loop, it would seem agents of social control are more adept at seeing the total relevance of therapeutic activities than are the drunks:

> Well, getting your leg set after it is broken is painful. Getting rabies shots after being bitten by a dog is painful. It [the agent's noncompassionate professionalism] doesn't mean that we don't care about the men. We have to do what is necessary . . . in order to really help them. [A38]

The average Skid Row alcoholic experiences the pain but not the compassion. He sees himself as surrounded by hard-hearted professionals who seem only to be using him for experimentation and self-aggrandizement. The Skid Row alcoholic's perspective is directed towards the local relevance, as this composite quotation illustrates:

> Well, you see, they said they were going to help me, but all they really did was use me . . . I volunteered for some of their experiments . . .

I sat in the therapy groups so that the leader could feel superior . . . Him and his airs . . . What does he know about getting high . . . What do they care about what I feel?

Gratitude

Despite all the services they render, agents of social control report little gratitude is forthcoming from the alcoholics who receive help. Rather, the professionals feel exploited and ill-used by the alcoholics and their favors wasted. Alcoholics, on the other hand, deny any need for gratitude, with the possible exception of that gratitude which they feel is owed to *them*.

Gratitude can be defined as thankfulness, an outward display of an inward state of being grateful for favors received. Simmel has stated that it is gratitude that holds society together. It supplements the legal order to ensure reciprocity. It is mankind's moral memory. It aids the continuation of a relationship and it gives pleasure by its very existence.[16]

But gratitude does not stand alone, it is connected with certain reciprocal actions [17] as well as feelings of thankfulness. Like compassion, its existence is not without complications, particularly in the areas of definitions and status expectations.

The definitional problem of the parties involved is slightly different from *compassion*, however. There the issue was of determining who was worthy and whether the action by the agent of social control constituted help or hurt. For gratitude, the definitional problem is focused on whether the aid offered by the professionals can be considered a *gift, or merely the fulfilling of an obligation*.

Strictly speaking, a favor is supposed to be freely given, a gift without obligation. It is the granting of a concession, privilege, or help. Which acts fall within these definitional boundaries will vary by the perception of the person who defines the situation.

The definition of gratitude, of course, suggests that gifts are not really gratuitous and free of obligation. In all societies, quite aside from the obligation to be grateful, there is between the parties to the favor further understanding that a social bond has been created. Like all bonds, it is supposed to establish a certain amount of purchase for each participant upon the other, that is, the favor-doer has enhanced his social credit status by his act, and expects both gratitude and the return of the favor in a suitable form. At the same time, the favor-receiver has the right to assume that the door is now open for similar favors from the grantor, should he request them. Thus the repayment of obligation by a return-favor reinforces the bond between the giver and the receiver, rather than cancelling the relationship. In addition, the gift bestows status superiority on the giver. Nor does the repayment of the favor equalize the status of parties to the transaction. Many theorists, Simmel among them, have pointed out the advantage remains forever with the first to give. Some degree of indebtedness and need to show deference becomes the permanent burden of the original receiver. As Simmel puts it:

> It [the favor] creates an unequal relationship which can never be redeemed; it puts the receiver into a position of being lower than the giver.[18]

How do the processes by which a gift is defined or a status bond denied, shape the giver-receiver relationship on the loop?

THE PROBLEMATIC NATURE OF GIFT-DEFINITION ON THE LOOP   Most staff members at stations on the loop see themselves in the role of *benefactors* in that they have planned their activities during a good part of the day around the needs of chronic problem drinkers.[19]

For instance, admission to the helping institution can be seen as the bestowal of a favor, inasmuch as this increases the case (work) load. Nurses in emergency wards, policemen on the beat (who have the choice of ignoring drunks or taking them in), judges, psychiatrists who run therapy groups, and Christian Missionaries and their staff, all have some leeway as to whom they will help and whom they will turn away.

The providing of certain services (bed, food, therapy, clothing, or medical attention without charge) is felt by the administrators to involve acts of benevolence for which gratitude is an obvious expectation. This includes the granting of welfare checks, bus tickets, food tickets, and hotel arrangements to these homeless men. Even giving an alcoholic man a work assignment in the institution is thought to be a kindness since it allows a virtually "unemployable" man to know again the satisfaction of doing a job well.

An even greater favor, so far as the agent of social control is concerned, is to arrange employment for their charges with some firm on the outside. This is because of the difficulties of placing "ex-" alcoholics in *any* job.

It follows, then, that these agents of social control would expect a show of gratitude for almost all services provided through them by their institution, whether voluntarily received or not.

Such comments as, "We do a lot for these guys . . . ," followed by a recital of institutional services, is a common conversational refrain of agents of social control when talking about Skid Row men to an outsider. It is indicative of the personal-favor basis on which professionals view their official activities. A sampling of common complaints about lack of gratitude includes:

> Alcoholics are likely to leave an institution without going through any formal termination or without saying "goodbye" or "thank you" to the persons there who have worked with them and tried to help them.[20]

Alcoholics are the most ungrateful men in the world. They don't appreciate a thing you do for them. You can work your heart out over them. [A24]

One thing you get pissed-off about is the ungratefulness of these guys who complain that the Christian Missionaries' workshop is "taking advantage of them." Actually, they couldn't do any other kind of work and couldn't get hired if they could anyway. [A38]

I sent him [an alcoholic] out on a job and it took a lot of doing to get the company to try him, and all he did was complain about the pay and that they asked extra things of him. He had no idea what I went through to get him that job. [A43]

The belief by professionals that they have done the alcoholic a *personal* favor also causes longer-lasting anger at his ungratefulness, because it is then seen as a *personal* affront.[21]

Clearly Skid Row alcoholics have a different set of criteria by which they judge whether an act or service performed is a favor for which they are beholden to the donor. On the basis of numerous interviews conducted at the institutional way stations on the loop, several attitudes concerning favor-definition emerged. Primarily, the alcoholics feel they need not be grateful for aid granted on what is claimed to be universalistic criteria—help that *must* be dispensed to persons who pass the objective tests set down for such assistance. The down-and-out drunk is aware that all institutions have screening rituals with certain criteria (such as residence, sincerity of purpose, lack of personal resources, and deteriorated physical condition) for admission. The mere act of acceptance (into an institution, a therapy program, to get medication, to get welfare checks, food coupons, free clothing, or whatever is being applied for) is seen as an indication the alcoholic *qualifies* for such aid by meeting the criteria and therefore cannot logically or legally be denied it.

To be grateful to a paid employee for doing his job—even well—in an agency created to aid those who qualify for such aid seems unnecessary to the alcoholic and analogous to being grateful to a librarian who checks out a book after seeing the properly-authenticated library card.[22]

Such statements as the following are often made by the Skid Row alcoholics:

I went down to the welfare and of course I qualified for aid; I've been a resident of the city for 20 years.

I was pretty down and I felt pretty bad . . . and I ran into a friend and asked him for a buck so I could get something to drink and a room . . . and he told me that I probably qualified for the welfare. So I went down and talked to them and I did.

The way I see it, the city hospital and emergency wards have no right to refuse aid to anybody. They are set up to help the person who lives in certain areas and qualifies for the help. It's not up to them nurses on the desk to decide who should be admitted and who should not. I got rights like any other citizen.

I don't feel I owe them anything for taking care of me. That is what they are there for. If you qualify for the aid, that's all there is to it.

These attitudes are reinforced in two ways. First, current practice of calling a charity case a "client," instead of a "patient" or a "case," supports the idea of qualification and tends to negate the overtone of benevolence in assistance rendered. Second, for social security, disability payments, old-age pension, and unemployment compensation, qualification *is* the universalistic criterion and person-to-person gratitude is neither expected nor extended. The Skid Row man (usually poorly educated, as discussed in a previous chapter) sees little difference between qualifying for social security and qualifying for welfare aid or hospital admission. Such statements as the following are often heard in tandem:

If you haven't been back to Welfare Home for Homeless Men for 90 days, you qualify.

I always see to it I qualify for unemployment compensation (or disability benefits at State Hospital) by working the minimum each year.

Alcoholics do recognize that some assistance given by agents of social control does reach the status of the *true* favor, which makes them beholden to the favor-doer. In the main, however, these are restricted to acts that the alcoholic feels are clearly "above and beyond the call of duty." Furthermore, the benefactor must not receive any recompense for this true favor, and should, in fact, be out of pocket for it.

A good example of a true favor as defined from this recipient-perspective is quoted below:

A man was suffering from an infected cyst and needed a hot water bottle, but there was not one available in the jail. This was not really an emergency, but a guard went to town on his own and spent his own money to get a bottle for him. In my eyes, this was a beautiful act. [15] [23]

In the same vein, in the area of employment aid, rather than feeling grateful for their first outside job, alcoholics often point to the gross differences in the wages they are paid in comparison to those paid to nonalcoholics. Thus the location of such a job can hardly be seen as an example of *extra effort* on the part of the professional since it is considered easy to find exploitative employers.

They [the agents of social control] get you into places that pay a menial salary rate. For instance, I'm a painter and they usually pay a painter

$5.65 an hour, but for me they paid $1.50 and expected me to do all sorts of things besides. It's disgusting. [47]

THE DOUBLE INDEMNITY OF THE STATUS-BOND OF DEVIANTS   It has been noted that any person who receives a gift is automatically at a status disadvantage. However, in the case of institutions that deal with deviants, another dimension must be added, that is, the lower status afforded automatically to deviants by reasons of their departure from normative behavior.

To most agents of social control, and the average citizen as well, any man who must be institutionalized loses some status as an adult citizen. Such a man is too sick physically, mentally, morally, or economically to maintain himself; therefore he is unable to discharge his responsibilities to others (family, friends, neighbors in the community). For those whose jobs require they help these deviant men, the assumption of superiority of the giver is much greater than might be expected in ordinary helping relationships. In these cases, there is the social class differential coupled with the impossibility of ever receiving adequate payment for such benevolence from such inadequate persons.

As one agent of social control put it:

> You know what we [the administrative staff] are—we are just a bunch of mothers. That's what these guys [the alcoholics] need—a mother! [A42]

Another indicator of this attitude is to be found in the practice of the former director of the Welfare Home for Homeless Men, who often referred to his clients as "my little men" and gave them small change for spending money out of his own pocket.

However, agents of social control rarely get the deference they feel is their due from these deviant men who have been unable to meet normal adult obligations. Rather, their superiority is often challenged, and thus they complain as follows:

> They don't like to take advice about how long to stay in treatment and so on. They think they know better.[24]

Some agents of social control feel the lack of gratitude they experience is the direct result of the alcoholic's attempt to deny his lower status:

> They don't appreciate what we do for them here. Have you ever known anyone who appreciated getting help? Look at how the United States is treated by countries who get our foreign aid. [A11]

> Alcoholics hate the Christian Missionaries because it [the help] forces them to be grateful and they don't want to be. It forces them to see the truth about themselves. They know they are indebted to it [the Missionaries] for sustenance and we always hate persons who patronize us. [A55][25]

The alcoholics have an entirely different view of what is the proper nature of the bond between themselves and the men whose occupation it is to help them. They sense the superiority that agents of social control feel to them. A poem, written by one Skid Row man, illustrates the resentment the indigent alcoholic feels at what he believes to be the unnecessary and lofty manner in which many agents dispense their services.[26]

The Establishment
(by a resident at Welfare Home for Homeless Men)

An attentive ear
Is required here.
Sit up straight
While I relate
Rule and regulation
For your elucidation.

Paupers have no privileged choice
Nor any right to clamorous voice
Our sufferance is your substance, Mack,
We'll tolerate no talking back!

According to our humor's vein
We dispense both boon and bane
Ours is the choice to arbitrate
If you don't like it, there's the gate!

As the Skid Row men see it, the institutions and the agents of social control who run them are "in the miseries business," and therefore have no right to act as though they are better than the source of their livelihood. Actually, professional helpers owe their very existence to the fact that there is a plentiful supply of miserable people needing help.[27] Alcoholics back up this viewpoint in a number of ways.

First of all, Row men are aware that the internal management of most of the helping institutions has been adjusted to take some advantage of the free labor offered by prisoner-patients-clients in order to (1) keep the men busy; and (2) forestall complaints from taxpayer-citizens that available manpower is going idle while the men live "in luxury" in tax-supported institutions. Whatever the original reason, the labor of the alcoholic quickly becomes a part of the institution's economic resources and could not be dropped without budgetary reorganization.[28] At the jail, the mental hospital, the Christian Missionaries' Center, the Welfare Home for Homeless Men, all able-bodied alcoholics are put to work, negating any acceptance of lowered status because of any charitable helping hand. As the men put it:

I don't feel as though the hospital should act like I owe them something. After I got through the first few bad days, I worked every day. I was there. Often I worked nine hours a day. The hospital would close down without our work. [44]

Look at all we do for this place. Most of the time for no pay and sometimes for a pack of cigarettes a day. [54]

I turn out $1000 worth of upholstery work a month for the Christian Missionaries. They are making money on me. [36]

I worked on the farm while I was in jail. Considering they spent about 22 cents a day feeding me, I guess they didn't lose any money on me. [18]

Even more important to feelings of status, however, is the realization by the men that an institution without clients would have to close down:

Where would the Christian Missionaries be without us, I ask you? Nowhere. They need us. They are vultures, feeding off of us. They tell the state what they do for us and then get a lot of funds. [31]

It is us alcoholics who support the police. On the County Jail Road Camp in Capital City they had 65 deputies who did nothing but sit around and watch 350 men. [60]

I suppose you know that they have to keep a certain number of us out here to justify their existences. Those social workers are actually parasites existing because of the miseries of others. [43]

There are four or five policemen on Skid Row whose jobs depend upon us. [38]

Alcoholics are aware of and talk freely to new arrivals about the fact that every institution must maintain a certain client load or its budget allocation will be jeopardized. This, of course, is further support for their belief that no favor is involved in their admission to the institution and no bond of deference exists between them and agents of social control.

The director has admitted to us that he has to keep a certain bed level in order to keep the place operating. He can only discharge a person if a replacement arrives. [38]

They have to keep a certain number at the jail or the guards would be out of work. That's why they have an agreement with the judge. [59]

When a new guy comes into the Welfare Home for Homeless Men, you should see the celebrating! It means some guy's going to get released on vouchers [welfare checks] and we all move up one. The director's as happy as we are. He has to keep 70 percent occupancy in order to justify his budget, and he hates to keep a man who wants to go. When a new guy comes in, it means that they [the administrators] will tell another man they think he is ready to go now. [49]

This belief in their value to the bed count is reinforced when they overhear *inter-station* administrative arrangements made to assist in maintenance of a desired bed-level:

I just got a call from the Church home halfway house. They are down a bed or so [bed assignments]. They wanted to know if we could spare them a couple of men. [A32] [29]

Both Heider [30] and Blau [31] have suggested that one person's lot is the function of another's. The existence of the alcoholic means that the agent of social control has a job and a career; and as a professional helper, his status is higher than his client. Thus if agents of social control did not have alcoholics to work with, perhaps they would have to invent them.[32]

Trust between Benefactor and Beneficiary

Charges of betrayal are made by both the alcoholic and the agent of social control and each can offer evidence, valid from his point of view, that is damning.

Although compassion and gratitude are usually thought of as the essential emotional elements in an interchange between the giver and the receiver, the entire transaction could not take place unless mutual trust were implicitly present. Trust can be defined as reliance on another's integrity, confidence in the good will of another.

Of the place of trust in social relations, Blau has said:

Social exchange is distinguished from strictly economic exchange by the unspecified obligations incurred in it and the trust both required for and promoted by it.[33]

Wherever there is an implicit promise and acceptance of the promise at face value, therefore, betrayal is possible.

Betrayal as a specific subject of inquiry has not been in the mainstream of sociological analysis. Trust, as an ingredient that holds society together, has been studied only by implication, except for the discussions by Garfinkel.[34] Studies of norms and the way in which they create mutual expectations plus the sanctions that follow when a norm is ignored do focus on the problem, but usually these discussions imply that the *definitions* of trust and betrayal are nonproblematic.

The analysis here will therefore move one step back in the sequence of action. The point at which an actor decides he has *grounds* for trusting must be examined. Next, there is the point at which the actor re-assesses the situation and decides he has made a mistake—often costly—and that the assumed grounds for trust were either not present in fact or were insufficient to prevent what he *defines to be* betrayal.

THE ASSUMED GROUNDS FOR TRUST   To accept aid from the giver, the receiver must trust enough to feel reasonably sure that the aid is *intended* as just that. To offer aid to the receiver, the giver must trust enough to be reasonably certain his aid will be wisely used and he will not be harmed by the recipient.

Simmel has pointed out that in social transactions, where the people involved are not personal friends, the trust—reliance—must be on the *role* of the other.[35] Therefore, most people will tentatively trust a doctor they have selected from a phone book, should they be taken ill in a strange town, because the doctor's role projects an image of trustworthiness that transcends geographic boundaries. Likewise, the doctor will treat them as patients although he does not know them, because of the trusting patient role presented. The reverse is also true: once betrayed by someone in a given role, the role itself (and all persons in it) become suspect.

In the specific case of the Skid Row alcoholic and the stations on the loop, both the men and the agents of social control have good reasons to feel—upon naïve first contact—that they can trust each other in terms of the roles each presents.

Service institutions implicitly assure the following:

Go along with the program here and it will help you. The staff knows what it is doing and will put all its talents to work on your case.

The patient also makes an implicit promise:

I sincerely want and need help and will do my utmost to cooperate with your expert efforts.

Often, by the time the association is terminated, they both feel betrayed. More importantly, the reaction to this defined betrayal is reflected in the caution with which each handles the other, or *subsequent persons in that role*. Each feels the other is probably lacking in *sincerity* when stating his aims and is therefore *untrustworthy*.

THE ABSENCE OF SINCERITY   As previously mentioned, agents of social control frequently complain about the lack of sincerity (in therapeutic terms) on the part of the alcoholics seeking help. Alcoholics likewise feel they are being dealt with by hypocrites.

Sincerity has many indicators on the world of the loop. For the professional, the emphasis is always on an expressed willingness to be honest about real *personal* problems. If concerned about his pattern of drinking and possible motivations for this action, the alcoholic is seen as sincere. If concerned about his current existential problems—no place to stay, no money, no contacts, no job, the alcoholic is considered to be *insincere* about wanting to stop drinking.

Because of previous disillusioning experiences, agents of social control often doubt the sincerity of the Skid Row alcoholic from the moment an intake interview begins. According to social workers:

> They'll come to you and they'll answer that they want to stop drinking, that they know it's killing them, and that they've got to do something before it does. But I've seen it too many times to believe it. They sound sincere but they don't really mean it. [A44]

> You can assume they lie at intake, just to get in. (A repeated statement at every station on the loop.)

If the alcoholic does mention real problems, if he cooperates with his therapist but still returns to drinking, then he is considered guilty of a far more serious type of insincerity—manipulation. This is particularly true if he made some obvious secondary gain during his stay at the institution—medical aid with withdrawal, board and room, a new suit, or a stake. Only the professional helper is supposed to be manipulative in a giver-receiver situation. Thus when the charge is manipulation, the discussion is much more venomous than if the lack of sincerity had been apprehended earlier.

> I think alcoholics are the lowest form of humanity. They are *bums*. They are cunning and conniving. They manipulate and con you. They are whiners. They ought to be put in the stocks—not treated. They are not ill—just weak. [A55]

> These men have the mentality and morals of children. You must watch them all the time. When they seem the most sincere is probably when they are putting you on the most. They think it is a joke. Often they are not really serious about stopping their drinking. [A34]

The alcoholic also has his case for lack of sincerity on the part of the agents of social control:

> Those Christian Missionaries are strictly a bogus outfit. I put it plain—a bogus outfit. [48]

> I was brought to the Welfare Home for Homeless Men under false pretenses. They said that if I went out for 30 days, I could qualify for vouchers [welfare checks]. But when I got out there and stayed 30 days and then asked to go, they said, "Sorry, there's ten guys ahead of you." It was the same story in 60 days. I've been here all summer. [49] [36]

They said they wanted to help me. Actually, I found myself working for free for them. [41]

Drunk court is no court at all. It is a travesty on American justice. [58]

MUTUAL ABSENCE OF TRUSTWORTHINESS   Agents of social control who help down-and-out alcoholics have a catalog of misdemeanors they cite to show how they are injured by their untrustworthy clients:

Complaints against Skid Row alcoholics
They steal things from the institution.
They try to con you out of extra issue of clothing so they can sell it.
They take extra food.
They hide out from work assignments.
They smuggle in liquor.

However, the Skid Row alcoholics also cite evidence in support of their charges of harm. Their claims are best summarized by Deutsch, who argues that if an actor doubts another person has his welfare at heart, the actor cannot develop trust in him.[37] Alcoholics generally believe the agent of social control cannot be trusted because he continues to offer ("with a straight face") assistance he actually is unable to deliver. Therefore the alcoholic doubts the good intentions of agents of social control.[38]

Complaints against Professional Rehabilitators
We're "sentenced to therapy" at the jail and there is none.
We go to the hospital for "the cure" and they have none.
We go to the Christian Missionaries for charity and there is none.

The men further complain their job-getting ability is almost irreparably damaged by the stigma of having been in an institution that claimed to help them.

Thus the Row men do not feel they are acting wrongfully when they goof-off on work assignments, steal small items, smuggle in liquor, or take off. They ask: What does a betrayed person owe his betrayers?

Both the agents of social control and the Skid Row alcoholics thus learn to have distrustful *expectations* of each other that color all their future interactions and tend to be reinforced with each new breach of the ideal giver-receiver model. As agents process alcoholics, they are "on their guard," ready to ascribe the actions or conversations of the drunks with the characteristics of an "ungrateful, untrustworthy manipulator." The alcoholic has ready-made role categories for the activities of his would-be rehabilitators: "untrustworthy, cold fish, hypocrites."

It takes little imagination to visualize the spiraling hostilities that have emerged. Like Lemert's "Paranoia, the Dynamics of Exclusion," [39] each protagonist gets what he expects, in part, by acting as though he expects it (although there are often some grounds for the original expectations).

WHOSE DESCRIPTION OF REALITY PREVAILS?

As the situation is formally constructed, and by the essential nature of the institutions on the loop, the agents have almost all of the power and can therefore impose their definitions of situations while the receivers have little recourse. Agents of social control are usually especially trained for their work. They know current theories of causes and cures for alcoholism. It is within their power to offer or decline therapy, to designate release or expulsion dates. During the time the alcoholic is in the institution, they can mete out rewards and punishments. Most important of all, they have the rights of screening for admission.

Screening is the strongest weapon for maintaining the semblance of the benefactor-beneficiary image—it keeps out dissidents and challengers who might arouse others to rebellion. The search for sincerity can be easily translated into a search for men who will appear to accept current definitions of institutional activity at face value.

Alcoholics are not, however, totally powerless against the definitions of the establishment. They often are able to manipulate themselves from an undesirable loop station to a desirable one. They can sometimes force admission to a reluctant station. They can, at times, misbehave in a loop station and not be expelled. Most important of all, they can maintain some role distance [40] despite the low status into which agents of social control cast them. From where does the power to achieve these desirable strategic objectives come?

A major source of tactical power is the knowledge of the location of weakness in the opposition. Most Skid Row alcoholics are far from naive clients and they quickly locate the weaknesses of the opposition with the characteristic fortitude of men who have successfully survived in the back alleys and tenement hotels of Skid Row.

There are four major sources of weakness inherent in the structure of the loop that can be used by the Skid Row alcoholic to create power for himself so he can buttress *his* definition of the beneficiary-benefactor situation: (1) the alcoholics have access to all stations on the loop, including backstage areas [41]—although range of access depends, in part, on length of stay at a given station; (2) the alcoholics are aware of the nature of various theories of alcoholism and cures for it, and they are further aware that these theories are, for the most part, unvalidated; (3) they have a special awareness of station dependency on them to maintain the bed count; (4) jealousy among various agents of stations and competitiveness between stations on the loop leads to information leaks about other stations, their faults, and the human (often private) frailties of their staffs.

Knowledge of these weakness areas on the loop will be discussed in terms of the power-leverage it offers to the Skid Row alcoholic to resist official designations of what is happening, or to use the expectations created by these definitions to their own advantage.

Access to All Stations on the Loop

In chapter 2, it was observed the Skid Row alcoholic is more sophisticated than agents of social control about informal machinations on the loop. He has seen all or most of the stations on the loop, while the agent usually is limited to experience at his own station.

As a result of making the loop, Skid Row alcoholics are in a position to make comparisons about the validity of different claims for an activity as therapeutic, or of an institutional agent as compassionate. More importantly, the alcoholic is in a unique position to develop awareness of *the relativity of truth* [42]—i.e., what is claimed as true is indeed a result of *subjective evaluation* rather than "fact." This is perhaps the best single insulator against accepting the claims of the professionals as to what is really going on.

These men see definitions of the truth as being so flexible that during an interview one said:

They [the judges, policemen, jailers] don't follow the law. They just find something they don't like and they look around for a law to slap over it. [12]

And another said:

I think that anyone who has arrived at the point in life where he has to live on Skid Row has already taken such a beating by life that he is not going to worry too darn much whether the judge or anybody else *is being accurate or fair or anything else; because they do what they want to do with you, and then try to persuade you it was for your own good.* [40] (Emphasis mine.)

The State of Knowledge on Alcoholism as a Source of Power to the Alcoholic

There is nothing more eye-opening to the possibility something is not really as its label states than to see that it has been given several different labels by different people. Alcoholism is described at various times as a disease, an addiction, an illness, a moral weakness, and a crime. As a result, Skid Row drunks who make the loop become somewhat cynical about the name given to their uncontrolled drinking and the presumed cures offered for it. Furthermore, the men perceive an internal inconsistency within each subfield of alcoholism. For instance, professionals who claim alcoholism is an illness are not consistent in their treatment of men who frequently slip off the wagon. Rather than viewing these recidivists as sicker than most men and therefore needing more attention than most, they begin to refer to them by such terms as "unmotivated," or "troublemakers." The agents who claim to believe the illness theory eventually will deny access to the stations on the loop to their "most seriously ill," that is, the recidivist patients. The same inconsistency occurs among those who see alcoholism as a moral or spiritual weakness. Recurrence of drinking behavior can disqualify a man for aid—rather than get him more help. *In the same vein, getting caught drunk can cause a man to be put in an institution if he is not in one, and thrown out of one if he is in.*[43] These incongruities in the system make the men doubt what officials say about the nature of pathological drinking.

Awareness of Bed-Count Dependency

As previously mentioned, men who make the loop become aware of their dollar value in the population maintenance of a given station (and thus to the station budget). The Row men know that for this reason (especially in the summer when admissions drop off), they are often most welcome—whether or not they seem to accept the definition of the situation offered by the professionals. This knowledge gives the man who is seeking entry into a station the power to have his definitional way because of seasonal exigencies. These seasonal limitations suggest the problems that affect the criteria for screening at any time. If the criteria were strictly applied, few Skid Row alcoholics would be admitted to any station or therapy after one or two times around the circle.

Jealousy among Professionals

Because all loop stations service the same clientele, there is some competitiveness among professionals on the loop, even while they cooperate with each other to some extent. This competitiveness, or even jealousy, works to the advantage of the alcoholic in locating areas of presumed hypocrisy. Making the round of institutions, he often is told about the faults and weaknesses of *other* institutions or well-known staff members at other institutions. For instance:

At the Christian Missionaries, a staff member said:

I think the Christian Missionaries do a lot more for the alcoholic than the State Mental Hospital does.

An officer of the Missionaries said:

We have been in the rehabilitation field long before these agencies [other agencies at the jail] ever thought of it. They are beginners compared to our experience.

At the Welfare Home for Homeless Men, a staff member stated:

We do a lot more for these men that is of practical help to them than the State Mental Hospital. And as for the Christian Missionaries—they are a cancer in the field of rehabilitation!

At the County Jail, a deputy sheriff says:

I think we do as much or more for these men as the mental hospital and the city welfare department.

At the State Mental Hospital, a staff member says:

They [other stations on the loop] are all learning from us. We are the pioneers and leaders in the field of alcoholism therapy. Just the other day we gave some of the staff members from agencies in Pacific City a tour of our alcoholism unit.

At County Hospital, a physician says:

They [jail guards and clinic personnel] are doing nothing for these guys at the jail except keeping them away from alcohol and drying them out. They are sitting on their fannies. Some of these guys die in withdrawal before they get attention.

Along with these pieces of information, the gossiping agents are purveyors of another type of useful information—the *personal* (and often private) weaknesses of their peers, the various well-known officials who operate stations on the loop. Stories of "scandalous" activities in the personal lives of the men in charge of alcoholics become, whether true or not, a part of the folk lore and are passed along the loop grapevine in much the same way that agents share "the file" on their mutual clients.[44] These weaknesses need not necessarily be directly related to the giver-receiver relationship. Some flaw that discredits the person so that he cannot be morally better than his beneficiaries is sufficient:

We all have to laugh at Bill _____ [the social worker] mincing around here, we know what he really is . . . And he sets himself up as better than us and tries to give us advice . . . He's not even a real man.

Did you know that the man in charge of this place ———— [station on the loop] had an affair with another official's wife? Got busted for it, too. Who is he to talk to us about our sins and slips, anyway?

You know who is in charge of that place? Some ex-lushes. And everyone knows there is nothing more depressing and more lacking in understanding toward lushes than an ex-lush.

Did you hear about the time the deputy took some of the prisoners into town with him and they all went to a tavern and got drunk? They were so bad off someone had to pick them up. But it was all hushed up.

There's a psychologist here working with alcoholics who has taken LSD six or eight times.

A sort of halo effect occurs with these recitations: if the agents have been adjudged phony good guys then their therapy (and the terminology used to describe it) must be phony too. The power this gives the down-and-out alcoholics is definitional as to their own status as well as to that of the givers of assistance. The alcoholic can say, in effect, "Who are *they* [the agents of social control, the representatives of square society] to be sitting in judgment on me?" This is followed by a recitation of some known weakness or scandal heard about the official.

Euphemisms as a Method of Social Control

As is apparent, the battle of the loop is a battle of words and definitions. When its protagonists disagree about the content of their relationship (Who owes gratitude? Who lacks compassion? Who is betrayed?), a major approach to situation control is that of definition control.[45] Like propaganda experts, each would like to bring out what he believes to be the most positive description of who he is and what he is doing in order to persuade the other of his worthiness. An attempt at such influence by linguistic means can be detected by listening to the euphemisms used to describe actions, treatments, and decisions when the Row alcoholic and the professional benefactor meet (or talk behind each other's backs).

Euphemisms are words or phrases used to reduce and ease the psychological pain, tension, or outrage that are expected as reactions to potentially unpleasant persons, objects, places, situations, or activities. The euphemism is, in fact, a valuable social lubricant and its presence can be taken as *prima facie* evidence that a touchy situation exists.

Euphemisms, of course, are found in abundance when topics considered socially delicate (like sex, excretion, and death) are discussed. For example, pelvic examinations are often spoken of as "the doctor wants to take a peek at you," or "let's take a look down here." [46] Contraception is called "family planning," or "planned parenthood." Sexual intercourse is called "going to bed with" or "having relations with." Bathrooms are called "powder rooms." Excretory products are called "BM's." Death is called "passing away." This substitution of emotionally neutral for emotionally loaded terms occurs in varying degree, in all societies, according to anthropologists.

In addition to being used in socially delicate situations or to refer to socially delicate topics, euphemisms are often used in a more Machiavellian sense—as *miscues* to manipulate people. The term "miscues" refers to the deliberate distortion of existential facts to create an illusion about a situation and thus to seduce significant others into action they might not otherwise have considered.[47]

In the case of organization and institutions, euphemisms and miscues are used by the staff to make outsiders or newcomers define the observed official activities as congruent with an official perspective or goal.[48] Clients of organizations also use such devices to persuade the staff of their worthiness to receive aid or to challenge or neutralize staff euphemisms.[49]

Actually, two types of touchy situations exist in the world of the loop that both agents of social control and the alcoholic men gloss over with euphemisms. The first includes such unpleasant but officially-supported activities as painful therapy and work assignments. This type of touchy situation includes topics relating to the absence of any cure or even criteria for improvement in alcoholism. The second refers to the area of personal antagonisms that develop between agents and drunks out of the violations of expectations on the gratitude-compassion-trust axes already described.

Not surprisingly, miscues or euphemisms are often used where an interaction involves something crucial to both participators—a lowering of status for the alcoholic that must be managed smoothly. On the loop, such euphemistic designations are made—and can be challenged—in the situations previously referred to as defining encounters:

1. Admissions or screening (in order to protect the decision from appeal)

2. Assignments

3. Therapy

4. Discharge.

In each of these situations, the giver and receiver confront each other and each would like to show the other compassion, instill trust, and permit gratitude to be shown without risking betrayal and ingratitude. In each situation, a status struggle is involved. In each, euphemisms and miscues become a major weapon. This weapon is only partly successful, however, since everyone involved soon comes to understand and parry the euphemisms of the other party.

Professional staff euphemisms are listed in Table 21, according to type of defining encounter in which they are used most often and classified by the type of giver-receiver problem with which they seem to be attempting to cope. The translations in the table are of two types: (1) the meaning the staff attaches to the euphemism and (2) the meaning the seasoned loop-traveler automatically assumes.

TABLE 21. Staff Euphemisms and Miscues

Euphemism: You are accepted/admitted.

Staff Meaning	*Client translation*
Not all applicants are accepted. You have passed our selective screening and seem like a good risk. We are here to help you.	1. Their bed count is low. 2. They could use some skill that I have. 3. I have a pretty good reputation here. I've never given them much trouble. I do my work and don't smart off to the staff.

Euphemism: We have a dedicated staff here.

Our staff is not antagonistic to alcoholics. In fact, it does its best to help them, despite the difficulties these men present.	A staff is composed of persons who get paid for working in institutions where alcoholics are sent or go voluntarily.

Euphemism: We are here to help you.

We are professionals and understand your problem better than you do.	As long as you consider what we are doing for you as help, we will allow you to stay here.

Euphemism: You have been (committed, sentenced, referred) here so that we can help you.

Do not look at (going to jail, going to State Mental Hospital etc.) as a punishment or a disgrace. Those places are set up for the purpose of helping men like you.	1. Your relatives can't handle you anymore. 2. You are annoying the upright, tax-paying citizens. 3. We want you to think we are offering help so you will be docile about going.

Euphemism: Making progress. (Also referred to as "getting insight.")

A man who is making progress is usually discussing past mistakes and hang-ups openly. He shows contrition for these and deference to the staff for their wisdom in helping him locate the mistakes.	1. You have been very cooperative with the staff. 2. You have yelled, cried, and demeaned yourself in group therapy.

Euphemism: Getting the program.

A person who takes part in all the institution's activities—both therapeutic and social.	Volunteering to help out with chores and acting grateful to the staff.

Euphemism: We'll give you another chance (Usually said in connection with a client being caught drinking).

We try to be understanding about "slips." We realize your anxiety level gets the better of you.	You will not be thrown out this time because . . . 1. We have an unusually low bed count. 2. We need every hand we can get.

Staff Meaning

Client translation

3. You have a skill that is needed here.
4. You are one of our favorites (because you seem to be "getting the program").

Euphemism: You will be given an industrial therapy/work assignment.

Work is good for everyone. It helps you build up physically and gets your mind off your troubles mentally. (This is intended to show a continuing interest in the client and reassure him that he is working on his problem daily.)

1. Work.
2. We are short a (whatever the skill is involved in the assignment).

Euphemism: Beneficiary

This program is being run for your benefit. We are here to offer you the kinds of aid that will be helpful with your alcoholism problem.

1. This is our way of letting you know that you do not have employee status, despite the amount of work you do. Further, it is a way of reminding you that you are the object of our "charity."
2. Do not expect minimum wages, overtime, or any of the other benefits and protections offered employees by state law.

Euphemism: Gratuity

Even though we do not have to, we pay you a small sum for the work you do here. This is in addition to your board, room, and clothing. We feel that all men should have a little spending money. Your gratuity will also provide an incentive to do well on the program, for it will be raised on that basis. (Intended to show compassion.)

1. Slave wages.
2. Money for liquor if another source of pin money (i.e., pension, disability pay, etc.) is available.

Euphemism: Therapy

Activities (the "specialty of the house," so to speak) intended to cure a man of his need to drink compulsively and heavily and to rehabilitate him for return to "normal" society.

Any activity so designated.

Euphemism: We are going to deal with your *real* problems here.

We are interested in helping you find your long-term psychological or social hangups that cause you to drink. We are not referring to short-term needs such as food, shelter, a job, and someone to relate to.

The type of problems with which the staff prefers to work.

Euphemism: You aren't ready to hunt for work on the outside yet.

It has been our experience that men who leave the program too soon start drinking right away.

Our bed count is down; we need you here.

Euphemism: We don't like to let a man out on pass until he has a substantial lead on a job.

Job hunting is usually an excuse to go out

The less time a man is allowed to look

Staff Meaning
and get drunk. Also, if a man has no specific appointments, he is likely to wander around, get discouraged, and get drunk. Men often come back from job hunting drunk and then we are faced with the decision of whether or not to throw them out.

Client translation
for a job, the longer he can be kept working for the organization.

Euphemism: You are ready for discharge.

We have done all we can for you. We have developed a standard length of time for most clients here and you have completed that length of stay.

1. You have been here a long time.
2. Our bed count is up now.
3. We need your bed for new admissions.
4. You are a troublemaker.

The Skid Row grapevine is a very efficient source of information about the proper form of euphemism to use to obtain admission to or discharge from an institution, get good quarters, soft jobs, better food, and other special favors. Little by little, piecing together the information gained by others during their trips on the loop, plus his own experiences there, the alcoholic learns the presenting "symptom" that will get him a job in the kitchen of City Jail instead of going to County Jail; how to seem to be "safe" on the Christian Missionary program; how to be a welcome addition to the Northern State Mental Hospital atmosphere, and how to show sincerity on demand. In other words they learn the proper responding euphemisms.

As the men explain it:

If the judge says, "I haven't seen you for a while," you say that you've been on the wagon. Never admit you've been out of town. Then he assumes you've been drunk the whole time.

If the judge says, "Have you got a job to go to?" you say, "Yes." It's a better way to get a kickout.

If you want a pass to go look for a job, tell them your brother is very sick.

If you want to get into State Mental Hospital, tell them that you heard they have a wonderful program.

If you want to go to the hospital instead of the jail, act like you are having hallucinations.

Always go to the Christian Missionaries around the first of the week. Tell them you have some kind of skill that would be good in the salvage business.

It is quite possible that when people speak of manipulative alcoholics, they are referring to attempts on the part of the alcoholic to use what seems to them to be professional dodges that are enormously successful.[50] Alcoholics, becoming aware that some ways of expressing their needs are more acceptable than others, attempt to meet these middle-class expectations. Thus, as can be seen in Table 22, alcoholics have also developed euphemisms by which they hope to convince agents of social control of their sincerity and their need for aid. Wary agents also offer their own translations.

TABLE 22. *Alcoholics' Euphemisms and Miscues*

Euphemism: I've got to stop drinking and I'm ready to do *anything* you suggest.

Alcoholic's Meaning	*Agent's Translation*
Right now, I really mean it.	I want to impress you with my sincerity so that I can get in your institution for a while.

Euphemism: I'm sick.

I'm desperate. I'm sick and I have no money. I feel so awful that I'm afraid I might die.	I've been drinking heavily and now I'm out of booze and money and going through withdrawal.

Euphemism: I'd like to pull myself together.

I feel as though I've lost control over myself. I don't know what to do. I can't think.	I'd like to stop drinking, dry myself out, build myself up, and then start drinking again.

Euphemism: I'm an epileptic.

I have seizures that are like epilepsy and Dilantin helps.	If I claim epilepsy, I get to take some barbiturates.

Euphemism: I'm working on my problem.

I am trying to do what is expected of me here. (Shows trust in staff.)	(Usually accepted at face value)

Unhappily for alcoholics, they lack both the resources and the talents (and perhaps the inclination) to manage these fictions for long. The fact that alcoholics are known as manipulators (while agents of social control are not) is testimony to their lack of skill in the use of euphemistic niceties. A successful mesmerizer never gains a reputation as a charlatan.

SELF-GENERATING ASPECTS OF THE LOOP

As can be seen, not only can many things go wrong in the relationship of the benefactor and the beneficiary, but the distortions, once initiated, can be self-enhancing and self-perpetuating.

At the heart of the matter is the problematic nature of definitions.

A gift is only received as such when it is defined as such by the recipient. Whether response to a gift indicates betrayal or maintenance of trust, depends on complementarity of definitions. Where this is not present, persons involved may turn sour and commit acts that escalate initial bad feelings.

The attempt to control the confronting situation by the use of euphemisms is only sporatically successful. The agents and alcoholics become locked in a transactional struggle to see whose euphemisms are more viable. Although there is no doubt the agents retain most of the power, it is not as total as might be expected by looking only at the formal structure. Down-and-out drunks have found chinks in the armor of the loop that give them leverage for strategy.

Agents of social control view their clients with a combination of exasperation, anger, and despair. The Skid Row alcoholic sees the operators of loop in which he is moving as heartless, insincere, and lacking in compassion for his problems. Professional rehabilitators say:

> I get *so* discouraged. I keep seeing the same men over and over . . . I've almost stopped trying.[51]

And the Skid Row alcoholics say:

> We're all going around—every alcoholic's running around in a squirrel cage and some of 'em just feel defeated. I do most of the time. You try all these different approaches and you get lost.[52]

Appendix: Methodology

INTRODUCTION

The methodological task of this study has been to apprehend and reconstruct, as closely as possible, the perspectives of persons from two very different social worlds—one deviant by middle-class criteria, the other professionally involved in the enforcement of middle-class expectations. Special emphasis has been placed on the evaluative definitions they develop of each other.

The deviant world is that of the Skid Row alcoholic. This world is in a subordinate position to the occupational world of the agents of social control, who are trying to rehabilitate these chronic drunkenness offenders. Despite the fact these groups intersect on a regular basis as a result of declared goals, each maintains its cultural integrity. A complicated, self-regenerating, symbiotic relationship has evolved that appears to prevent either complete assimilation or total disengagement from the perspectives and normative understandings of the other.

As indicated in the Preface to the main report, an important way to analyze the relationship between these protagonists is to trace histories of the very different commonsense frameworks through which each views the world in general and the other in particular. Then, using the perspectives generated by these frameworks as a guide, an attempt can be made to understand resultant defining encounters between representatives of each group.

The goal of this study differs markedly from efforts at statistical measurement of attitudes or characteristics of subsocieties—that is, the standard survey research-multivariate analysis. Multivariate analysis is a frequently-used approach in sociology to infer causality and is methodologically well developed. Holistic descriptions of cultural perspectives, such as this study, present the investigator with problems that are different from those of survey research. Although there have been many attempts to build theory for this approach, few practitioners have attempted to codify their methodology. Thus the investigator, lacking established directives, is often forced to develop strategies for uncovering the actor's views that have little precedent and are difficult to test for validity and reliability.

What follows here then is a discussion of the methodological problems encountered in this study and the strategies used in an attempt to overcome them. It is hoped this description will aid the reader in assessing the strengths and weaknesses of the study, while also serving as a worthwhile addition to existing materials on the goals and methods of naturalistic field work.

DECIPHERING THE ACTOR'S PERSPECTIVE

What is the actor's perspective and how can it be located?

Becker and Geer suggest this definition, used in their study *Boys in White:*

> We use the term "perspective" to describe a set of ideas and actions used by a group in solving collective problems. The content of a group's perspective includes a definition of the environment and the problems it presents as seen by group members, an expression of what members expect to derive from the environment, and the ideas and actions group members employ in dealing with the problem situation.[1]

In many ways, the researcher's objective of ascertaining and perceiving the actor's perspective is quite similar to what any social actor does [2] in order to conduct himself as properly as possible in a foreign setting and thus avoid sanctions:

1. He observes everyday action and attempts to reconstruct the definition of the situation on which "natives" appear to base their activities.
2. He asks questions of "the natives" to find out "what is going on" and what sort of action is expected to ensue as a result.[3]
3. He finds special informants.[4] These are people who, by virtue of some official capacity in the world under study, or because of some marginal status that makes them unusually sensitive to everyday expectations,[5] can give the researcher a great deal of insight (the real "low down") about some society.
4. He *tests* both the answers received to direct questions and the interpretation he makes of the action observed to see if, in the context they were made, the perspective he is developing "works." That is, he sees if his analysis would enable a person to participate intelligently in the setting and to reasonably understand and predict the reactions of others.[6]

The approach of the researcher differs significantly from that of the naive actor participating in the situation, however, in that the researcher is attempting to organize the bits and pieces of social structure and culture he gathers into a *comprehensive whole.* This is not to say that the participant does not attempt to organize his findings; but for his purposes this enterprise can stop short of a general description of a way of life. Cavan makes this distinction in her ethnography of a Hippie community. Paraphrased, her point is this:

> The research enterprise is different from the activity of the regular participant whose reason for observing is practical—to organize those portions of ongoing life

that are immediately relevant. The [researcher] observer is looking for integrated systems, a description of the "world view" constituted by a systemization of segments of immediately relevant matters.

This is not to say that the observer will see something the members can never see. If at any time the participating members were to stop participating, and reflect back upon what they had participated in, they too would be provided with the organized perspective utilized by the observer.[7]

This study on Skid Row alcoholics goes beyond *one* "world view." It attempts to present *two perspectives on the same social scene* and the effect that each has on the other's maintenance and development. Real-life participants also attempt to do this in order to predict the actions of someone from another world with whom they must interact. As with their other efforts at understanding and predicting, most individual actors proceed on a pragmatic, piecemeal basis. They do not try to assume the total perspective of the other or to perceive *his* rationale. In fact, as Garfinkel has shown, the social actor constructs logical, but often distorted, reasons for the acts of others, which usually do not coincide with the logic used by the actor in question.[8]

A general description of the methodological approach to this joint world reconstruction would be the following: Skid Row problem drinkers and agents of social control were interviewed at length about their daily activities, their opinions about their peers, and about each other. They were also observed as they interacted in various settings. These observations ranged from those in which both parties knew a "stranger" (i.e., the investigator) was present, to those where only one party knew, to those where neither party knew and the observer was passing as a participant. This variety in approach, in part, was dictated by the goals of the study, as well as necessitated by various problems of institutional security and cooperation.

The foregoing, however, gives the reader little idea of the actual details of the field work. Inasmuch as the final results of research are dependent upon numerous interim activities and decisions, it seems fitting that a chronology of these events, and the rationale behind them be presented.[9]

RESEARCH DECISIONS AND DEVELOPMENTAL STAGES

Becker and Geer have suggested that the *methodological operations* that are carried on during a field investigation of the type undertaken in this report, can be divided into three stages:

1. Select and define problems, concepts, and indices
2. Check on the frequency and distribution of phenomena
3. Incorporate individual findings into a model of the organization under study.[10]

Becker and Geer further suggest that each of these stages is mutually exclusive and follows in logical time sequence. In this study, however, the goals of the research required moving back and forth between analytic operations of all stages. Attempts to apprehend and reconstruct the belief systems or perspectives of another may involve both induction and deduction. That is, first an attempt was made to reason from parts of the perspective to wholes; then, in later stages, when large "portions" of a model of the world view of the subjects and how it works have been pieced together, the researcher can begin to reason from the general to the particular. This may cause further adjustments so the researcher will revert to working in the other direction again.[11] Nash makes this same point when he discusses the problems of a methodological marriage between ideographic and nomothetic approaches in anthropology:

> The theory strives for a nomological form—it attempts to state laws, but it must account for the facts gathered. That is, it is an uneasy mixture between deductive and inductive nomological theories. . . .[12]

Nevertheless, Becker's paradigm is useful as a scheme for presentation in this report; it assists in organizing research operations of this type of study into logical categories; further, the implied time sequence is *loosely applicable*.

Stage 1. Selection and Definition of Problems, Concepts, and Indices

Initially this study was limited to life of the Skid Row alcoholic from his point of view.

The city that was selected for the study is the hub of a large metropolitan area with approximately 8.5 million population. Skid Row in this city was one of those investigated by Bogue in his demographic and attitudinal study, *Skid Row in American Cities*.[13] In keeping with National Institute of Mental Health protocol on the protection of research subjects,[14] the names of the city, its rehabilitation organizations, as well as the respondents themselves, have been replaced by pseudonyms.

The first investigative steps taken were participant observation on Skid Row (with the aid of a paid "guide," a Skid Row hotel clerk who knew the area), and interviewing of Skid Row alcoholics at a cooperating institution, a shelter provided by the City Welfare Department. This latter approach afforded the opportunity to talk at length with these men while they were in a state of sobriety.

The subjects interviewed were chosen from those institutionalized at least three times for a drinking problem. They had lived within the boundaries of Skid Row in Pacific City during the previous three years.[15] Bogue's criteria for determining Skid Row boundaries were used to delineate the area under study.

Becker and Geer have pointed out that "during the first stages of analysis, the observer looks for problems and concepts that give promise of yielding the greatest understanding of the (social) organization he is studying, and he looks for items which may serve as useful indicators of facts which are harder to observe." [16] This is exactly what occurred in this research and illustrates the usefulness of their advice.

Early in the course of the interviewing, it was ascertained that few of the alcoholics spend an uninterrupted year on the Row. Instead, they travel a circuit from institution to institution, voluntarily or involuntarily, seeking or having forced on them, shelter and/or therapy for their drinking problem. The discovery of the loop constituted, in Becker's terms, a concept that gave promise of yielding the greatest understanding of the social organization of the lives of Skid Row alcoholics; therefore, the focus of the research was broadened to include institutions on the loop.

As the study progressed, more and more "stations," as the institutions are referred to in the study, were mentioned by respondents as being part of the loop. There were so many such stations, in fact, that it became apparent the field work could not possibly be expanded to undertake an investigation of them all. The next research decision, therefore, was to *categorize* the stations by type and to limit the number of stations studied to those considered exemplars of the most popular approaches to the treatment of alcoholism—the punitive-correctional (County Jail), the psychological-physiological-therapeutic (therapy at the Jail and the State Mental Hospital), and the paternalistic-spiritual (Christian Missionaries). The stations selected were also considered to represent major stations on the loop of any large metropolitan area. Other unique but important stations mentioned in the study include the City Hospital, the Out-Patient Therapy Clinic, and the Welfare Home for Homeless Men.[17]

Where more than one branch of an institution was available to the Pacific City Skid Row alcoholic, the one that received the largest proportion of these men on a *long-term* basis was selected for study. On this basis, the second County Jail branch, the State Mental Hospital, and the Christian Missionaries' Work and Residence Center (rather than that organization's other missions) were selected.

Following the decision to devote a good deal of research time to exemplar stations on the loop another unexpected finding shaped the study. When the Skid Row men spoke of or described the loop, they pictured it as a haphazard cluster of institutions, with no particular intermural organization or relationship, but with many informal links. Furthermore, the stated grounds upon which men were sent (or committed) to institutions were seen by them as highly idiosyncratic.

On the other hand, when discussing the loop with a doctor at City Hospital, I realized he saw the connections between these institutions rather differently than the "clients." His description—and indeed a rough drawing he made for me—depicted an orderly, planned relationship between institutions in which an alcoholic went to one institution for a specific purpose, was referred to another for another purpose, and finally was referred to another for aid in "returning to society." A city public health department chart of the relationship between these institutions confirmed the doctor's view of the presumed orderliness of the stations as the official one, a great contrast to the absence of order the alcoholics themselves perceive.

Confronted with this obvious difference in perceptions, I became interested in comparing the view that the agents of social control had of their work with the alcoholics' description. It was then that a study of the *two* perspectives was begun, along with an analysis of the resultant interactions, and the defining encounters that occurred between the representatives of each world.[18] With this expansion in focus, I began watching for parallel phenomena that could be compared for each perspective.

For example, the *movement* between stations and its rationale is visualized quite differently by the Skid Row men and their would-be rehabilitators.

Therefore, the analysis was expanded to include comparative views on paths into each of these stations and paths out—plus the formal and informal connections between them as reported by both types of participants.

As the study progressed, other important parallel concepts and constructs emerged. Alternative goals and ideologies maintained by agents of social control and Skid Row men in the face of a high rate of recidivism were investigated. Perceptions of gains and losses in terms of rehabilitation, and social consequences resulting from having made the loop were pursued. The phenomenon of screening criteria used by each "side" to protect himself from the presumed undesirable features of the other also became important parts in the investigation of defining encounters and their outcomes.

Stage 2. Check on the Frequency and Distribution of Phenomena

Becker and Geer describe the second stage of analysis as follows:

> . . . the observer, possessing many provisional problems, concepts, and indicators, now wishes to know which of these are worth pursuing as major foci of his study. He does this, in part, by discovering whether the events that prompted their development are typical and widespread, and by seeing how these events are distributed among categories of people and organizational sub-units. He reaches conclusions that are essentially quantitative, using them to describe the organization he is studying.[19]

This stage can best be discussed by addressing the problems of (a) the types of data collected, (b) the manner of processing it, and (c) the significance of a given phenomenon.

TYPES OF DATA COLLECTED Depth interviews and observations were the two major approaches to data collection. Records were examined where available to corroborate statements made during interviews. Each of these approaches gives the investigator access to a specific type of data, from which inferences about the scope and frequency of a given phenomenon can be drawn.

Asking the social actor to discuss the grounds on which he made certain decisions to act, or inferring these grounds from a recitation of his attitudes, has both advantages and drawbacks. Assuming frankness on the part of respondents, it does, of course, tap his conscious reasoning to some extent.[20] However, such a method puts much reliance on faulty memory, and the truthfulness or selective reactions of the respondent. Even more serious, the method may create data from obliging informants who instantly produce reasons where none may previously have been formulated.[21] Thus the investigator runs the risk of neglecting to assess the perspective that may underlie the decisions of the respondent, because the respondent is not consciously aware of it.

Observing encounters in action and inferring decision-making processes from them is an alternative approach to attitude collection and retrospective accounts of encounters. It draws on the ability of the sociologist to apprehend the pertinent aspects of the situation that could account for the actions of participants. The drawback here, of course, is that the investigator imposes his subjectivity onto that of the actor's.[22]

Although problems are inherent in each of these approaches, they were both used in this study in hopes that they would supplement each other, since there are no practical alternatives. Becker and Geer also appear to concur in this dual methodology. Although their statement refers to conversations overheard as well as answers to direct questions, it expresses the position of this study:

> If all the items consisted of observations of activity or if all the items consisted of statements made by students, our conclusions would be affected by this disproportion. If all items were observations of activities and there were no statements on the subject, we know nothing of students' views. Similarly, in the opposite case, we might conclude that the perspective was "all talk" and unrelated to the students' behavior.[23]

Interviews were unstructured and were an attempt to simulate the way in which any outsider tries to get to know "the ropes" in a strange culture—by asking questions. The interviews were thus "focused" around the problem for research. Respondents were often used as informants.[24]

As indicated, depth interviews were conducted initially at the Welfare Home for Homeless Men. Twenty individual depth interviews were conducted there and recorded on tape, five before the discovery of the loop. The average length of these interviews was one and one-half hours and covered all institutions respondents had experienced. With men who were very informative and cooperative at the Home, three-hour interviews (in two shifts) were held. Three 24-hour periods of observation were spent on Skid Row during this phase at two-hour or three-hour intervals, spaced through a day.

With the discovery of the loop and the decision to do research at stations on the loop, the interviewing approach expanded. Fifty-two depth interviews were conducted among significant agents of social control on the loop, and thirty-six among alcoholics at various stations. Topics covered in the latter included attitudes toward and experiences in all stations. Most of the interviews with Row men were taped.

In an attempt to rule out the idiosyncratic, while retaining that which was a portion of the collective perspective, some material was obtained by interviewing men in groups as well as singly. Group discussions were arranged covering the same stations as the individual interviews. Sixteen Row men in groups of two, three, four, and seven were interviewed. These were also tape recorded. Participant observers also joined various groups of men and listened to them discussing some of these subjects. Becker and Geer make the following point about the usefulness of group-generated data:

> . . . all items should be classified according to whether they occurred in the presence of the observer alone or when other members of the group were also present. If, for instance, the observer sees a student doing something in the presence of several other students who take it as a matter of course, he is entitled to assume that this kind of activity is legitimate enough to excite no comment from other members of the group. He could not make this inference if he saw the act performed when he was the only other person present. Similarly, if a member of the group makes a statement in conversation with other members of the group, we are

entitled to regard this as a legitimate way to view things more than if the statement is made to the observer alone.

We can argue that the appearance of terms of the perspective in the everyday conversation of group members indicates that they share the perspective, since they could not use these terms to communicate unless there was mutual understanding of them.[25]

Observational data gathering was both participant and nonparticipant. Care was taken that a time sampling was made of a given setting that obtained frequency of phenomena at different times of the day and week.

On Skid Row, observations were made both by myself in the company of a paid "guide," [26] and by paid male observers. My observations were confined to those activities in which a woman can take part on the Row without causing undue comment—walking around during the day, sitting in bars, eating in cafeterias, cafes, and shopping in grocery stores.

Four male observers walked the streets of Skid Row with the men at night, stood talking to them on the street, drank in taverns with them, and met them at the bus returning from jail. These observations were spread in time through one year. Findings were further supplemented by published observations of the Skid Row area by other researchers.

On Skid Row, I passed as a woman friend of a presumed resident there, as a woman looking for a lost boy friend, and as a woman who had returned to the area after some absence and was looking for a bartender friend. In Christian Missionary prayer meeting and in free soup lines, I merely joined the men and few women recipients. At the various screening sessions held at stations on the loop, agents of social control were kind enough to allow me to sit in and pass as a secretary who was taking medical notes.

In the Jail and the State Mental Hospital, no attempt to pass was made for two different reasons: in an all-male world like the Jail, it would be virtually impossible; in a calmly coeducational and research-oriented environment like the State Hospital, it seemed unnecessary. The first night at the Hospital, when I was introduced to the men in one of the alcoholic wards, they gallantly included me in a late night party based on food raided from the kitchen. From then on they treated me as one of the family.[27]

However, while there were a great many scenes I could observe, it became apparent that as a woman, or as a researcher, access was denied to some areas of the loop. Especially acute problems were presented by the County Jail and the Christian Missionaries (in addition to Skid Row at night where a woman attracts attention no matter how innocuously she is dressed).[28]

For these three areas, as well as a fourth (the courts), where time was at a premium, observers were hired. In jail, at the Christian Missionaries, and on Skid Row they were participant observers, unknown to their subjects as researchers. Recruiting observers for the Jail posed several problems. Obviously, I could not ask someone to commit a crime so as to be sentenced to the County Jail. On the other hand, there was a need for someone who could participate unnoticed in prisoner activities. The decision was to recruit within the jail. Young men who were not in jail for alcoholism were selected.[29] There were four observers in all. These men were not used simultaneously, but two were observing and recording for three weeks and then two others working for the same period of time approximately six months later—some time after the first two had been released. In this way it was hoped that collusion between observers would be prevented.

The directions given jail inmate-observers were purposely as general as possible to avoid bias in their reports. They were asked to keep diaries of all the occurrences at the jail involving the alcoholics. The alcoholics were easily identifiable for such observations because (a) a majority of them were older than the rest of the inmate population, (b) they were all housed on the same two tiers, and, (c) they were usually assigned only to certain jobs.

To solve the problem of inaccessible areas at the Christian Missionaries, an anthropologist (a student who had passed his orals for the Ph.D.) was hired to apply for admittance to the Work and Residence Center operated by the Missionaries. He lived and worked there, passing as an alcoholic with both staff and beneficiaries for seven days and nights. His primary function was to check out the scope and general validity of a considerable amount of data previously collected in depth interviews.

The fourth area in which hired observers were used was the municipal "drunk" court. Here, two observers were used—approximately one year apart. The first kept a diary of court procedures with special emphasis on conventional interaction among court officials. The second maintained a count of sentences and checked out some of the findings that had been developed from an analysis of the materials of the first. Their findings were supplemented by reports of Court observations made by other researchers of the same Court.

Although the collection and enumeration of statistical aggregates has not been the major approach to this study, there are some areas in which this information can aid in completion of a picture of structural exigencies. As Nash put it . . .

> There are gains in counting, even if the investigator must devise units. The largest is a shift in emphasis toward the *consequences* of patterns and structures as against the mere establishment of them. . . . (Emphasis mine.) [30]

Two types of statistical information, official and special, were collected and compiled in order to aid in establishing the frequency and distribution of a phenomenon. Official statistics were requested from the records of institutions on such items as the following:

Admittance and discharge of prisoners, patients, inmates, clients

Length of stay of prisoners, patients, inmates, clients

Weight gain and loss of prisoners (since food at the jail was a constant complaint).

Special informal counts of phenomena seldom recorded officially were made by observers or gathered in a special sub-study:

Jail sentences as meted out to various "social types"

Arrest patterns on Skid Row

Actual (versus claimed) daily menus in the jail

Patterns of travel on the loop made by Skid Row alcoholics.

PROCESSING THE DATA   The processing of the voluminous data that is gathered in most studies of this type presents a crucial step in ascertaining frequency and scope of phenomenon since conceptual categories are often perceived or further established at this stage. Categorizing of situations and activities is most difficult because they are often illustrative of more than one concept at a time.[31]

Furthermore, a serious problem is sometimes created by the very fact of organizing the material through coding or breaking it up into segments in that this destroys the *totality* of philosophy as expressed by the interviewee—which is closely related to the major goal of the study.

To circumvent this problem, taped interviews were typed in duplicate. One copy was cut apart and affixed, by subject matter, to hand sort cards and then further cross-coded by coders. Four coders handled the data and checked each other's work. A second copy of the interview was left intact to be read in its entirety. All cards were labeled with the name of the respondent, the place of the interview, as well as the subjects covered in each interview. (These cards were used only by professional coders and returned.)

Gross categories developed for use of the coders were most helpful in sorting the cards into chapter groupings and subsections. Then more refined sorts, re-sorts, and cross tabulations were utilized in the analysis and reporting of the data for each individual chapter, as well as for establishing general frequency and scope of some phenomena.

THE SIGNIFICANCE OF A GIVEN PHENOMENON   In a naturalistic study, significance is sometimes not indicated by either frequency or distribution of phenomena. A single act, by a person in power, may be far more significant than multiple acts by the powerless. Therefore, the significance of concern here was of the structural and cultural repercussions, as expressed and affected by collective belief systems.[32]

Thus the problem of Stage Two is not limited only to finding that which occurs with enough frequency to be allowed to remain in the analysis, but to make decisions as to what is significant because it has *significant social effects*. Put another way, the problem is: what data is *so* idiosyncratic that it should be omitted as of little consequence to the analysis of perspectives on social worlds? This is partially a matter of concept formation. Often what appears idiocyncratic can be recast as a specific type of a more general and frequently-appearing construct.

The search for frequency and distribution in this study was one of watching for a repeat of certain *total* patterns rather than isolated portions. For instance, it seems to be not so important to get a count and distribution on the different specific ways in which the Skid Row alcoholic gets food, shelter, or money, as to note that almost all methods are unorthodox and fraught with risk by middle-class standards. For these reasons, "data clusters" such as the following were collected, utilizing the intact copy of the interviews:

On the subject of Skid Row and the outside world:

Middle-class views of Skid Row (especially views expressed by agents of social control).

A typical day of any alcoholic on the Row.

Resources for existence of Skid Row alcoholics—how do they handle problems of money, shelter, food, clothing, liquor.

Activities leading to drinking again after abstinence in an institution.

On the subject of the loop and its stations:

For the agent of social control . . .
His general opinion of alcoholics.

His theories on alcoholism and the types of therapy that are most suitable.

His criteria for the "success" of therapy.

His day-to-day problems in working with alcoholics and methods of coping with them.

His view on how the men get into institutions; what screening procedures are used.

For the Skid Row man . . .
His perceptions of a given institution in terms of help received on alcoholism problem.

General treatment accorded to him while in an institution.

Opinion of persons who operate institutions; problems of dealing with them.

Perceptions of how he gets into and out of an institution.

Perceived consequences of being in an institution.

Stage 3. Incorporation of Individual Findings into a Model of Organization

Mannheim has said that group ideologies are understood only by "adding" the separate ideologies of its members or by selecting those that are common to the individuals in the group. The total conception, however, seeks to establish the integrated system of thought of a group that is implicit in the judgement of its members.[33] This view gives ultimate direction to the study.

In order to accomplish this, Becker and Geer's plan of action was adopted. They see the final analysis as the procedure of taking many partial models of the organization, and filling them out with data and then connecting them into a total model.[34]

The final state of analysis (construction of social system models) in the field consists of incorporating individual findings into a generalized model of the social system or organization under study or some part of the organization. . . . The kind of participant observation discussed here is related directly to this concept, explaining particular social facts by explicit reference to their involvement in a complex of interconnected variables that the observer constructs as a theoretical model of the organization. In this final stage, the observer designs a descriptive model which best explains the data he has assembled.[35]

The successful realization of these aims is tied to the problems of validity, reliability, and sampling, and thus these issues will now be considered.

Problems of Validity, Reliability and Sampling

In the usual survey-research approach, validity refers to whether or not the "data collected represent that which they purport to represent." Or to put it another way, the "extent to which the data corresponds with some criterion which is an acceptable measure of the phenomena being studied." [36]

In this type of study, however, the validity problem is not whether the empirical indicators used to operationalize concepts are indeed valid representations of this phenomenon from an objective or scientific point of view (or even the so-called rational or reasonable man's point of view), but whether or not the investigator has represented the social world of the actor as the actor himself sees it. The agreement of an "objective" investigator as to whether this is the "real" (and not distorted) social world is moot, by definition. In this study one man's reality could be another man's gross distortion. The question of validity remains, however, only it must be interpolated for the purposes of this type of study as follows:

1. Do the social actors in question build the concepts and constructs of *their* daily social reality out of the same data that the investigator has gathered and with the same general forms emerging?

2. How valid are the *conclusions* the investigator draws from the constructs he is using to depict this special social world he has selected to study? [37]

The investigative talents required to establish validity in each case are somewhat different. In the first, the researcher must be sensitive enough to apprehend the important ingredients of the constructs of another's social world. The second is the more sociological enterprise—the investigator must be able to *generalize* from particular constructs and causal inferences that emerge in *this study* to other instances of the same phenomenon in *other social worlds*, using sociologically technical terms. That is, he must be able to translate the meaning of this world into the vernacular of sociology, thereby allowing this world to be compared and contrasted with findings concerning other actor-constructed worlds. The validity of the latter is much more difficult to assure or demonstrate.

For the first type of validity testing, that of building of constructs purporting to have close resemblance to those of the social actor, two procedures were used. First, persons who had given information concerning a behavior setting were given an opportunity to read the chapter concerning that setting. They were invited to comment on the chapter and to suggest changes where they felt that the draft did not reflect "what was really happening." Both Skid Row alcoholics and agents of social control were given chapters to read where these chapters represented a world and a perspective with which they were thought to be familiar.

Second, a set of instructions was given to some of the later observers on how to dress and how to act so as to pass as a native at a given station on the loop—in this case Skid Row and the Christian Missionaries. Successful passing (i.e., unquestioned acceptance) was seen as validating the instructions and the perspective they reflected, to some extent at least.

In the second type of validity—that of the sociological conclusions that form the analysis—the problem was different. Here, the search is for sociologically parallel phenomenon or cause-effect relationships that are not of concern to the average social actor but only to the student of human group life. For instance, when interaction and activity on Skid Row were compared to that of a college campus, a list had to be made of those activities unique to a college campus as compared with other outdoor areas (i.e., street corners in the financial district, parks, playgrounds, stores and markets, etc.). Then the problem was to see if Skid Row did indeed manifest many of the same characteristics. Similarly, to claim that drunk court is operated like juvenile court, one must first locate the ideology of juvenile court and accompanying actions, then compare to see if similar behavior may not be found in drunk court.

Cause-effect inferences are much more problematic. I may posit that the Christian Missionaries treat the drunks as they do for a variety of reasons: that their reaction is a reflection of their Protestant ethic beliefs as to the nature of man; that part of their response is the result of the pressures of the salvage business, and part develops as a result of their interaction with the men. I am not suggesting by these statements, however, that the Missionaries are themselves fully conscious of the effect each of these considerations plays in structuring their motivation. In this case, the question was: "If I believed certain things about the nature of man and the nature of alcoholics, and if further, I had certain experiences with them, and was under certain business and economic pressures, what would my likely attitude toward Skid Row alcoholics be?" Following this imaginary reconstruction of motivation, the attitudinal and interactional data were examined to see if they bore out these suppositions. Where they did not, suppositions were reviewed and modified.

Reliability is a problem closely-connected to validity; for as Selltiz, *et al.*, say, "In general, any lack of reliability in a test lessens its validity; correspondingly, it lessens one's ability to demonstrate relationships between variables or to make precise distinctions among individuals who are similar in the characteristic one is trying to measure." [38]

Reliability refers to the consistency of the data obtained. In successive gatherings of data using the same instrument, would the same results be obtained? The concern here is that should another investigator choose to replicate the study, using the same approach, his findings (so far as the raw data collected are concerned) would not deviate sharply from that of the principal researcher. The reliability problem in this study has some unique aspects:

Does the data offered by the respondents in the form of attitudes, descriptions, and observed interactions constitute commonly accepted phenomena in this world, or is it idiosyncratic and not representative because . . .

1. The persons interviewed or observed are not truly representative of the social actors in this behavior system or

2. The person interviewed lies to the investigator or changes his behavior in the presence of the observer, or is a chronic complainer and a malcontent. (This second point is important because there is a widespread commonsense belief that alcoholics do a great deal of lying and unnecessary complaining.)

In the methodology of survey research, there are various sampling procedures that are accepted as insuring the representativeness of the sample in studies of this type. However, in a study where the *Weltanschauung* of a relatively unexplored behavior system is the goal, many kinds of sampling are required and the problem of their representativeness is complicated and interrelated. In an exploratory study of this type it is difficult to know in advance just *what the sample should be representative of.* For the Row men, is it age, sex, class, and education, those standbys of survey research, or should it be number of institutionalizations, attitude toward therapy, and liquor capacity? Should agents of social control be selectively sampled by age, sex, and education, or by staff position, attitude toward alcoholics, and years spent in a rehabilitation career?

Several kinds of samples proved necessary:

Skid Row alcoholics who make the loop.

Agents of social control who deal with them.

Stations on the loop as behavior systems for observation.

Time sampling for daily and weekly rounds of activities.

Information gained in each was used as a cross-check against possible sampling inadequacies of the other, but no attempt was made to obtain a "cross-section" of the composition of the populations of the two worlds under study in advance of knowing what characteristics that cross-section should be based on.

When there is no set number of interviews decided upon in advance and no structure to the questions, how does one decide when to stop gathering data? In the case of this study, interviewing concerning activities at a station and the two views of meaning of those activities continued until no new material was discovered for some time. By that time, both the general and detailed data to be obtained from an interview concerning a given station by either a Skid Row alcoholic or an agent of social control there could be more or less *predicted.*

At this point, I made a concerted attempt to locate deviant cases (i.e., persons who were not representative of the average case in a situation). These persons were interviewed to discover the range of the phenomenon under study and some of the factors that might lead to the appearance of such deviant cases.[42]

Tables 23, 24, and 25, which follow, indicate the locale of the interviews and their number and distribution among Skid Row alcoholics and agents of social control. A key to respondents, indicating site of the interview and position or former occupation, follows the tabular material.

Among agents of social control, questions concentrating on their view of their clients and the institution where they worked were asked of as many different types of agents as possible. For instance, at the Jail, the captain and the guards, the social workers and the psychologists, were interviewed; at the State hospital, a psychiatrist, psychologists, psychiatric social workers, a minister, and various researchers were interviewed. The results of these interviews served as a reliability check on each other; they also served as a check on the findings of the depth interviews with the alcoholics.

Becker and Geer have mentioned the usefulness of many kinds of evidence, as well as many kinds of items as a validity check:

> The researcher also takes account of the possibility that his observations may give him evidence of different kinds on the point under consideration. Just as he is more convinced if he has many items of evidence than if he has few, so he is more convinced of a conclusion's validity if he has *many kinds* of evidence. For instance, he may be especially persuaded that a particular norm is shared and affects group behavior if the norm is not only described by group members but also if he observes events in which the norm can be "seen" to operate. . . .[41]

Those individuals who lie to the researcher or who in some way distort the collective perspective and the individuals who are not representative of the majority of actors in a social world under study can be handled in a number of standard ways in traditional attitude studies that are not applicable in a study of this type.[39]

In order to be sure to avoid reporting mere idiosyncratic findings drawn from nonrepresentative alcoholics or clever liars and malcontents, several types of data were collected at each station on the loop.[40] As previously mentioned, men were interviewed individually and in groups concerning their current views of that station, and their retrospective views of other stations they had visited. Additionally, arrangements were made to meet men after discharge from an institution and (hopefully) before they went into another.

By collecting this information *at* several stations and *about* several stations simultaneously, comparative data was obtained that guided the elimination of that which seldom was mentioned or seemed, in the light of other testimony to the contrary, a deliberate lie. Disregarding the unlikely possibility of a great conspiracy that extended to all stations on the loop, information that came up repeatedly in many locales was assumed worth using in the study.

This approach resulted in another gain—that of being able to compare current attitudes with retrospective ones. The current data has the advantage of temporal propinquity but is somewhat problematic because men might be afraid to talk adversely about an institution where they are currently staying (even with assurances of anonymity); the retrospective data is plagued by problems of selective memory but offers more freedom from fear of retaliation (although men who make the loop realize that in all probability they will return to a given station at a later date).

TABLE 23. *Locale of Observations*

Skid Row
Hall of Justice where bus deposits men after release from jail
Municipal Court
County Jail
Jail Branch Clinic (limited observations due to limited activity)
Superior Court
State Mental Hospital
Christian Missionaries
    Work and Residence Center
    Beacon in the Darkness (limited to prayer meeting, dining room, and coffee lounge)
City Hospital and Screening Center
Welfare Home for Homeless Men
St. Joseph Kitchen
Seamen's Rest halfway house
Second Chance halfway house

TABLE 24. Distribution of Taped Depth Interviews by Locale and Subject with Skid Row Alcoholics

STATIONS DISCUSSED DURING INTERVIEW

Site of Interview	Total Interviewed	Skid Row*	County Jail	Jail Clinic	Mental Hospital	Christian Missionaries Work Ctr.	City Hospital	Welfare Home	Municipal Court	Superior Court	Other Christian Missionaries	Other Mental Hospital
Skid Row†	8	8	—	—	—	—	—	—	—	—	—	1
County Jail	10	8	10	8	—	6	1	—	10	1	3	1
State Mental Hospital	13	8	4	1	10	7	—	—	4	2	4	5
Christian Missionaries‡	5	—	—	—	—	5	—	—	—	—	—	—
Welfare Home for Homeless Men (Individual interviews)	20	20	9	5	12	9	6	5	6	1	2	8
Group interviews Two men	2	2	2	2	2	2	—	—	2	—	3	—
Three men	3	3	3	3	3	3	—	—	—	—	4	3
Four men	4	—	4	—	4	4	—	—	4	—	—	—
Seven men	7	—	7	7	7	7	—	—	—	—	—	—
TOTAL	72	49	39	26	38	43	7	5	26	4	16	17

* Including police action on Skid Row.

† Interviews on Skid Row were actually informal conversations and were not taped. Notes were made in the washrooms of bars. (See also sub-sample of patterns of travel through the loop, chapter 2, page 60.

‡ The Christian Missionaries did not encourage on-premises interviewing of beneficiaries. Interviews were not taped, but an attempt to take verbatim notes was made.

TABLE 25. *Distribution of Interviews * with Agents of Social Control †*

Locale and Official Capacity	Number of Officials
SKID ROW	
Police Captain	1 (interviewed twice)
Skid Row beat patrolmen	3
CITY JAIL	
Booking sergeants	3
MUNICIPAL COURT (Drunk Court)	
Judges	2
Court aide	1
COUNTY JAIL	
Captain	1 (interviewed three times)
Guards	2 (one interviewed twice)
Christian Missionary	1 (interviewed twice)
JAIL BRANCH CLINIC	
Head psychiatrists	2 (one was replaced during study)
Clinical psychologist	1
Social workers	2
Psychiatrist	1
SUPERIOR COURT	
Judge	1
Court Aide	1
STATE MENTAL HOSPITAL (alcoholism units)	
Psychiatrist	1
Head of alcoholism units	1 (interviewed twice)
Social workers and group therapy leaders	2
Minister	1
Research psychologists	2
CHRISTIAN MISSIONARIES	
WORK AND RESIDENCE CENTER	
Major	1
Captain	1
Psychologist	1
Clinical psychologist and counselor	1 (interviewed twice)
Vocational counselor	1
BEACON IN THE DARKNESS	
Captain	1
Aide	1
CITY HOSPITAL AND SCREENING FACILITY	
Social welfare workers	2
Physician	1
OUT-PATIENT THERAPY CLINIC	
Director	1
WELFARE HOME FOR HOMELESS MEN	
Director	1
Assistant directors	2
Social workers	2 (one interviewed three times)
URBAN RENEWAL	
City Planner	1
Man in charge of planning New Horizons Center	1

Locale and Official Capacity	Number of Officials
HALFWAY HOUSES	
Director, Seamen's Rest	1
Director, Second Chance	1
PACIFIC CITY DEPARTMENT OF PUBLIC HEALTH	
Officials	2
PRISONERS' AID	
Social worker	1
OTHERS QUOTED (See bottom of list, p. 290, A51–A55)	5
TOTAL	57

* In a few cases recorded remarks of informal conversations are cited.
† Interviews were not taped, because it was found that a tape recorder upset agents of social control; however, an attempt to take verbatim notes was made.

KEY TO IDENTITY OF RESPONDENTS

In order to obviate the need for an identifying footnote for each of the quotations used to illustrate various points made in this study, respondents are listed below along with an assigned number. The number of the respondent will be found after each quote in brackets [ ]. Alcoholics are assigned a number only; agents of social control have *their* number preceded by the letter A so that the reader may identify a quote as coming from a Skid Row alcoholic or an agent at a glance, without referring to the key.

In using this key, it should be kept in mind that *all names are pseudonyms.* Ages and past skills or occupations of alcoholics, where available, are also changed slightly or interchanged among respondents to avoid identification.

Alcoholics Interviewed

Location	Identifying Number
SKID ROW	
Bartender—"Big John"	1
Hotel Clerk—Steve Pearson	2
Three men in bar (no names exchanged)	3
Three men on street corner (no names)	4
Two men on street corner (no names)	5
Two men on park bench (one called himself "Indian Joe")	6
Man having breakfast in Skid Row restaurant (Mr. Dodds—approx. 62)	7
Two men having bowl of chili (no names)	8
COUNTY JAIL	
Mr. Innsbruck, 52, artist and hairstylist	9
Mr. Capwell, 40, factory worker	10
An Indian, 47, farmer	11
Mr. Pollak, 39, laborer and hospital aid	12
Mr. McFadden, 49, plumber's helper	13
Mr. Folmer, 48, electrician	14
Mr. White, 62, taxi driver	15
Mr. Ingalls, 64, kitchen helper	16

Location	Identifying Number
Mr. Shepard, 67, kitchen worker	17
Mr. Landon, 63, restaurant man and merchant seaman	18

STATE MENTAL HOSPITAL

Mr. Hanley, 54, electrician	19
"Jim," 62, hotel clerk	20
"Parkbench John," 51, longshoreman	21
Mr. Jonas, 32, artist	22
Mr. Thackery, 59, newspaperman	23
Mr. Murphy, 39, bartender and restaurantman	24
Mr. Wilburn, 32, laborer	25
Mr. McCandeless, 37, electrician	26
Mr. Lane, 41, laborer	27
Mr. Hochstatter, 60, odd jobs	28
Charlie Ince, 45, surveyor	29
Henry G., 32, odd jobs	30
Mr. Johnson, 53, chemist	31

CHRISTIAN MISSIONARIES

Mr. Johnson, 62, real estate man	32
Mr. Winter, 51, merchant seaman	33
Mr. Bales, 45, hotel clerk	34
Mr. Gentry, 39, laborer	35
Mr. Reed, 50, sheet metal worker	36

WELFARE HOME FOR HOMELESS MEN

Mr. Blumenshein, 41, Assistant Production Manager	37
Mr. Dennis, 50, kitchen helper	38
Mr. George Billings, 58, warehouseman	39
Mr. James Lee, 53, department store salesman	40
Mr. Jordan, 57, hospital attendant	41
Mr. Gene Burkett, 60, hotel clerk	42
"Burl," 42, painter	43
"Ferdie," 44, musician in dance band	44
Mr. Young, 62, prison guard and maintenance	45
"Bob," 61, tailor	46
Mr. Hansen, 45, butcher, housepainter	47
Mr. Martin, 51, warehouseman	48
Mr. O'Leary, 55, mailers' union	49
Mr. James Lloyd, 55, watchmaker	50
Mr. Dean, 48, sheet metal worker	51
Mr. Williams, 48, railroad laborer and odd jobs	52
Mr. Thompson, 63, upholsterer	53
Mr. Krause, 50, odd jobs	54
Mr. Schumacher, 56, piano tuner and repairman	55
Mr. McAteer, 58, surveying and drafting	56

GROUPS

Two men	57
Three men	58
Four men	59
Seven men	60

Interviews with Agents of Social Control Working with Skid Row Alcoholics

Location	Identifying Number

SKID ROW
Precinct Captain O'Brien   A1
Skid Row beat patrolman (known as "Friendly Joe")   A2
Skid Row beat patrolman   A3
Retired Skid Row patrolman (the first "Friendly Joe")   A4

CITY JAIL
Booking sergeant   A5
Booking sergeant   A6
Former booking sergeant   A7

MUNICIPAL COURT (Drunk Court)
Judge Darlington   A8
Judge Carmichael   A9
Court Aide Gerston   A10

COUNTY JAIL
Captain Jackson   A11
Guard O'Gara   A12
Guard Schultz   A13
Christian Missionary Officer, Brigadier Gomez   A14

JAIL BRANCH CLINIC
Psychiatrist-director Dr. Winterbottom   A15
Psychiatrist-director Dr. Whittaker (who replaced Dr. Winterbottom)   A16
Social worker Kennedy   A17
Social worker Mrs. Siebels   A18
Clinical psychologist Emory   A19

SUPERIOR COURT
Judge Lilly   A20
Court Aide O'Flaheraty   A21

STATE MENTAL HOSPITAL (alcoholism units)
Psychiatrist, Dr. Golden   A22
Director of alcoholism units Mr. Martin   A23
Social worker Mr. Green   A24
Social worker Miss Jordan   A25
Protestant minister, Dr. McLemore   A26
Research psychologist, Dr. Landon   A27
Research social psychologist, Dr. Pennell   A28

CHRISTIAN MISSIONARIES WORK AND RESIDENCE CENTER
Major Jenner   A29
Captain Burton   A30
Psychologist, Dr. Weinstein   A31
Clinical psychologist and director, Dr. Redson   A32
Vocational counselor, Mr. Develin   A33

BEACON IN THE DARKNESS
Captain Andrews   A34
Aide Jim Brown   A35

CITY HOSPITAL AND SCREENING FACILITY
Social welfare worker Mr. Guettarez   A36
Social welfare worker Mrs. Knox   A37
Physician, Dr. Anderson   A38

Location	*Identifying Number*
OUT-PATIENT THERAPY CLINIC	
Director, Dr. Forrester	A39
WELFARE HOME FOR HOMELESS MEN	
Director, Mr. Mannheim	A40
Assistant director Mr. Wood	A41
Assistant director Mr. Garner	A42
Social worker Mr. Houston	A43
Social worker Mr. Jones	A44
URBAN RENEWAL DEPARTMENT OF PACIFIC CITY	
City Planner Mr. Simpson	A45
Man in charge of planning New Horizon's Center	A46
HALFWAY HOUSES	
Director of Seamen's Rest	A47
Director of Second Chance	A48
OTHERS QUOTED	
Pacific City Public Health Official, Dr. Stevenson	A49
Prisoner's Aid Official, Mr. Jenner	A50
"The Rapper" (both a court aide and a patient at State Mental Hospital)	A51
Municipal Judge from another county (informal discussion)	A52
Trusty at County Jail (not an official interview, but an exchange of comments in the hall)	A53
Nurse at City Hospital (not formally interviewed)	A54
Psychiatrist at State Mental Hospital (not formally interviewed)	A55
Psychiatrist at Jail Branch Clinic (not formally interviewed)	A56
Director of Public Welfare, Pacific City (not formally interviewed)	A57

All alcoholics interviewed were Caucasian due to the fact that very few Negroes or Orientals make the loop. With the exception of the County Jail, I saw very few Negroes in institutions, and those designated as alcoholics were from areas other than Skid Row. In the County Jail, where I had a free hand at interviewing Skid Row alcoholics, none of those located by address were Negro. This does not quite reflect the proportion of Negroes living on Skid Row, however. According to a Pacific City Urban Renewal study, the population of the Skid Row there is 82 percent Caucasian, 4 percent Latin-American, 12 percent Negro, 1 percent Oriental and 1 percent other. (This is a much higher proportion of Negroes than the Chicago Skid Row population Bogue studied. He found only 3.6 percent of Skid Row there nonwhite, with 1.4 of that Negro.) [43]

Notes

CHAPTER 1

1. Sarah Harris, *Skid Row USA* (Garden City, N. Y.: Doubleday and Company, Inc., 1956), p. 16. The pictures of Skid Row used to illustrate the various books and studies about the area show what can only be described as squalor and filth. The faces of the men look resigned and expressionless.

2. Samuel E. Wallace, *Skid Row as a Way of Life* (Totowa, N. J.: The Bedminister Press, 1965), pp. 13–15.

3. Donald J. Bogue, *Skid Row in American Cities* (Chicago: University of Chicago Press, 1963), Ch. 1, reported the existence of 45 cities with identifiable Skid Rows.

4. As indicated by studies and the experience of cities, the Skid Row man will move to another Skid Row area in another city if his present area is destroyed. He may also move to other areas in the same city where food and rent is inexpensive or where social welfare agencies are available nearby, and gradually attract enough cohorts to establish a second Skid Row. Seventeen of the 41 cities mapped by Bogue had more than one separate and distinct Skid Row area. Bogue, *ibid.*

5. See, for example, Nels Anderson, *The Hobo, The Sociology of the Homeless Man* (Chicago: University of Chicago Press, 1923); Howard G. Bain, *A Sociological Analysis of the Chicago Skid Row Lifeway* (unpublished M.A. dissertation, University of Chicago, 1950); Sarah Harris, *Skid Row USA*; Elmer Bendiner, *The Bowery Man* (New York: Thomas Nelson and Sons, 1961); Bogue, *Skid Row in American Cities*; Philip O'Connor, *Britain in the Sixties, Vagrancy* (Baltimore: Penguin Books, 1963); Edward Rose, *et al.*, *The Unattached Society* (University of Colorado, Institute of Behavioral Science, Bureau of Sociological Research, No. 24, September 1965).

6. Wallace, *Skid Row as a Way of Life*, pp. 23–25.

7. Estimates as to what proportion of Skid Row residents are heavy drinkers vary with the investigator and the area under discussion. Wallace, *Skid Row as a Way of Life*, p. 182, suggests that almost *all* in the Skid Row of his study are heavy drinkers. Donald J. Bogue, *Skid Row in American Cities*, pp. 92–93, estimates that 65 percent of Chicago Skid Row residents have been arrested as drunk, but that only about 30–35 percent are alcoholics.

8. Organization of phenomena into something meaningful requires that man select data and then categorize his selections. Even these actions require some preexisting rules or grounds. The grounds for selection and categorizing are often called a "frame of reference," or a "standard for judging." The end result has been aptly called the "meaning of the object" or the "definition of the situation." When a person arrives at *this* point, he can begin to consider suitable action toward the object or situation. Although any number of frameworks may be used to organize phenomena, utilization of one frame of reference almost automatically results in the discard of any others. This is because the very act of selection and categorizing of phenomena means that some phenomena are *not* selected (in fact, often not taken cognizance of). As a result alternative definitions of the situation are at least momentarily impossible until the framework has shifted. For further discussions of this point see: Alfred R. Lindesmith and Anselm L. Strauss, *Social Psychology* (New York: Henry Holt and Company, Inc., 1956), especially "Perceiving as a Selective Activity," pp. 86–90; Peter L. Berger and Thomas Luckmann, *The Social Construction of Reality: a treatise in the sociology of knowledge* (New York: Doubleday, 1966); and George A. Kelly, *A Theory of Personality, the Psychology of Personal Constructs* (New York: W. W. Norton & Co., Inc., 1963).

9. The social pathology point of view is best explained in C. Wright Mills, "The Professional Ideology of the Social Pathologists," *American Journal of Sociology*, 49, No. 2, September 1943, 165–80. An alternative view, that a social problem is what men decide and define it to be, is found in Richard C. Fuller and Richard R. Myers, "The Natural History of a Social Problem," *American Sociological Review*, 6, June 1941, 320–29.

10. So cognizant are Pacific City's Urban Redevelopment leaders of the effect of deteriorated buildings on the property value of adjacent structures that they plan to have a sort of neutral or buffer zone (i.e., an area of improved buildings) between the remainder of Skid Row and that portion destined to be torn down and replaced with an expensive sports arena and shopping mall.

11. Not all social theorists agree that men will automatically and uniformly improve if their surroundings do. W. I. Thomas and Florian Znaniecki were among pioneer sociologists to point out a possible fallacy in the idea that men's behavior automatically and uniformly reflected their physical conditions. See "Methodological Note" in *The Polish Peasant in Europe and America* (New York: Dover Publications, Inc., 1918–20), p. 12. See Albert K. Cohen and James F. Short, Jr., "Juvenile Delinquency," in Merton and Nisbet (eds.), *Contemporary Social Problems* (New York: Harcourt, Brace and World, Inc., 1961), pp. 104–5 for a discussion of the lack of correspondence of delinquency rates with improvement of economic conditions in an area.

12. "Report on First Annual International Institute on Homeless Alcoholics" (Detroit, 1955).

13. Capt. Andrews, Christian Missionaries, "Report on Conference with Eastern City Center Team," (n. d.) p. 1.

14. Discussion of a return to Skid Row by Arthur Stine, Executive Director of the New Mexico Alcoholic Rehabilitation Commission, "Report on First Annual International Institute on Homeless Alcoholics," December 27, 1955.

15. Newspaper reporter for paper in Pacific City, 1956. Editor's introduction mentions that "Skid Row is an ugly world and the story he [the reporter] tells is not a pretty one."

16. Partial text of Pacific City Redevelopment Agency pamphlet (1966) designed to attract Skid Row residents to the agency for relocation assistance before their hotel was demolished.

17. Bogue, *Skid Row in American Cities*, p. 117.

18. *Ibid.*, pp. 116, 117.

19. By middle-class standards, the men on Skid Row do not appear to make lasting

social commitments. They have no family, no permanent employer, change hotel addresses often, and seldom have a roommate. (This latter appears partly to be a result of hotel rules.) The type of social relationships they do have appear to be extremely temporary (usually based on a bottle) and not dependent on what sociologists would term a primary group relationship. Yablonsky's description of the informal structure of the "near group" in connection with teenage gangs seems also to fit the structure of the bottle gang. See "The Delinquent Gang as a Near Group," *Social Problems*, 7 (1959). (See also footnote 21, this chapter.)

20. See especially Bogue, *Skid Row in American Cities*, Chap. 4, pp. 116–33.

21. For a detailed discussion of the undersocialization hypothesis, see James F. Rooney, "Group Processes Among Skid Row Winos, A Reevaluation of the Undersocialization Hypothesis," *Quarterly Journal of Studies on Alcohol*, 22, No. 3 (September 1961), 444–60. Pittman's discussion of undersocialization epitomizes this theory: "By undersocialization we mean that the person is characterized by limited participation in the primary groups which are necessary for personality formation, by minimum participation in social activities, and by inadequate opportunities for sharing experiences with others. His [the police case inebriate] life history is one that has been and continues to be deficient in membership in those associations of sharing that are found in the family of orientation and procreation, in the peer groups that stretch from preadolescence to old age, and in community activities." See David J. Pittman and C. Wayne Gordon, *Revolving Door: A Study of Chronic Police Case Inebriate* (New Haven: Yale Center of Alcohol Studies, 1958), p. 10. See also Robert Straus, "Alcohol and the Homeless Man," *Quarterly Journal of Studies on Alcohol*, 7, No. 3 (1946), 360–404.

22. For instance, a recent Health, Education and Welfare study of 1,343 patients in California alcoholic treatment centers found that: ". . . accidents kill seven times as many alcoholics as non-alcoholics, cirrhosis ten times as many, influenza and pneumonia 6.2 times, and suicide . . . 3.5 times. A sampling of 922 drinkers (532 known to be and 390 thought to be alcoholics) and 922 nondrinkers at E. I. du Pont de Nemours indicates that various other degenerative diseases, including some not popularly associated with alcohol, strike drinkers with measurably greater frequency than nondrinkers: e.g. hypertension 2.3 times as frequently, cerebrovascular disease 2 times, stomach ulcer 1.9 times, asthma 1.7 times. . . . More alcoholics . . . die of cardiovascular catastrophe than from all other causes combined." See Herrymon Maurer, "The Beginning of Wisdom about Alcoholism," *Fortune*, 67, No. 5 (May 1968), 176. Courtesy of *Fortune Magazine*.

23. Anderson, *The Hobo.*, pp. 133–36; Bogue, *Skid Row in American Cities*, pp. 199–223; and Wallace, *Skid Row as a Way of Life*, pp. 119–21, all suggest that the Skid Row man's health problems are usually much more serious than those of the average population of the same age.

24. Wallace, *Skid Row as a Way of Life*, p. 164.

25. The term "Skid Row" apparently originated in Seattle and referred to the trail down which logs were skidded to the saw mill. Soon a lumberjack community of flop houses, saloons, and other commercial enterprises serving homeless men was established on either side. The term "to skid" has come to mean downward social mobility. The implication, of course, is that Skid Row is social and economic bottom, and persons arrive there from higher stations in life. See, for instance, Harold L. Wilensky and Hugh Edwards, "The Skidder: Ideological Adjustments of Downward Mobile Workers," *American Sociological Review*, 24, No. 2 (April 1959), 215–31.

26. Of all the investigators of the Skid Row man, only Wallace clearly differentiates between original causation (i.e., why a man first arrives on Skid Row) and how he happens to stay there, or even resists attempts to rehabilitate him out of Skid Row. Using a careers model outlined by Howard Becker (*The Outsiders* [Free Press of Glencoe, 1963]), Wallace suggests the Skid Row "recruit" must be gradually socialized into the ways of the area, while at the same time being gradually isolated

from contact with the "outside world." Eventually, he becomes socialized to Skid Row society and unfit to live elsewhere. Wallace, *Skid Row as a Way of Life*, pp. 172–77.

27. Bogue, *Skid Row in American Cities*, p. 406.

28. *Ibid.*, p. 27.

29. H. Warren Dunham, *Homeless Men and Their Habitats* (Detroit: Wayne University, 1953), pp. 13–15. Clausen and Kohn criticize this approach because its lack of longitudinal data results in unwarranted assumptions about cause and effect of personal and social pathology. See "The Ecological Approach in Social Psychiatry," *American Journal of Sociology*, 60 (September 1954), 140–51.

30. Irwin Deutscher in private conversations with me.

31. The parallel with police treatment of Negro juveniles in reservation maintenance is ably discussed by Carl Werthman in his unpublished Master's thesis, "Delinquency and Authority" (University of California, Berkeley, 1965).

32. Harris, *Skid Row USA*, pp. 57–58, 104.

33. Boris M. Levinson, "Some Aspects of the Personality of the Native-born White Homeless Man as Revealed by the Rorschach," *Psychiatric Quarterly Supplement*, 32, No. 2 (1958), 278–86.

34. Stanley Rosenman, "The Skid Row Alcoholic and the Negative Ego Image," *Quarterly Journal of Studies on Alcohol*, 16, No. 3 (1955), 448.

35. David J. Pittman and C. Wayne Gordon, *Revolving Door: A Study of the Chronic Police Case Inebriate* (New Haven: Yale Center of Alcohol Studies, 1958), p. 11; and Robert Straus, "Alcohol and the Homeless Man," *Quarterly Journal of Studies on Alcohol*, 7, No. 3 (1946), 360–404. The quotation is actually from "Report on First Annual International Institute on Homeless Alcoholics," p. 2, but both make substantially the same points.

36. Pittman and Gordon, *Revolving Door*, p. 11.

37. Robert K. Merton, *Social Theory and Social Structure* (Glencoe, Ill.: The Free Press, 1949), pp. 134, 153–54.

38. Bogue, *Skid Row in American Cities*, p. 403–4.

39. *Ibid.*, pp. 405–6. Elmer Bendiner (a journalist) refutes all social and psychological theories as not necessarily connected in a causal way to Skid Row residence and suggests the area offers a retreat from the status struggle, from failure and defeat, a sort of tranquility, and that it attracts men who seek a limbo existence. See Bendiner, *The Bowery Man*, pp. 91–103.

40. Anderson, *The Hobo*, p. 61–86.

41. During the course of an interview, a majority of the alcoholics would volunteer the information that they were ordinarily socially shy but that liquor helped them overcome this feeling and enjoy the company of others. Such an announcement usually came as a surprise to me inasmuch as most of the men seemed completely at ease while talking to me, and had, in fact, more than the average amount of charm.

In recalling early drinking experiences, many of the men stated that alcohol gave them feelings of great social and physical prowess:

The kids dared me so naturally I took the drink, three or four shots of I. W. Harper and then maybe a sip of beer, and I remember that I felt like I could fly. I said to myself, "I can do anything!" That put me on the great quest. From then on I started looking for that feeling. [30]

My first time was at a school dance and I was so nervous, and some guys came along during intermission and said, "Let's go up to Bushes' Grove and get a drink." Well, this sounded like a wild idea so I went and maybe had three, no more, and when I came back to that dance, why the problem of cutting in on a girl was gone. I thought, "Why, what a marvelous elixir this thing is." [40]

42. According to Raymond G. McCarthy, *Drinking and Intoxication* (Glencoe, Ill.:

The Free Press, 1959), pp. 28, 29. Alcohol taken in moderation produces a general physical euphoria (sometimes described as bodily pins and needles, itching sensations of a rather pleasant and eroticized nature) and a general feeling of lethargy, somnolence, relaxation from anxiety or tension. Functioning as a depressant, alcohol sometimes appears to have the opposite psychological effect because it is accompanied by an increase in spontaneity and gaiety. A well-known television comedian who is known for his heavy drinking has been quoted as saying, "I drink because it removes pimples and warts—from the faces of others."

43. See chapter 6, footnote 42.

44. See, for instance, Aldous L. Huxley, *The Doors of Perception* (New York: Harper, 1954), in which enhancement of awareness of beauty is considered to be an advantage of taking hallucinatory drugs. (In the early days of LSD experimentation, subjects were often told to select a favorite flower or musical recording so while under the effect of the drug they might enjoy its beauty as though greatly magnified.)

45. See, for instance, Oscar Lewis, *The Children of Sanchez* (New York: Random House, 1961), and Egon Bittner, "The Police on Skid-Row: A Study of Peace Keeping," *American Sociological Review*, 32, No. 5 (October 1967), 705–6. This lack of future orientation may be the result of severing most of the social ties that encourage planning for the future—wife, children, job. Bittner has suggested this results in every act considered in isolation on a sort of ad hoc basis.

46. This may also be a part of the culture of the very poor. See, for instance, Walter B. Miller's "Lower Class Culture as a Generating Milieu of Gang Delinquency," *Journal of Social Issues*, 14 (1958), 12, 13.

47. Nutritionally, the alcoholic who drinks a pint of whiskey per day gets all the calories he needs and thus exhibits an almost total disinterest in food, according to the California School on Alcoholism, University of California, 1963. Alcohol does not provide vitamins, however, and thus drinking without eating results in vitamin deficiency problems. Alcoholics I interviewed testified to drinking a minimum of two fifths of whiskey per day, plus wine in large tumblers or from the bottle, "just like it was water."

48. Herbert Blumer was the first to point out to me that there is no fixed sum of social power divided between protagonists, but power can be created by a clever person where none existed previously merely by the redefinition of existing arrangements or the insertion of a neglected issue or object. Herbert Blumer, "Lectures in Sociological Theory" (University of California, Berkeley, 1965).

49. Edmund G. Love, *Subways Are for Sleeping* (New York: Signet Books, 1956).

50. During my visits on Skid Row I noted the following prices: hamburgers, 50 cents; cheeseburgers, 60 cents; soup, 30 cents; plate luncheons, 60 cents to 90 cents; milk, 15 cents.

51. This is a standard practice in all cities. A recent item in a Pacific City newspaper referred to the revolt of men in a neighboring city's Skid Row mission who refused to "sing for their supper" (as the newspaper story phrased it) there.

52. Pacific City has no so-called cubicle hotels, although some rooms come very close to this. The cubicle hotel is a building that has been subdivided into the smallest single rooms possible so as to house a maximum number of men. A typical cubicle is seven-foot long, five-feet wide, has no windows, but rather a chicken-wire ceiling for air. See Bogue, *Skid Row in American Cities*, pp. 79–86.

53. The term refers to Pacific City Social Welfare rent vouchers and are a sort of promissory note by the Welfare Department to pay the lodging of a man who has been granted welfare aid. This means the man himself does not handle the money; he gives the voucher to the hotel manager who then turns it back to the Welfare Department and receives a check from them. The purpose of this approach is to keep the man from using the money for something other than intended— such as liquor.

Men talk about "graduating" from vouchers to welfare assistance checks (which they are given after they have proved themselves to be trustworthy). A welfare assistance check goes directly to the client so he is allowed to cash it and handle the money himself. However, hotel managers in Skid Row do manage to get some control over this check as well, as is explained in a later part of the chapter.

As previously mentioned, Social Welfare does not officially "aid" alcoholics; it aids indigents and ill persons who are unable to work and support themselves. However, aid often goes to alcoholics, with the unofficial knowledge of the social worker that without such aid the man may possibly starve. The Welfare Home for Homeless Men was created for the express purpose of serving humanitarian ends by providing shelter and food for the homeless man, while at the same time avoiding direct subsidy of an alcoholic habit.

54. The term most frequently applied to men who pretend conversion is "mission stiff," and can be found in most of the literature concerning the religious meetings on Skid Row.

55. See Love, *Subways Are for Sleeping*, pp. 24–26. George Ray also discusses the use of the bus depot by Skid Row men on the bum in "Observations at the Greyhound Terminal" (unpublished paper, University of California, Berkeley, 1965).

56. Goffman, *Asylums* (Garden City, New York: Doubleday Anchor Books, Inc., 1961), pp. 243–49.

57. Field notes from interviews at the Pacific City Welfare Home for Homeless Men, Skid Row, and the Northern State Mental Hospital.

58. This appears to be true in all cities as noted by Anderson, *The Hobo*, p. 13; Bogue, *Skid Row in American Cities*, Ch. 7, pp. 199–230; and Wallace, *Skid Row as a Way of Life*, pp. 119–20.

59. Goffman's discussion of money and money substitutes in total institutions has many parallels in Skid Row. See *Asylums*, pp. 264–74. Goffman quotes Dostoevski that "money is coined freedom" and thus ten times as dear to a man deprived of all other freedom. From *Memoirs from the House of the Dead*, trans. Jessie Coulson (London: Oxford University Press, 1956), pp. 355–59.

60. Lewis, *The Children of Sanchez*.

61. All of these methods of converting objects into cash were mentioned numerous times in the course of interviews with Skid Row alcoholics.

62. See Bogue, *Skid Row in American Cities*, Chap. 6, pp. 172–98.

63. One man told me that he was shaking so badly from drinking that he could not sign his name so as to match his signature on file at the bank; further, even though the bank knew him, they insisted he keep trying to sign until he could steady his hand enough to give them a specimen they could accept. As he described it:
    The teller was very understanding. She kept saying, "Come on, Mr. Lane, try to match your signature here." [27]

64. Goffman also points out the problem persons in total institutions have in finding a safe and accessible place to save money. See *Asylums*, pp. 264–74.

65. This symbiotic relationship between the blood bank and the Skid Row alcoholic occurs in most major cities and is usually mentioned wherever ways of earning money are discussed. See, for instance, Wallace, *Skid Row as a Way of Life*, p. 119; and Bain, *A Sociological Analysis*, p. 119.

66. A few men also peddle items like needles, little American flags, pencils, or thread. Anderson, *The Hobo*, p. 50, suggests there is quite a bit of status antagonism between panhandlers and peddlers.

67. This is a problem faced by all persons who operate outside the law to get others to part willingly with their money. See David W. Maurer, *The Big Con* (New York: Signet Books, 1962).

68. That stealing somehow enhances self-respect, or at least is not the blow to it that begging is, is also mentioned by George Orwell in *Down and Out in Paris and London* (New York: Harcourt, Brace & World Company, Copyright, 1933 by

George Orwell. Copyright renewed, 1960 by Sonia Pitt-Rivers.), p. 75. Reprinted by permission of Brandt & Brandt. Orwell quoted a man who said, ". . . I steal, just to show my independence." Wallace, *Skid Row as a Way of Life*, p. 177, quotes Mayhew on the greater welcome thieves received in a group of down-and-out men, as compared to the reception of self-proclaimed beggars.

69. In many areas of life, routine tasks are lightened by contests. Husking bees, sheep-shearing contests, war bond drive competitions, and charity fund drive competitions are but a few examples.

70. Rooney, "Group Processes," pp. 440–60.

71. The cavalier refusal to take a steady job may be a rationalization. Bogue, *Skid Row in American Cities*, p. 192, found a majority of the men, when pressed, said they would prefer steady work if they could get it. See chapter 8 for a discussion of the difficulties Skid Row alcoholics encounter when they do try to find steady, permanent work.

72. Field notes during Skid Row observations.

73. Erving Goffman, "Regions and Region Behavior," in *The Presentation of Self in Everyday Life* (Garden City, New York: Doubleday Anchor Books, 1959), Chap. 3, pp. 107–40.

74. Skid Row men are most successful with the type of woman in whom they have the least interest for long-term relationships, however. At institution dances they feel as if they are dancing with their "own kind" (alcoholic women) and thus suffer no shyness. However, with so-called respectable women they confess often to being at a loss. Wallace mentions the insecurity the men feel in the presence of these women in *Skid Row as a Way of Life*, p. 174.

75. Many Skid Row alcoholics showed a change of address to a nurse's residence.

76. I experienced it, as did all my hired observers. Several of my students who went to the area to gather material for research papers reported on this friendliness with a tone of amazement.

77. Bain, *A Sociological Analysis*, p. xiii.

78. The same sentiment is to be found in the words of the folk song of the poor, "Hurry sundown, see what tomorrow bring . . ." From *Hurry Sundown* by Clarence Williams and Richard Huey, © copyright 1940 by MCA Music; copyright renewed 1967 and assigned to MCA Music, a division of MCA Inc.; all rights reserved. Used by permission of the publisher. (This was also used as the title for a novel about the poor of the South: K. B. Glidden, *Hurry Sundown* [New York: Signet Books, 1966].)

79. Bain, *A Sociological Analysis*, p. 40.

80. Matthew P. Dumont, "Tavern Culture, The Sustenance of Homeless Men," *American Journal of Orthopsychiatry*, 37, No. 5 (October 1967), 938–45, noted in his observations of Skid Row tavern conversations that the drinkers discussed causes of cancer, men who had recently died of it, inadequacies of the city hospital, ways of predicting life span, urban renewal, and the causes of the depression in the thirties.

81. Phillip L. Harriman, *Modern Psychology* (Ames, Iowa: Littlefield, Adams & Co., 1958), p. 89.

82. Bogue, *Skid Row in American Cities*, p. 463.

CHAPTER 2

1. Charles Clapp, *Drinking's Not the Problem* (New York: Thomas Y. Crowell Company, 1949), p. 85.

2. Every major city in the country has a portion of its jail facilities devoted to the chronic drunkenness offender, as well as emergency psychiatric and drying out

wards in public city hospitals. Additionally, city officials can arrange voluntary or involuntary commitment to a state mental institution of a person designated as an alcoholic. Welfare agencies also deal with alcoholics, as do church groups and missions. There are numerous halfway houses for alcoholics in all large cities.

3. Official estimates of the proportion of Skid Row alcoholic men to be found in any one agency in Pacific City at any one time, selected at random, are given below. (These estimates are based on checks of addresses in records or, where these were not available, use of census tracts in which Skid Row is found.)

OFFICIAL ESTIMATES
PERCENT SKID ROW ALCOHOLICS
OF TOTAL INMATE POPULATION

Institution	Percent
County Jail	45 *
City Hospital (in- and out-patient)	(Not available) †
City Screening Facility	60
State Mental Hospital	20 *
County Welfare Home	80–90
Christian Missionaries	80

* Represents a majority of all *alcoholics* using facility.
† City Hospital keeps no records of the number of Skid Row alcoholics *per se* who are bed patients at any one time. Many come with other presenting symptoms—pneumonia, broken limbs, concussions, ulcers, or malnutrition, and are not counted as alcoholics.

4. The Alcoholics Anonymous organization holds meetings in the County Jail, the Christian Missionaries, the State Mental Hospital, the Welfare Home for Homeless Men, and many halfway houses. Skid Row alcoholics, for the most part, attend these meetings only if it is required, or—where voluntary—on a sporadic basis, if at all.

5. See, for instance, George B. Vold's discussion of hedonistic criminality, in *Theoretical Criminology* (New York: Oxford University Press, 1958), pp. 15–18.

6. See chapter 3 for an expanded discussion of the Pacific City public drunkenness ordinance.

7. Arrest, sentence, and jail can be seen as the *formal* extensions of informal methods used by family, employer, and friends to punish an alcoholic for what is defined as his own weak will.

8. See chapter 3 for an extended discussion of psychological therapy.

9. Ingestion of considerable amounts of alcohol will ultimately result in one of the following: regurgitation, sleep, blackout, or death. Death due to an "overdose" of alcohol *can* result from the following: respiratory depression, cardiovascular repression and shock, or severe irritation of the gastro-intestinal track causing bleeding, hemorrhaging, and increasing shock. *Withdrawal symptoms* in the form of delirium tremens result from abstinence from alcohol after dependence has been developed. Physical symptoms are: agitation, tremors, paresthesias, nausea, vomiting, muscle cramps, quivering, diarrhea, sweating, and epigastric burning. See Arnold Pfeffer, *Alcoholism* (New York: Grune and Stratton, Inc., 1958), p. 22.

10. Although the initial effects of light, or even heavy drinking if it is sporadic, are to bring about a pleasant euphoric state of mind, continued overindulgence over a period of years does not sustain this result. A particularly depressing pattern of ever-increasing fear, anxiety, paranoia, guilt, sense of impending danger, pervades all psychological developments. Hallucinations also occur. Paradoxically, in order to avoid these unpleasant reactions and to maintain a normal facade, the alcoholic finds that he must maintain a certain level of alcohol in his system. *Ibid.*, pp. 24–27.

11. State agencies, for instance, are attempting to develop formal screening criteria for this factor, as is indicated by a study in Westcoast state entitled, *The Development of a Screening Device for Risk Populations,* November 1961.

12. The captain of the jail estimates that 85 percent of the chronic drunkenness offenders who serve time are repeaters. The Christian Missionaries estimate they have a national repeater rate of 40 percent. No estimates were available from State Mental Hospital, but staff members acknowledge a high rate of returnees.

13. See Robert Merton, "The Unintended Consequences of Purposive Social Action," *American Sociological Review,* 1 (December 1936), 894–904. See also Phillip Selznick, "Foundations of the Theory of Organization," *American Sociological Review,* 13 (February 1948), 25–35.

14. Melville Dalton's study of bureaucracies, *Men Who Manage* (New York: John Wiley and Sons, 1959), presents informal conduct norms as instrumental in the smooth operation of business as a whole, for they take care of petty grievances in a way prohibited to the formal institution—through petty graft.

    Gresham M. Sykes' study of the prisoner community, *The Society of Captives* (New York: Atheneum Publishers, 1965), esp. Chap. 3, pp. 40–62, depicts the interlocking character of the formal organization with the informal. The small number of guards charged with maintaining order among a large number of prisoners resulted in informal delegation of authority to some prisoners; then followed the generation of a series of special favors and conduct norms suitable to the rather ambiguous situation of power these prisoner leaders found themselves facing.

    Goffman's concept of the inevitable development of an institutional "underlife" growing out of the formal restrictions in a mental hospital, simultaneously modifying and aiding the official interaction allowed, are also of the same genre. See Erving Goffman, "The Underlife of a Public Institution: A Study of Ways of Making Out in a Mental Hospital," in *Asylums* (Garden City, N.Y.: Doubleday & Co., Inc., 1961), pp. 171–320.

    The social power imbedded in these informal networks was illustrated by Roethlisberger and Dickson in their pioneering study of informal peer group norms growing out of the work situation. In this case, the group challenged the power of the company norms of production, won by pitting fear of group ostracism against an increased paycheck, and forced deviant "rate busters" into line. See F. J. Roethlisberger and W. J. Dickson, *Management and the Worker* (Cambridge: Harvard University Press, 1939), Part IV.

15. The term "referral" has several meanings and it is sometimes difficult to ascertain which is being used. It can range all the way from actual arrangements being made for the transfer of the person from one institution to another with concomitant financial arrangements, or it can mean a suggestion to the man that he go to a certain agency for help. In between are letters or cards of referral or recommendation that aid the men in gaining entrance to institutions.

16. There is some evidence that the availability of this constellation of free agencies is one of the recruiting attractions of Skid Row. In his pioneering study of the Chicago Skid Row, *The Hobo,* p. 48, Nels Anderson cites both the charitable and medical agencies as an attraction:

    There are men who make a specialty of "working" charity organizations. Some of them are so adept that they know beforehand what they will be asked and have a stereotyped response for every stereotyped question. These men know a surprising amount about the inside workings of the charitable agency and they generously hand their information on to their successor.

17. The respondent is an ex-alcoholic and considers himself "wise" to their ways. His reference is to Eric Berne's *The Games People Play* (New York: Grove Press, Inc., 1967), a popular discussion of the devious strategies people use to obtain unsuspected goals.

18. At best, this tabulation of patterns through the loop is very crude. Respondents had a difficult time remembering all the institutions they had been in, which they had visited more than once, or the order of the visits.

19. See John Irwin, *The Felon* (Englewood Cliffs, N.J.: Prentice-Hall, Inc., forthcoming 1970).

20. A check was made of these flow charts with both agents of social control at the various processing centers and the Skid Row problem drinkers themselves. Each group essentially agreed with the chart pertaining to their perspective. However, it should be mentioned that the charts present oversimplified perceptions of both groups, but in opposite directions:

Agents of social control are aware of the informal routing practices directly connected with their own agency. Therefore, they accept the idealized chart only for agencies other than their own. Figure 2 represents their *innocence* rather than their sophistication because innocence as to the circle dominates their perceptions.

Skid Row problem drinkers vary as to their experience with the circle. Some make attenuated circles. However, all are aware of more informal linking between processing centers than are agents of social control. Figure 3 represents *sophistication* rather than innocence of the Skid Row drinkers, because sophistication concerning the circle dominates their perceptions.

21. This tendency of welfare and public health organizations to share clients by reciprocal trade agreements, or otherwise, has been noted by Wilensky and Lebeaux in *Industrial Society and Social Welfare* (New York: The Free Press, 1965), p. 235. The authors note that this results in the passing of clients from agency to agency.

This phenomenon is also noted by Elliott A. Krause in "After the Rehabilitation Center," *Social Problems*, 14, No. 2 (Fall 1966), 197–206.

"The loop" is not an entirely new discovery. Other researchers have mentioned it in various terms; however, none has attempted to see it as an environmental progression as it looks from the Skid Row alcoholic's point of view.

Jay N. Cross, Assistant Director of the U.S. Public Health Service Alcoholism Project, speaking on "The Public Health Approach to Alcoholism Control," at the American Public Health Conference in 1966, made the following statement:

It is said that the effects of one alcoholic patient are felt by community agencies ranging from general hospitals through social welfare agencies, correctional institutions, churches, industry, and public health agencies.

Arthur Stine, Executive Director of the New Mexico Alcoholic Rehabilitation Commission, quotes Straus about the loop:

In American society, Dr. Straus stated, the young person is faced with a challenge of "social weaning." This should occur in the late teens and early twenties, and for many young people it is very difficult. The homeless derelict seems in general to be a person who never accomplishes this weaning process. He tends to become an "institutional addict" and surveys show many of these men have a regular cycle of movement from one institution to another during the year: jails and veterans' hospitals, quite commonly. They may also follow a geographical cycle around the country. (p. 2)

The study done by David J. Pittman and Muriel W. Sterne, *Alcoholism: Community Agency Attitudes and Their Impact on Treatment Services* (Bethesda, Md.: U. S. Department of Health, Education, and Welfare, June, 1963), is devoted to an analysis of the various institutions serving alcoholics, the differing perspectives of each, and the problems of keeping clients long enough to "do them some good." An earlier, longer version of this report was published under the title, "The Carousel: Hospitals, Social Agencies and the Alcoholic," (prepared for the Missouri Division of Health, 1962), a title that shows awareness of the loop.

Albert F. Wessen in "The Apparatus of Rehabilitation: An Organizational Analysis," in Marvin B. Sussman (ed.), *Sociology and Rehabilitation* (American Sociological Association, 1965), made the following statement in connection with rehabilitation services in general:

. . . patients are often carried through the process of rehabilitation on a chain of referrals. (p. 167)

Nils Christie in "The Scandinavian Hangover," *Trans-action,* 4, No. 3 (January-February, 1967), said:

A major trend in recent social and criminal policy is toward *combining* the different control disciplines. I doubt the fruitfulness of this approach, certainly when dealing with alcoholics. (p. 37)

Howard G. Bain, *A Sociological Analysis,* noted that:

Few Skid Rowers can long avoid passing through the hands of the Chicago missions, Welfare Department, police, or Cook County Hospital. (p. xviii)

CHAPTER 3

1. Herrymon Maurer, "The Beginning of Wisdom About Alcohol," *Fortune,* 77, No. 5 (July 1968), 177.

2. Source: "Pacific City" arrest statistics, 1967.

3. Source: "Pacific City" arrest statistics for 1967.
   Although Pacific City has no figures on the number of repeaters involved in repeat arrests, the figures from other cities indicate that they represent approximately one-fifth of the number of arrests. For instance, Pittman points out that in Portland, Oregon, 2,000 individuals accounted for 11,000 arrests; in Baltimore, 11,340 convictions for drunkenness involved only 7,176 repeaters (and if the arrest rate were used for contrast, the ratio would probably be close to Portland's). See David J. Pittman, "Public Intoxication and the Alcoholic Offender in American Society," *Task Force Report on Drunkenness, The President's Commission on Law Enforcement and Administration of Justice* (Washington, 1964), pp. 8, 9.

4. On a "Pacific City" police map of reported crimes, the Skid Row area and the adjacent Tenderloin area have by far the most numerous dots indicating location of a reported crime.

5. Egon Bittner, "The Police in Skid-Row: A Study of Peace Keeping," *American Sociological Review,* 32, No. 5 (October 1967), 701–6.

6. *Ibid.,* pp. 702 and 707–8.

7. This ability to "spot one" of a certain group or type of persons is a phenomenon which is prevalent but little understood. David Mechanic discusses this in connection with spotting the "mentally ill." See "Some Factors in Identifying and Defining Mental Illness," in Thomas J. Scheff (ed.), *Mental Illness and Social Processes* (New York: Harper and Row, 1967), pp. 23–31. David Sudnow also discusses how police spot trouble and identify possible crimes in "Normal Crimes: Sociological Features of the Penal Code in a Public Defender's Office," *Social Problems,* 12 (Winter 1965), 255–76. Skid Row men also feel they have a better than average ability to spot "marks" for panhandling. (See chapter 1, this text.)

8. According to Pacific City policemen and officials of Alcoholics Anonymous interviewed, alcoholism is such a problem with the police force that they have their own branch of AA with one policeman permanently assigned to maintain in membership those officers thought to need it. This is not unique to Pacific City, according to reports received subsequently.

9. Bittner, "The Police in Skid Row," 710–14.

10. Source: "Pacific City" arrest statistics, 1967.

11. In addition, the number of policemen assigned to Skid Row was reduced from time to time due to an industrial strike during which management demanded police protection for its properties.

On the other hand, if the Skid Row area is to come under unusual public scrutiny, arrests are often increased. During the New York World's Fair, according to some reports, arrests of Skid Row men were greatly increased to keep them from upsetting tourists who had to pass through a part of the Skid Row area to get to the fair.

12. The foregoing arrest criteria are not idiosyncratic to "Pacific City," but are general to all large cities. In the introduction to *Task Force Report on Drunkenness, The President's Commission on Law Enforcement and Administration of Justice,* the following point was made:

> The police do not arrest everyone who is under the influence of alcohol. . . . It is when he appears to have no home or family ties that he is most likely to be arrested and taken to the local jail.

One policeman assigned to a Skid Row precinct in a large eastern city recently described how he decided whom to arrest:

> I see a guy who's been hanging around, a guy who's been picked up before or been making trouble. I stop him. Sometimes he can convince me he's got a job today or got something to do. He'll show me a slip showing he's supposed to go to the blood bank, or to work. I let him go. But if it seems to me that he's got nothing to do but drink, then I bring him in. (p. 2)

13. The fact that police can be pulled on and off Skid Row duty without too many undesirable repercussions means that the area offers the police department a way to deploy men during "slack periods" much in the same way that the "continuing project" offers companies a means of employing men in between rush periods when they have specific contract work to complete. Research firms often use this device to maintain consistent staffing regardless of the ebb and flow of more imperative work.

14. Jerome H. Skolnick, *Justice Without Trial* (New York: John Wiley and Sons, 1966), p. 6.

15. *Ibid.*, p. 232.

16. Gresham M. Sykes and David Matza discuss ways of neutralizing the guilt produced by committing an illegal act in "Techniques of Neutralization: A Theory of Delinquency," *American Sociological Review,* 22 (December 1957), 664–70. See also William Westley, "Violence and the Police," *American Journal of Sociology,* 59 (July 1953), 33–41, for a justification of violence as a method of preventing trouble.

17. Bittner, "The Police in Skid Row," p. 713.

18. Police, jail captain, judges, and professionals at the City Screening Facility claim this to be true.

19. Information gained during interview of City Screening Facility official.

20. Apparently, arrests of Skid Row residents for public drunkenness are among the few where there is little attrition between the arrest and the appearance before the judge except for those informally dismissed by the booking sergeant or sent to the hospital. For instance, on other crimes, a number of cases are "lost" before conviction (through various legal and informal maneuvers that are never attempted on behalf of homeless alcoholics). See a discussion of attrition in the legal process by Philip H. Ennis, "Crime, Victims, and the Police," *Trans-action,* 4, No. 7 (June 1967), 40.

21. Actually, very few "atrocity tales" were heard about police brutality aside from complaints about being arrested when not drunk. Men often spoke of *fearing* a beating if they resisted, but apparently few resist to test the theory. See, however, Albert J. Reiss, Jr., "How Common is Police Brutality?" *Trans-action,* 5, No. 8 (July/August 1968), 10–19.

On the other hand, there does appear to be some evidence that some police will roll a drunk. Both Donald J. Bogue, *Skid Row in American Cities* (Chicago: University of Chicago Press, 1963), pp. 493–94, and Samuel E. Wallace, *Skid Row as a Way of Life* (Totowa, New Jersey: The Bedminister Press, 1965), p.

97, mention this. Wallace claims to have been rolled by a policeman when he pretended to be passed out on the sidewalk drunk and was arrested. He quotes the police officers as saying, "They'll never know the difference, and nobody will believe 'em anyhow."

22. According to state law, arrested persons are not allowed to pay their own bail. All money that a person may have in his possession at the time of arrest is put in safekeeping by the booking desk and cannot be used to pay bail. Most persons call their family, their lawyer, or a friend to arrange bail for them. The Skid Row man usually has none of these resources. Persons who are able to make bail arrangements do not usually appear for sentencing, but rather forfeit bail. There is no limit on the number of times they can do this, according to court aides.

23. "Dead time" is time spent in jail while awaiting trial; it does not count toward the sentence to be served. Sometimes judges will permit this time to be converted to "good time" served, thus shortening the sentence. In the case of the Skid Row alcoholic, the dead time he may serve is often longer than the sentence he would get, so that conversion to "good time" is of little solace.

CHAPTER 4

1. Newspaper interview with municipal court judge who handles public drunkenness cases, Pacific City.
2. William Petersen and David Matza, "Does the Juvenile Court Exercise Justice?" in Petersen and Matza (eds.), *Social Controversy* (Belmont, Calif.: Wadsworth Publishing Company, 1963), p. 107.
3. There has been pressure, in the form of a U.S. Supreme Court case, and a bill before Congress, to have alcoholism legally declared an illness. Neither effort has made much headway. The court case was based on the claim that it should be illegal to jail the steady, compulsive drinker for drunkenness inasmuch as he is suffering from an illness. The courts refused to make this judgment, saying there is no agreement currently as to the type of disease alcoholism is.

    As part of his decision on this case, Justice Thurgood Marshall said:
    It would be tragic to return large numbers of helpless, sometimes dangerous, and frequently unsanitary inebriates to the streets of our cities without the opportunity to sober up adequately which a brief jail term provides.

    The bill, the Federal Alcoholism Act of 1966 (S 3089), would define alcoholism as an illness and establish a Control Administration to work on the problem. It has not yet passed.

    For a discussion of the issues involved see Gerald Stern, "Public Drunkenness: Crime or Health Problem," *Annals of American Academy of Political and Social Science*, 374, (November 1967), 147–56.
4. Frederic S. LeClercq, "Field Observations in Drunk Court of the Pacific City Municipal Court" (unpublished memorandum, 1966), p. 1.
5. These observations were made almost two years after LeClercq made his.
6. LeClercq, "Field Observations in Drunk Court," p. 12.
7. Harold Garfinkel, "Conditions of a Successful Degradation Ceremony," *American Journal of Sociology*, 61 (March 1956), 420–22.
8. Source: "Pacific City" official arrest statistics.
9. From information received in the course of interviewing numerous Skid Row alcoholics while in institutions on the loop.
10. The use of a "Rapper" is apparently not a local phenomenon. Bogue notes it also in his study of the Chicago Skid Row. See Donald J. Bogue, *Skid Row in American Cities* (Chicago: University of Chicago, 1963), p. 414.

11. When the Rapper started drinking again, he was not replaced; rather court officers and an official of the Christian Missionaries, fulfilled his duties.

12. The Rapper was under treatment again for alcoholism at State Mental Hospital when he made this statement. The lack of compassion deviants show each other if they get into positions of authority is noted again in chapter 7. Kurt Lewin discusses this phenomenon of rejection of one's own (if they are a minority group of some type) in "Self-Hatred Among Jews," Chap. 12 of *Resolving Social Conflict* (New York: Harper Publishing Company, 1945).

13. LeClercq, "Field Observations in Drunk Court," p. 11.

14. *Ibid.*, pp. 6–7.

15. "The fundamental idea of the (juvenile court) law is that the state must step in and exercise guardianship over a child found under such adverse social or individual conditions as develop crime. . . . It proposes a plan whereby he may be treated, not as a criminal, or legally charged with crime, but as a ward of the state, to receive practically the care, custody, and discipline that are accorded the neglected and dependent child. . . ." *Report Committee of Chicago Bar*, 1899, footnote in Gustav L. Schramm, "Philosophy of the Juvenile Court," in Petersen and Matza (eds.), *Social Controversy*, p. 109.

16. Reported by inmate in County Jail on public drunkenness charge.

17. Source: Captain, County Jail.

18. LeClercq, "Field Observations in Drunk Court," p. 7.

19. As previously mentioned, the chief deputy of County Jail puts the number of recidivists at 85 percent of the total admissions in any one year.
A small "loop," made by the chronic drunkenness offender who goes between municipal jail and Skid Row has been well chronicled by Pittman and Gordon in *The Revolving Door* (Glencoe, Ill.: The Free Press, 1958).

20. Statement made by Municipal Judge from city near Pacific City.

21. Their feelings are not unlike those that Matza in *Delinquency and Drift* (New York: John Wiley and Sons, 1967), p. 135, imputes to juveniles who are appalled at the arbitrariness and seeming unfairness of the juvenile court system: Hypocrisy . . . and . . . favoritism . . . [are] imputed (from the way the juvenile court is operated). [Why do] they insist, as they frequently do, that it is not what he [the delinquent] did—which strikes delinquents and others as a sensible reason for legal intervention—but his underlying problems and difficulties that guide court action? Why do they say they are helping him when patently they are limiting his freedom of action and movement by putting him on probation or in prison? What on earth could they possibly be hiding that would lead them to such heights of deception?

22. Not all the Skid Row alcoholics hated the Rapper. Some men felt he saved them from a harsher sentence. However, when Northern State Mental Hospital staff learned of the Rapper's impending arrival, they called a meeting of the male alcoholics and asked them to treat the Rapper with kindness rather than vengeance.

23. Matza draws the same parallel between bed space and probability of sentence to juvenile hall or probation in his study, *Delinquency and Drift*, p. 126.

24. As a member of the city screening team put it:
We often send one of our social workers to court to see to it that the judge goes along with our decision on the guy. Often, the social worker can speak up and clarify our position. [A36]

25. In Bittner's paper on peace-keeping in Skid Row, some incidents suggest a basis for the belief among Skid Row drunks that a quota exists for each round of the paddy wagon. For instance:
Sometimes drunk arrests are made mainly because the police van is available. In one case a patrolman summoned the van to pick up an arrested man. As the van was pulling away from the curb the officer stopped the driver because he sighted another drunk stumbling across the street. The second man protested

saying that he "wasn't even half drunk yet." The patrolman's response was "OK, I'll owe you half a drunk." (Egon Bittner, "The Police on Skid Row; A Study of Peace-Keeping," *American Sociological Review*, 32, No. 5, [Oct., 1967].)

26. Allen also discusses this sentiment, which he feels is ignored by laymen and re-habilitation professionals, in favor of considering jail euphemistically as a reform or rehabilitation institution. See Francis A. Allen, "Criminal Justice and the Rehabili-tative Ideal," in Petersen and Matza, *Social Controversy*, pp. 119–20.

The Skid Row alcoholic has his own sarcastic way of expressing this:
When the judge sees a man standing before him, dirty, ragged, and maybe in withdrawal, why it brings out the "humanitarian" in him. He says to himself, "I'll do this poor fellow a good deed and send him to jail." [13]

CHAPTER 5

1. A seizure is a "fit" not unlike the epileptic fit. It results from being taken too suddenly off alcohol after prolonged heavy drinking.

2. See chapter 6 for discussion of rehabilitation activities in the "Pacific City" County Jail, especially quote from Bulletin, page 134 of this study.

3. Gresham M. Sykes, *The Society of Captives* (New York: Atheneum Publishers, 1965).

4. Erving Goffman, *Asylums* (Garden City, New York: Doubleday Anchor Books, Inc., 1961).

5. Donald Clemmer, *The Prison Community* (New York: Holt, Rinehart and Winston, 1940; paperback, 1965).

6. This is apparently characteristic, not only of prisons, but of other institutions such as the mental hospital and the medical hospital reported on below:
To see that the [mental] patients are regularly fed, clothed, and do not escape or harm one another takes considerable patience and effort. There is little time left to attend to the problems of the individual patient in any therapeutic sense.
See Nick J. Colarelli and Saul M. Siegel, *Ward H, An Adventure in Innovation* (Princeton, New Jersey: D. VanNostrand Co., Inc., 1966), p. 12.

Rose L. Coser reported similarly on the medical hospital. From her observations, nurses actually had very little opportunity to do "supportive nursing" because this interfered with the running of a "smooth ward." See *Life on the Ward* (East Lansing, Michigan: Michigan University Press, 1962), esp. Chap. 5, "Mother or Career Girl," pp. 70–79.

7. Everett Hughes discussed this ambivalence in his article, *Good People and Dirty Work*, in Howard S. Becker (ed.), *The Other Side* (New York: The Free Press, 1964), pp. 30, 31.

8. This is actually in keeping with current medical practices, especially where a large group of persons who use the same physicians and equipment is involved. Dr. Harold F. Newman, who administers the largest closed-panel medical plan, the Group Health Cooperative of Puget Sound in Seattle, Washington, has mentioned that in this day of advanced technology, it is a waste of a doctor's time to make house calls when most of the diagnostic equipment used is at the hospital. Ac-cordingly, house visits are discouraged and ambulance trips to the hospital are encouraged through the rate schedule. (Dr. Newman in private conversations with me.)

Somers and Somers also make this point in *Doctors, Patients, and Health Insurance* (Garden City, New York: Doubleday Anchor Inc., 1962), Chap. 9, "Changing Patterns of Utilization," especially the section, "Factors Affecting Hospital Use," pp. 152–159. (See also footnote 38, this chapter.)

9. A typical official menu for "Pacific City" County Jail is shown in part below:

OFFICIAL MENU—COUNTY JAIL (FEBRUARY 20)

Breakfast	Lunch	Dinner
cornmeal	minestrone soup	Boston beans with pork
milk	cole slaw with	stewed prunes
sugar	oil and vinegar	cornbread
bread	coffee	coffee
coffee	bread	

10. Technically, County Jail is for persons whose crimes have been defined as a mis-demeanor, even if they originally were defined as felonies and "reduced" to misdemeanors. The actual inmate composition, as described by the captain, probably is contrary to the popular stereotype of the County Jail as an institution for persons who commit petty crimes, such as persons who fish out of season or become involved in barroom brawls. Note this item from "Pacific City" newspaper:

Spokesmen for home owner improvement groups in the vicinity of the [County] jail . . . cited the influx of tough felony prisoners in the dangerously-under-staffed medium security jail, originally designed for alcoholics and minor offenders.

They said they will ask . . . officials to "do something because the jail has become a grim little (state prison) right in our backyards."

11. In previous years, men could be "committed" to the County Jail on a Health, Education, and Welfare commitment by a judge. Such a sentence was an alterna-tive to mental hospital commitment. (This practice has been virtually halted.)

According to the Chief Deputy, although men committed to County Jail were not there for any crime (actually they had often been persuaded by a relative to appear in Superior Court and request a mental hospital commitment), they were treated "just like anyone else at the jail."

12. Among the alcoholics, only those on a pension or receiving some form of govern-ment subsidy have money for commissary purchases.

13. Being homeless males, few of the alcoholics receive letters while in jail.

14. The captain claims to review all lockups and lost time ordered by guards. The inmates doubt this, however, saying that it would be physically impossible, and that too few such orders are rescinded to have received any review. On the other hand, men have told me cases of the captain's intervention in what they felt to be an unfair lockup.

15. Skid Row alcoholics rarely have anyone to write to, although they sometimes need to notify some hotel management that they are incarcerated and ask that belong-ings be saved for their release. Furthermore, men must buy their own stationery and postage, and often the Skid Row alcoholic comes in penniless or nearly so. Alcoholics have told me that if they are arrested with less than a dollar on them, this amount would be taken from them because City Jail would not keep books for any amount under one dollar.

16. Most Skid Row alcoholics serve their entire sentences without having a single visitor. A three months' count of weekend visitors revealed that of the 50 or 60 who were registered each visiting day, only two or three visited with men incar-cerated on a public drunkenness charge.

17. Of course, many Skid Row alcoholics could not handle an office job; but they could handle some of the other jobs available, such as running an elevator, working in the kitchen, working in the laundry, serving as trusty, and so on. Persons who work in the kitchen, the commissary, or the front office sleep in a dormitory as part payment for their services, a bit of freedom that the man serving a public drunkenness charge is denied.

18. Official "Pacific City" arrest and sentence statistics.

19. Thus if rehabilitation is looked at in terms of preparing a person to be self-sup-porting in the community, the jail certainly offers little in the way of job experience

to make alcoholics self-sufficient. The inside jobs they get are of the most menial variety and the outside jobs are not usable training for men who prefer an urban environment. Once in a while, after release, these men are offered employment at schools and other institutions that have grounds to maintain, but they seldom stay for long because they miss the city.

20. Outdoor work long has been considered to be a panacea for alcoholism, although there is, as yet, no empirical evidence that the fresh air is any better for the chronic drinker than any other environment in which a man is kept away from a liquor supply, given regular meals, and required to do regular physical exercise. Certainly, reading the brochures of private sanitariums for alcoholics, one becomes aware of this attitude. Almost all of them carry descriptions or pictures of the fine grounds where patients may stroll, getting all the fresh air they want, presumably improving with every breath.

21. It should be mentioned that when the Captain read this manuscript, he denied alcoholics were singled out for the more undesirable jobs in the jail. However, the notes made of his discussion indicate he did say it.

22. This is a policy in many small towns and rural areas where every man is known by name.

23. This is a policy in many major cities according to well-traveled Skid Row men. New York, Chicago, and Boston have been mentioned by Skid Row alcoholics, who travel extensively, as using this approach to public drunkenness.

24. It should be mentioned that one of the guards who read this manuscript questioned the validity of the statement concerning the need for farm labor because he felt that the farm is virtually inactive at present.

25. Records kept of inmates' weight upon entering the jail and leaving indicate claims by the jail administration of "building the chronic drunk up" are an exaggeration, at least so far as weight increase is concerned. (Nor do the men lose any considerable amount of weight as *they* sometimes claim.) A sampling of the records indicate that the men's weight changes but little for the most part, although when it does, it is usually in the direction of a slight gain. Food served has a high starch content and the inmates are quite sedentary, so one wonders at the quantity of starchy food that could result in so small a weight gain.

COMPARISON OF WEIGHT ON ARRIVAL IN JAIL AND
AT RELEASE, SHOWN BY HEIGHT

Weight upon arrival	Weight upon release	Height
120	124	5'6"
137	138	5'8½"
114	118	5'4½"
153	154	5'4"
130	130	5'8"
125	131	5'8½"
155	162	5'9"
136	140	5'7½"
171	171	6'
133	141	5'6½"
167	164	5'7"
149	160	5'10"
141	148	6'¼"
190	194	5'9"
127	131	5'6½"

(Taken at random from County Jail records, last names starting with A's and M's.)

Men may, of course, be in better shape from adequate sleep, abstinence from liquor, and an outdoor job.

26. When one of the guards read this, he wrote on the manuscript, "This is ridiculous."

27. Sykes, *The Society of Captives*, pp. 67–70.

28. Inmates claim that the official menu often bears little resemblance to the food actually served both as to items and portions. Furthermore, the men claim that sometimes its taste is so bad that it "comes up" on them.

SAMPLE OF CHRONIC DRUNKENNESS INMATE'S
RECORD OF MEALS RECEIVED AT COUNTY JAIL
(SAME MONTH AS OFFICIAL MENU; SEE FOOTNOTE 9)

Breakfast	*Lunch*	*Dinner*
Cornmeal mush	Baloney	Boiled rice
Coffee	Cheese	Chicken gizzards
(no sugar; no milk)	Lettuce	Jello
	Tea	

(A City Health Department nutritionist's report found that Pacific City Jail food was deficient in calcium, Vitamins A and C, and protein, and below the State's minimum jail standards, according to an item in the Pacific City daily paper.)

29. Although this may be true, records (see footnote 25) seem to indicate that most inmates' weight remains fairly stationary. Furthermore, it is only fair to point out that inadequate as jail fare may be by civilian standards, it probably is better than most of the Skid Row alcoholics were eating on the outside just before their incarceration.

30. Divided trays have been provided since the recent Grand Jury investigation.

31. As previously mentioned, the longer the sentence, the more dangerous the person (in terms of a hold for other crimes or an interest in drug [pick-ups]), the more likely that man is to get a "good" inside job. Since many Negro prisoners qualify on the above counts, they are more likely to become trusties.

Some men claim that men with a sentence of 30 days or less (often given for public drunkenness violations) are ineligible to become trusties at all. The Chief Deputy has said that this is not necessarily true, that it depends on the composition of the jail population on hand when an opening comes up.

Regardless of the reason for trusty appointments, the fact remains that the "tougher" inmates get them and that they often take advantage of the older, alcoholic inmates—at least by the alcoholics' testimony.

32. The captain claims that the cereal is presweetened. Undoubtedly the amount provided does not satisfy the exceptionally strong cravings for sweets that many alcoholics claim to have.

33. It should be stated, however, that most alcoholics who live on Skid Row tolerate a level of sanitation there much lower than that afforded by the jail.

34. Mattresses did look dirty to me; they are *not* sterilized between uses, jail officials state.

35. Some time after the field work for this study was completed at the County Jail (and following the most recent Grand Jury investigation) a male nurse was hired for the jail to supplement the medical attention afforded by the doctor. He is on duty eight out of 24 hours a day.

36. The "squirrel cage" is a special padded cell for men suspected of being on the verge of a seizure, or for men suffering a seizure, so that they may fall or suffer convulsions without bruising themselves.

37. Captain Jackson gave these reasons for the confiscation of drugs (primarily claimed to be Dilantin and Phenobarbitol):

1. the officials cannot be certain that there are not illegal drugs in the bottles;
2. there is no way to know that the man who is in possession of the drugs is actually to have them. He may have someone else's prescription or switched labels;
3. it is difficult to keep the men from peddling such drugs to other inmates.

Therefore, all drugs are confiscated and a doctor must represcribe and dole out drugs in small quantities. Unfortunately, the doctor is often a bit slow in doing this.

38. Shortly after this claim was made, a former Pacific City Jail inmate brought suit against the city for the harm he claimed to have incurred when his Dilantin was taken from him during his incarceration and he suffered a seizure.

This prisoner was informally advised by the chaplain that he might get six months added to his sentence if he insisted on such trouble-making. Approximately two years later, *an ex-inmate* of the County Jail brought suit in Superior Court in an attempt to force a ruling on the required presence of a physician at the jail. His case is still pending.

39. Goffman, *Asylums*, p. 186.

40. An alcoholic who had been in the jail of a nearby county reported the following "indoctrination speech."

You go to this brief orientation meeting and a guy tells you to keep your nose clean and you'll get along fine. But, he says, "You've seen that sign out in front and it says 'Central City Rehabilitation Center.' That looks real pretty and it looks good to people driving by, but, as far as I'm concerned and any other deputy here, I don't care what you're here for. You're in jail, period. You're an inmate, period. And that is it." [26]

41. The captain insisted, upon reading this comment, that it is inaccurate and that undergarments are provided all inmates, although perhaps old and sometimes torn. Of course, while the jail garb is in bad shape, the clothes most alcoholics arrive in are in even worse shape. These garments are often stained with vomit, infested with lice, torn, and ill-fitting. Many men leave the jail in donated clothing that looks better than the clothing they wore on arrival.

42. Three North is a combination receiving tier and homosexual tier. All men go there when they first arrive. Homosexuals are kept there because it is closest to the rotunda where a deputy is always on duty. Ninety percent of the new men are moved off within two or three days. The receiving cells are adjacent to the homosexual cells so that heterosexuals form a rotating and transient population and have no chance to build up any relationship with a homosexual.

43. According to the psychiatrist at the jail, the alcoholic men do not like being so close to homosexuals because it brings out their own latent homosexuality.

44. As mentioned, the alcoholic, with his usually shorter sentence, has fewer of the opportunities to work the system and create a self-saving existence through the use of such secondary adjustments as were described by Goffman in *Asylums*, in "The Underlife of a Public Institution," p. 188–319.

45. Recent testimony at an investigation of the Pacific City County Jail indicated that men sometimes spend six months in cells without exercise due to shortage of guards for the exercise area.

46. Farber, Harlow, and West have hypothesized that living under conditions of "debility, dependency, and dread" for any length of time has an adverse effect on the self-concept as well as on such processes as time-attention span and responsiveness to stimuli. Although this study was centered on the Chinese Communist prisoner-of-war camps, and attempted to explain the phenomenon of "brainwashing" on the above grounds, it also is probably applicable, to a modified extent, to the alcoholic's position in County Jail. They arrive in a condition of physical debilitation, they are totally dependent upon their "captors," and they also have a situation of dread of both guards and other prisoners whom they must live in contact with 24 hours a day. See Farber, Harlow, and West, "Brainwashing, Con-

ditioning, and DDD (Debility, Dependency, and Dread)" in Theodore R. Sarben (ed.), *Studies in Behavior Pathology* (New York: Holt, Rinehart and Winston, 1961), pp. 106–16.

47. The term "hypes" refers to drug users.

48. The recent prison scandals in the South in which hundreds of bodies, with broken limbs, of men thought to be inmates were found buried in unmarked graves in the jail yard give some credence to this fear.

49. The ride to Pacific City and the 15 cents carfare were not always supplied to inmates discharged from County Jail. These departure aids are the direct result of complaints of merchants and residents near the jail (which is located outside the county it serves) that men were being discharged penniless and without transportation and were panhandling their way back to the city.

CHAPTER 6

1. This is akin to the core philosophy of Alcoholics Anonymous, although they prefer to call the problem an allergy. Paradoxically, this organization does not believe that hospitals, sanitariums, medical doctors, or psychiatrists can aid the alcoholic in getting well, but rather that he must do it through the help of God, other AA members, and his own willpower. See E. M. Jellinek, *The Disease Concept of Alcoholism* (New Haven, Conn.: Hillhouse Press, 1960) and *Alcoholics Anonymous* (New York: Alcoholics Anonymous Publishing, Inc., 1955).

2. Tranquilizers and paraldehyde are used to ameliorate withdrawal symptoms; vitamins to build health. Somewhat more exotic approaches to the medical treatment of alcoholism are reportedly being tried at other institutions on the loop, such as getting "poisons" out of the body through steam baths, and the use of spinal taps. (One Skid Row alcoholic reported that he was offered extra days in City Hospital if he would submit to an experimental spinal tap. He protested that he did not want to do this but that he was still too sick and weak to leave. When he refused the spinal tap, he was discharged.)

3. The turmoil in the field of alcoholism as to what is a fruitful approach to the problem can be seen from such articles as H. Krystal and R. H. Moore, "Who is Qualified to Treat the Alcoholic?" *Quarterly Journal of Studies on Alcohol*, 24 (1963), 705–20, and the comments which followed in Vol. 26, No. 2 (1965), 310–16 by Joseph Thinmann, Jean J. Rossi, and John Clancy. See also, Moore and Ranseur, "Effects of Psychotherapy in an Open Ward Hospital on Patients with Alcoholism," *Quarterly Journal of Studies on Alcohol*, 21 (1960), 233–53; and P. O'Hollaren, "Symptom Analysis of Alcoholism," *Medical Times*, 87 (1959), 520–24, and O. William's discussion of this problem in *Quarterly Journal of Studies on Alcohol*, 21 (1960), 360–61. See also Reginald A. H. Robson et al., *An Evaluation of the Effect of Treatment on the Rehabilitation of Alcoholics* (Alcoholism Foundation of British Columbia, Vancouver, B.C., 1963; mimeographed).

4. There are many approaches to and theories supporting these therapies, which are discussed briefly below:

Aversion therapy or conditioning therapy is intended to create an association of something unpleasant with the use of alcohol so that the drinker is deterred by the automatic memory of the unpleasantness. Prominent among the approaches to such conditioning is the use of an electric shock whenever the patient reaches for a glass of alcohol, which is set in front of him, and inducement of violent vomiting after the patient has ingested alcohol. This latter is the basis of the Antabuse treatment.

Somewhat more fanciful was the anectine experiment, first tried by doctors in Queen's University, Canada. They injected succinylcholine chloride (anectine, quelcin) directly into the blood stream of a subject immediately after he had been given some of his favorite drink. Sudden, total, paralysis results, including cessation of breathing. The subject is administered an antidote before he dies; the purpose of the treatment is for him to associate feelings of impending death with alcohol. This experiment was repeated at State Mental Hospital with volunteers. Some of the volunteers were Skid Row alcoholics who later were interviewed at Welfare Home for Homeless Men. When asked if the treatment kept them away from liquor for any time one answered. "No, but I sure as hell stay away from that anectine." [49]

LSD and CO_2 therapies are more closely tied in with Freudian theory. Both are intended to induce hallucinations from which the alcoholic may get insights into his personality and social problems. Often the patient is asked to describe his hallucinations to a therapist for analysis much as a man would tell his dreams to a psychoanalyst.

For discussions of aversion therapy see:
Walter L. Voegtlin, "The Treatment of Alcoholism by Establishing a Conditioned Reflex," *American Journal of Medical Sciences*, 199 (June 1940), 802–10; and R. E. Sanderson, D. Campbell, and S. C. Laverty, "An Investigation of a New Aversion Conditioning Treatment for Alcoholism," *Quarterly Journal of Studies on Alcoholism*, 24 (1963), 261–75.
For discussions of LSD therapy:
N. Chwelos, D. Blewett, C. Smith, and A. Hoffer, "Use of LSD in the Treatment of Alcoholism," *Quarterly Journal of Studies on Alcoholism*, 20 (1959), 577–90.
S. Jensen and R. Ramsay, "Treatment of Chronic Alcoholism with LSD," *Canadian Psychiatric Association Journal*, 8 (1963), 182–88.

5. Among the most difficult to establish rates is that of alcoholic recidivism. First of all, much of this recidivism does not come to the attention of agents of social control and is therefore "unofficial." Secondly, "official" recidivism is not kept track of in any systematic way. The reason for this probably lies in the enormous bookkeeping problems. As was noted in chapter 2, alcoholics do not always return to the same institution when they lapse; they make a round of institutions. Therefore, to keep a record of official recidivism with any accuracy at all, there would have to be much more cooperation and information exchange between institutions on this subject than there is at present.

Some institutions keep rates on "repeat admissions," but this obviously ignores the inter-institutional action between visits to a given institution. Nevertheless, these rates do give some idea of the high rates of recidivism of alcoholism among adult males. (See chapter 2, footnote 12.)

6. W. R. Bion, *Experiences in Groups and Other Papers* (New York: Basic Books, Inc., 1959), p. 11.

7. On this point, group therapy is not unlike Alcoholics Anonymous meetings. See the description in R.H. Blum and E.M. Blum, *Alcoholism* (San Francisco: Jossey-Bass, Inc., 1967), pp. 163–66. AA probably attaches less importance to sexual "hang-ups" than do less religiously-oriented therapy groups. For a version of therapy groups oriented to sex and other personality problems that is possibly (though not necessarily) exaggerated, see the fictionalized account in Jerry Sohl, *The Lemon Eaters* (New York: Dell Publishing Co., 1967).

8. Discussions with Lloyd Meadow, psychologist with a special interest in group therapy as a rehabilitative tool, and J. Maurice Rogers, psychologist with a special interest in rehabilitation of deviants. See also S. R. Slavson, *Fields of Group Psychotherapy* (New York: International Universities Press, 1954), p. 83.

9. In the area of teaching, for instance, see Miriam Wagenschein, "Reality Shock" (unpublished Master's thesis, University of Chicago, 1950), pp. 58–59; Howard S. Becker, "Social Class Variations in the Teacher-Pupil Relationship," *The Journal of Educational Sociology*, 25, No. 8 (April 1952), 451–65; and Willard Waller,

"What Teaching Does to Teachers," *The Sociology of Teaching* (New York: John Wiley and Sons, Inc., 1932), pp. 375–409.

Students also suffer reality shock. See Howard S. Becker and Blanche Geer, "The Fate of Idealism in Medical School," *American Sociological Review*, 23 (February 1958), 50–56.

In the area of politics, see Seymour Martin Lipset's *Agrarian Socialism* (Berkeley and Los Angeles: University of California Press, 1950). On the institutional level, see Charles Perrow, "Reality Shock: A New Organization Confronts the Custody-Treatment Dilemma," *Social Problems*, 10, No. 4 (Spring 1963), 374–82; and Charles Perrow, "Reality Adjustment: An Institution Settles for Humane Care," *Social Problems*, 14, No. 1 (Summer 1966), 69–77. See also Robert A. Scott, "The Selection of Clients by Social Welfare Agencies: The Case of the Blind," *Social Problems*, 14, No. 3 (Winter 1966), 256–58.

10. This problem is ably discussed by Seymour L. Halleck in his book, *Psychiatry and the Dilemmas of Crime* (New York: Hoeber Medical Books and Harper and Row, 1967).

11. David J. Pittman and C. Wayne Gordon, *Revolving Door: A Study of the Chronic Police Case Inebriate* (Glencoe, Ill.: The Free Press, 1958), pp. 141–42.

12. A demonstration project is exactly what the words imply. It is intended, in this case, to demonstrate to local and state officials what could be done for the chronic alcoholic as an alternative to mere incarceration. Presumably such a project would be operated with a joint research-action approach and some predetermined criteria for success or improvement over previous methods, but these attributes were not, so far as I was able to determine, built into this demonstration project.

13. These funds are also used for treatment of alcoholic inmates at Northern State Mental Hospital and the use of the same fund for both the jail and the hospital is at least one indication that their rehabilitation services were considered equivalent.

14. Actual quotation from the "Bulletin of Pacific State Mental Health Bureau." (pseudonym)

15. Actual quotation from the *Pacific City Public Health Annual Report*. (pseudonym)

16. A basic antagonism apparently exists between most lower-class patients and their therapists. August B. Hollingshead and Frederick C. Redlich make the point that lower-class patients rarely see any value in psychotherapy and their therapists rarely understand the lower-class patients' general outlook on life. The former sees the "talk therapy" as useless; the latter sees such patients as hopeless. See *Social Class and Mental Illness* (New York: John Wiley and Co.; Science Editions, 1958), pp. 301–2.

17. Social workers apparently are becoming less and less interested in the traditional material aid they can dispense to clients and rather prefer to offer "therapy" to them. The head psychiatrist at the Jail Branch Clinic complained to me of this trend.

Everyone wants to get into the group therapy act. These social workers here don't want to do social work, they want to engineer character change. It's ridiculous. I'd like to get them off their duff and busy helping these guys out with their real dependency problem—having no financial resources when they get out of jail. [A16]

18. This is apparently a common complaint of professionals who work with alcoholics; it highlights the dichotomy of physical and mental aid for chronic alcoholism. Some therapists fear that modern chemotherapy so reduces the amount of withdrawal suffering an alcoholic must undergo that fear of withdrawal no longer provides him with any incentive for cessation of excessive drinking.

19. The staff of the Jail Branch Clinic includes:

A woman psychiatric social worker who is at the jail four days per week and divides her time between the men and women's units;

A male psychiatric social worker who devotes 18 hours per week to the jail;

A male psychologist who is at the jail five half-days per week;

A male psychiatrist who spends eight hours per week at the jail;

A male psychiatrist who is at the jail late Monday and Wednesday afternoons for a total of nine hours in all. Much of his time goes to administration, as he is director of the branch staff.

20. For instance, see Perrow, "Reality Adjustment: An Institution Settles for Humane Care," *Social Problems*, Vol. 14, 69–77.

21. See Robert A. Scott, "Selection of Clients by Social Welfare Agencies," *Social Problems*, Vol. 14, p. 251, in which he discusses the selection of blind clients for rehabilitation therapy who will probably do well (children and employable adults), and the avoidance of those who probably will not (elderly blind persons).

22. Sincerity or "true motivation" on the part of most Skid Row alcoholics to be rehabilitated is doubted by a majority of veteran workers in the loop institutions who see man after man proclaim his determination to stop drinking—only to return to heavy imbibing almost immediately upon release. As a social worker at Welfare Home for Homeless Men put it:

They come and *seem* sincere when they say they've got to stop drinking, that they are determined to do so, and they want your help to do it. But they *aren't* sincere because they start drinking the minute they leave here. They are just saying what they think you want to hear. You cannot believe or trust them. [A44]

23. The material on screening criteria that follows is a composite of conversations with various members of the Jail Branch Clinic staff. Not all therapists could verbalize their criteria for admission of an inmate to a therapy group. The former Branch Clinic Director refused to discuss any of the criteria he used for evaluating the motivation of possible group therapy members. When asked this question, he replied somewhat heatedly:

You can't ask that! That sort of thing is up here (tapping his head). It's part of my knowledge in this field. It can't be put into so many words. [A15]

24. The records used to check on the number of alcoholics in therapy groups were those kept in compliance with state funding of the Jail Branch Clinic. It is difficult to imagine that the staff expected the State to peruse these records, even cursorily, as they were very carelessly filled in, lacking in uniformity of attention to items and, for the most part, not filed. (The Clinic was dependent upon prisoners for clerical assistance.) In order to confirm the number of alcoholics in therapy groups, I asked each group leader for this information. The reply was either that there were none, or that some of the men in the group might have a drinking problem in addition to the offense for which he was sentenced. It was during one of these conversations that a staff member said, "We are thinking of starting a group for the alcoholics."

I was able to locate two public drunkenness offenders (with the aid of a psychiatric social worker) who had received some therapy-counseling from the Center on previous confinements. One was quite noncommittal about whether it had helped him and the other showed some enthusiasm, saying it helped him to understand some of his problems and the reasons for his drinking. None of the men interviewed at the jail or in other institutions had received any therapy at the jail whatsoever during their time there.

25. The new director instituted many policies the Pacific City Health Department saw as controversial. Finally, he was asked to resign and was replaced by a more conservative director. It is difficult to tell at this time whether or not this change in executives has had any great effect on treatment of alcoholics at the Jail Branch Clinic.

26. Such inmates are usually quite verbal and, further, have mastered the rudiments of Freudian psychology to the extent that they know how to describe their lives in such a manner as to titillate the interest of the group leader. Both psychologists

in the Pacific City Public Health Department and guards at the County Jail suspected that the therapists preferred the more glamorous prisoners to the duller alcoholics.

27. See chapter 5, footnote 40.

28. Ken Kesey makes much the same point in his novel about a mental hospital, *One Flew Over the Cuckoo's Nest*, pp. 54–66. In Kesey's fictionalized account of his experiences in a mental hospital, one patient likened group therapy to a pecking party by a flock of dirty chickens, who, when sighting blood, rip one chicken to bits. When he described the psychiatric nurse who led the group as a "ball cutter," another patient replied: ". . . [she's] accused me of having nothing between my legs but a patch of hair . . .! Ball-cutter? Oh, you *underestimate* her!" (p. 62)

29. It seems inadvisable to take space in the main text of this chapter to discuss the content of the therapy sessions since so few alcoholics are involved. The sessions are, nevertheless, worth a footnote.

In a therapy meeting attended by the author there were two alcoholics and four drug users. The drug users did most of the talking. With the exception of one who had been treated at the State Mental Hospital, the drug users wanted to talk about their current existential position—the quality of the food, the problem of getting out, the bum rap that put them there. On the other hand, the therapist wished to guide the conversation into a search for deep emotional problems that presumably caused the alcohol and drug abuse.

Social worker: Are you willing to admit you still have problems to work on?

Drug user: My problem right now is getting out of here. I'm going to IBM school. I have my own doctors for my emotional problems.

2nd drug user: The real issue here is that the food is slop and we have to eat it while the stirs [guards] downstairs are eating steak.

Social worker: That isn't what we are here today for. We are here on another issue.

3rd drug user: State Mental Hospital has a pretty effective program for the addict. They gave me a chance to talk out my problems. I learned that I take drugs because of these problems and I learned from the other guys how they licked their problems temporarily.

Alcoholic: At State Mental Hospital, I learned that I drink because of some problem I have.

1st drug user: How can anyone say to me "Why don't you try this?" These psychiatrists told me that I like to stick things in my arm because of sexual experience. How do they know? They haven't made the scene. They don't even know the vocabulary. I find contentment in my fantasy—just like Walt Disney did.

It should be mentioned that the therapy sessions at the jail are carried on against overwhelming physical odds. The room is an old classroom and is adjacent to an echoing hall where there is much activity. Much of the time it was difficult for members of the group to hear one another speak.

30. Halleck in *Dilemma of Crime*, p. 289, mentions the problem the prison psychiatrist faces in asking the prisoner to "adjust" to a miserable situation for his own good.

31. "Turning sour" is a strategy used by otherwise fairly helpless persons to fight the sanctions being applied to them for some deviation from group norms. Employees often do this, limiting their activities to what they absolutely have to do on a job and no more; Negroes do this to whites through sullen and only minimal attention to assigned tasks. I am indebted to Erving Goffman and Herbert Blumer for calling my attention to this strategy by which the weak sometimes defeat the strong.

32. These complaints actually focus on the failure of alcoholics to meet the role responsibilities of "good patients." See Talcott Parsons' discussion of the role of patient in "Definitions of Health and Illness in the Light of American Values and

Social Structure," in Jaco (ed.), *Patients, Physicians, and Illness* (Glencoe, Ill.: The Free Press, 1958), pp. 165–87, esp. pp. 176–77.

33. This fear of "wasting" therapy on the unresponsive is even reflected in the commitment code and suggests that although mental institutions are willing to wrestle with some personality problems, they see others as beyond their therapeutic scope.

    "Before a person is committed to a state hospital, however, satisfactory evidence shall be submitted to the trial judge, showing that the person to be committed is *not of bad repute or bad character*, apart from his habit for which commitment is made, and that there is reasonable ground for believing that the person, if committed, will be permanently benefited by treatment." (Emphasis mine.) (From state code on commitment to mental hospital.)

34. Max Hayman, *Alcoholism: Mechanism and Management* (Springfield, Ill.: Charles C Thomas, 1966), pp. 137–38.

35. In Pacific City, the main reason for involuntary commitment of alcoholics to State Mental Hospital was to allow the state to arrange for the transportation of persons to the hospital who might otherwise not be able to afford it. Therefore, more indigent alcoholics were likely to be committed (by their own request, usually) than men who could raise the bus fare for the trip.

36. Jellinek's types are the best known. He divided alcoholics into five types based on disease processes or symptoms: alpha, beta, gamma, delta, and epsilon alcoholism. See E. M. Jellinek, *The Disease Concept of Alcoholism*, pp. 36–41.

37. The World Health Organization has suggested that there are four phases or stages of alcoholism: prealcoholic, prodromal, crucial, and chronic. They correlate these phases with both drinking behavior and development of dependency on alcohol. See "Expert Committee on Mental Health: Report on the First Session of the Alcoholism Sub-committee," *World Health Organization Technical Report Series, No. 42 (September 1951).*

38. Hayman, *Alcoholism: Mechanism and Management*, pp. 137–38.

39. Ivan Belknap, *Human Problems in a State Mental Hospital* (New York: McGraw-Hill Book Co., Inc., 1956).

40. See Erving Goffman, *Asylums* (Garden City, New York: Doubleday Anchor Inc., 1961), and Alfred Stanton and Morris S. Schwartz, *The Mental Hospital* (New York: Basic Books, Inc., 1954).

41. Roy Turner, *Talk and Troubles* (unpublished Ph.D. dissertation, University of California, Berkeley, 1968).

42. An excellent description of the type of program inaugurated by State Mental Hospital, along with its theoretical rationale, may be found in Robert N. Rapoport, *Community as Doctor: New Perspectives on a Therapeutic Community* (London: Tavistock Publications, 1959; and Springfield, Ill.: Charles C Thomas, 1960). For an appraisal of such a program in action, see Anselm Strauss, *et al.*, *Psychiatric Ideologies and Institutions*, esp. Chaps. 6, 7, 8.

43. Rapoport, *Community as Doctor*, pp. 272–73, also questions what he terms "the acceptance of slogans as attainable goals rather than ideological tenets." He also notes that these ideologies tend to be held with a "fervor and conviction for somewhat autonomous reasons."

    A danger this poses is that they may become goals in themselves. Being "democratic" or "permissive" comes to be the *summum bonum, the more fundamental question of how such behavior contributes to any patient's therapy may be lost sight of.* (Emphasis mine.)

44. Despite this avowed absence of certainty as to proper treatment or predicted results of work with alcoholics, State Mental Hospital also has a "hopeful" flow chart—not unlike the official flow chart cited in chapter 2—depicting the so-called steps in alcoholism rehabilitation terminating in "a functioning and responsible citizen."

45. Professional loyalty to group therapy may be tied in with the amount of personal

investment an agent of social control feels he has in the method. As one said when asked how he would feel if group therapy were proved useless:

What would I do if I thought my approach did nothing for the alcoholics? I don't know what I would do. My whole professional life is developed around this approach. I haven't seen anything that works any better. Everything I know, all my skills, are concentrated on this approach. It must be doing some good, men still come to the hospital for help. [A24]

46. The so-called gut-level or marathon-group therapy session is growing in popularity. In general, the term refers to continuous 24-hour meetings in which members of the group are encouraged to insult each other and to react to such insults emotionally. Again, the purpose is to "strip away pretenses" of persons and make them "see themselves as they actually are." The presumption is they will be better people and better able to relate to others as a result. Gut-level or marathon-group therapy sessions are used for such disparate groups as divorcees and Vista volunteers, as well as alcoholics. See Bill Davidson, "Help Me, I'm Alone," *Saturday Evening Post* (September 10, 1966); and "Judy Lewis Reaches People and is Reached and is Loved," *Look* (December 27, 1966), for popular but accurate descriptions. The assumed advantages of such sessions appear to be an article of faith with participants. Empirical studies of effectiveness have not been made to my knowledge.

47. There is the belief among some that if an alcoholic returns to drinking after a remission—even as long as 20 years—his drinking will be at the stage it would have been had he drunk continuously during those sober years because the "disease" is progressive whether he consumes alcohol or not.

48. Lillian Roth (with Mike Connolly and Gerald Frank), *I'll Cry Tomorrow* (New York: Frederick Fell, Inc., 1954), pp. 208–9.

49. Although the City Hospital is ostensibly in existence to aid indigent patients with their medical problems, a hierarchy of moral qualification is invoked in the acceptance and treatment of patients that works to the detriment of the Skid Row alcoholic. Quite simply, the hospital staff feels that the alcoholic is ill by his own hand and not worth their time. The following overheard quotes are illustrative:

Doctor, to man in drying-out unit:

For Pete's sake! Are you back again? I thought I told you not to drink anymore, that another bout might kill you. They ought to put you guys on a slow boat to China [this loud enough for all patients and nurses to hear]. I don't know what else can be done when you deliberately go out and drink again after what you were through the last time. Don't you have *any* sense?

Nurse to social worker on drying-out unit:

I get so discouraged. We keep seeing the same men over and over. Don't they know they are killing themselves? There must be something wrong with them that makes them act like this.

In his ethnography of emergency room treatment, David Sudnow also noted that possible DOA's (dead on arrival) were given little if any emergency treatment to save their lives if they were thought to be alcoholics. See "Dead on Arrival," *Trans-Action*, 5, No. 1 (November 1967), 38–39.

50. The men also have their own idea as to who makes a good group therapy leader, although this is not one of the concerns that they state voluntarily when asked to assess the State Mental Hospital:

There are two kinds of therapists. The first is medical-psychiatric; you can't get a straight answer from them. They talk above your head. They tend to diagnose you or use you for an experiment. They try to pry things out of you. They have no feeling for the individual.

The other kind of guy, you are comfortable around him. You can't con him. He talks straight to you. He helps you plan the future—like if you lost your car because you were so drunk you don't remember where you parked it. He won't bother you with motives—he calls the highway patrol to help find it.

The best kind of therapist was Robertson. He was a good guy. He used to take our group fishing up at the lake.

There are only a few good therapists here. The rest try hard, but they are too professional. I want a guy who can get on my level. [28]

51. This was a frequent comment and often used by the men as the criteria for differentiating a good hospital from a poor one.

52. This attitude is, of course, contrary to the middle-class view of welfare aid as the voluntary beneficence of those persons who earn and thus deserve their wealth, toward those who are unable to earn it and are therefore outside the legitimate reward structure. The implication is that no one *qualifies* for such aid, rather they receive it as a result of the charitable attitudes of others. See Bernard Beck, "Welfare as a Moral Category," *Social Problems*, 14, No. 3 (Winter 1967), 258–77. (See also discussion of benefactor and beneficiary in chapter 9.)

53. As previously mentioned, many alcoholics commit themselves to State Mental Hospital when they receive a long probation from the courts following an arrest, knowing that when they are picked up again, they will go to hated County Jail for three months. Usually, they stay during the entire risk period at Northern State Mental Hospital.

CHAPTER 7

1. The Christian Missionaries was started by a minister as a means of spiritual revival for the masses, with the belief that the problems of the world are created by men ignoring the divine laws of God.

2. All official activities of the Christian Missionaries, both in this country and abroad, in the fields of rehabilitation of handicapped (alcoholic) men, are standardized and regulated by the Christian *Missionary Manual*. Unlike codebooks for jail administration, or descriptions of the demonstration project at the Jail Branch Clinic, where official descriptions fit the actual activities loosely, if at all, the concordance between the operation of the Pacific City Work and Residence Center and the Missionary Manual directives is striking. It is obvious that the Manual is taken much more seriously by the Missionaries than codes for jail operation are by jail administrators, or judiciary promises of therapy for alcoholics in the jail by judges, social workers, and psychologists.

(Inasmuch as page citations of the manual are useless unless it is properly identified, and this is not possible due to NIMH protocol, no pages numbers will be given and no direct quotations from the manual are made. References to parallels between activities at the Center and exhortations of the manual will be mentioned, however.)

3. See, for instance, the discussion of the beliefs about blind persons as they affect original and changing goals of workshops for the blind in Robert A. Scott, "The Factory as a Social Service Organization: Goal Displacement in Workshops for the Blind," *Social Problems*, 15, No. 2 (Fall 1967), esp. 160–61.

4. This is assumed by the Missionaries to be the result of Adam and Eve's fall from grace, a consequence of which is that all men have become sinners and justly exposed to the wrath of God.

5. This is well expressed in a Missionary magazine article, which indicated that to speak of God's forgiveness means to speak of that which is unearned and unremitting and, in fact, exists before the sin is committed, since the very nature of God is love.

6. This theory is also espoused by social workers. See Howard J. Clinebell, Jr., *Understanding and Counseling the Alcoholic* (New York: The Abingdon Press, 1956), p. 104.

7. The *Missionary Manual* also suggests this combination approach of social, psychological, and medical aid.

8. Old age is usually considered to be 60 or older by the Missionaries, although there is no hard and fast exclusion rule on this if a man is in good physical condition.

9. The *Manual* emphasizes that motivation and self-insight into the path one's life is taking are absolute musts for rehabilitation.

10. The official attitude, as carried in the *Missionary Manual*, also reflects this ambivalence toward repeaters and rounders. The *repeater* is defined as the man who repeatedly leaves for any number of reasons and returns asking for readmission, while the *rounder* is said to be the man who repeatedly wanders from center to center. It is estimated that as high as 40 percent of the applicants to a center at any one time may have been in some center previously. Although it is felt there is a danger the center becomes an assistance to men who have no desire to lead a responsible life, a number of repeaters have suddenly "taken the program" and rehabilitated themselves.

Because of the ever-present possibility that a man may find himself eventually, the policy is not to restrict men from returning to the Center after previous stays.

11. This demonstration project seems to have been decidedly more research-oriented than was the one at the County Jail Branch Clinic (described in chapter 6). Before and after treatment, records were kept. Effect of different treatment modalities on length of sobriety was reported. These articles cannot be cited without revealing the name of the organization, but some of the project results will be mentioned later in this chapter.

12. The *Manual* also notes this point as well, noting that studies have indicated that the average Skid Row man sees God as punishing rather than forgiving and loving.

13. At Beacon in the Darkness, testimony by men on the program is a more formal part of the services. Advance arrangements are made and men who are going to testify sit on the stage. (This does not preclude unscheduled testimony from the audience, however.) Men on the program are also expected to participate in street services, usually by singing hymns. (Some have told me that while they are singing, empty cans and bottles are tossed at them in jocular fashion by former drinking companions.)

14. Staff members at the Work and Residence Center readily acknowledge that pressure to testify is often exerted at other Missionary centers. Public testimony has always been considered to be an important part of a Missionary service. At Beacon in the Darkness, men are rewarded with candy bars if they can quote Scripture correctly.

15. Of the need for meditation by the alcoholic, the *Manual* says that it is the first step to get the man to face his problems and do something about his own defects, instead of being concerned, as usual, with his physical and immediate needs.

16. Beacon in the Darkness uses more direct pressure for self-denial contributions. A chart is posted with the men's names and the total expected from them during a campaign, along with their weekly progress toward their goals. Both staff and residents are listed and, of course, contributions expected of staff are much larger.

17. The Missionaries believe, along with some social psychologists, that the Skid Row alcoholic is grossly "undersocialized" and needs direction in development of responsibility for the welfare of others, a presumably desirable trait of the "socialized person."

18. The *Missionary Manual* recognizes the problems inherent in self-revelation, but Missionaries prefer to view it positively as a test of readiness for rehabilitation, with those who cannot take such self-revelation eliminating themselves from the program.

19. The *Manual* quotes the founder of the centers on the subject of work as a necessity for maintenance of the men's self-respect and as the means of avoiding the creation of a new institution designed to merely give a handout.

20. Under a new policy, the cost of the snack bar ticket is deducted from the gratuity and given to the beneficiary, regardless of the level of pay he has reached.

21. This policy is in keeping with what the *Manual* directs on the therapeutic use of the gratuity.

22. The *Manual* stipulates the necessity for, and the general content of, these gratuity meetings. For bad behavior, reduction in gratuity is suggested.

23. Although it is true that the Missionaries supply these benefits to the men, it is in the role of middleman rather than at retail cost to the Center. The clothing is donated by merchants of the area who get tax write-offs by donating to a charitable institution. The medical and psychiatric attention is also underwritten by grants to some extent, and serious medical cases are referred to County Hospital. The men, of course, are aware of this. See pages 196–97 of this chapter.

24. The *Manual* in its directive on leisure-time program and facilities suggests that they serve the two-fold purpose of providing alternative activities to drinking, plus giving a chance to relate socially to others.

25. I also observed very little socialization across beneficiary-staff or Missionary lines and what there was had the forced-friendly quality of the boss as he talks to employees:
    Clinical director to men as they struggle to get a donated mattress onto an elevator:
    "If they make beds any bigger, we'll have to get a bigger elevator, eh?"
    Major to man waiting table in dining room:
    "Do you want your gratuity this week? Then you'd better get my dinner out here right now!" (This said in jocular fashion.)
    On the other hand, when I checked this manuscript with the Missionary staff, they insisted that Missionaries play pool with the men whenever their schedules permit.

26. The current tendency for social workers to abandon their more traditional tasks of material aid and advice and move into therapy—especially group therapy—can be noted on almost all stations of the loop. Social workers at the Jail Branch Clinic were attempting this transition as was noted in chapter 6. Additionally, the man in charge of screening alcoholics at County Hospital told me he was running some "gut-level therapy sessions" in his spare time with some of the drug users and alcoholics whom he had screened. The director of the Welfare Home for Homeless Men also runs discussion sessions in addition to handling his administrative tasks. It should be mentioned, however, that counseling on problems connected with employment rather than job placement is more in line with the *Missionary Manual's* directive on the subject.

27. The Center does maintain a working relationship with the State Department of Vocational Rehabilitation, which has a specific section devoted to alcoholics. Where it seems practicable, a man with a combination alcoholism and vocational problem can be given training so that he qualifies for some occupation more in demand than his present talents or which gives him more satisfaction. Legally, *any* man who claims to have an alcoholism problem is eligible for inclusion in a training program if he applies for it; actually, only a few men at the Center (three or four at any one time) are recommended for this program by the Center. From the criteria for acceptance, it can be seen that few of these are Skid Row men. As the vocational counselor explained it:
    The key word is *feasible*. I try to recommend men who seem like good bets— like they will make it. ("Making it," refers to a man who will stay sober, finish the training, and then do well on a job arranged for him.) Of course there's a little subjectivity in the decision. Take a man 52-years old, who has been to nine centers, no sobriety for a year—he's not a good bet. [A33]

28. According to the Major and some of the long-time beneficiaries, there has been some relaxation of the requirement to make up all time lost—especially among resi-

dents who have been at the Center more than six months and have been good workers.

29. This rule is relaxed around old-timers who can be trusted not to be stealing from the salvage area or stashing a bottle in their locker.

30. I received conflicting reports about the exact number of locker shakedowns performed in a given period. Old-time residents report that sometimes weeks go by and lockers are not inspected. Others suggest lockers are inspected on a random basis (much as traffic tickets are given out) in order to keep everyone wary of developing stashes. The Major declared all lockers are inspected once a week and that two men are delegated to this task to prevent charges the inspector stole from a locker he was supposed to be inspecting or planted a bottle in the locker of an enemy.

31. The MMPI refers to the Minnesota Multiphasic Personality Inventory, a self-administered check list of attitudes, activities, likes and dislikes, somewhat projective in character, which, when answers are combined, is considered to form a "personality profile" of the subject. The Wechsler Adult Intelligence Scale is an intelligence test. Timothy Leary's Interpersonal Diagnosis of Personality is a test of interpersonal relationship proclivities of subjects, such as whether they are usually leaders or followers.

32. Consistent with reports from other stations on the loop, Alcoholics Anonymous is not popular with the beneficiaries at the Missionary Center.

33. Recently the Center instituted a plan whereby it will maintain a man who has terminated to take outside employment until his first paycheck arrives. He is, of course, expected to repay the cost of his board and room at that time. Furthermore, only long-time residents are eligible.

34. The *Missionary Manual* also suggests that time off to go "outside" not be granted automatically but that such requests be used as a time for a review of the man's entire situation. It is suggested the staff ask the man to honestly appraise his readiness to move out of a sheltered environment, to get and keep a job, and most importantly of all, to cope with his personal problems and temptation to drink.

35. This is by no means an isolated phenomenon. Becoming an employee of the Center occurs in all centers to such an extent that it is referred to in the *Missionary Manual* (along with finding a job on the "outside") as "graduation."

36. The result, of course, is that ego receives conflicting descriptions of the same act or object. The current phrase, "Tell it like it really is," used by dissident youth and other minorities, is a charge not of digression from accepted norms and values but of *denying* the digression.

37. The cultural patterns described by anthropologists are usually thought to be an idealized version of activities and interactions to which all members of a culture subscribe, even though they may fail to enact some or most perfectly. Such divergence around the presumed mode is both tolerated and expected, and thus is not enough in and of itself to result in charges of hypocrisy.

38. H. L. A. Hart, "The Ascription of Responsibility and Rights," in Anthony Flew (ed.), *Essays on Logic and Language* (Garden City, New York: Doubleday Anchor, Inc., 1965).

39. Actually, five men were initially recommended by the Missionaries as being successful on the program, but three disappeared during Christmas holidays and were not available for an interview. Other men who were complimentary in their comments about the Center's program were located in other institutions to which they were subsequently admitted and they are quoted also.

40. As an organization, the Missionaries are aware that intake based on center needs is indeed a temptation. The *Manual* contains an admonition to officers to remember that the man's need always comes before that of the center and that to admit men on the basis of what is expedient for the operation of a center is inconsistent with its purpose.

41. The "dose" of religion at the Center is mild compared to that given at the Missionaries' Beacon in the Darkness Shelter. There, the men must attend five services on Sunday plus devotion services every evening, a special Bible class on Monday, and a special prayer-fellowship meeting Wednesday night.

42. Salaries paid to officers in the Christian Missionaries are minimal, averaging around $200 per month. However, this amount is suppplemented by housing, which is furnished by the organization, furniture from the salvage operation, and medical and educational benefits. Additionally, since both husbands and wives are required to be active Missionaries, there is the assistance of a double income.

43. This includes such heavy items as stoves, refrigerators, rugs, and washing machines.

44. Long-time residents of the Center say this rule has been relaxed somewhat under the new Major's administration.

45. The statistics are indeed impressive. According to the Major:
    Of all the social rehabilitation agencies, the 125 Christian Missions throughout the country are the only ones that have live-in rehabilitation. Every night in the United States over 20,000 people are under the Christian Missionary roof. At this Center, we had a bed complement of over 11,000 people in 1965 and served over 8 million meals. [A29]

46. This is a reference to the Major who was in charge of the Center prior to the appointment of the present one. From numerous remarks made during interviews of Skid Row alcoholics, it seems safe to say the previous Major was disliked by the men because he seemed much more interested in business operations than the welfare of the beneficiaries.

47. This is another reference to a former Major. However, on the wall of the current Major's office there are several colorful charts indicating the fluctuating state of the salvage business by month at various outlets. There were no religious pictures or symbols that I could discern.

48. The fact that psychologists rarely discuss the "diagnosis" or "prognosis" that presumably results from the "tests" they do on the alcoholic is a common complaint of these men. (See chapter 6.) The staff psychologist at the Christian Missionary Center tells me that such discussions are rarely held in any patient-psychologist relationship, which is, of course, an important digression from the medical model that psychologists and psychiatrists attempt to emulate otherwise.

49. Actually, final results of the demonstration project indicated that men who had been in group psychotherapy (as it was called in the final report) did only slightly better on improvement of work and sobriety than did those men who had had no group therapy. Approximately 52 percent who had no psychotherapy improved their sobriety record, while 55 percent of those who had participated in group therapy showed such improvement. In the area of work improvement, 43 percent of those who had not participated in psychotherapy showed improvement, while approximately 50 percent of those who were group members improved. The greatest improvement was shown among those beneficiaries who had at least five or more sessions of vocational counseling. Although those without such counseling presented a picture similar to that of the no-psychotherapy results, those with five or more vocational counseling sessions showed 88 percent and 78 percent improved in the sobriety and work areas respectively. (Source of report cannot be cited without disclosing name of organization.)

50. For instance, while waiting near the desk one evening to meet a man I was to interview, a man in work clothes went up to the desk clerk and said to him, "Now don't throw out so many men tonight that I can't get started in the morning! Remember, I have to have *some* work force!"

51. This is an interesting parallel to the phenomenon that the class immediately above the lowest class (i.e., poor whites to Negroes) is the most overtly prejudiced against it. See John Dollard, *Caste and Class in a Southern Town* (Garden City, N.Y.: Doubleday Anchor, Inc., 1957), pp. 75–77. (See also chapter 4, footnote 12.)

52. For instance, a long-time beneficiary who does clerical work said:
    We have such a turnover that I do all the clerical work in pencil for both
    beneficiaries and employees. For instance, we have a new driver about once a
    week.

53. According to the Major:
    A man must be here at least 30 days before he can get medical, optical, or
    psychiatric care. Otherwise, we'd have men checking in and out just to get a
    new pair of glasses or something. You know these guys are in a lot of fights,
    lose or break their glasses and their teeth. We have to make them stay here 30
    days before we help with that or all we'd get was guys needing glasses and dental
    work. [A29]

54. Bogue has a few cautious words to say about the exploitation of Skid Row alco-
    holics by missions:
    By making a tie-in arrangement between salary and room or board, the man gets
    paid less than the minimum wage, even when his pay check and benefits are
    given their combined cash value. Unfortunately, many missions are guilty of this
    practice, too, in the employment they offer. Often their workers are not sinners
    or drunks but just desperately poor. While they are getting "rehabilitated," they
    refinish furniture or do other productive work at substandard wages. . . . It is
    admittedly difficult to draw the fine line between charity for the poor and
    economic exploitation of a man who is penniless, discouraged, and frightened.
    (See Donald J. Bogue, *Skid Row in American Cities* [Chicago: University of
    Chicago, 1963], p. 492.)

CHAPTER 8

1. This differs only slightly from the goal usually mentioned in connection with physical deviants—which, as stated for the blind—is as follows: "to maximize their
   ability to perform independently . . . to restore [them] . . . to the fullest physical,
   mental, social, vocational, and economic usefulness of which he is capable." (See
   Robert A. Scott, "The Selection of Clients by Social Welfare Agencies: The Case
   of the Blind," *Social Problems*, 14, No. 3 [Winter 1967], 256.)

2. See, for instance, "Welfare Home for Homeless Men Offers Skid Row Alcoholic a
   Chance to Regain Reality," *Westcoast State Alcoholism Discussions* (Westcoast
   State Department of Public Health, 1961), pp. 66–67. The cover story is also a
   variation of the same theme, "How You Can Help the Loneliest Man in Town
   . . . the Alcoholic."

3. See, for instance, the following statement concerning the concept of interlocking
   of personal and social rebirth in rehabilitation:
   Social rehabilitation would aim to restore a person to maximum usefulness to
   himself, his family, and his community. *Special Education and Rehabilitation*
   (U. S. House of Representatives, 87th Congress, 1st Session), p. 97; Statement
   of the American Public Welfare Association at hearings before the Sub-Committee on Education of the Committee on Education and Labor (August 1961).

   The holistic concept of behavior stresses an organic and/or functional relationship, a continuing interaction, and a fundamental interdependence among the
   traditionally defined "parts" or "areas" of human behavior.
   (Biological, personal, environmental, social, and cultural areas must be taken into
   account, according to this discussion.)

   From Robert Straus, "Social Change and the Rehabilitation Concept," in Marvin
   B. Sussman (ed.), *Sociology and Rehabilitation* (Washington: American Sociological Association, 1965), pp. 31–32.

4. See J. Kob, "Definition of the Teacher's Role," in Halsey, Floud, and Anderson,
   (eds.), *Education, Economy, and Society* (New York: The Free Press, 1961), pp.
   559 and 575.

5. See for instance, Esther Lucile Brown, "Meeting the Patients' Psychosocial Needs in the General Hospital," in Skipper and Leonard (eds.), *Social Interaction and Patient Care* (Philadelphia: J. B. Lippincott, Co., 1965), pp. 6–15; and Phyllis A. Tryon and Robert C. Leonard, "Giving the Patient an Active Role," *ibid.*, pp. 120–27.

6. Captain Andrews (pseudonym), "Report on Conference with Eastern City Center Team," (which is working with alcoholics).

7. "Welfare Home for Homeless Men Offers Skid Row Alcoholics a Chance to Regain Reality," p. 67.

8. Donald J. Bogue, *Skid Row in American Cities* (Chicago: University of Chicago, 1963), Chap. 1.

9. Edward Blacker and David Kantor, "Half-Way Houses for Problem Drinkers," *Federal Probation* (Washington, D. C., 1960), p. 2 of the reprint.

10. The frequent charge of insincerity leveled at alcoholics assumes free will on the part of the patient, a point of view that is both tautological and particularly interesting in the mental health field where "compulsions" over which the patient is considered to have no control are such an important part of the theoretical framework.

11. Inasmuch as there is no established length of time an alcoholic should undergo treatment to receive maximum benefit, it is difficult to ascertain when treatment stops prematurely. As was mentioned in earlier chapters, length of treatment or residence in an institution appears to rest most heavily on such nontherapeutic factors as eligibility of the institution for government aid, needs of the institution to maintain a certain inmate-client load, and labor-force needs. Termination procedures vary greatly from that of a set sentence at the Jail to no termination procedure at the Christian Missionaries.

    Sometimes the charge of premature termination of stay at an institution is rephrased to suggest that the sudden change from the institution to the "outside world" was too hard on the alcoholic. The halfway house was specifically created to ameliorate this problem. It is interesting to note that halfway house proponents worry about the shock their residents will experience when leaving the halfway house as well! Note the following quote: ". . . And in any case, opportunities for the use of the recreational and physical facilities (of the halfway house) should be made available to successful "graduates" of the program, *so that discharge does not come as a kind of weaning shock.*" (Emphasis mine.) See Blacker and Kantor, *Federal Probation*, p. 6 of the reprint.

12. For a discussion of the grounds on which accounts of action are socially acceptable or not, see Marvin B. Scott and Stanford M. Lyman, "Accounts," *American Sociological Review*, 33, No. 1 (February 1968), 46–62. By their criteria, alcoholics seldom offer "acceptable" accounts for their resumption of heavy drinking.

    The sample sentiments presented here were expressed so often that it is difficult not to give them credence. They outnumbered by at least ten to one "real reasons" for starting to drink again—such as the loss of a girl friend, and death of a loved one, the loss of a job. Apparently the decision to drink after being dried out is not the agonizing one that the nonalcoholic would like to think it is, nor is it usually triggered by some unexpected tragedy.

13. C. Wright Mills, "The Professional Ideology of the Social Pathologist," *American Journal of Sociology*, 49, No. 2 (September 1943), 165–80, esp. 173, 179, 180. See also Frances A. Koestler, *Portrait of Median City, A Capsule View of Social Welfare Programs in the United States* (Washington, D. C.; Department of Health, Education, and Welfare, n.d.).

14. See, for instance, David Matza's discussion of the importance of the "home situation" as reported by the social worker in the judge's decision as to whether to grant probation to a juvenile offender, *Delinquency and Drift* (New York: Wiley and Sons, Inc., 1967), pp. 116–17. See also Frances L. Feldman and Frances H.

Scherz, *Family Social Welfare: Helping Troubled Families* (New York: Atherton Press, 1967).

Discussions to be found in social welfare texts or descriptions of social welfare research often describe the "ideal family" by implication. See, for instance, Scott Briar's discussion of "Social Disorganization in the Family," and "The Multi-Problem Family," in Henry S. Maas (ed.), *Five Fields of Social Service* (New York: National Association of Social Workers, Inc., 1966), Chap. 1, "Family Services," esp. pp. 33–47.

15. The term "disreputable poor" refers to the attitude of the working members of society that there really is *no* excuse for an able-bodied man not to work for a living; only victims of an undeserved stroke of fate constitute the "worthy poor." Furthermore, the worthy poor, unlike the disreputable poor, are desirous of changing their condition and willing to take the advice of their "betters" as to how this might be done. See David Matza, "Poverty and Disrepute," in Merton and Nisbet (eds.), *Contemporary Social Problems* (2nd ed., New York: Harcourt, Brace and World, Inc., 1966). See also Chap. 1, "Go to the Ant, Thou Sluggard . . .," in Edgar May's discussion of Social Welfare, *The Wasted Americans* (New York: Harper and Row, 1964), pp. 1–16; and Paul Jacobs, *Prelude to Riot* (New York: Random House, 1966), esp. pp. 63–78.

Most adoption procedures forbid the placement of a child in the home of a working mother, despite the fact that many children of natural parents grow up successfully in such an environment. Research in this area is contradictory. See "Maternal Deprivation" and allied areas of research discussed by David Fanshel, in Henry S. Maas (ed.), *Five Fields of Social Service*, pp. 86–88.

16. See, for instance, David Matza, "Poverty and Disrepute," *Delinquency and Drift*, pp. 646–47, and Samuel Mencher, "Public Welfare," in Henry S. Maas, *Five Fields of Social Service*, pp. 135–36. Families attempting to adopt infants usually must be able to assure social workers that there will be a separate room for the child, that surroundings will be clean, etc. A home with a yard is preferable to an apartment. See also Paul Jacobs, *Prelude to Riot*, pp. 63–78, on the demands of social workers that their Aid to Dependent Children clients keep their homes clean.

17. See Minuchin, *et al.*, *Families of the Slums: an Exploration of their Structure and Treatment* (New York: Basic Books, 1967); Strauss, *et al.*, *Psychiatric Ideologies and Institutions* (London: The Free Press of Glencoe, 1964); and Ruth E. Smalley, *Theory for Social Work Practice* (New York: Columbia University Press, 1967), esp. Chap. 4, "A Psychological Base for Social Work Practice," pp. 61–87.

18. Robert S. Lynd and Helen Merrell Lynd, *Middletown* (New York: Harcourt, Brace and Co., 1956; first published in 1929).

19. Arthur J. Vidich and Joseph Bensman, *Small Town in Mass Society* (Garden City, N.Y.: Anchor Books, 1960).

20. James West, *Plainville, U.S.A.* (New York: Columbia University Press, 1945).

21. August B. Hollingshead, *Elmtown's Youth* (New York: John Wiley and Sons, 1949).

22. W. Lloyd Warner, *et al.*, *Yankee City* (New Haven: Yale University Press, 1963).

23. Sociologists, to some extent, have attempted to overcome this bias recently by (1) acknowledging the similarities between so-called deviant groups and conforming groups, and (2) by emphasizing studies of methods whereby assignment to a deviant group is accomplished, and the effect of such an assignment on the individual so assigned.

24. S. M. Miller has referred to this portion of the laboring class as "the stable poor" and "the copers." They manage to hold their families together and remain a part of the community, serving its need for semiskilled and manual labor. They are the "poor but proud" who receive approval of the middle-class. See S. M. Miller, "The American Lower Classes: A Typological Approach," in Shostak and Gomberg

(eds.), *New Perspectives on Poverty* (Englewood Cliffs, N. J.: Prentice-Hall, 1965), pp. 27–30.

25. Captain Andrews (pseudonym), "Report on Conference with Eastern City Center Team," p. 1.

26. Men who are considered "better risks" (likely to try to get a job and keep it and stay away from heavy drinking for a time, anyway) are granted vouchers that vary from $71.50 to $105.60 per month. The amount differs primarily in the allowance for rent. On the first, rent allowance is $30.00, food is $32.40, and miscellaneous is $9.10; on the second, rent allowance is $60.00, food is $33.00, and miscellaneous is $12.60. As one welfare worker put it:

> We give the larger amount to a person with a plan, a man who seems to be striving for self-support. He needs more support than the "drifter." [A43]

Thus, the less chance a man seems to have to "make it," the less help he is given.

27. My concept of *margin* is closely akin to the concept of *social credits* that originated with Erving Goffman and *deviance credits* that originated with E. P. Hollander. Social credits refer to those social attributes that, when a person can claim them or is known to possess them, allow him a certain unquestioned latitude of action denied to the stranger or person lacking an acceptable biography. (Erving Goffman in private conversations with me.)

Deviance credits refer to the degree of idiosyncratic behavior of an individual tolerated by a group, and the variation in their award to each person. See E. P. Hollander, "Conformity, Status, and Idiosyncrasy Credit," in *Psychological Review*, 65 (1958), 120.

28. In his study of Skid Row, Howard G. Bain, *A Sociological Analysis of the Chicago Skid-Row Lifeway* (unpublished M.A. thesis, Chicago: University of Chicago, 1950), pp. 52–60, illustrated, through life histories of Skid Row men, their vulnerability to becoming public charges. Often such a man was able to hold out no longer than ten days after losing a job before being totally without resources.

In a study on which I served as a consultant, the purpose of which was to establish differences between families who "coped" with the aid of welfare assistance and those who were unable to cope even with such an allotment, the major difference between copers and noncopers was the extra-family resources (i.e., credit, help from friends, relatives, etc.) upon which the copers could call in an emergency.

29. George Orwell in *Down and Out in Paris and London* (New York: Harcourt, Brace & World Company, copyright, 1933 by George Orwell, copyright renewed, 1960 by Sonia Pitt-Rivers. Reprinted by permission of Brandt & Brandt), pp. 14–15, describes most vividly how continually close to disaster the person without social margin must travel:

> You discover the extreme precariousness of your six francs a day. Mean disasters happen and rob you of your food. You have spent your last eighty centimes on half a litre of milk, and are boiling it over the spirit lamp. While it boils, a bug runs down your forearm, you give the bug a flick with your nail, and it falls, plop! straight into the milk. There is nothing for it but to throw the milk away and go foodless.
>
> You go to the greengrocer's to spend a franc on a kilogram of potatoes. But one of the pieces that make up the franc is a Belgian piece, and the shopman refuses it. You slink out of the shop, and can never go there again.

30. His helplessness in the face of "preventative" arrests and platoon sentencing discussed in chapters 3 and 4 are cases in point.

31. See Scott Briar and Irving Piliavin, "Delinquency, Situational Inducements, and Commitments to Conformity," *Social Problems*, 13, No. 1 (Summer 1965), 38–41, for a discussion of the phenomenon of "stake."

32. As one man put it in trying to explain why he returned to drinking:

> You can't just straighten out by yourself. You've got to have a purpose in life. You've got to *want something* and have some chance of gettin' it, besides just drinking. [A12]

Orwell in *Down and Out,* p. 16, has noted this situation often dulls rather than excites initiative to escape it.

> And there is another feeling that is a great consolation in poverty. I believe everyone who has been hard up has experienced it. It's a feeling of relief, almost of pleasure, at knowing yourself at last genuinely down and out. You have talked so often of going to the dogs—and well, here are the dogs, and you have reached them, and you can stand it. It takes off a lot of anxiety.

33. Julius A. Roth discusses this interlocking of steps in employment career advancement in *Timetables* (Indianapolis: The Bobbs-Merrill Co., Inc., 1963), pp. 82–85.

34. This is not to say that professional rehabilitation workers are not sincere in their feelings of friendship toward their patients or clients. It is rather that these friendships are not of the type to carry past quitting time, when the off-duty professional usually prefers the company of persons of his own educational and social background.

Alcoholics are not the only persons to mistake professional friendliness for the genuine thing. The following was overheard at County Jail between ex-state prison inmates who were discussing parole officers:

> At least those guys who go by the book, you know what they are going to do. You don't overestimate their show of friendliness and get out of line and get slapped down. (Overheard while observing in the Jail.)

35. See, for instance, William Schofield, *Psychotherapy, the Purchase of Friendship* (Englewood Cliffs, N.J.: Prentice-Hall, 1964), plus the discussion of the therapeutic community in chapter 6.

36. See Robert Rapaport, *Community as Doctor: New Perspectives on a Therapeutic Community* (London: Tavistock Publications, 1959; and Springfield, Illinois: Charles C Thomas, 1960), for a discussion of the deliberate creation of a permissive, security-oriented atmosphere that is no doubt helpful in reducing anxieties in patients but bears little resemblance to the less well-planned outside world.

37. For the middle-class returnee, the problem is one of breaking down the counterrole relationships that were built up during the heavy drinking period when they were "irresponsible," according to middle-class standards. The middle-class ex-alcoholic's problems in overcoming the dependency relationships he helped to create have been well-chronicled. See Joan K. Jackson, "Family Structure and Alcoholism," *Mental Hygiene* (July 1959), 403–7. Jackson points out that "if the husband does stop drinking, he is usually permitted to exercise his family roles *only on probation*." (Emphasis mine.)

38. At least, there usually are no relatives to whom he is willing or able to return. Sometimes this is by choice. As one man put it:

> I got to straighten myself out *before* I go to see my family. I can't let them see me this way. [26]

Another said:

> Most of us would starve rather than call our relatives. That relationship is *over*. [41]

39. This is not intended to suggest that the Skid Row alcoholic was not of some higher status before coming to Skid Row. By the very term "bottom of the barrel" Skid Row residents suggest they were higher at *some* time, at least in their own eyes. However, both Bogue, in *Skid Row in American Cities,* pp. 320–22 and Howard M. Bahr, *Homelessness and Disaffiliation* (New York: Columbia University Bureau of Applied Social Research, 1968), pp. 220–30, indicate that these men started out in the lower portion of the status continuum and rose only slightly before losing status. As previously mentioned, skidding from high status to Skid Row happens in only a few well-publicized cases.

Pittman and Gordon's study of the chronic police case inebriate produced the following socio-economic characteristics, scarcely indicative of middle-class status:

> Approximately . . .

90 percent are skilled and unskilled workers (as compared with 59 percent of the general population)

75 percent had only a grade school education (as compared with 41 percent of the general population)

85 percent had no permanent residence, lived at a mission or shelter, a hotel or shelter, a hotel or rooming house (as compared with 21 percent of the general population).

See David J. Pittman and C. Wayne Gordon, *Revolving Door* (Glencoe, Ill.: The Free Press, 1958), Chap. 2, "The Sociocultural Profile," pp. 16–58.

Bogue, *Skid Row in American Cities*, pp. 13–14, reports that, "in comparison with the adult population of the city of Chicago as a whole, the . . . Skid Row men are:

  a. Foreign born white or "other nonwhite" race (American Indian).
  b. Single, widowed, or divorced: half have never married.
  c. Middle-aged or older men, concentrated in the ages of 45–74.
  d. Very poorly educated, with more than one-fifth being "functionally illiterate" (having completed fewer than five years of elementary school).
  e. Unemployed. The unemployment rate among the Skid Row men was more than eight times that of the general population.
  f. Not in the labor force, with "unable to work" as the primary reason.
  g. Employed as wage or salary workers.
  h. Of extremely low income, with almost one-half living on less than $90 per month. Almost one-fourth of the men had received less than $500 in cash during the preceding year.

40. Agents of social control report a large proportion of Skid Row alcoholics keep in contact (usually through correspondence) with their mothers. (Maintenance of this mother-son tie is often cited by those Freudianly inclined group therapy leaders as evidence many alcoholics have not passed the oedipus crisis successfully, are latently homosexual as a result, and thus drink to forget the guilt attached to this perversion. Of course, there are no comparative figures on the proportion of non-alcoholic males who maintain contact with their mothers.)

41. The fact there are an infinite number of mental frameworks, and a given individual may use more than one on the same phenomena, was discussed in chapter 1 to explain how Skid Row may be seen as both a disgusting and exciting place in which to live.

The point is that motivation to act is not, as seen by conventional psychological theory, the result of either inner personality characteristics or external cues alone but is rather the result of the way in which the situation is defined by the actor. The "wisdom" of a given plan of action is dependent upon the ground rules for such wisdom—that is, the theoretical framework by which the ingredients of the situation are "understood." When presumably intelligent individuals do things and later admit they "should have known better," they are referring to the fact they are now viewing the action from another, less sympathetic framework.

42. Joan Emerson has suggested the Skid Row alcoholic (often accused of being a con-artist) apparently does not know how to lie sensibly in an employment interview situation. He either lacks the middle-class job-seeker's training in fictionalizing his job experience and covering up embarrassing spots with plausible excuses, or he has become out of practice in such activity.

43. As mentioned in chapter 1, Skid Row men are often exploited by employers who pay them below-standard or state-minimum wages, taking advantage of their desperate need for work and money. Bogue, in *Skid Row in American Cities*, p. 492, also noted this in his study of the Chicago Skid Row and incorporated the following into his recommendations for eliminating the area:

The minimum-wage laws are openly broken, both in spirit and in deed, along Skid Row. Some industries . . . manage to get their work done at rates as low as fifty cents an hour, by declaring the men . . . are independent operators. Skid Row hotels and restaurants also pay very low wages to night watchmen, janitors, and dishwashers. By making a tie-in arrangement between salary and room or board, the man gets paid less than the minimum wage, even when his pay check and benefits are given their combined cash value. . . . A careful review of minimum-wage compliance should be made of every hotel, restaurant, mission, employment agency, and firm known to employ numbers of Skid Row men.

44. It seems strange that Pacific City Welfare officials do not see any contradiction in returning an alcoholic to live in a Skid Row hotel after he has been dried out and his health rebuilt at their Welfare Home for Homeless Men. When I was first granted permission to interview men at the Welfare Home for Homeless Men, the director said, as he bemoaned the high rate of recidivism among alcoholics:

   If you can tell us why, after all we try to do for these men, that they go right back to Skid Row and drinking, you will be doing a great service with your research project. [A57]

45. Earl Rubington has done some of the few analyses of the problem of operating or living in a halfway house. (The tone of most literature on halfway houses reads like annual reports—glowingly successful.) Rubington outlines the problems faced by ex-alcoholic administrators in "Organizational Strains and Key Roles," *Administrative Science Quarterly*, 9, No. 4 (March 1965), 350–69, and the panhandling problems Skid Row alcoholics face within the halfway house itself. See "Panhandling and the Skid Row Subculture," paper read at 53rd Annual Meeting of the American Sociological Society (Seattle, Washington, August 28, 1958).

46. My limited visits to halfway houses seem to confirm this. They are *very* quiet and the atmosphere is "cold." At one co-educational house, men and women could not eat meals at the same table. There was little talking in either the lounge or the coffee room. The alcoholism units at State Mental Hospital were swinging places by comparison.

47. As mentioned in chapter 1, these subjects constitute a substantial proportion of small talk among Skid Row men.

48. Howard M. Bahr has been engaged in some well-constructed tests of generally-accepted hypotheses concerning life on Skid Row with special emphasis on the area of socialization. His findings seem to indicate Skid Row men develop a rather strong attachment to Skid Row drinking companions, which aid in their identification with the Row and their feelings of alienation off the Row. See Howard M. Bahr and Stephen J. Langfur, "Social Attachment and Drinking in Skid-Row Life Histories," *Social Problems*, 14, No. 4 (Spring 1967), 464–72. Also, see Howard M. Bahr, "Drinking, Interaction, and Identification: Notes on Socialization into Skid Row," *Journal of Health and Social Behavior*, 8, No. 4 (December 1967), 272–85.

49. The experience of being "on the other side" apparently does not leave a man unmarked psychologically and, paradoxically, although it is degrading, it is simultaneously a source of pride to have survived it. As a survivor, a man actually feels superior to those who have not had this experience, and this creates a chasm between deviants and nondeviants that may never be closed again. John Irwin, in his study, *The Felon* (Englewood Cliffs, N.J.: Prentice-Hall, 1970), speaks of "the enduring affinity" ex-convicts have for each other—others with the same experience. It is also said that drug addicts at Synanon still consider themselves "hipper" than the nonuser.

50. Samuel E. Wallace, *Skid Row as a Way of Life* (Tottowa, N.J.: The Bedminister Press, 1965), p. 174.

51. George Orwell, in *Down and Out*, p. 148, speaks of "the degradation worked in a man who knows that he is not even considered fit for marriage. . . . Cut off from the whole race of women, a tramp feels himself degraded to the rank of a cripple or a lunatic. No humiliation could do more damage to a man's self-respect."

52. Additionally, trying and failing to gain acceptance is much more ego-debilitating than not trying at all. Like going through college rush week and not getting a bid

from a sorority or fraternity, there is no longer any doubt about your social acceptance with a group deemed desirable. The Skid Row alcoholic, in his efforts to get back into society may also encounter a "reality shock" not intended by his rehabilitators—that of finding that he is socially undesirable to the society he seeks, regardless of his efforts to the contrary.

53. Before it happens, the thought of being sent to jail for drunkenness, or going to a mental hospital for "the cure," seems like one of the worst experiences that a man can have. However, when he finds he *can* survive it, going through the same thing again holds fewer terrors. At times he even feels strengthened by the experience. Jack Black, a confessed thief of all trades, explains this phenomenon in terms of his reactions to the whipping post (*You Can't Win* [New York: The MacMillan Co., 1927], p. 278):

> As a punishment, it's a success; as a deterrent it's a failure; if it's half and half, one offsets the other and there's nothing gained. The truth is I wouldn't have quit no matter how I was treated. The flogging just hardened me more, that's all. I found myself somewhat more determined. . . . I had taken everything they had in the way of violence and could take it again. Instead of going away in fear, I found my fears removed. *The whipping post is a strange place to gather fresh confidence and courage, yet that's what it gave me.* . . .

See also Orwell's comments on "going to the dogs," Footnote 28, this chapter. Furthermore, while the quest for society is fraught with uncertainty, life in an institution offers security of rules and regulations plus provisions for all the exigencies of living which are a problematic struggle on "the outside."

54. Howard Bahr's analysis of the relationship of drinking and social disaffiliation to presumed "institutionalization" indicates that it is not the simple one-to-one relationship some persons have thought. Rather, it is a complicated, interactive process. Howard M. Bahr, "Institutional Life, Drinking, and Disaffiliation," a paper read at the 1968 annual meeting of the Society for the Study of Social Problems in Boston.

55. It could be the grinding monotony of regular but boring and often physically demanding work, the lack of desirable or interesting companions, and the bleakness of his living quarters contribute to a certain "flatness" of experience quite unlike the little adventures the Skid Row alcoholic has enjoyed both in institutions and on the Row. Just as soldiers returning from the war find civilian life flat at first so may the Skid Row man find the square life dull.

56. It is indeed a paradox that the Skid Row man must return to an *ad hoc* existence (where neither his past nor his future is seriously affected by present adventures) to feel he is accepted as a real person. Only on Skid Row, where times of pleasure are momentarily "sealed off" from their consequences, can he enjoy himself. When he is working at his low-status job and living his ascetic "attempting-to-make-it" life, he has all the burdens of responsibility to the past and cognizance of the future without any of the rewards.

57. See, for instance, National Institute of Mental Health, *Experiments in Culture Expansion*, Report of proceedings of a conference on "The Use of Products of a Social Problem in Coping with the Problem" (Norco, California, July 1963), and *Offenders as a Correctional Manpower Resource*, Report of a seminar convened by the Joint Commission on Correctional Manpower and Training (Washington, D. C., March 1968).

Erving Goffman has called the phenomenon of the deviant using his stigma to advantage as "going into business for himself." "Twelfth-step work" in Alcoholics Anonymous and Synanon (for drug users) are other examples of this phenomenon.

58. An excellent description of the way in which the ex-alcoholic seeks to identify with agents of social control to the extent that he is actually rude to ex-drinking partners is to be found in Earl Rubington's "Grady 'Breaks Out': A Case Study of an Alcoholic's Relapse," *Social Problems*, 11, No. 4 (Spring 1964), 372–80. This phenomenon of upwardly mobile low-caste persons turning with vehemence upon

those who were formerly "their own kind" has been noted by many sociologists and psychologists, and has been given many labels including "identification with the aggressor," and "self-hatred of one's membership in a despised group."

Note also the sanctimonious anger of the Rapper toward other alcoholics, chapter 4, pp. 94–95, and footnote 12. See also chapter 7, pp. 205–6.

CHAPTER 9

1. For a discussion of agents of social control who admit dislike for their "clients" see chapters 2 and 6 particularly. There also may be the agent of social control who does not admit, perhaps even to himself, that he dislikes his charges, but nevertheless appears to gain a satisfaction from humbling them. See, for instance, footnote 27 in this chapter.

2. Peter M. Blau, *Exchange and Power in Social Life* (New York: John Wiley and Sons, Inc., 1967), p. 12, quoting Georg Simmel (trans. Blau), *Sociologie* (Leipzig: Duncker and Humblot, 1908), p. 6.

3. See, for instance, Bronislaw Malinowski's discussion of the principle of give and take in *Crime and Custom in a Savage Society* (London: Routledge & Kegan Paul, Ltd., 1932), pp. 39–45; Claude Levi-Strauss, "The Principle of Reciprocity," in Coser and Rosenberg (eds.), *Sociological Theory* (2nd ed., New York: The Macmillan Co., 1967), pp. 74–84; Marcel Mauss, *The Gift* (London: Cohen & West, 1954); and Alvin W. Gouldner, "The Norm of Reciprocity: A Preliminary Statement," *American Sociological Review*, 25, No. 2 (April 1960), 161–78.

4. St. Luke 10:30–37.

5. The issue of conservation of emotion has been variously discussed by Talcott Parsons as a part of his pattern variables (affectivity-affective neutrality as a dichotomous choice of emotions). See Talcott Parsons and Edward A. Shils (eds.), *Toward a General Theory of Action* (New York: Harper Torchbacks, 1951), pp. 76–98.

   George Homans has suggested that, like more tangible things, emotions can be "invested" and "expended." He cites as part evidence the well-known phrase, "He took a lot out of me." See Homans, *Social Behavior, Its Elementary Forms* (New York: Harcourt, Brace and World, Inc., 1961), p. 13.

   Affect control in the medical profession has been discussed by Morris J. Daniels, "Affect and Its Control in the Medical Intern," *American Journal of Sociology*, 66, No. 3 (November 1960), 259–67.

6. This phenomenon of worthiness for compassion has been reported in a number of studies on human suffering. See, for instance, Barney A. Glaser and Anselm L. Strauss, *Awareness of Dying* (Chicago: Aldine Publishing Co., 1965), p. 38, for the concept of "social loss" as an explanation of why some patients' dying results in more sympathy than others. David Sudnow, *Passing On* (Englewood Cliffs, N.J.: Prentice-Hall, 1967), stresses the normative underpinnings for compassion, as do Julius A. Roth and Elizabeth M. Eddy, in *Rehabilitation for the Unwanted* (New York: Atherton Press, 1967).

7. Fritz Heider, *The Psychology of Interpersonal Relations* (New York: John Wiley & Sons, Inc., Science Editions, 1967), pp. 278–79.

8. This is also a characteristic of the sick role, as discussed by Talcott Parsons. See Talcott Parsons, "Definitions of Health and Illness in the Light of American Values and Social Structure," in Jaco (ed.), *Patients, Physicians and Illness* (Glencoe, Ill.: The Free Press, 1958), pp. 165–87.

   See also Clyde Kluckhohn and Dorothea Leighton, *The Navajo* (Cambridge: Harvard University Press, 1960), p. 175, for discussions of illness traced to witchcraft seen as blameless, whereas illness traced to breaking of a taboo is seen as the fault of the ill person.

9. It may be awareness of the advantage this type of account gives the individual patient with the professionals that causes Skid Row alcoholics to concoct appropriate "sad tales" when explaining their drinking. However, I heard only two or three such tales during my entire field work. Many of the men interviewed were heavy drinkers early in life. (Some started as early as ages 5, 8, and 11, and were given wine as part of a picnic lunch when they went fishing!) Others started in late teens or early twenties. See also footnote 13, chapter 8, concerning the absence of acceptable accounts for *resumption* of drinking after therapy.

10. This comment is typical of those made by both agents of social control and the average layman when discussing the alcoholic.

11. Heider, *Interpersonal Relations*, p. 264.

12. See for instance, Parsons' discussion of the sick role in Jaco, (ed.), *Patients, Physicians and Illness*: Howard S. Becker, *et al.*, discussion of "docs and crocks" in *Boys in White* (Chicago: University of Chicago Press, 1961), pp. 317 and 327–29; and Rose Coser's discussion in *Life on the Ward*, in which a "good" patient is to be passive and conform to rules, (East Lansing, Mich.: Michigan University Press, 1962), p. 9.

13. "Dr. X" (pseudonym), *Intern* (Greenwich, Conn.: Fawcett Publications, Inc., 1965), p. 290.

14. Wilensky discusses this problem in connection with social workers. See Harold L. Wilensky and Charles N. Lebeaux, *Industrial Society and Social Welfare* (New York: The Free Press, 1965), pp. 300–301.

15. Heider, *Interpersonal Relations*, pp. 254–55.

16. Georg Simmel, "Faithfulness and Gratitude," in Kurt Wolfe (ed.), *The Sociology of Georg Simmel* (London: The Free Press of Glencoe, 1950), pp. 387–92. See also Levi-Strauss, in Coser and Rosenberg (eds.), *Sociological Theory*, p. 79.

17. See Gouldner, "Reciprocity."

18. Georg Simmel, in Kurt Wolff (ed.), *The Sociology of Georg Simmel*, paraphrased; from pp. 390–95. Simmel suggests that one reason for this permanent status discrepancy is that the first-given gift has the quality of being initiated by the giver, while subsequent gifts are contaminated by a sense of obligation.

19. For instance, Paul Jacobs suggests that civil servants in the welfare bureaucracies often take a benefactor's tone to the clients they serve. See *Prelude to Riot* (New York: Random House, 1967), "The Welfare Bureau," pp. 59–96, especially pp. 83 and 87. This is not an isolated phenomenon. Persons who are in any of the helping services appear to expect gratitude from their "clients" or "customers," as well as a salary or a fee from them or their employer. A restauranteur likes to be known as a "host," even though he charges for his meals. Funeral home proprietors speak of "years of service to Pacific City families" in their advertisements. Despite an adequate fee schedule, doctors often admit to feeling they are doing a personal favor to their patients by treating them.

20. This is a very common complaint everywhere on the loop.

21. Heider, *Interpersonal Relations*, p. 256.

22. Heider, *Interpersonal Relations*, also makes this point:
    Thus *p* will not feel grateful for a benefit, and will not feel obligated when he accepts it, if he thinks that it was owed to him by *o*, and that *o* ought to benefit him, that it was *o's* duty to benefit him.

23. Anything done by the agents beyond the routine services of the institution is considered to be an *extraordinary favor*, which should call forth an unusual degree of gratitude. This would include such things as making a phone call for a man, getting him an extra ration of anything (pills, clothing, blankets, etc.), arranging for a "good job" within the institution for him.

24. A comment very frequently made.

25. Agents have their own methods of handling those persons who would attempt to escape the feeling of indebtedness:

    Mr. Adams told me he was going to scrub the kitchen floor every day and in that way pay for his room and board and be beholden to no man. Well, I told him I knew he was a physical culturist and was scrubbing the floor so he could build up his physique. You have to let them know you are on to them. [A43]

26. George Orwell recounts such hostility of penniless men toward one mission, The Salvation Army in England. See *Down and Out in Paris and London* (New York: Harcourt, Brace and World Company, copyright, 1933 by George Orwell; copyright renewed, 1960 by Sonia Pitt-Rivers), pp. 111–15, 152, 155. Reprinted by permission of Brandt & Brandt.

27. The term "miseries business," was used by one of the first interviewees [51] at the Welfare Home for Homeless Men.

28. In a recent investigation of the state mental hospital system, the labor-force saving that the hospital was able to make by utilizing alcoholics was mentioned in testimony to the Westcoast State Legislature. Some administrators estimated alcoholics do 40 percent of all labor below the professional level.

29. Overheard by observer at Christian Missionaries and said in the presence of beneficiaries.

30. Heider, *Interpersonal Relations*, pp. 284, 285.

31. Peter M. Blau, *Exchange and Power in Social Life*, p. 15.

32. The apparent need of agents of social control for deviants to control has many parallels. Howard S. Becker discusses the issue of "Moral Entrepreneurs," in *The Outsiders* (New York: The Free Press, 1963), pp. 147–63. Becker points out that one of the dilemmas moral entrepreneurs face is that they must show some measure of success in eradicating the problem (which they, themselves, have publicized)— but not so much improvement in the situation as to put themselves out of business! The National Polio Foundation did just that a few years ago, but saved its existence by finding a new problem with which to maintain itself—birth defects.

33. Blau, *Exchange and Power in Social Life*, p. 8.

34. See Harold Garfinkel, "A Conception of and Experiments with 'Trust' as a Condition of Stable Concerted Actions" in O. J. Harvey (ed.), *Motivation and Social Interaction* (New York: The Ronald Press, 1963), pp. 187–238; and "Studies of the Routine Grounds of Everyday Activities," *Social Problems*, 11 (1964), 225–50.

35. Georg Simmel, in Kurt Wolff (ed.), *The Sociology of Georg Simmel*, pp. 318 and 319.

36. In all fairness, it should be mentioned that these men are not being held at Welfare Home for Homeless Men against their wills. There are no gates or fences to keep them in. They could walk away at any time—but without any promise of future financial aid from the Welfare Department.

37. See Morton Deutsch's discussion of this point in "Cooperation and Trust, Some Theoretical Notes," in Schein, Berlew, and Steele (eds.), *Interpersonal Dynamics* (Homewood, Ill.: The Dorsey Press, 1964), pp. 564–82.

38. This absence of trust of agents of social control is compounded by the sense of unfairness that Skid Row alcoholics develop concerning their treatment by police, the courts, and in the jail. It is a feeling that pervades many agent-client relationships and is found in other institutions concerned with the control of deviant behavior, as well. See, for instance, John Irwin, "Correctional Treatment and the Inmate Sense of Injustice," paper delivered at Spring 1968 session of the Pacific Sociological Association, San Francisco; and David Matza, *Delinquency and Drift* (New York: John Wiley and Sons, Inc., 1964), Ch. 4, "The Sense of Injustice," pp. 101–51.

39. Edwin M. Lemert, "Paranoia and the Dynamics of Exclusion," in *Human Deviance, Social Problems, and Social Control* (Englewood Cliffs, N.J.: Prentice-Hall, 1967), pp. 197–211.

40. See Erving Goffman's delineation of role distance in *Encounters* (Indianapolis: The Bobbs-Merrill Co., Inc., 1961), pp. 85–152.

41. Erving Goffman, *The Presentation of Self in Everyday Life* (Garden City, New York: Doubleday Anchor Books, 1959), Ch. III, "Regions and Region Behavior," pp. 106–40.

42. I am indebted to Wilson Van Dusen for first calling my attention to this secondary gain from making the loop.

43. This same phenomenon was also noted by Elliott A. Krause in his study of vocational rehabilitation centers in "After the Rehabilitation Center," *Social Problems*, 14, No. 2 (Fall 1966), esp. 202:

    Good performance could result in quick discharge and job placement . . . [or] might result in extension and more training at the center. *Poor* performance might lead to the same alternatives of discharge or extension!

44. These quotes cannot be credited to preserve a confidence. The "truth" concerning these items of gossip is not known. The fact that they are frequently told tales, and thus influence behavior, is the reason for their inclusion.

45. Even persons with total power over individuals resort to definition control as a means of social control; witness the Nazis' ruse of calling the gas chambers "delousing showers" so that the Jews would enter them docilely.

46. I am indebted to Joan Emerson for these euphemisms, gathered by her in the course of studying humor in hospitals for her unpublished Ph.D. dissertation, *Social Functions of Humor in a Hospital Setting*, University of California, Berkeley, 1963.

47. Marvin B. Scott and Stanford M. Lyman discuss extensively how adolescent gangs use linguistic social mechanisms such as miscues as a way of protecting territory, or "turf." See "Territoriality: a Neglected Sociological Dimension," *Social Problems*, 15, No. 2 (Fall 1967), 236–49.

48. Sherri Cavan offers a revealing analysis of the disjunction in perspectives experienced by naive recruits to institutions when the idealized version of what will be done for them there collides with their actual experiences. Paper, "Recruitment Betrayal," delivered at the Pathways to the Mental Hospital Conference, sponsored by San Francisco State College, Spring 1967.

49. Richard M. Stephenson and Frank R. Scarpitti, "Argot in a Therapeutic Correctional Milieu," *Social Problems*, 15, No. 3 (Winter 1968), 384–95, suggest that euphemisms actually have therapeutic value in the way they redefine situations for delinquent boys.

50. This brings us to another point of conjecture where little or no research has been done: To what extent do people actually *believe* the euphemisms they use? In the loop, for instance:

    Does the judge *really* believe there is therapy at the jail?
    Doesn't he know what jail conditions are?
    Do group therapists *really* believe that "talking it out" will affect alcoholism?
    Do the welfare workers in the jail *really* think the Missionaries are rehabilitative as is suggested during County Jail orientation?
    Do the Christian Missionaries *really* believe that they are giving spiritual rebirth to alcoholic men?

    There are several theories worth entertaining in this area:

    First of all, it is possible that agents of social control do not know what goes on in the loop from the alcoholic's point of view. Judges rarely visit jails; psychologists and welfare workers rarely concern themselves with the existential situation in jails—they just do not see it. True rehabilitation is difficult to measure, as is the effectiveness of programs of therapy.

    The second possibility—and this is the most popular with the Skid Row men—is that agents of social control *do indeed know what is going on*. In fact, they are co-conspirators in maintaining the status quo because this is where they obtain their salary. There is some evidence that this is, at least in part, true. For instance, an official in the city's Mental Health Department made the following statement in connection with the arrest of alcoholics and the absence of therapy at the jail for them:

> Listen, we all know what is going on with these drunks. We know that they are sentenced in platoons. We know that there is nothing at the jail for them. But what can we do? If one of us were to expose the whole thing it could mean his job and a lot of other people's jobs as well, and it probably wouldn't end the sentencing procedure anyway.

Two professionals in two different stations on the loop claimed that everyone in the rehab business "knows what is really going on at the Christian Missionaries," but one said . . .

> What can you do? We are all in the United Crusade. It would look like we wanted to stab a fellow organization in the back.

Despite the cited evidence that many officials knowingly make a living off the alcoholic's misery, it seems to me that a third possibility should be considered. This is as follows: That the agents of social control do know what is "really" going on, but they consider themselves to be educated enough to *reconceptualize* a mundane activity into a "therapeutic" one. That is, they pride themselves on the ability to think *abstractly*. If what looks like just plain work is reconceptualized as work-therapy, the educated professional has no trouble moving to this level of abstraction and seeing work as a therapy. If the jail experience is redefined as "rehabilitative," the judge feels able to grasp that as a concept also.

51. A frequently-made remark by agents of social control.

52. This is a well-stated version of a frequently-made remark.

METHODOLOGY

1. Howard S. Becker and Blanche Geer, "Participant Observation: The Analysis of Qualitative Field Data," in Adams and Preiss (eds.), *Human Organization Research* (Homewood, Ill.: The Dorsey Press, Inc., 1960), p. 280. The reference in the text is to Becker, Geer, Hughes, and Strauss, *Boys in White* (Chicago: University of Chicago Press, 1961).

2. For a discussion of the methodological aspects of this approach to data collection see Charles H. Cooley, "The Roots of Social Knowledge," *American Journal of Sociology*, 32 (July 1926), 59–79.

3. Becker and Geer note that general questions were also of use to them in the study, *Boys in White*. The favorite, apparently, was "What's happening?" which they report was productive of important preliminary information. See Becker and Geer, "Participant Observation: The Analysis of Qualitative Field Data," p. 286.

4. See, for instance, Kurt W. Back's discussion of this approach in, "The Well-informed Informant," in Adams and Preiss (ed.), *Human Organization Research*, pp. 179–87.

5. Many sociologists have noted the heightened sensitivity to the social structure of the "detached" or "marginal" person, and not a few methodologists have urged that the researcher exploit this. See for instance, David Riesman, "Some Observations Concerning Marginality," *Phylon* (2nd quarter, 1951); pp. 113–27; "Marginality, Conformity, and Insight," *Phylon* (3rd quarter, 1953), pp. 241–57, and "A Philosophy for 'Minority' Living," *Commentary*, 6 (1948), pp. 413–22. Aaron Cicourel discusses this as a research method in his book, *Methods and Measurement in Sociology* (New York: The Free Press, 1964), Chap. II, esp. pp. 64, 65.

6. Karl Mannheim suggested this as a test of a theory:

> A theory then is wrong if in a given practical situation it uses concepts and categories which, if taken seriously, would prevent man from adjusting himself at that historical stage.

See *Ideology and Utopia* (New York: Harcourt, Brace and World, Inc., 1966), p. 85.

Anthropologist Charles O. Frake has pointed out that Goodenough's definition of an ethnography should be a guide to the study of any culture: ". . . it [an ethnography] should properly specify what it is that a stranger to a society would have to know in order to appropriately perform any role in any scene staged by that society. See "How to Ask for a Drink in Subanun," in Gumpertz and Hymes (ed.), *The American Anthropologist, The Ethnography of Communication,* 66, No. 6 (Part 2, 1964), 127–32.

7. Sherri Cavan, "Hippies of the Haight," pp. 1 and 2 of unpublished manuscript.

8. Harold Garfinkel, "Common Sense Knowledge of Social Structures," in J. Scher (ed.), *Theories of the Mind* (New York: The Free Press, 1962), pp. 689–712.

9. Glaser and Strauss discuss the importance of the *interaction* between theoretical development and data gathering in "Discovery of Substantive Theory: A Basic Strategy Underlying Qualitative Research," *The American Behavioral Scientist* (February 1965), pp. 5–12. See also, Robert K. Merton, "Some Notes on Problem-Finding in Sociology," in Merton, Broom, and Cottrell (eds.), *Sociology Today* (New York: Basic Books, Inc., 1959), pp. ix-xxxiv.

10. Becker and Geer, "Participant Observation: The Analysis of Qualitative Field Data," p. 271.

11. See Glaser and Strauss, "Discovery of Substantial Theory," for a discussion of this approach.

12. Manning Nash, *Primitive and Peasant Economic Systems* (San Francisco: Chandler Publishing Company, 1966), p. 10.

13. Donald J. Bogue, *Skid Row in American Cities* (Chicago: University of Chicago, 1963), Chap. 1, pp. 1–45.

14. See for instance, National Institute of Health memorandum, "Investigations Involving Human Subjects, Including Clinical Research: Requirements for Review to Insure the Welfare of Individuals" (July 1, 1966). See also, Herbert C. Kelman, "Human Use of Human Subjects: The Problem of Deception in Social Psychological Experiments," *Psychological Bulletin,* 67, No. 1 (1967), 1–11.

15. This need not have been constant residence; the subjects were often out making the loop, as the study indicates.

16. Becker and Geer, "Participant Observation: The Analysis of Qualitative Field Data," p. 272.

17. The Welfare Home for Homeless Men was not included as an exemplar station in this study, because I was uncertain as to whether its counterparts in other cities were as truly comparable as in the case of those institutions selected.

18. As mentioned in the acknowledgements, the author is indebted to Andie Knutson, Director, Behavioral Sciences in Public Health, University of California, Berkeley, for suggesting this important addition to the analysis.

19. Becker and Geer, "Participant Observation: The Analysis of Qualitative Field Data," p. 275.

20. A good deal of methodological controversy both in sociology and psychology centers around this point. There are those who believe that the human subject is incapable of telling an investigator how he *really* feels about anything because he is unaware of the pressures on his construction of reality. This point of view has some strange bedfellows: Sigmund Freud, of the psychoanalytic school of thought; John B. Watson, the behaviorist; and Aaron Cicourel, Harold Garfinkel, ethnomethodologists; as well as Erving Goffman, whose brilliant existential observational techniques defy categorization. On the other hand, attitude researchers such as Herbert Hyman, M. Brewster Smith, Paul Lazarsfeld, and the public-opinion pollsters place great faith on the gathering of attitudinal data as viable indicators of human feelings.

21. See especially Harold Garfinkel, *Studies in Ethnomethodology* (Englewood Cliffs, N.J.: Prentice-Hall, Inc., 1967), see esp. Chap. 3, pp. 76–103; and Aaron V. Cicourel, *The Social Organization of Juvenile Justice* (New York: John Wiley and Sons, Inc., 1968), esp. Chap. 1, pp. 1–21.

    See also Herbert Blumer, "Attitudes and the Social Act," *Social Problems*, 3 (1955), 59–65.

22. See, for instance, Theodore Abel's discussion, "The Operation Called Verstehen," *American Journal of Sociology*, 54 (November 1948), 211–17.

23. Becker and Geer, "Participant Observation: The Analysis of Qualitative Field Data," pp. 286–87.

24. For example, see Walter Miller's discussion of the use of informants in his studies of lower-class culture. "Lower Class Culture as a Generating Milieu of Gang Delinquency," *Journal of Social Issues*, 14, No. 3 (1958), 5–19. See also Robert K. Merton and Patricia L. Kendall, "The Focused Interview," *American Journal of Sociology*, 51 (1946), 541–57.

25. Becker and Geer, "Participant Observation: The Analysis of Qualitative Field Data," p. 286.

26. The term "escort" might be more suitable here than "guide." The function of a male companion during my observation on Skid Row was primarily to reduce the amount of attention received from the police if I went to the area alone. The Skid Row men also seemed more at ease if I were accompanied by a man. There were three guides in all. The first was a hotel clerk on the Row who, I learned later, was involved in drug traffic and was forced to "hole up" in his room so long that he developed a severe case of malnutrition and was sent to Veterans' Hospital. The second was a man who had served a sentence for manslaughter for the jealousy-slaying of his wife. While in my employ, he shot and killed his second wife because she, like the first, was unfaithful to him. The third "guide" was a divinity student.

27. On the other hand, at a dance at the hospital, a mental patient, upon learning that I was a sociologist, left me in the middle of the floor with the remark, "This is typical of my luck!"

28. My "uniform" in Skid Row and at the County Jail was a grey dress, one size too large, a raincoat, flat black shoes and a head scarf. In other institutions, however, I dressed more attractively, as it seemed to be expected in those settings.

29. Recruits were contacted by notes I placed in prayer books during jail devotions I was allowed to attend. The notes suggested that the reader request to see me for an interview. During the course of the interview, which was conducted in private (in the lawyer's room), I asked them to work for me.

30. Nash, *Primitive and Peasant Economic Systems*, p. 11.

31. See Becker and Geer, "Participant Observation: The Analysis of Qualitative Field Data," pp. 280–81.

32. In survey research studies using a standardized questionnaire, the frequency and distribution of a phenomenon is established statistically, and well-accepted tests of significance increase confidence in the usefulness of such findings. In naturalistic studies where the attempt is to get at the perspective of the actor, the hope is to reconstruct his world as a whole. Statistical fragments, although very useful at getting specific information (such as IQ, level of formal education, and so on) often do not reflect the actor's common sense approach to categorizing his world.

33. Mannheim, *Ideology and Utopia*, pp. 49–53.

34. Becker and Geer, "Participant Observation: The Analysis of Qualitative Field Data," p. 278.

35. Ibid., pp. 276–77. According to Becker and Geer (p. 277), the most common kinds of statements at this level include:

    1. Complex statements of the necessary and sufficient conditions for the existence of some phenomenon.

2. Statements that some phenomenon is an "important" or "basic" element in the organization.

3. Statements identifying a situation as an instance of some process or phenomenon described more abstractly in sociological theory.

36. From Julius Gould and William L. Kolb (eds.), *Dictionary of Sociology* (New York: The Free Press of Glencoe, 1964), pp. 742–43, definition by Raymond V. Bowers (paraphrased to some extent).

37. For a discussion of this point see Aaron V. Cicourel, *Methods and Measurement*, p. 18, Nash, *Primitive and Peasant Economic Systems*, p. 9 and Mannheim, *Ideology and Utopia*, p. 85.

38. Selltiz, Jahoda, Deutsch, and Cook, *Research Methods in Social Relations* (New York: Holt, Rinehart, and Winston, 2nd ed., 1964), p. 178.

39. Survey research analysts have devised "trick questions" to catch liars. Questions that have no answer, such as, "Who is the cabinet member in charge of urban affairs?" are asked. If the respondent invents a name, as he would have to do, inasmuch as the post does not exist yet, he is suspected of perhaps lying on other portions of the questionnaire. On long questionnaires, *consistency* between questions is checked as persons often forget to maintain a false stance all the way through a particularly long interview. An unusual pattern of answers (not fitting general response configurations) may also be suspect and checked out in some way or other—perhaps by interviewing another member of the family.

40. I am indebted to Anselm Strauss for this suggestion. He also used this method in the study, *Awareness of Dying*. See Barney G. Glaser and Anselm L. Strauss (Chicago: Aldine Publishing Co., 1965), and discusses it in Glaser and Strauss, *The Discovery of Grounded Theory* (Chicago: Aldine Publishing Co., 1967).

41. Becker and Geer, "Participant Observation: The Analysis of Qualitative Field Data," p. 276

42. *Ibid.*, p. 287 and 288.

43. Donald J. Bogue, *Skid Row in American Cities* (Chicago: University of Chicago Press, 1963), p 14.

Index